MARCO POLO

D0513150

PRAGUE

www.marco-polo.com

Sightseeing Highlights

The list of sights in Prague is long. Old City Square, Hradčany or Charles Bridge are definitely not to be left out. For the rest of the sights we've put together a list of the most important highlights. After all, a prophecy was made about the city early on, that »its fame would one day touch the stars«.

❶ ✶✶ Old Town Square

After the Hradčany this square with an area of 9000m2/97,000sq ft and the monument to the reformer Jan Hus in the centre is Prague's most historic place.
page 258

❷ ✶✶ Old Town Hall

The town hall's main attraction is the 16th cent. astronomical clock. The 69m/227ft-high tower of the town hall offers the best view of the Old City Square.
page 260

❸ ✶✶ Prague Castle

Over the centuries almost all of the past rulers have immortalized themselves in various buildings.
page 273

❹ ✶✶ St Vitus Cathedral

The brilliant cathedral master builder Peter Parler created his masterpiece here – an early monument to himself.
page 282

❺ ✶✶ Old Royal Palace

Another highlight on the Hradčany – the defenestration from one of its rooms made history once. Not only art historians go into raptures at the sight of the Vladislav Hall.
page 284

❻ ✶✶ Josefov

Today the former Jewish quarter of the city is practically an open air museum. The many synagogues and the Old Jewish Cemetery tell the long story of the Jewish community in Prague.
page 207

❼ ✶✶ Charles Bridge

The row of Baroque statues along the city's oldest bridge are what give it its huge impact. It is also a popular meeting point for street artists and strollers.
page 181

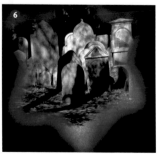

❽ ✳✳ Karlštejn Castle

Located 40km/24mi south-west of Prague, the most famous Bohemian castle was built to be the place where the Bohemian royal insignia would be kept. Do not miss seeing Holy Cross Chapel with the panels by Master Theoderich.
page 222

❾ ✳✳ St Nicholas

On the Lesser Quarter Square, this is an example of the ultimate in high Baroque; enjoy the best view of this neighbourhood's rooftops.
page 230

❿ ✳✳ Loreta

Prague owes this copy of the Casa Santa to the veneration of Mary – sculptures and reliefs show the life story of the mother of God.
page 235

⓫ ✳✳ Strahov Monastery

The 25 frescos in the theological library hall symbolize the struggle for wisdom in connection with the love of science and literature. In the philosophical hall a mighty ceiling fresco by Franz Anton Maulbertsch can be seen.
page 303

⓬ ✳✳ Vyšehrad

According to legend Vyšehrad was the seat of Duchess Libussa (Czech: Libuše), who predicted that Prague's fame would reach the stars. The first Přemyslid rulers were also supposed to have lived here.
page 319

Do You Feel Like ...

... Prague just the way you like it? Then these tips will certainly help you discover the most different sides of the city on the Vltava.

VIEWS AND DISTANCES

BEAUTIFUL ILLUSION(S)

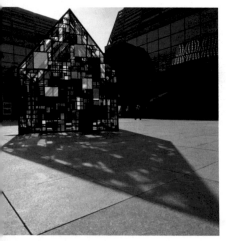

ART & ProvoCation

NIGHTCLUBBING

BACKGROUND

ENJOY PRAGUE

TOURS

SIGHTS FROM A TO Z

Charles Bridge: Kings once walked over these stones on the way to their coronation

Travelling by tram is one of the best means of transport in Prague

PRICE CATEGORIES
Restaurants (main dish
without a drink)
€€€€ = over €50
€€€ = €30 – €50
€€ = €20 – €30
€ = up to €20
Hotels (double room)
€€€€ = over €250
€€€ = €120 – €250
€€ = €80 – €120
€ = up to €80

Note
Billable service telephone
numbers are marked with an
asterisk: *0180…

PRACTICAL
INFORMATION

BACKGROUND

Clear and concise, easy to follow, handy for quick reference: everything worth knowing about the land and its people, the economy, politics and history of the city of a hundred spires, where the Old Town has been granted protection as a UNESCO World Heritage Site.

The Mother of All Cities

Virtually unaltered in over a thousand years, »Prague, the mother of all cities« (Praga mater urbium) paints a truer picture of its history than almost any other European metropolis. But Prague is more than just a historic city, it is a modern, vibrantly cosmopolitan metropolis which beguiles at first sight: magnificent panoramic views may be enjoyed from each and every vantage point. First impressions promise an unforgettable experience – and Prague truly delivers.

Kafka summed it up nice and succinctly: »Prague doesn't let go.« Perhaps the most beautiful description, however, was penned by the author Lenka Reinerovà, like Kafka a native of Prague and writing in German as he did: »Prague, in Czech the feminine Praha, can be as moody as a woman. She too has plastered too much make-up onto her face in recent years. Too flashy, yet merely superficial, a concession to the deplorably commercial habits of the day. The true countenance of the city is untroubled by such undesirable alterations, my home knows its history and remains as it ever was, our wonderfully mad Prague«.

Church of Our Lady before Týn, from Old Town Square

In order to learn more about the true features of this face, there can be no substitute for seeing them at first hand – the sooner the expedition begins, the better.

A ROMANTIC DISCOVERY

One tower rises up after another amidst a myriad of rooftops, elegant bridges arc across the Vltava, townspeople take a stroll along splendid riverside promenades. On arrival in Prague, check into the hotel as quickly as possible, there is no time to waste. Save unpacking for later and head straight out into the streets, experience Prague with all of your senses. Touch the old stone walls, breathe in the flair of yesteryear, confront the present. The key to unlocking the romance of Prague lies in the Lesser Quarter. Our journey through time begins at the »Malostranskà« metro station, ascending some 105 feet on the escalator to emerge alongside a Roman fountain. A statue of St Adalbert is flanked by playful elves, fauns and kobolds who dance and play the flute – a cheery scene. It makes sense to follow the locals at this point! Those who work in the Lesser Quarter disappear through a »mousehole« in the wall. Around a sharp corner at the end of the path, a door – open from April to October – leads directly into the Wallenstein Garden. This park is one of Prague's magical places, adorned with roses and sculptures, home to an aviary for owls and a grotto. If this jaunt into the past is unexpected, it

Prague in full bloom:
Palace gardens (Lesser Quarter)

would seem almost natural to see General Waldstein appear in his garden to serenade visitors – with Beethoven's Moonlight Sonata, of course!

MAGICAL PLACES IN STOP AND GO MODE

Magnificent palaces and picturesque squares can be found at every turn, a wonderful backdrop to give free rein to one's imagination. The age of Mozart never felt closer, the court life of the nobility never more vivid. Prague, as soon becomes apparent, is a consummate work of art. Changes can be observed in the detail. Traditional taverns now serve fancy gourmet cuisine, ladies in precariously high heels stand in front of Art Nouveau houses. Cocktail and beer glasses are equally tall, club music overflows onto the street. David Cérný, »Mr Black« himself, drags the spirit of Kafka into the third millenium with his faceless tower babies. Interest is growing in »alternative Prague«, the less well-known, predominantly industrial parts of the city where artist studios, designer lofts and hip clubs are in the ascendancy. Nevertheless, the historic centre remains the ultimate tourist magnet. The Charles Bridge groans under the weight of stop and go pedestrians. Access to Golden Lane, leading up to Prague Castle, demands a fee. Yes, it should be noted that Prague is becoming an increasingly expensive pleasure!

Facts

Population · Politics · Economy

In the Middle Ages, Prague stood alongside Rome and Constantinople as one of Europe's greatest metropolises. Emperor Charles IV ruled over the Holy Roman Empire from Hradčany, Emperor Rudolf II over the Habsburg Monarchy. Many sought their fortune in the Golden City. Industrialization brought about the next upturn in the 19th century. Today, following the 1989 transition which became known as the »Velvet Revolution«, this multifaceted city is one of the continent's most popular travel destinations.

When Emperor Charles IV first made Prague the capital of the Holy Roman Empire in the 14th century, the city on the Vltava had approximately 40,000 inhabitants. Bohemia's importance to the Empire waned under Charles' successors to the extent that, after the losses of the Thirty Years' War, the population was still around 40,000 towards the end of the 17th century. From that time on, however, it did begin to rise. By 1786 Prague's numbers had grown to 73,000 and reached 193,000 by 1890. This upsurge is attributable largely to the process of industrialization. Thousands of Bohemian villagers descended on Prague to seek their fortune. Entirely new city districts sprang up, such as Karlín and Žižkov. In 1920 legislation was approved for the incorporation of further districts: Greater Prague's population thus leaped 677,000. The million mark was reached at the beginning of the 1960s. Further incorporations in the 1970s brought the number of Prague's inhabitants up to the 1.2 million it registers today, a figure on which the political events of 1989 had negligible impact.

Development

Abraham ben Jacob, a Spanish Jew and envoy of the caliph of Cordova, described Prague as a »city of many stones« as long ago as the 10th century already. Stones were, at that time, a symbol of wealth. Only the rich could afford to build houses from such materials. The first construction boom under Emperor Charles IV ushered in the initial wave of migration in 1346. The father of the nation sought out bronze casters, stonemasons and other craftsmen in Franconia. Bavaran nobles dispatched their offspring to Prague to face the challenge of establishing new businesses. Germans tended to settle in the Old Town, Czechs in the New Town which Charles IV founded for them, complete with its own town hall. In 1492, Ferdinand the Ca-

Ethnic composition

Baroque houses on the south side of the Altstädter Ring: they have colourful names like »At the storks« or »At the blue fox«.

▶ Czech

Praha

Location:
Prague is located in the central western Czech Republic on the Vltava River.

Area:
496km²/191sq mi

Population: **1.26 mil.** (2015)
Compared to:
Czech Republic
10.5 mil.
Berlin **3.5 mil.**
London **8.5 mil.**

14° 27' 17"
east longitude

Berlin ■

280km/
169mi

50° 05' 19"
north latitude

Prague ■
278km
168mi ■ Ostrava
187km/
112mi ■ Brno

©BAEDEKER

▶ Religion

0,05 Jews
1 Hussites
Other
Catholics
None

| 14.65 |
| 26 |
| 58.3 |

▶ Coat of arms

The coat of arms contains three golden towers on a golden city wall on a red background. The number of the towers and the bricks stands for the 112 cadaster quarters of the city. The armour-clad silver arm holding a sword symbolizes combat strength and fidelity.

▶ Administration

The 70-member city representative body votes for one of ist members to be head mayor (Primátor) for five years; he is he head of the 11-member city council (Rada).

22 administrative districts und 57 city districts.

The city districts **Prague 1** consists of the former districts Old City (**Staré Město**), New Town (**Nové Město**), Lesser Quarter (**Malá Strana**), **Hradčany** and (**Josefov**).

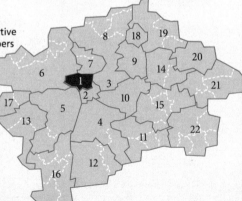

▶ Economy

C. 5.5 mil. tourists

with an average
3 overnight stays (2015)

Unemployment rate (2014):
Prague c. **2.5%**
Czech Republic **6.1%**

European cities with good or
very good employment
opportunities (European
Commission/Gallup 2016, in %)

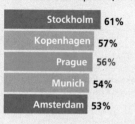

Stockholm	61%
Kopenhagen	57%
Prague	56%
Munich	54%
Amsterdam	53%

0   10   20   30   40   50   60   70   80

▶ Climate in Prague

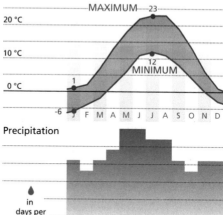

MAXIMUM ---- 23
20 °C
10 °C
MINIMUM
0 °C
-6   J F M A M J J A S O N D

Precipitation

in days per month

7 6 7 8 10 10 9 9 7 6 7 7

in hours per day

2 3 4 6 7 7 7 5 4 2 1

J F M A M J J A S O N D

▶ Prague's twin cities

The city district Prague 6 has been
twinned with Bayreuth, Germany
since fall 2008.

Brussels (2003)
Drancy (1995)
Hamburg (1990)
Bamberg (1991)
Saint Petersburg (1991)
Moscow (1995)
Berlin (1995)
Prague
Bratislava
Paris (1997)
Frankfurt (1990)
Nuremberg (1990)
Tirana (1995)
Jerusalem

Not on the map
Chicago, USA (1990)
Phoenix, USA (1992)
Taipeh, Taiwan (2001)
Kyoto, Japan (1996)

The Czechs and the Czech Republic

Created on 1 January 1993 by dividing up Czechoslovakia, the Czech Republic unites three historic countries in Bohemia, Moravia and Czech Silesia. The Czechs who live here (calling themselves Češi) are a West Slavic people who migrated in the second half of the 6th and the first half of the 7th centuries to what is now Czech territory. The name of the Czech people – first recorded by the historian Cosma of Prague around the year 1120 – is thought to date back to the mythical leader Čech, who is believed to have led the various West Slavic tribes to their new home in the period of migration. Here they subsequently merged into one people, one ethnic group. Today, the Czechs represent the largest share of the population with 90.1%, augmented by 3.7% Moravians and Silesians, 1.8% Slovaks, 0.5% Poles, 0.4% Germans and 3.4% miscellaneous. Romanies are estimated at somewhere between 200,000 and 250,000.

tholic expelled the Jews from Spain; every Jew who refused to convert to the Christian faith had to leave the country within three months. The ensuing exodus brought many Jews to Prague which henceforth flourished as a »European Jerusalem«. Large numbers of immigrants also arrived from Italy – master builders, carpenters and stucco plasterers who settled in the Lesser Quarter. A street named Vlašská – meaning »Romans« – serves as a reminder of their presence. But craftsmen and artists, adventurers and mercenaries were not the only new arrivals in Prague. The »Hussite King« George of Poděbrady (1420 – 1471), from a noble Moravian family, was the last Czech monarch to occupy the throne. Subsequent rulers were all »foreigners« without exception, from 1471 until the founding of Czechoslovakia in 1918. Vladislav II and his son Ludvík II came to Prague Castle from Poland; the son was succeeded by the Madrid-born Ferdinand I, a Habsburg who inherited the Bohemian Crown through complex hereditary relations.

Ethnic composition of Prague

When the Counter-Reformation forced the rebellious Hussites to their knees after the Thirty Years' War, the political significance of the Germans in Prague continued to grow. Not until the middle of the 19th century did they lose their majority on the city council. At the beginning of the 20th century, Prague's total population of 400,000 included some 30,000 Germans, many of whom were Jews. After the founding of Czechoslovakia in 1918 many Germans left the city; others were driven out in 1945, after World War II. Only 4000 of Prague's Jews survived the Holocaust. Today, the Jewish community comprises around 1600 members. The largest minority is represented by approximately 18,000 Romanies – discriminated against under socialism and denigrated as »gypsies« long after the events of 1989. Some 15,000 Vietnamese constitute the second largest minority. The Italians, once the ethnic soul of the Lesser Quarter, returned to their Catholic homelands a hundred years ago. Still, their love for Prague has not deserted them – the »amici italiani« like to buy renovated apartments in the Old Town as a capital investment, but often leave the properties empty.

The transition of 1989 opened up new perspectives. An estimated 55,000 Ukrainians migrated to the city to find work – and they stayed, now representing the largest group of migrants. The new Russian wave is an ironic twist of fate: the despised occupying forces not so very long ago now bring the largest sums of money into Prague. A good 20,000 Russians reside permanently here on the Vltava, whilst at least half a million Russian tourists splash their cash to boost the economy every year. Russian couples love getting married in Prague and stretch limousines can frequently be seen ferrying brides in white from one glorious monument to the next for memorable photo opportunities. A distinctive feature of Prague is the strong US community: around 20,000 young Americans flocked to the city on the Vltava after 1989, attracted by the »Velvet Revolution« and »poet-president« Václav Havel; several thousand have stayed on permanently.

Migrants old and new

STATE AND SOCIETY

The Czech Republic modelled its parliamentary system on the USA administration. Tomáš Garrigue Masaryk (1850 – 1937), the founder of the Republic, was married to an American pianist and was a strong admirer of the USA. The Czech parliament comprises two chambers: the Chamber of Deputies (»Sněmova« in Czech) and the Senate. Both chambers are voted for and legitimated by the people. The 200 members of the lower chamber serve four year terms and are elected through a party-list proportional representation system. A 5% minimum threshold guards against parliament fragmenting into too many smaller parties. The Senate, or upper house, has 81 senators elected by majority vote for six years (minimum age 40); voting takes place in one third of the 81 constituencies every two years. Both chambers – and the government –can initiate legislation, but it is the president who has the final say. He has the power of suspensive veto, along with a host of other prerogatives, much like his American counterpart. His powers include the appointment of the prime minister as elected by parliament and also that of the cabinet ministers proposed by the prime minister. He also appoints the nation's supreme judges as representatives of the judiciary – separate from the legislature (parliament) and the executive (president).
Initally the president was elected by the two chambers of parliament for a five year term (minimum age 40, allowed to stand for a maximum of two terms). A change to the constitution in 2012 meant that

Welcome to Everyday Life

»Czechs are not friendly, but they are human« (Philip Roth): For those who wish to experience Prague away from the throngs of tourists and meet completely »normal« people, or perhaps meet Prague locals in person, the Baedeker editorial team has prepared some useful tips.

EARN A BACHELOR'S DEGREE

Study by day, party by night. Prague is a lively student city with international appeal. The University of New York in Prague (UNYP) offers a broad range of educational programmes for senior executives of the future in the fields of administration, finance and IT. Courses are taught in English, a little bit of Czech can be absorbed later on in the bars and taverns. There are plenty of service jobs available to keep the bank balance healthy.

www.unyp.cz

HOMESTAY

Staying with a host family is always a good way to meet local people and to get to know the locality better.

www.homestaybooking.com

PRIVATE GALLERY VIEWING INVITATIONS

What are Prague people like? Get to know them through art, jazz, action and happenings. The Prague scene throws up no end of crazy ideas. A fridge with a hole you can stick your head through? Trying to sit on a two-legged wobbly chair? – Get into the swing of things and enjoy the fun. How to get in? Usually a few simple words are enough. There are over 300 galleries in Prague, almost one for every day of the year. A party for every night of the week. Trendsetters flock to Mánes, DOX, Meet-Factory. The cultivated crowd confer at the Arthotel Kempinski.

www.meetfactory.cz, www.dox.cz, www.praguepost.com/night-and-day

GRAPE HARVEST AND TANGO

Alongside Paris and Vienna, Prague is the third capital city in Europe to produce its own wine. Pinot Noir, Portugieser, Müller Thurgauer all thrive on the slopes of the Grébovka in the district of Vinohrady. Helping hands at harvest time are always welcome.

Sign up via Email: sklepgrebovka@seznam.cz

A pretty pavilion at the top of the vineyard promises panoramic views. This is where tango aficionados meet in summer: La Cumparsito, olé!

www.sklepgrebovka.cz, www.tango inprague.cz, www.milongaprague.cz

IN THE BELLY OF THE WHALE

A bizarre mix of Prague originals – many film students, journalists, bearded 1968 veterans and long-haired beatniks – populate Kavárna Velryba (The Whale Café). Catch a whiff of the atmosphere through the large cellar windows from the pavement. Inside, anything goes except for mainstream. Waiting staff will not split the bill for groups of four or more people. Weekend nights can go on and on: numerous bars in the neighbourhood stay open until 4am.

Quartier Latin, Opatovická 24
Tel. 22493 1444
www.kavarnavelryba.cz
daily 11am–midnight

future presidents would be voted in by the public. The five year term remains, as does the maximum of two terms candidacy. The first president to be elected under the new system was the former prime minister Miloš Zeman, winning a run-off against the incumbent foreign minister Karel Schwarzenberg in January 2013 and succeeding Václav Klaus who had held office from 2003.

Driving force of the »Velvet Revolution« was the »Civic Forum«, which emerged in the stirring November days of 1989. The leader, and indeed the symbolic figurehead, was dramatist Václav Havel and first president after the collapse of the Communist system. This »revolutionary league« soon divided into several splinter groups. The Občanská demokratická strana, ODS, the democratic citizens' party, secured a new, broad basis of support. Its leader, economist Václav Klaus, was regarded as the father of privatization. He was prime minister from 1993–1997, but following a corruption scandal was forced to resign by his former comrade and subsequent critic Václav Havel. In 1998 Česká strana sociálně demokratická, the social democrats (CSSD) took the helm. Theirs was not a newly formed party, having been founded in 1878 and banned by the Communists in 1948. Miloš Zeman was the first Prime Minister to come from their ranks, in office from 1998 to 2002. His successor, Jiří Paroubek, only served for two years (2005 – 2006), leaving the party in 2011 before becoming chairman of the newly founded National Socialists – Left of the 21st Century (Národní socialisté – levice 21. Století, NS-LEV 21 or LEV 21) in November of the same year. Whilst domestic politics were in a state of disarray, the Czech Republic took over the EU Presidency on 1st January 2009. Its own government was brought down in Prague four months later, losing a vote of no confidence. Czechs suffered the embarrassment of seeing Europe lose its leadership. The consequences were felt in the last parliamentary elections of June 2010: Karel Schwarzberg was chosen as leader of the new TOP 09 party, founded in 2009, in a veritable landslide of an election, positioning him as kingmaker in the new government – and taking up the post of foreign minister for the second time (TOP stands for »tradice, odpovědnost, prosperita« tradition, responsibility, prosperity). The

Democracy in a feudal framework

Prague is both the national capital and the seat of government. The prime minister operates in the sweeping Straka Academy on the left bank of the Vltava river, parliament sits in the Thun Palace, where Mozart once waved his conductor's baton. The Senate enjoys the most beautiful residence, the Baroque splendour of the Wallenstein Palace. Inside, an ostentatious ceiling fresco adorns the main hall. The Duke and Commander Wallenstein is depicted as Mars, the god of war, riding his chariot above the senators …

leading candidate of the democratic ODS party, Petr Nečas, took up the post of prime minister. Radek John, a former television presenter, snapped up the ministry of the interior position, using his on-screen popularity to found and win support for Věci veřejné, VV, the party for »public affairs«. He campaigned without a manifesto, offering his services as a controller to »see everything is done properly«. The bearded orator, a combative character, may have risen to interior minister, but he was obliged to resign as early as 2011 on account of irregularities in his department. He also failed, in the same year, as deputy prime minister and as head of a government committee set up to tackle corruption. This spelled the end for his VV party, its remaining members regrouping in a newly created liberal democratic party (liberální demokratié, LIDEM). Led by Karoline Peake, the party managed to stay in government. Alongside the Czech Social

Chapel of the Holy Cross in the 2nd Prague Castle courtyard – the official residence of the President of the Czech Republic

Democratic Party (ČSSD), the Communist Party of Bohemia and Moravia (Komunistická strana Čech a Moravy, KSČM) is also represented in parliament. The latter replaced the party's red star with a new red-green collective emblem (two red cherries on a green stalk), but neither the »reds« nor the »greens« have (thus far) entered a coalition with the neo-communists. The Green Party (Strana zelených, SZ) failed to win any seats in either chamber in the 2010 elections, picking up just 2.4% of the vote, well short of the 5% barrier. They recovered sufficiently to re-enter the Senate in 2012. Founded in June 2009, the Czech Pirate Party (Česká pirátská strana, CPS) introduced the political freebooter phenomenon, already on the wane elsewhere, to the Czech Republic. Their manifesto calls for an »open state«, demanding maximum transparency and the publication of confidential acts of state. Using public happenings to provoke a reaction, the Pirates occupy a single seat in the Senate, won in the 2012 election.

The Czech Republic and the EU

Overall, the division of Czechoslovakia on 1 January 1993 went smoothly, bringing the Czech Republic more advantages than disadvantages. It freed the economically stronger republic from the need to make balancing payments to Slovakia, and sped up its approach to becoming a member of the European Union. On **1 May 2004** the Czech Republic joined the EU, as the union expanded to include ten new member countries from Eastern Europe. In 2007, the Czech Republic signed up to the Schengen Agreement, removing all border controls. Checks on travellers who arrive from outside the Schengen Area only continue at international airports.

But the Czech stance on the European Union divides the Republic. President Václav Klaus, a eurosceptic, developed a reputation as an obstructionist in European politics. First he blocked the Lisbon Treaty, then the Czechs dragged their heels with regard to their obligation to join the eurozone. This although the country profits from extensive support from the EU in developing infrastructure, plus financial support for weaker economic regions. Last but not least, the Czech Republic receives millions of Euros for conservation and protection of monuments. There are earnest grounds for Czech euroscepticism, dating back to the Munich Agreement of 1938. Decisions were taken on Czech state sovereignty – without the Czechs. France, the United Kingdom and Italy agreed on the annexation of territory within the Czech Republic in favour of Hitler's Germany. The current Czech protestations against common EU programmes has to be seen in this historical context: »Never again about us, without us«. This fear of heteronomy in whatever form it may take is still deeply ingrained in the Czech psyche. Overcoming old prejudices through the power of reconciliation presents a challenge for an entire generation.

ECONOMY

During the first half of the 1990s, Czech economic policy was consi- Upswing
dered to be exemplary for the whole of Eastern Europe. Unemploy- after 1989
ment was just 3.5%, exports showed a surplus, and the national budget showed a profit. In Prague, where more than 10% of production
is concentrated, there were not enough people to fill all the jobs. Numerous foreign businesses set up in the Czech Republic after 1989,
competing with one another for highly qualified young employees.
When the Czech Republic joined the EU, Prague was the only region
to enjoy living standards above the EU average. Large public companies were privatized, but the state, or the banks it controlled, continued to maintain large shareholdings. In order not to endanger his
re-election, prime minister Václav Klaus prevented these companies
from going into liquidation. Wages rose more sharply than produc-
tivity, hence the price advantage of Czech products abroad was lost.
By the late 1990s unemployment had risen to 10%. A slowdown occurred only when the Social Democrats, having won the 1998 parliamentary elections in 1998, renewed the privatization process. It took
the global financial crisis of 2008/2009 to put the brakes on the ex-
port-oriented Czech economy.

The number of civil servants employed in government, ministries, Viva activa:
administration and other state organizations in Prague could rival daily life in a
the Greeks. As a university metropolis with a strong tradition in edu- changing city
cation and the arts, many academics, doctors, computer scientists
and media specialists live and work in the city. The »black Prague« of
smoking chimneys – once the industrial heart of Czechoslovakia, one
of the ten leading industrial nations of the world in the 1930s - has
long since been swept away. In the Karlin and Vysočany districts,
what was once the largest tram factory in the world has been transformed into artist studios, designer lofts and event locations. Loco-
motive and carriage workshops have been replaced with shopping
centres and luxury apartments, trendy clubs and galleries. The former industrial harbour of Libeň has been developed into a prestigious river park with offices, penthouses, educational facilities and a
marina for Vltava's yachts. Publishers and advertising agencies have
moved into the old red brick industrial courtyards. The transformation into a high-tech metropolis is thus complete, where the IT, financial and logistics sectors reap rewards. Mechanical engineering, phar-
maceuticals, electronics and foodstuffs production account for
roughly one third of jobs.

The Czech Republic also sees itself as an important energy supplier Energy and
in the future. In spite of vehement protests from neighbouring coun- the economy
tries, Temelín Nuclear Power Station is undergoing expansion. In the

autumn of 2012, US foreign minister Hillary Clinton travelled to Prague to recommend the Westinghouse company as a nuclear reactor specialist. Clinton noted: »The Czech Republic deserves to get the best and safest nuclear technology from America«.

Tourism Unable to meet demand with local staff, the hotel industry has looked to Kazakhstan to supplement chambermaid numbers – tourism is booming to such an extent that comparisons with Venice are not out of place. Like the lagoon city, Prague is creaking under the masses of tourists, although the boost in terms of currency and employment softens the blow (for now): 2015 saw some 5 million guests spend an average of three nights in the city.

Film production in »Hollywood of the East« If the city's status as a World Heritage Site is one significant factor in making Prague so immensely attractive, the prolific film industry also plays its part. The »Hollywood of the East« (▶MARCO POLO Insight p. 112) not only boasts marvellous »locations«, it is also home to one of the oldest, largest and – according to Roman Polanski

Which way forward for Prague? Tourism is the engine room for jobs – it has become the most important sector of the Czech economy.

– finest film studios in the world. Founded by the Václav Havel family, the Barrandov Studios celebrated their eightieth anniversary in 2011. Production costs here are approximately 30% lower than in the west (at present), adding to the appeal. There is no lack of expert talent either: founded in 1941, the Film and TV School of Academy is renowned the world over.

Foreign investment

Prague Experience: English is a prerequisite for getting on in business in Prague. Over 300 foreign companies have entered into Czech joint ventures. Over 300 British companies are operating from Prague. The British Chamber of Commerce opened its business centre in Prague in June 2014. Foreign professionals and lecturers for economics, trade, marketing and languages are in high demand. The IT branch is booming – the Czech Republic is one of Europe's leading nations for computer software and security systems.

The new Bohemia

And if none of the above fits the bill, international arrivals – Americans, Norwegians and Indians among them – have also made a successful entry into the gastronomy scene. Prague's first Michelin star was awarded to an Italian, Andrea Accordi, for his Restaurant Allegro – two Czechs, Roman Paulus at the Alcron and Oldřich Sahajdá of the Degustation Bohême Bourgeoise also received the prestigious award in the Golden City in 2012.

History of the Golden City

Four assassinations, two defenestrations, one act of treason – what happened in Prague has always influenced the fate of Europe. The history of this city reflects the image of a small nation which was remarkably capable of holding its own against the major powers close by – often with revolutionary ideas ...

PREHISTORY

c800	Prague founded by Princess Libuše
921	St Wenceslas (Václav) becomes ruler
973	Boleslav II founds the diocese of Prague and the first monastery
1198	Přemyslid prince Otakar becomes king
1230	Prague receives municipal charter
1306	End of Plemyslid dynasty rule

Human settlers probably inhabited the area covered by today's city of Prague from the early Stone Age (Palaeolithic era); the earliest known traces of settlement date from several hundred-thousand years before the common era. In 4000 BC a few tribes advanced from Bohemia, the heartland of European settlement, over the Moldavian heights towards the region that became Prague. During the next 3000 years the area alongside the Vltava ford below Hradčany was settled by merchants; it was the intersection point of the Amber Road and the Salt Road. At the beginning of the most recent Ice Age, from 400 BC (La Tène culture), the **Celtic Boii** (from whom the region of Bohemia takes its name) overran Bohemia and gradually subjugated the earlier population; there is a large Celtic oppidum on Závist mountain on the southern edge of Prague. During the Roman era, in the year 10 BC, the Boii were subjugated by the Marcomanni, whose chieftains were assumedly Germanic. In the course of the period of migration, in the 6th century, **West Slavs** occupied the terrain of the current Czech capital. Settlements arose on what is now the castle hill (Hradčany), and in Malá Strana.

Early settlers

Legend has it that Prague, which in AD 800 comprised several small fortified settlements, was founded by Princess Libuše, who had the

Foundation Myth

The astronomical clock, mounted on the southern wall of the Old Town Hall, installed in 1410 and completed around 1490.

gift of prophecy. As she had foreseen in her vision of a city which would one day be famous the world over, the princess's retinue found the spot where Prague would be founded on the banks of the Vltava: a spot at which a man was chiselling the threshold (»práh«) of his house. When, after several years, the people tired of female leadership, Libuše sent her companions to the river Biela. There, close to Stadiz – as the princess had said they would – they met a young ploughman named **Přemysl Oráč** who became Libuše's husband and the first Přemyslid prince.

Přemyslid Rule Duke Bořivoj, the first historically attested representative of the Přemyslid dynasty, subjugated the Czech tribes. Prague Castle (Pražský hrad) was built at this time. In 874 Bořivoj was baptized by Methodius, who brought Christianity to the Slavs. After Bořivoj's death, his widow Ludmila, who had also been baptized, was murdered in the course of family feuds. She is regarded as the country's first martyr, and is venerated as a patron saint of Bohemia. The duke **St Wenceslas (Václav)**, a grandson of Ludmila, came to power in 921. A Christian ruler, he established close contact with the Saxon court of King Heinrich I. In 935 he was murdered by his brother Boleslav I, the Cruel, in Stará Boleslav. After his canonization he was venerated as a patron saint of Bohemia, and became the symbol of unity and independence for his country, which often suffered under arbitrary foreign power.

Boleslav II Under Boleslav II, the Pious, the diocese of Prague was established in 973, and the first monastery (of St George) was founded. Bohemian rule extended as far as the borders with Kiev territory. Jewish and German merchants settled in Prague, as did those from France and Italy. In 993 St Adalbert, bishop of Prague, founded the Benedictine monastery of Břevnov (Klášter Břevnov). In 1085 Duke Vratislav II became the first king of Bohemia (Vratislav I) and moved his royal seat from Hradčany to Vyšehrad.

Vladislav II Duke Vladislav II was declared King of Bohemia in 1158. Construction of the first stone bridge over the Vltava (Judith Bridge; later replaced by Charles Bridge) secured Prague's pre-eminence as trading metropolis for a lengthy period. In 1178 Duke Soběslav II decreed that German merchants should operate according to German law, be exempt from military service, and enjoy tax privileges, measures intended to keep the colonists in Prague. In 1198 the emperor crowned Duke Přemysl Otakar I King of Bohemia. This gave the rulers de facto right to royal status, and from 1212 (Sicilian Golden Bull) this was confirmed de jure as a hereditary right. From 1289 to 1806 the Bohemian king also bore the title of Elector of the Holy Roman Empire. The town of Prague was fortified in 1230 and received its municipal charter in the same year. In 1257 King Přemysl Otakar II founded Malá Strana (the Lesser Quarter) for German colonists; it was administered according to Magdeburg law. In the years that followed Otokar was able to extend his kingdom to Austria and large parts of northern Italy, but his attempts to become emperor were in vain. The first Prague groschen were minted c1300. The groschen went on to become the most important coin in Eastern Europe. The murder of King Wenceslas III in 1306 brought to an end the Přemyslid dynasty, which had lasted for more than 400 years. With the king's demise, the direct Přemyslid line died out.

THE LUXEMBOURG RULERS

1344	Building of St Vitus Cathedral
1346	Charles IV becomes King of Bohemia, Prague becomes the »Rome of the North«
1348	Founding of Charles University (Karolinum)
1355	Charles IV becomes emperor of the Holy Roman Empire
1419	First Prague defenestration
1420	Battle of Vitkov Mountain
1458	Under George of Podebrady, Prague loses its pre-eminence as economic centre

After a period of confusion, during which the Habsburgs were able to stake their first claim to the Bohemian throne through the brief reign of Rudolf I (who died in 1307), the German king Heinrich VII, of the house of Luxembourg, was able in 1310 to arrange for the marriage of his son John to the Přemyslid heiress Elisabeth, thus securing the Bohemian crown for the Luxembourgs, with support from France and the church.

Archdiocese of Prague

Charles IV governed Bohemia. In 1344 the building of St Vitus Cathedral began on castle hill – the cathedral of the newly created archdiocese of Prague. In 1346 Charles IV became King of Bohemia, and in 1347 official German king (from 1346 king in opposition). Brought up in France, well educated, cultured and nurturing a pious interest in religious relics, this ruler made Bohemia the heartland of the German empire, and brought Bohemia, Moravia and Silesia together under the Bohemian crown. As the metropolis of the Holy Roman Empire, Prague became the **»Rome of the North«**. The city attracted scholars and artists from all over Europe. In rapid succession, scarcely pausing for a moment, Charles IV commissioned the Gothic masterpieces which made medieval Prague famous. His leading master builder was **Peter Parler**, summoned to Prague from Germany at the age of 22. Charles commissioned the Church of Our Lady of the

Charles IV

Snows (Marie Sněžné), on which construction began in 1347, and the castle of Karlštejn (1348 – 1357). In the year 1348 Charles University (the Karolinum) was founded as the first university in central Europe. Nové Město was designed on a large scale, with imposing squares (Wenceslas Square, Charles Square), wide streets, harmonious churches and monasteries, and extensive fortifications which include the Gothic enclosure around Vyšehrad. This meant that for several centuries it was possible to accommodate the growing population, above all people working in crafts and trades, without further expansion; in terms of area as well as population Prague was the largest city in central Europe. In 1355 Charles IV became emperor of the Holy Roman Empire, and two years later he commissioned the building of the Charles Bridge and the Old Town Bridge Tower.

Political and religious tensions Following the death of Charles IV (1378), grave social and religious tensions developed under Wenceslas IV, as well as controversy regarding succession to the throne. In 1400 Wenceslas was deposed as German king, but continued to be King of Bohemia. Master Jan Hus persuaded Wenceslas to curtail the rights of Germans in favour of Czechs at the universities in 1409; some 2000 German students and many teachers left the country, and founded several universities, including the University of Leipzig.

HUSSITE WARS

Jan Hus at the stake The aims of the reformer Jan Hus and many who shared his views were initially moderate – they wanted only to return to the original source of Christianity and eradicate corruption in the church. Yet this developed into a religious, social and national movement which made increasingly radical demands, and became even more volatile when Hus refused to recant at the Council of Constance. He was publicly burnt at the stake, his death in 1415 triggering an anti-ecclesiastical uprising in Bohemia. On 30 July 1419 a crowd led by Jan Želivský stormed the town hall in Nové Město, freed the Hussites who had been imprisoned there, and threw two Catholic councillors out of the window. This **first Prague defenestration** signalled the beginning of the Hussite Wars, which lasted until 1436. Wenceslas IV died that same year.

Hussite victory at Vitkov Mountain In 1420 Pope Martin V issued a bull which proclaimed a crusade against the heretics in Bohemia. On 14 July the Hussite army under Jan Žižka vanquished King Sigismund's much larger crusader army at the Battle of Vitkov Mountain (▶Žižkov), enabling the Hussites to prevent the capture of Prague. Thereafter the Hussites even went on the offensive under Procopius Holý and launched retaliatory campaigns against Bavaria, Brandenburg, Saxony and Austria. The Hussites lost the war, but were successful in some of their demands (among them, dispossession of the church's secular property).

After a short interregnum under Albrecht of Habsburg and a 13-year vacancy of the throne, a Bohemian nobleman with Hussite leanings – George of Poděbrady – became first regent and then, from 1458, King of Bohemia (until 1471). Under his rule, construction work in Prague continued (Týn Church). The dispossession of church property had made the nobility rich, and the nobles gained in influence at the expense of the cities; Prague's position as centre of the economy declined as towns close to the frontier grew more important. The significance of the university also declined increasingly. In 1490 the lands of the Bohemian crown were united with Poland and Hungary. King Vladislav Jagiello (Vladislav II) moved the royal seat from Prague to Budapest. Prague's significance decreased hugely at this time. Feuding between the aristocracy and the city intelligentsia inhibited further development.

Loss of influence

HABSBURG DYNASTY

1526	Prague falls to the Habsburgs
1556	Ferdinand I becomes German emperor
1618	Second Prague defenestration leads to Thirty Years' War
1621	The 27 leaders of the nobles' revolt are executed
1641	Prague forfeits its cultural and economic significance
1784	Hradčany, Malá Strana, Staré Město and Nové M:sto are united in a single administrative unit

After the death of Vladislav II's son Ludvík in 1526, at the Battle of Mohács fought against the Turks, Ludvík's Habsburg brother-in-law **Ferdinand I** was chosen as king. Wide-ranging rights were granted to the country, and especially to the city of Prague (the restoration of the archdiocese, and of Prague as royal residence). In 1547 these rights were set to be curtailed, and there was an uprising of towns and Estates led by Prague against the king. After the revolt had been put down, the capital and many other Bohemian towns were severely punished by loss of privileges, authority and income.

Battle of Mohács

From 1549 an influx of Germans of Lutheran persuasion strengthened the opposition to the Counter-Reformation taking place under the Catholic Habsburgs. Ferdinand I became German emperor in 1556. He summoned the Jesuits to Prague; they busied themselves with new buildings, and educated a new generation of strictly Catholic noblemen and burghers. These measures, and repeated attempts

Counter-Reformation

Trigger for the Thirty Years' War: in 1618 two imperial governors were tossed out of the window of Prague Castle

on the part of the king to restrict the religious freedom guaranteed in 1436, were the basis for ongoing disputes between the Bohemian Estates and the house of Habsburg, which also overshadowed the reign of Maximilian II (1564 – 1576). In Prague Castle, Maximilian's son **Rudolf II** lived for his art collection and for his scientific and astronomical studies; to assist him he had brought the scholars **Tycho Brahe** and **Johannes Kepler** to Prague. He had to call on his brother Matthias and the Bohemian Estates for help in resisting an attack by his nephew, the archduke Leopold. In return for the nobility's help he confirmed to them the guarantee of religious freedom in the »royal charter« of 1609. In 1611 Rudolf II abdicated; his brother Matthias became king.

SECOND PRAGUE DEFENESTRATION

Beginning of the Thirty Years' War
Renewed controversy over freedom of religion and the rights restored to towns and Estates led to the second Prague defenestration of 23 May 1618, effectively the signal for a revolt of radical Protestant noblemen against the Catholic Habsburgs, and the start of the Thirty

Years' War. The Bohemian Estates proclaimed the deposition of Habsburg monarch Ferdinand II in 1619, and chose the Palatinate Elector Friedrich V as king. Ferdinand II vanquished the Palatine Friedrich, the »Winter King« (1619–1620), on 8 November 1620 at the **Battle of the White Mountain** and re-established his hereditary rights.

The »Old Town Square execution« took place on 21 June 1621, with the leaders of the nobles' revolt – 27 Bohemian representatives of the uprising against the Habsburgs – losing their lives. The Protestant aristocracy and wealthy citizens were disempowered or banished, and the non-Catholic clergy driven out.

Execution of the rebels

In the year 1624 Ferdinand moved the Bohemian chancellery to Vienna. In the »revised constitution order« of 10 May 1627, Bohemia's heritability was anchored in the Austrian house of Habsburg. Catholicism was the only permitted religion. The monarch was given prime legislative rights, and was enabled to make appointments to high office and to reverse parliamentary decisions. This constitution for Bohemia and Moravia destroyed the power of the Estates irrevocably; it forced the majority of the educated class to leave the country and deprived Prague of its intellectual and cultural pre-eminence. In the year 1631 Wallenstein repelled the Swedes, who had advanced as far as Prague during the course of the Thirty Years' War. Shortly after the Swedes had occupied Malá Strana in 1648 came news of the end of the war. The Thirty Years' War was a catastrophe for Bohemia. The country lost almost half its population, and continued to be subjected to oppressive taxation during subsequent Habsburg wars. This resulted in the irretrievable loss of Prague's cultural and economic significance.

Prague surrenders its intellectual supremacy

In the Battle of the White Mountain, 1620, the Bohemian army was crushingly defeated

During the War of the Austrian Succession, 1740 – 1748, Prague was occupied by Bavarians, Saxons, French and Prussians. In 1757, during the Seven Years' War, Frederick the Great of Prussia defeated the Austrians outside Prague, but did not raise the siege of the city after his own defeat at Kolín. In 1781 Joseph II introduced reforms with his patent for the abolition of serfdom, revival of religious freedom and introduction of the German elementary school in Bohemia. Use of the German language was further encouraged. In the year 1784 the

War of the Austrian Succession

four previously independent city districts of Hradčany, Malá Strana, Staré Město and Nové Město were joined into a single administrative unit. The Jewish district Josefov was added in 1850. In 1845 the railway link between Prague and Vienna was opened. The Czech national revolution, centred on Prague, failed. František Palacký declined to take part in the national gathering in Frankfurt in 1848. In the same year there was a meeting of the Slav congress. Tensions between Germans and Czechs intensified.

Reduction of German influence

Since the late 18th century a new Czech movement had been gradually gaining momentum, with impassioned adherents particularly in intellectual and artistic circles. This led to repression of the German language, after violent parliamentary debates. In 1861 the Germans lost their majority in Prague city council for the first time. The 1866 **Treaty of Prague** brought an end to the war between Prussia and Austria over control of Germany. In 1886 the Germans left parliament, but continued to dominate the economy. The industrial exhibition of 1891 took place in Prague. Through industrialization, especially in areas of German settlement, Bohemia became a key industrial centre for the Austro-Hungarian Empire. In 1913 national tensions made it impossible for parliament to function. During World War I Bohemia was administered under emergency legislation.

REPUBLIC OF CZECHOSLOVAKIA

1918	Founding of the Republic of Czechoslovakia (ČSR)
	Philosopher and politician Tomáš Garrigue Masaryk (»little father«) becomes lifelong president.
1939	On 15 March, German troops march into Prague,
	proclaiming the Protectorate of Bohemia and Moravia
	Pro-fascist Slovakia declares independence.
1942	SS Obergruppenführer Reinhard Heydrich, Deputy/Acting Reich-Protector is assassinated.
	The villages of Lidice and Ležáky are obliterated in an act of retribution.
1945	Prague uprising against German occupation on 5 May.
	Arrival of the Red Army on 9 May. Prague's Germans and Hungarians are driven out of the city.
1948	Communist coup d'état
1960	New constitution: Socialist Republic (ČSSR)
1969	»Prague Spring«
1989	»Velvet Revolution«, Václav Havel elected president
1992	Peaceful division into Czech Republic and Slovak Republic. Prague's historic centre is granted UNESCO World Heritage status.

The Republic of Czechoslovakia (ČSR) was founded as the Slav successor state to the Austro-Hungarian monarchy (28 October 1918). Its founding president was **Tomáš Garrigue Masaryk**. Constant tensions between the national groups (Czechs, Slovaks, Germans, Magyars, Poles) put the multiracial state at risk. The municipal area of Prague was considerably extended by incorporation of outer suburbs, and in 1922 it was divided into 19 districts. As a consequence of the **Munich Agreement** of 1938 – in which Czechs had no voice – the borderlands of Bohemia and Moravia (Sudetenland) settled by Germans became part of the National Socialist (Nazi) German Reich. In 1939 the remaining Czech territory was incorporated into Hitler's »Greater Germany« as the »Protectorate of Bohemia and Moravia«. On 26 May 1942 the deputy Reich Protector, Reinhard Heydrich, was fatally wounded in an assassination attack. The Nazis retaliated with the total destruction of the villages of Lidice and Ležáky, brutally suppressing any form of Czech resistance.

Foundation of the ČSR

According to the »Košice programme« of 22 March 1945 announced by Social Democrat Zdeněk Fierlinger, the Czech state borders of 1937 were to be restored, and the country was to be ruled on a socialist popular front model. The uprising of the people of Prague on 5 May in the same year spreaded throughout the whole country; the expulsion of Sudeten Germans began. On 25 May Edvard Beneš returned to Prague from exile in London –holding the office of state president until his retirement on 7 June 1948. The Communist Party (KPČ) came to power in 1948: Czechoslovakia became a »people's republic«. President Klement Gottwald prescribed a radical »purge«. 1960 saw the founding of the Czechoslovakian Socialist Republic (ČSSR), with the city now divided into into ten districts.

Socialist state

PRAGUE SPRING

During the so-called »Prague Spring« of 1968 the Czech Communist Party under First Secretary **Alexander Dubček** who had been elected in January, strove for »socialism with a human face«. Their programme for liberalization and democratization was supported by the people. On 21 August the USSR and four other Warsaw Pact states put a violent end to the Prague Spring by sending in troops. The USSR asserted its right to keep troops stationed in Czechoslovakia for an unlimited period. In 1968 the municipal area of Prague was extended to include 21 outlying districts. On 16 January 1969 the 20-year-old philosophy student **Jan Palach** poured petrol over himself and burnt himself to death on Wenceslas Square in protest

Socialism with a Human Face

… was the idea of the Czechoslovakian reformers of the Prague Spring. They planned deep-reaching liberalizations of the economy and society; and the Communist Party was not to be excluded. But the Soviet Union though that their hegemony was being threatened.

Ludvik Svoboda
(1895 – 1979)
President of the ČSSR from 1968–1975. Opinions on him are divided as he made it possible for the reformers to take part in the negotiations with the Soviets, but forced them to sign the Moscow protocol.

▶ **Chronology of events**

June: writers criticize the Novotný regime **Oktober:** student protests	Novotný resigns, Dubček succeeds him	Dresden Conference: anti-reform alliance (Soviet Union, Poland, GDR, Hungary, Bulgaria) founded	»The Two Thousand Words«: intellectuals demand the unconditional continuation of the reform	Censorship revoked
1967	**Jan 6**	**April 23**	**June 27**	**June 29**

1968

Alexander Dubček
(1921–1992)
Secretary general of the
Czech Communist Party
and head of the reformers.
Lost his position in April
1969 and was expelled
from the party in 1970.

Jan Palach
(1948–1969)
This student lit a beacon
on Wenceslas Square on
January 16, 1969 with his
self-immolation. His death
on January 19 started mass
demonstrations across the
country.

Leonid Brezhnev
(1907–1982)
The secretary general of
the CPSU sent in tanks. On
November 12, 1968 he
proclaimed the Brezhnev
Doctrine, which stated:
»The sovereignty of
socialist nations is
limited.«

C. 200,000 soldiers along with 2,000 tanks
marched into Czechoslovakia on the
night from August 20 to 21, 1968.
Within a few hours all of the
important positions were
occupied.

▶ **Invasion troups**
Albania and Romania
refused to send troops.
The GDR gave logistic
support and kept two
divisions on the alert.

▶ **Casualties**

Invasion troups:
more than 100 dead

Czechoslovakian civilians:
more than 100 dead

»Appeal of the
citizens to the
presidium«
with about 1 mil.
signatures

**Czechoslovakia occupied by
Warsaw Pact troops**

from 11.30pm on
»The anti-reform
alliance« marches in,
protest strikes begin

»Moscow
protocol«,
end of reform
process

Censorship
reintroduced

About 100,000
people emigrate
after the Prague
Spring is put down

July 26   **Aug 20**   **Aug 24**   **Aug 30**   **from about Sep 1968**

against the arrival of Warsaw Pact troops. Six weeks later the 18-year-old schoolboy Jan Zajíc took his own life there in the same manner. A new constitution determined the federation of the Czech state (ČSR) and the Slovakian (SSR), with their own state parliaments and governments in Prague and Bratislava (Pressburg), and a joint parliament attached to the seat of the federal government in Prague.

Treaty of Prague

In 1973 a treaty was signed regarding mutual relations between the ČSSR and the Federal Republic of Germany. Among other things, it declared the Munich Agreement of 1938 null and void, agreed renunciation of force on both sides, and established diplomatic relations. Prague was enlarged considerably through the incorporation of rural areas. Prague's first underground railway (Metro) opened in 1974.

CHARTA 77

Demonstration for freedom and civil rights

In 1977 a civil rights group under the leadership of former foreign minister Jiří Hajek, dramatist **Václav Havel** and philosopher Jan Patočka published »Charta 77 «, which included demands for freedom of opinion and religious conviction as granted in the constitution. On 21 August 1988, the 20th anniversary of the occupation by Warsaw Pact troops, thousands of demonstrators protested against the occupation and in favour of freedom, civil rights and the rehabilitation of supporters of the Prague Spring who had suffered political discrimination. On 28 October, in Wenceslas Square, police put a brutal end to demonstrations critical of the regime; these demonstrations commemorated the founding of the first Czechoslovakian republic in 1918. Prior to the day of national celebration there had been large-scale harassment of respected members of the civil rights movement.

In 1989 several demonstrations marking the 20th anniversary of the self-immolation of Jan Palach in Wenceslas Square were terminated by massive police deployment; protest rallies by the civic rights movement »Charta 77« were prohibited (January). The might of the state reacted to people's growing discontent with even harsher repression, culminating in the callous intervention of state security forces in a university students' procession commemorating the death in 1939 of student Jan Opletal. This proved to be the final trigger for the **»Velvet Revolution«**, which ultimately, without the use of force, led to the overthrow of the Communist domination which had lasted more than 40 years. The first milestones on the way to a new democracy in Czechoslovakia were the appointment of a new »government of national understanding« (10 December) and the election of Václav Havel as president of the republic (29 December).

Truth and Love ...

... triumph over lies and hate: Václav Havel's words in November 1989 at a demonstration on Wencelas Square. The inexorable disintegration of the Eastern Bloc was at hand.

Mikhail Gorbachev introduced glasnost and called for perestroika, whilst cracks began to appear in Moscow's totalitarian powers. East German citizens provided the catalyst, gathering at the Austro-Hungarian border in their thousands, yearning for freedom of movement. It was here that the Iron Curtain swayed and fell in the summer of 1989. In October, some 5000 East Germans who had taken refuge in the garden of the West German embassy in Prague were permitted to leave the country and head towards freedom. In Poland, the »Solidarnosć« union took over from the Communists, in Bulgaria the Communist Party's General Secretary Todor Zhivkov was ousted on 12 November. In Prague, the peaceful transition to a new system took almost six weeks: from 17 November to 29 December 1989.

The switch from a dictatorshop to a democracy was effected without any bloodshed, hence it would become known as the »Velvet Revolution«. If the name sounded rather like a pop song, it is fitting that a courageous singer, Marta Kubišová, joined Václav Havel in lighting the fuse of change at the mass demonstrations in Prague. She had been banned from performing, excluded from her profession, for 20 years, but now she sang »A Prayer for Marta«, a symbol of resistance against the Soviet occupation of 1968. The crowds joined in by rattling their keys – a gesture which matched their demands: open up! Yes, the time had come to liberate an imprisoned nation. The pathway to the first free elections since 1948, since the »dictatorship of the proletariat« had been cleared.

To mark the 20th anniversary of the »Velvet Revolution«, a symbolic »Iron Curtain« is burned on Prague's Národni třida on 17 November 2009.

POLITICAL CHANGE

New federal republic

The ČSSR was re-named ČSFR (Czechoslovakian Federative Republic, 29 March 1990) and, at the insistence of the Slovaks, the name was soon changed to **»Czech and Slovak Federative Republic«**. In free parliamentary elections (8 June 1990), the civil rights movements came out on top in both Czech and Slovak Republics; they formed the nucleus of the new »government of national sacrifice« (27 June 1990). Václav Havel was again elected head of state (5 July 1990). In the subsequent parliamentary elections of 1992, the Democratic Citizens' Party (ODS) in the Czech Republic and the Movement for a Democratic Slovakia (HZDS) in the Slovak Republic gained the most votes. Václav Havel was not able to win the presidential election at this point.

DIVISION INTO TWO INDEPENDENT STATES

On 27 August 1992 the Czech prime minister and his Slovak counterpart agreed that the Czechoslovakian Federation be divided into two independent states from 1 January 1993. The division law was passed by the federal government in Prague on 25 November, though not without a struggle. On 7 November 1992 Alexander Dubček (born 1921), leader and icon of hope for the Prague Spring suppressed by force in 1968, died of injuries received in a road accident. With effect from 1 January 1993 the two successor states, the **Czech Republic** and Slovak Republic (Slovakia), replaced the ČSFR.

THE CZECH REPUBLIC

1993	Prague becomes capital of the Czech Republic, Václav Havel is elected as the first president of the Czech Republic
2003	Václav Havel is succeeded by his arch-rival Václav Klaus as leader.
2004	Czech Republic joins the EU
2007	Czech Republic signs up to the Schengen Agreement
2009	First Czech EU presidency
2011	Death of the poet president Václav Havel shocks the world
2013	Miloš Zeman becomes the new president

New beginning

On 26 January 1993 Václav Havel was elected as the first president of the Czech Republic; he was re-elected five years later. In 1999 the Czech Republic becomes a member of NATO, alongside Hungary and Poland. In August 2002 the Vltava river floods parts of the town, including the Metro, with a century-high record of 4m/15ft; fortunately, Staré Město (the Old Town) was not affected. In June 2003 Václav Havel's presidency comes to an end. The new elections are accompanied by a succession of embarrassing situations as the former parties in government fail to push their advance their candidates. After a tough struggle, Václav Klaus is finally able to organize a small majority. Political irony indeed: Václav Havel is replaced as leader by his political adversary. In May 2004 the **Czech Republic joins the EU** as one of ten new entrants, most of them from the Eastern bloc. In December 2007 the Czech Republic signs up to the Schengen Agreement, removing border controls. In 2009 the Czech Republic takes on the presidency of the EU, but a government crisis in Prague forces Mirek Topolánek to resign. In May of the same year, US President Barack Obama calls for world peace in Prague.

»Thank you, Václav« read a banner carried through the streets of Prague in December 2011, when more than 10,000 people gathered to pay their respects to the »poet president« in a funeral procession. The obsequies represented the largest act of state in Czech history. They lasted for a whole week.

»Thank you, Václav«

The presidential elections to succeed Václav Klaus, who retired after two terms in office, came down to a straight race between former prime minister Miloš Zeman on the left and Karel Schwarzenberg, the incumbent foreign minister. As the run-off drew closer, the campaign escalated. Ex-communists on Zeman's side attacked Schwarzenberg for his comments on the expulsion of Sudeten Germans which contravened international law. President Václav Klaus came out strongly in support of Zeman whilst still in office. The latter had previously made a deal with him, backing his left-wing socialist minority government when in opposition, getting minister posts for his centre right leaning ODS party. In his acceptance speech after the election, the 68-year-old Zeman promised that he did not intend to be a »president of the top ten thousand, but of the bottom ten million« – quite a claim in a country with a population of 10.5 million. When Václav Klaus came to the end of his tenure, the Senate went before the Supreme Court in Brno to charge him with high treason. Amongst the reasons given was the controversial general amnesty which Klaus had announced on New Year's Day. A possible punishment would have been the loss of office – but Klaus had already stepped down officially in March 2013. Miloš Zeman succeeded him.

The old and the new

Arts and Culture

Art History

Bohemia developed into a renowned region for arts and culture under Charles IV. With the help of sculptor and master cathedral mason Peter Parler, important milestones were laid down. The influence of the Bavarian Dientzenhofer family on the city was notable in the Baroque era. Above all, Prague's Art Nouveau legacy, paving the way for Cubist architecture, is very much in evidence until today. The »dancing house« on the Vltava is, however, the work of a later architect, the modernist Frank O. Gehry.

The earliest remains of stone-built Christian churches in the present-day Czech Republic date back to the days of the missionaries to the Slavs, Cyril (Constantine) and Methodius, and are located in what was then the Great Moravian Empire. A pre-9th-century fortified settlement with five sacral buildings was situated in southern Moravian Mikulčice. In the Old Town of Uherského Hradiště Staré (the »Veligrad« of Great Moravia), three 9th-century churches have been identified. The Přemyslid duke Bořivoj (circa 850 – 895), who had been baptized at the Great Moravian court, brought Christianity to Bohemia, and during the first half of the 9th century he founded St Clement's Church on the river Vltava, to the north of what is now Prague. After the ducal seat had been moved to Prague, the Church of Our Lady was built (894). The foundation walls of this small round building are in the castle gallery.

Early ecclesiastical architecture in the Great Moravian Empire

ROMANESQUE ARCHITECTURE

Under Vratislav (circa 905 – 921) St George's Basilica was founded in Hradčany in 912. Notwithstanding the alterations of 1142 – 1150 (to the towers, east and west choir and crypt), it still remains the best-preserved Romanesque building in Prague. An important building in the history of sacred structures, the St Vitus Rotunda, was erected under St Wenceslas from 926 to 930. The round Ottonian design, with four apses in place of the Wenceslas Chapel in the modern St Vitus Cathedral, served as the pattern for several single-aisled round churches (»Bohemian rotundas«) characteristic of Bohemia, such as the Staré Město Chapel of the Holy Cross (circa 1100), St Martin's Chapel in Vyšehrad (mid-11th century) and the

Stone witnesses of time

Art Nouveau is everywhere to be seen in the city on the Vltava – here House Koruna at 1 Wencelas Square

Longinus Chapel (12th century) in Nové Město. The St Vitus Rotunda was replaced in about 1060 by St Vitus Basilica, which has two choirs, a west transept and two crypts, similar to St Emmeram in Regensburg. At around this time Prague Castle (Pražský hrad) had a Romanesque ducal palace; the remains (9th – 12th century) have been preserved beneath Vladislav Hall. In the second half of the 11th century there was already a Romanesque stone castle in Vyšehrad with several sacral buildings (remains of the St Lawrence Basilica). In the monasteries founded from the late 10th century (973, castle monastery of St George; 993, Břevnov; 1148, Strahov) arts and crafts flourished, and in their scriptoria valuable manuscripts were produced, the most famous being the Codex Vyšehradiensis of 1086.

GOTHIC ART AND ARCHITECTURE

New style of building

The Cistercians and Mendicant Friars were the first to bring the Gothic style to Bohemia, in the second quarter of the 13th century. The new manner of building was extended to non-ecclesiastical buildings such as the Gothic palace in Prague Castle (around 1250 – 1400). The Old-New Synagogue (Staronová synagóga) in Josefov (1273) is another example of Gothic architecture. The aspiring burghers used the new style for buildings designed for pomp and ceremony, such as the old town hall (from 1338) in Staré Město.

Late Gothic

Under Charles IV (1346 – 1378), a ruler open to arts and to the world, the Bohemian lands were put on the map of central European art and architecture; the transition to Late Gothic was made. Initially French influence was strong; changes to Prague's Royal Palace were modelled on the French palace on the Île de la Cité in Paris, where Charles had grown up. For the new building of **St Vitus Cathedral** (foundation stone laid 21 November 1344), Charles first summoned **Matthias of Arras** from papal Avignon, whose design followed the characteristic pattern of French cathedrals (choir with radiating ambulatory chapels). However, after Matthias' death (1352) **Peter Parler** (1330–1399) took over the building project with his sons, and introduced entirely new, original aspects (emphasis on the south side with Wenceslas Chapel, transept portal and tower). His constant flow of ingenious ideas gave Prague architecture a dynamism all its own, and the influence of »Parler Gothic« on architecture and sculpture was extensive, reaching as far as Italy and Spain. The Parler workshop created further cathedrals in Kolín and Kutná Hora. The Old Town Bridge Tower in Prague, not completed until the beginning of the 15th century, was also constructed from Parler's drawings.

The court art of Charles IV's era anticipated important features of the Renaissance: the first ribbed vaulting and effigies (triforium busts in St Vitus Cathedral), and the first free-standing equestrian statue (St George at Prague Castle), by the brothers Martin and Georg Klausenburg.

Court art

A distinctive and independent school of painting, evident in all genres, grew out of a synthesis of foreign (especially Italian) and specifically Bohemian characteristics. The leading artists of this fraternity, the so-called Prague »Malerzeche« were the Master of Hohenfurt, active in Prague c1350, Master Theoderic (documented 1359 – 1380) and the Master of Wittingau (documented 1380 – 1390), who mainly created altar panel paintings (St Agnes Monastery, Karlštejn Castle). Also characteristic are the Bohemian »pictures of grace«, half-figure portraits of the Madonna with child by anonymous masters, which show Byzantine influence. The most important wall-paintings, usually difficult to assign to individual artists, are found in Emmaus Monastery in Prague, founded in 1357, and at Karlštejn Castle (1348 – 1357), where the Strasbourg master Nikolaus Wurmser (documen-

Prague »Malerzeche«

The master of Litoměřice painted the polychrome pictures in St Wencelas Chapel, St Vitus Cathedral

ted 1357 – 1360), and probably also Tommaso da Modena (circa 1325 – 1379), were active. Outstanding illuminated manuscripts were produced, frequently commissioned by the Silesian humanist John of Neumarkt, under whom a standard written form of German began to establish itself as the language of the Prague chancellery. After the death of Charles IV (1378) and Peter Parler (1399) the arts declined. Contrasting with the rather realistic approach of the Prague »Malerzeche«, there now arose the »International« and »Soft« styles, a subtly refined manner of painting found mainly in pictures of the Madonna circa 1400 (Sights from A to Z, St Agnes Monastery). Charles IV's activities as planner and patron are evident in Prague to this day (founding of Nové Město, Charles Bridge, Na Karlově Church). However, he was not able to complete all his ambitious projects. The eruption of the Hussite revolution (1419, First Defenestration of Prague) put an abrupt end to the unparalleled flowering of the city, and some buildings remained unfinished, either for ever, such as the Church of Our Lady of the Snows (Marie Sněžné) or for a long time (St Vitus Cathedral, Týn Church).

Architecture in the 15th century

After the Hussite Wars, the character of Bohemian art – now almost entirely Czech – remained conservative and eclectic until the end of the 15th century. The most important Czech architect of the time was Matthias Rejsek, who was responsible for the Powder Gate (Prašná brána) in 1474. The most important artist invited to Prague under

House »At The Minute« with sgraffito ornamentation

King Vladislav II (1471 – 1516) was Benedikt Ried. His designs were used for Vladislav Hall in Prague Castle's Royal Palace, one of the most magnificent secular interiors of the time (1493 – 1502), and for the nave of St Barbara's Church in Kutná Hora (1512 – 1547), with arguably the most beautiful late Gothic ribbed vaulting to be found anywhere. The sculpture and painting of the period, like many of the buildings, belong by and large to the Renaissance; they reflect almost all of the important schools and trends of the Dürer epoch. The most remarkable of the Czech artists is the master of the Litoměřice altar (Sights from A to Z, St Agnes Monastery), who participated in the painting of the upper part of Wenceslas Chapel in St Vitus Cathedral in around 1509; he himself painted the most important scenes from the Wenceslas legend.

RENAISSANCE

Italian Renaissance art was probably established earlier in Prague than anywhere else in central Europe, except Hungary. As early as the period 1538 to 1555 the Belvedere colonnade in Prague Castle's royal garden was constructed from plans by Paolo della Stella. This was commissioned by Ferdinand I (1526 – 1564) for his wife Anna, and is one of the purest examples of Renaissance architecture north of the Alps. Archduke Ferdinand also provided the idea for the bizarre Star Summer Palace, Letohrádek hvězda, constructed by Italians in the years 1555 – 1558 on a star-shaped ground plan. After the mid-16th century Bohemia's leading architect was the imperial court master builder **Bonifaz Wohlmut** from Überlingen on Lake Constance (organ loft in St Vitus Cathedral, 1557 – 1561; Ball-Game Hall in Prague Castle garden, 1568; ribbed vaulting in castle Assembly Hall, 1559 – 1563; stellar vault dome in the Church of Our Lady and Charlemagne, Nové Město, 1575). The new style developed features specific to Prague. After the great fire of 1541 which destroyed large parts of Prague Castle and Malá Strana, several aristocratic residences were built, such as Martinický Palace (late 16th century) and Schwarzenberský Palace on Hradčany Square, both in the Bohemian Renaissance style that saw the façades adorned with lavish sgraffito ornamentation. Such sgraffiti also decorate many civic buildings of the Renaissance, such as the houses of »The Three Ostriches« (1585) near Charles Bridge and the »At the Minute« (late 16th century) next to the town hall in Staré Město. Here the façade ornamentation shows scenes from antiquity and the Bible, and allegories of the virtues.

Architecture

Under the Habsburg ruler Rudolf II (1576 – 1611), a keen art collector, Prague once more became an imperial seat and a centre for Mannerist works. The emperor drew artists of the most diverse of origins

Mannerist works

to his court: the sculptors and bronze-casters Benedikt Wurzelbauer and Adriaen de Vries (whose work anticipated many Baroque features), and the painters Hans of Aachen, Bartholomäus Spranger, Jan Brueghel (»Velvet Brueghel«), Guiseppe Arcimboldo, Roelandt Savery, Joseph Heintz, Hans Rottenhammer and Aegidius Sadeler. Sadeler left a prospect of Prague, 1606, consisting of nine engravings, an overview of the architecture of the time. Yet Mannerist art served the interests of the court alone, and did not resonate widely in Bohemia. The Czech engraver Wenzel Hollar (1607 – 1677) and still-life painter Gottfried Flegel (1563 – 1638) both made a name for themselves, abroad as well as at home, as representatives of a Bohemian art of the period rooted more strongly in their native country. St Roch Chapel in Strahov shows that Gothic influences were retained right down to the late Renaissance. It exhibits an exciting synthesis of Gothic features such as pointed arches and buttresses with Renaissance motifs.

BAROQUE

Italian influence

The Counter-Reformation finally triumphed through the Catholic victory at the Battle of the White Mountain (Bílá hora) in 1620, and brought Baroque architecture to Prague, largely from Italy in the early stages. For approximately half a century Italian craftsmen dominated almost all construction work. They were organized into fraternities, and most of them came from the Como region. For their own community they built the »Italian Chapel« as early as 1590 – 1600, the first Baroque central-plan building in Prague. Palace and castle construction In the 17th century the emphasis initially was on the building of palaces and castles. The most important patrons among the Prague magnates were Albrecht of Wallenstein, for whose enormous Valdštejnský Palace (1623 – 1630) an entire district of the city had to be demolished, and Humprecht Count of Černín (Černínský Palace, 1669 – 1692). Church building was at first strongly influenced by the Jesuits' church in Rome »Il Gesù«; this was the model for the alterations in 1611 – 1616 to what had been the Protestant Church of St Maria de Victoria (Kostel Panny Marie Vítězné). The most prolific experts in this Jesuit style were Carlo Lurago (Church of St Ignatius or Kostel sv Ignáce, 1665 – 1678) and Giovanni Domenico Orsi de Orsini (Jesuits' house, Church of St Nicholas (Chrám sv Mikuláše) in Malá Strana, 1673). However, some church buildings continued earlier Czech traditions (galleries, wall pillars), such as St Salvator's Church (Kostel sv Salvátora) in Knights of the Cross Square (Křižovnické náměstí).

Painting and sculpture

In the fields of sculpture and painting, by contrast, Czech artists, or migrants from nearby countries, continued to dominate the scene.

The original figures on the Charles Bridge – most of which have since been replaced with replicas – were crafted by Prague's finest Baroque sculptors

The most important sculptors from the mid-17th century were Johann Georg Bendl (circa 1630 – 1680; statues on the façade of St Salvator's Church and Vintners' Column in Knights of the Cross Square, St Wenceslas in the old deanery at Prague Castle); and Hieronymus Kohl (1632 – 1709; statues on the façade of the Church of St Thomas (Kostel sv Tomáše) in Malá Strana, fountain in the second courtyard of Prague Castle). The most prominent painters were Karel Škréta (1610 – 1674), born into an aristocratic Bohemian family, who emigrated for religious reasons and returned as a convert; and Michael Leopold Willmann (1630 – 1706), a pupil of Rembrandt (works in the Bohemian art collection from the time of Rudolf II to the Baroque era, in St George's Monastery).

Late Baroque reached its peak in Prague during the first half of the 18th century, the most productive era for the arts since the time of Charles IV. The Frenchman Jean Baptiste Mathey (circa 1630 – 1695), who had trained in Rome, was the first to make the link with European developments: in church architecture, with the central plan of the Knights of the Cross Church (also, the Church of St Francis of Assisi, 1679 – 1688); in secular building with Troja Chateau (1679 – 1685). This brought Italian hegemony to an end. Soon Prague's own artists were able to take the lead, after assimilating the formative influence of Austrian and Bavarian architecture of the time.

The National Theatre displays historic neo-Renaissance architecture; it reflects Czech cultural self-assurance

Dientzenho-fer Baroque The Viennese court architect Johann Bernhard Fischer von Erlach worked on Clam-Gallas Palace from 1707 and left several pupils in Prague. Christoph Dientzenhofer (1655 – 1722) came from a family of Bavarian architects who were active in many locations. He settled in Prague, and with his brilliant son Kilian Ignaz Dientzenhofer (1689 – 1751) created **Dientzenhofer Baroque**, a synthesis of the traditional Bavarian wall-pillar system and the baldachin principle of Guarino Guarini; this was the prerequisite for the last, supreme phase of central European ecclesiastical architecture.

Works begun in rather conventional manner by the father were often perfected architecturally and stylistically by his more gifted son. This was the case in Břevnov Monastery, in the Church of the Nativity of Our Lord (behind the Loreta), and especially in the Church of St Nicholas (Kostel sv Mikuláš) in Malá Strana, one of the most important late Baroque church edifices anywhere in central Europe with regard to historical development and urban architecture. Christoph Dientzenhofer had planned the dome according to the Bavarian wall-pillar system. His son gave it the space-creating conch motif, and with the asymmetrical exterior dome-scape he deftly added a crucial ingredient to Prague's silhouette.

The overall view of Prague and the wider Baroque cultural landscape of Bohemia would be unthinkable without Kilian Ignaz Dientzenhofer's contribution. Further important buildings of his are: Villa Amerika, the Church of St Nicholas in Staré Město, the Church of St John Nepomuk on the Rock (Kostel sv Jana Nepomuckého na Skalce) and the Ursuline nunnery in Kutná Hora; furthermore, he carried out the remodelling of the Church of St Thomas in Malá Strana. He also designed the plans for Goltz-Kinský Palace and Sylva-Taroucca Palace, both of which show early Rococo features. Giovanni Santini-Aichl (1667 – 1723) designed Morzinský Palace and Thun-Hohenštejnský Palace; in sacral building he subscribed to a historicizing Baroque Gothic style (Church of Our Lady at Sedlec, Kutná Hora), as did Octaviano Broggio (1668–1742). Other architects of the period included František Maximilian Kaňka (1674 – 1766), whose designs included the terraces of the Vrtba Garden (Vrtbovská zahrada) and various parts of the Klementinum; and Giovanni Battista Alliprandi (1665 – 1720).

One of the most important of the many sculptors active in Prague around 1700 was Matthias Wenzel Jäckel (1655 – 1738), whose works included statues for Charles Bridge and the former Church of the Knights of the Cross (also, the Church of St Francis of Assisi, on Křižovnické náměstí). Ferdinand Maximilian Brokoff (1688 – 1731) was another sculptor responsible for several groups of figures on Charles Bridge. Matthias Bernhard Braun (1684 – 1738) brought the influence of Bernini to Bohemia, and his works represent the high point of Bohemian Baroque sculpture. Some of his figures, too, are found on Charles Bridge, others in the Vrtba Garden (Vrtbovská zahrada) and by the portal of Thun-Hohenštejnský Palace.

Sculpture

There is some representation of the Rococo style in Prague; yet in Bohemia, as in Austria, it never became an independent variant as it did, for instance, in Bavaria, Franconia and Potsdam. Empress Maria Theresa's chief court architect, Nicolo Pacassi, was in charge of the 1753 – 1775 extension of Prague Castle; Johann Joseph Wirch was responsible for the extension of the archbishop's palace, 1764 – 1765. Prague owes the design of the Estates Theatre (Stavovské divadlo), realized between 1781 and 1783 by Anton Haffenecker, to the cavalier architect Count von Künigl. It was here that Mozart's »Don Giovanni« was first performed in 1787. The leading sculptors in the third quarter of the 18th century in Prague were Johann Anton Quittainer (1709 – 1765), Ignaz Platzer the Elder (1717 – 1787), whose works included the design for the façade ornamentation of the archbishop's palace, and Richard Prachner (1705 – 1782). The Church of St Nicholas in Malá Strana has works by Platzer and Prachner. The painter Norbert Grund (1717 – 1767), a proponent of the »Feinmaler« technique, made a name for himself well beyond Bohemia; during his lifetime his works were forged and several times they were reproduced by means of engravings.

Rococo

»Open the Windows to Europe«

The year 1891 was an important one for Prague, both in terms of politics and architecture. The arboretum on the east side of the Letná Gardens played host to the »Bohemian National Exhibition«, a trade fair designed to document Bohemia's ascent to industrial nation status.

The buildings constructed for this exhibition were clearly designed with an eye cast towards England, Europe's »first« industrial nation, and to the culturally pre-eminent France: the Hanavský Pavilion, moved in 1898 to its current position on the Letná plateau, was constructed from pieces of wrought iron, as were the modern glass and iron constructions of English exhibition architecture; and the 60m/200ft viewing-tower built by the Czech tourist club on Petrín hill was nothing other than a copy of the Eiffel Tower in Paris.

Yet in spite of these progressive signs at the beginning of the 1890s, Art Nouveau did not become widely established in Prague until the turn of the century – relatively late. Art Nouveau architects active from the very beginning included Otto Wagner's pupil Jan Kotěra, who exerted an enormous influence on the younger generation, both as architect (for instance, of Peterka House erected in 1899/1900 at 12 Wenceslas Square), and as a teacher. »Open the windows to Europe« was his motto, and it fired Prague's artists with enthusiasm

Art Nouveau spread to architecture as well as decorative arts

for the most recent developments in western Europe. Art Nouveau architecture spread in Prague from the turn of the century, especially along Wenceslas Square, which had been developing into a generous metropolitan boulevard from the mid-19th century, and along neighbouring Na přikopě (On the Moat) – the two together forming the »Golden Cross«. The new style was used in hotels and cafés, insurance offices, large stores, ornate assembly rooms and association headquarters. One of the best addresses on the square was number 29, the »Archduke Stephen«, built in 1903, now the Grand Hotel Evropa; its gabled façade is distinguished by clear structure and lavish moulded decoration. The sumptuous interior of the coffee house on the ground floor is still (almost) entirely authentic. Two years before the hotel opened in 1901, the building of Prague's main railway station had begun. In spite of various later alterations, there is still no denying its Secession character.

Pomp and ceremony

House Koruna, on the corner of Wenceslas Square and Na přikopě, was built between 1911 and 1914 from plans by Antonín Pfeiffer, and is clearly recognisable by its lofty tower. It houses offices and business premises, and embodies the more Constructivist version of Prague Art Nouveau. On Národní are two particularly good Secession buildings by Osvald Polívka: the Topic publishing house; and directly adjacent, the former »Praha« Insurance Company (1903 to 1905),

whose name is prominently inscribed in large letters artistically looped around the oval windows on the façade. At the east end of Na přikopě, the Municipal House, built between 1906 and 1911 according to plans by Antonín Balšánek and Osvald Polívka, takes up a whole block. However, the magnificence of this building cannot disguise the fact that it is just as close to late 19th-century neo-Baroque as it is to Art Nouveau, which in fact had passed its peak by the time the Municipal House

Glass mosaic in Obecní dům (Municipal House)

was completed. One of those involved in the design was Alfons Mucha, who had already made a name for himself in Paris as a painter, illustrator and poster designer. Just behind the Municipal House is the luxury hotel Palíô (U obecního domu 1), which has an impeccable, elaborately restored Art Nouveau interior; a look at the elegant entrance hall should not be passed up.

19TH CENTURY

Classicism   Unlike the Baroque, to which Bohemians clung longer and more pas-
sionately than did other central Europeans, Classicism was relatively
insignificant, at least as far as fine arts were concerned. The former
Customs House, »U hybernú« (Municipal House), was given its Empire façade in 1808 – 1811 by Georg Fischer. It is one of the most
remarkable architectural achievements of the period.

Romanticism   Romanticism was the first movement to be kindled in Bohemia after
Herder's ideas had contributed to the awakening of the Czech nation.
Yet the Czechs' attainment of cultural independence resulted also in
the decline of supranational »Bohemian art«; from the second half of
the 19th century there was an increasingly decisive drift into separate Czech and German components. The most important of the Romantic and post-Romantic painters were Joseph von Führich (1800
– 1876), Josef Mánes (1820 – 1871) and Mikoláš Aleš (1852 – 1913),
as well as Gabriel Max, pupil of Piloty, and Václav Brožík. Important
representatives of neo-Gothic were Joseph Kranner (high altar in St
Vitus Cathedral, 1868 – 1873) and Joseph Mocker (extension of St
Vitus Cathedral, 1859 – 1929). The Czech pupil of Semper, Josef Zítek, designed the magnificent National Theatre (1868 – 1881) in ostentatious Czech neo-Renaissance style, but after a great fire it had to
be replaced by architect Josef Schulz (1840–1917); it re-opened in
1883. Josef Schulz also directed the building of the »Rudolfinum«,
arguably the most important building of this era in Prague. In sculpture, a school influenced by French art was founded by Josef Václav
Myslbek (1848 – 1922; equestrian statue of St Wenceslas on Wenceslas
Square, bronze statue of cardinal Schwarzenberg in St Vitus Cathedral). Distinguished students included Jan Štursa (1880 – 1925), Bohumil Kafka (1878–1942; Mánes memorial in front of the Rudolfinum), and Otto Gutfreund (1889 – 1927).

FROM THE 20TH INTO THE 21ST CENTURY

Architecture   Scarcely any other city can rival Prague for **Art Nouveau** buildings.
The best example of »Prague Secession style« is the splendid Municipal
House (Obecní dům), built from 1906 – 1911 according to plans by
Osvald Polívka and Antonín Balšánek. Among the forerunners of mo-
dern architecture in the 20th century were Josef Maria Olbrich (1867
– 1908), Josef Hoffmann (1870 – 1956) and Adolf Loos (1870 – 1933),
whose main work, however, was carried out in Darmstadt (Olbrich) or
Vienna (Hoffmann and Loos). »House Müller« by Adolf Loos, in
Prague-Střešovice, was built between 1928 and 1930. In it Loos realized
for the first time his »space plan« – a concept of living space based on

the principle of individual rooms varying in height, arranged around the central axis of the house. Cubism The final move to modern architecture in Prague was made by Josef Gočár (1880 – 1945), who built the Cubist »House of the Black Madonna« (dům U černé Matky Boží) on Celetná in 1911/1912; Pavel Janák and Josef Chochol. Chochol's Cubist architecture is a Prague speciality that can be interpreted as a counter-trend to Functionalism. Villa Kovařovič at Libušina 3 or the residential building Neklanova 30 (Sights from A to Z, Vyšehrad) transfer the vividness and dimensionality of Picasso's paintings to architecture. The Functionalist Trade Fair Palace (Veletržní palác) by Oldřich Tyl and Josef Fuchs today houses part of Prague's National Gallery; the monumental building was erected between 1925 and 1928, and it impressed even Le Corbusier. Prague Castle The architect Josip Plečnik was commissioned by Tomáš Garrigue Masaryk, co-founder of the (first) Republic of Czechoslovakia, to modernize Prague Castle – an undertaking that was not completed until 1928. He adapted historic elements and aimed for a dialogue between past and present, tending towards a style that might now be described as postmodern.

The Futurist television tower (1987–1990) by Václav Aulický was initially hugely controversial; it is a vital component of Žižkov's skyline today. The highlight of contemporary architecture in the city is the »Dancing House« (Tančící dům) of 1996 by architects Frank O. Gehry and Vlado Milunić, which stands on the corner of Jirásek Square (Jiráskovo náměstí) and Rašín Quay (Rašínovo nábřeží) alongside the Vltava (see p.17). The eccentric glass and concrete building, also called »Ginger & Fred« after the twinkle-toed stars of the Hollywood musical, filled a gap on the bank of the Vltava left by World War II. The undulating façade of the seven-storey building fits in very cleverly alongside Rococo, Renaissance and Art Nouveau façades. Frenchman Jean Nouvel is another architect of international renown who has left his mark on Prague: the »Zlatý Anděl« commercial and office building. *The present*

Conservative art trends in Prague are represented, for instance, by the painter and illustrator Max Švabinský (1873 – 1962), whose works include beautiful glass paintings in St Vitus Cathedral (1946 – 1948); and Heinrich Hönich, a pupil of Wilhelm Leibl. There were important exponents of Expressionism as well as Cubism. German-speaking artists were more numerous among the Expressionists (Oskar Kokoschka, Alfred Kubin, Josef Hegenbarth), Czechs among the Cubists (Emil Filla, Václav Špála). The monumental Jan Hus memorial of 1915 on Old Town Square is by Ladislav Šaloun, who also designed allegorical sculptures for several buildings in Prague. The art pedagogue and theoretician Adolf Hölzel (1853 – 1934) from Olomouc is one of the founders of abstract painting. *Conservative art trends*

Strong Emotions, Strong Art

Born in Prague, the sculptor David Černý is a master of productive disquietude. His sculptures are not only hot topics of conversation, they can sometimes be the source of scandal.

Portrait of the artist as cheerful provocateur: David Černý

A red double decker bus doing push-ups, a parody on sport as the Czech contribution to the Olympic Games 2012. David Černý's »London Booster« huffed and puffed itself fit with push-ups in the Islington district of London and was as controversially received as most works by Mr »Black« (Černý in Czech). Three years earlier, in 2009, to mark the Czech presidency of the EU, he created an allegorical map of Europe which was intended to go on display in the Council's atrium for six months and then hang in the National Theatre in Prague for the next six months. In formal terms, the piece had got rather out of hand, measuring some 16m/52ft square and weighing some 8 tons. With regard to content, certain elements of his »Entropa« collage transgressed every possible boundary of state-related political correctness. Germany was represented as a network of motorways, arranged in a manner which vaguely resembled a swastika. Denmark was constructed from Lego bricks, with the face of the Prophet Muhammad discernible in the landscape.

Legends

More than a few critics saw what he was up to – taking national prejudices and making caricatures of them to the point of unmistakable satire – and were upset. Černý caused further outrage when it became apparent that the legend accompanying the work, meticulously documenting each of the 26 participating artists from each of the EU states, was itself a work of fiction. Černý had created the whole thing with just the help of his two assistants and had invented the names and biographies of the 26. He owned up to this »misunderstanding«, claiming he had merely intended to inject an element of humour into his sculpture. In Brussels, the entire sculpture was hastily dismantled. For a while it was parked in the DOX Centre for Contemporary Art in Prague, before moving to its current location at

Černý sets out to prove that basic laws can be turned on their head – his inverted equestrian monument in the Lucerna Palace.

the newly opened Techmania factory museum in Plzeň. Černý, labelled the »bad boy of Czech art« by the critics, is no longer just a phenomenon in Prague, but in the whole of the Czech Republic.

The Pink Tank

Born in the year 1967, Černý had not dreamed of becoming an artist. »My parents were artists themselves. As a child there was nothing I hated more than being dragged to all those exhibition openings« he recalls. He first studied design and graphic design, but art won out in the end. Černý loved extremes too much to be satisfied with sketching tables, chairs and sofas. His works were garish from the very beginning, turned down by one gallery after another. He tried his luck at Prague's largest open air gallery, the Charles Bridge, but found no takers for his pictures and objects. A protest action in September 1989 made a star of him overnight – quite literally in fact, as the »Pink Tank« was created overnight. Černý and his assistants painted a Russian tank pink. This monument to the liberation of the city by the Red Army in 1945 had, over the next four decades, become a symbol of the despised Soviet occupation. Now, painted pink, it symbolized a non-violent act of liberation: the »Velvet Revolution«. At that time, the Eastern Bloc was in a state of upheaval and Černý drove his political point home: his golden Trabant on four legs (»Quo Vadis« – inspired by the East German citizens who fled to the West German embassy in

Prague) established him on the international stage. Today he is described as the »Kafka of sculpture«, his style a »mix of Damien Hirst and Fernando Botero«. The latter is in relation to his black babies (»Miminkas«). Černý's contribution to the Prague scene is his own »MeetFactory« art centre, alongside the tracks of the Smíchov railway station. There is a good chance of meeting Černý in person here. The art millionaire is instantly recognizable with his unkempt bird's nest hair, clad in black T-shirt and worn out military parka. He is often to be found at the entrance, a beer in one hand and smartphone in the other. Of an evening, he listens in on the live bands: left of centre, electro and indie, audio vitamins. Just what Mr Black ordered.

Černý Sculpture Walk

Those wishing to follow the art trail in Prague should make sure they have a half day at their disposal.

Miminkas – eight black babies scale the Žižkov TV tower (Vinohrady, Mahlerovy sady (metro line A: Jiřího z Poděbrad)

Horse – Wencelas astride his upside-down steed – in the Lucerna Palace at Wencelas Square.

Hanging out – Sigmund Freund swinging from an iron beam above a narrow cobbled street in the Old Town (Na Perštyně, U Medviku brewery; metro line B: Národni).

Brownnosers – two headless, five metre/16 foot high rear ends are bent over against a wall, The giants can be climbed by means of a ladder. A video plays inside the cavernous hole, Queen's »We Are The Champions« reverberates in the belly of the sculptures. Ex-president Václav Havel can be seen inside, a punchline which the duped dignitary took with good grace – Černý enjoys a jester's licence (Futura art gallery, Smíchov, Holečkova 49, Mon–Sun, 11am–6pm; tram 4, 9, 10, 16: Bertramka).

Mimi Kampa – three black monster babies, their mouths stapled shut, crawl outside the entrance to the Kampa Museum (Lesser Quarter, Kampa Island; tram 9, 20, 22: Újezd).

Quo Vadis – golden Trabant on four legs (German Embassy garden, Lesser Quarter, Vlašská 19; tram 12, 20, 22: Lesser Town Square).

Piss (Proudy) – two mechanical aluminium men urinate on a map of the Czech Republic (outside the Kafka Museum, Lesser Quarter, Cihelná 2b, metro line A: Malostranská).

Meat – two red limousines hang like meat from the façade of the MeetFactory, Smichov, Ke Sklárně 15 (tram 12, 14, 20: Lihovar). Is it art or a scandal? Černý is the subject of heated debate – and always good for a surprise.

From top to bottom: Černý's »MeetFactory« at Smíchovské nádraží; one of his monster babies at the museum on Kampa Island; »Piss« in front of the Kafka Museum

Famous People

MADELEINE ALBRIGHT (*1937)

From the Vltava to the Potomac River, from Prague to Washington, **First woman**
D.C.: born on 15 May 1937 in Prague, the daughter of a Czechoslova- **to become**
kian diplomat and future professor of politics in the USA, Marie Jana **United States**
Korbelová was the first woman to become United States Secretary of **Secretary of**
State, a position she held from 1997 – 2001. In 2012 she published a **State**
book under the title of »Prague Winter« which recounted her childhood memories, further noting that up until the moment she entered
office as Secretary of State, she had no idea that she came from a Jewish family which lost over twenty members in the National Socialists' Holocaust. Why did her father, whom she adored – »I was the
perfect daughter. I still am today, even though he is dead« – never talk
to her about the darkest chapter in their family's history? She doesn't
know. The family fled to London in 1939 and only returned to Prague
after the war had ended in 1945. Young Madeleine spent part of her
childhood in Serbia, where her father worked for the Czechoslovakian
embassy in Belgrade. But the family was forced to take flight once
again after the Communist coup d'état in 1948. This time they went to
America, where the young emigrant studied political science, law and
international relations. She became a US citizen in 1957 and two years
later married the journalist Joseph Medill Patterson Albright. Her un-
precedented career saw her employed on the National Security Council from 1978 – 1981; under Clinton she became US Ambassador to
the United Nations in 1993 and continued until 1997 when she became the first female US Secretary of State. The »Velvet Revolution«
engendered new hope in her for old homeland. »All my life«, she wrote in her memoir, »I had believed in the virtues of democratic government, the need to stand up to evil, and the age-old motto of the Czech
people: Pravda vítězí or Truth shall prevail«.

TYCHO BRAHE (1546–1601)

When the Danish astronomer Tycho Brahe came to Prague in 1597 **Astronomer**
he was already famous; from 1599 he served as Emperor Rudolf II's
court astronomer. Brahe had built an observatory in Denmark; his
astronomical instruments were the largest of the time – the telescope
had not yet been discovered. Though his observations yielded the
empirical foundations for Kepler's laws of planetary motion, he remained an opponent of the heliocentric world picture. For a long
time Tycho Brahe's system of the world, which continued to place the
earth at the centre of the universe, competed with that of Copernicus.

**Prague-born Madeleine Albright at a book presentation in the city on
the Vltava**

CHRISTOPH (1655 – 1722) AND KILIAN IGNAZ DIENTZENHOFER (1689 – 1751)

Christoph Dientzenhofer came from a large family network of Bavarian architects. Having moved to Prague, he never worked anywhere else. With his genius son Kilian Ignaz he created Dientzenhofer Baroque, a synthesis of the early Bavarian wall-pillar system and the baldachin principle of Italian Guarino Guarini. This was the prerequisite for the final, supreme phase of Baroque sacral architecture in central Europe. The father's works were often begun in a rather conventional manner and then brought to architectural and stylistic perfection by the son. This is the case, for instance, in Břevnov Monastery, in the Church of the Nativity of Our Lord (behind the Loreta), and especially in St Nicholas Church in Malá Strana, one of the most significant late Baroque sacral buildings anywhere in central Europe with regard to historical development and urban architecture. The Church of St Nicholas in the north-west corner of Staré Město is also the work of Kilian Ignaz Dientzenhofer. Further important buildings of his are: Villa Amerika, the Church of St John Nepomuk on the Rock and the remodelled Church of St Thomas. He also designed the plans for Sylva-Taroucca Palace and Goltz-Kinský Palace.

VĚRA ČÁSLAVSKÁ (*1941)

Gymnast One courageous woman stood alongside the men who resisted Communism – the gymnast Věra Čáslavská. She won three gold medals at the 1964 Olympic Games in Tokyo, four more gold and two silver medals in Mexico four years later. Using her triumph as a political demonstration, she protested against the Soviet invasion and dedicated her Olympic medals to the tragic hero of the Prague Spring, Alexander Dubček, who sought to create »socialism with a human face« but was forced to resign by Moscow. The Olympic queen paid dearly for her courage, banned from the gymnastics association and prohibited from training other gymnasts. She was eventually rehabilitated after the events of 1989 and engaged by the president Václav Havel as a sporting advisor.

JÁRA CIMRMAN (CIRCA 1854 – ?)

»The greatest Czech of all time« »Jára Cimrman will outlive us all«, Václav Havel once wrote on a scrap of paper which now lies in the Cimrman Museum. The collection is dedicated to the »greatest Czech of all time«. How to make sense of that? The Swiss have their William Tell, the East Germans their Till Eulenspiegel and the Czechs have Cimrman, an entrepreneurial spirit who is full of ideas and zest for action. A biography exists for the man whose name is an onomatopoeic transcription of »Zimmermann«, but it is riddled with inconsistencies. Starting with his date of birth. A footnote states: »The clerk was drunk«, a portent of more absurdities to come. Introduced in 1966 via a radio show entitled »The Spider Non-alcoholic Wine Bar«, Cimrman is a phantom, invented by the authors Ladislav Smoljak and Zdeněk Svěrák, who consistently concocted new stories for their fictional character over a period of 40 years. Examples: who made the suggestion to the US government to build the Panama Canal? The Czech Cimrman! Who gave Gustav Eiffel the idea of building a panoramic tower in Paris? All-rounder Cimrman! Who invented yoghurt and the bikini? Cimrman of course!

Cimrmania reached its peak in 2006. Whilst the British voted Winston Churchill as the greatest figure in their history and the Germans chose Konrad Adenauer, Czech television's equivalent show added Cimrman to their shortlist more in jest than as a serious candidate. But the Czechs indicated every possibility that they would vote for Cimrman – at which point Czech TV bosses insisted on historical fact as a condition, handing victory to Charles IV. In Žižkov, a district of Prague, there is not only a Cimrman museum, but also a Cimrman theatre. Here Cimrman appears as the perenially misunderstood, unrecognized genius, a tormented dreamer in an ungrateful world. Condemned to fail, he masters his odyssey with humour and stoicism. Cimrman's creators themselves proved to be successful in their own right, winning an Oscar in Hollywood for the comedy »Kolja«. Written by the father Zdeněk Svěrák and directed by his son Jan, it really is a must see film.

Cimrman versus Charles IV

ANTONÍN DVOŘÁK (1841 – 1904)

The works of Antonín Dvořák continue to be performed today with great regularity in concert halls the world over. With his numerous chamber music compositions and great symphonies, he is regarded as a trailblazer of independent Slavic music. The composer was born in Nelahozeves close to Prague; in 1875 he was awarded an Austrian state scholarship, thanks in part to a recommendation from Johannes Brahms.
From 1884 Dvořák travelled to England several times, and from 1891 he was professor at the Prague Conservatory. During his three-year stay in America as head of the National Conservatory in New York (1892 – 1895) he influenced many young American composers. His most famous work, the New World Symphony (1893), is full of impressions garnered at this time; elements of American folklore are

Composer

united with Bohemian and Moravian folk music. Dvořák also made a name for himself as a composer of operas.

KAREL GOTT (*1939)

»The golden voice of Prague«

In 1968 the Vltava Prague Cafe was always completely packed to the rafters whenever the beguiling singer in a tight-fitting sports jacket delivered a message from the west: »Rock Around the Clock«. Backed by Karl Krautgartner's band, Karel Gott was bold enough to plaster a kiss curl on his forehead like Bill Haley and swivel his hips like Elvis, a hot property in the Cold War era. Having studied opera as a tenor at the Prague Conservatory, Gott would cover an astounding range of musical styles in the decades that followed: jazz, chanson, tearjerkers, swing, ballads, folk songs and Christmas carols. And »Maya the Bee«, of course. Canny American promoters labelled him the »Sinatra of the East« when they brought him to Las Vegas for a casino opening. His big breakthrough in Germany came courtesy of a TV appearance in 1968 for Kulenkampff. Forty years later he would perform a duet with Berlin rapper Bushido, who perhaps felt drawn to the Prague tenor by an unconscious yearning for an untroubled world. The duo performed their song »Für immer jung« live at the Brandenburg Gate with such gusto that even the Hells Angels had to wipe away a tear or two.

JAROSLAV HAŠEK (1883 – 1923)

Author

Hašek created in Josef Švejk an immortal figure whose disarming naivety exposes the stupidity of the world; the work is an anti-militarist satire on the Austro-Hungarian monarchy, although this means rather less to the current generation. Those who engaged in passive resistance after the »Velvet Revolution« only punished themselves. Under a Communist dictatorship, this stance had been a necessary means of self-protection, whereas in the spirit of a new democracy it represented a poor alternative to active participation. In his day, Hašek and his friends ran a cabaret in the »Cowshed« bar, located in the Vinohrady district; each of them wrote his own part in the afternoon, ready to play same the evening. Hašek's talent for improvisation proved very useful when he appeared as chairman, candidate and main speaker for the »Party of Moderate Progress within the Bounds of Law« which he had founded. In 1915 he was conscripted into the 91st Infantry Regiment, but defected to the Russian side before the year was out. He returned to Prague under a false name in 1921, and the first adventures of »The Good Soldier Švejk«, created out of his experiences of the war, appeared in March the same year. Initially no publisher could be found, so Hašek published it himself and hawked it around in pubs. Each week he produced a new chapter but when alcoholism led to his death in January 1923, Hašek had not completed Švejk's story: his name became famous only after his death.

VÁCLAV HAVEL (1936 – 2011)

From politically persecuted author and dissident to first representative of his Czech homeland – the career of Václav Havel, native of Prague, reads like a modern fairy-tale. During the Prague Spring, Havel was chairman of the »Club of Independent Writers« and became one of the most prominent spokesman of dissident intellectuals. Forbidden to publish in his own country after their attempts at reform had been crushed, his plays for theatre and radio were performed to great acclaim elsewhere in Europe.

Poet president

His activities as spokesman for and co-founder of »Charter 77« led to harassment, house arrest and a total of 50 months in prison. Yet despite health problems Havel would not budge. In the year 1989 he was elected chairman of the newly founded Civic Forum, and 40 days later he was unanimously chosen as the first democratically elected state president of the Czechoslovakian Republic. Although he was elected to this office a second time in the Czech Republic, the »poet-president«, who coined the phrase the »Velvet Revolution« to capture the events of November 1989, found his international esteem offset by dwindling support at home. Following the political transition, he resembled a character from one of Hrabal's comic novels. Which president takes care of state business from his own home? Havel did just that at first, as well as driving a modest, bottle green Renault 21 instead of the usual luxury limousine, receiving the Pope and pop stars alike. When Bill Clinton came to Prague, Havel played the drums in the »Reduta« jazz club whilst his American counterpart played saxophone. His inability to prevent the breakup of the Czechoslovakian Republic marks him as a tragic hero. Increasingly isolated in the political landscape, he owed his third term in office to a wafer-thin majority of two votes. In 2003 his presidency came to an end. Havel died on 18 December 2011 at the age of 75. The valedictory act of state which followed was like nothing Prague had ever seen before.

Those who knew Havel well perhaps remember him as a man to whom words and thoughts were closer than office. He always carried two pens with him: a green one for autographs and a red one to draw hearts alongside his name.

BOHUMIL HRABAL (1914 – 1997)

Author

»For thirty-five years I've been compacting wastepaper«, writes Bohumil Hrabal. Those wishing to find out more about socialism would do well to read his tale »Too Loud a Solitude«. Alongside Jaroslav Hašek (Švejk) and Karel Čapek (R.U.R), Bohumil Hrabal is one of three great Czech authors of the twentieth century. He came to fame with his novel »Closely Watched Trains« - filmed as »Closely Observed Trains«, an Oscar winner in Hollywood in 1968. His greatest literary success, the picaresque novel »I Served the King of England«, was also made into a film. Hrabal's death is something of a mystery. Was it an accident or suicide? Feeding the pigeons, he fell from a topfloor window of a Prague hospital. At the U Zlatého tygra, his favourite Prague pub – the Golden Tiger – in the Old Town, the locals believed »he had had enough of life«. A fourth Prague Defenestration was also mentioned, this time without any warlike repercussions. The secret millionaire Hrabal, who always took a carrier bag with him rather than a briefcase, was buried in a plain coffin with the inscription »Polná Brewery«, where his father had worked as a bookkeeper.

JAN HUS (CIRCA 1370 – 1415)

Reformer

The Czech church reformer Jan Hus was born of peasant stock in Husinec in the year 1370. Ordained as priest in 1400, Master Jan Hus taught at Charles University and preached in Bethlehem Chapel against papal authority, criticized the secular possessions of the church and demanded a Bohemian national church. He consolidated his ideas for reform in culture by helping to bring more Czech emphasis to Prague's university, where he was the first rector from 1409 – 1410.

The reformer was supported by the people as well as by King Wenceslas, but he was excommunicated by the pope in 1411. In his polemic »De ecclesia« (Regarding the Church) of 1413, Hus painted a picture of the church as a non-hierarchical assembly of believers who recognized as their leader only Christ, not the pope. With a guarantee of safe conduct from the German king Sigismund, Hus answered a summons to the Council of Constance in 1414, where he was charged with heresy. Since Hus did not recant, he was burnt at the stake in Constance in 1415. His death sparked violent conflict in

Bohemia between the Hussites (moderate Utraquists and radical Taborites) and the country's Catholics, who supported the king, and in 1420, after the First Defenestration of Prague, the conflict finally led to the bloody Hussite Wars.

MILENA JESENSKÁ (1896 – 1944)

Milena Jesenská's name is usually mentioned in connection with Franz Kafka – her career as a journalist who worked for equal rights for women and on behalf of German immigrants is less well known.

Milena grew up in Prague. Her father, an irascible, fervent nationalist, was a failure as a parent; her mother died when Milena was 17 years old. In order to end her relationship with the writer Ernst Polak, her father sent Milena to an asylum. Nevertheless, she married Polak and went with him to Vienna. Milena began writing in 1919. She translated Kafka's tale »The Boilerman« into Czech and started to correspond with him. Her return to Prague in 1925 – Kafka died in 1924 in Klosterneuburg – and her separation from Polak saw her gain fresh self-confidence. Furthermore, she was commissioned by the highly regarded Prague newspaper Národní listy to run the women's page. She joined the Communist Party and re-married in 1926 – her new husband was the Bauhaus architect Jaromír Krejcar. She fell ill while pregnant and became addicted to morphium. Her second marriage, was also a failure. In the year 1939 Milena was arrested by the Gestapo for helping people to escape; she died in 1944 in Ravensbrück concentration camp. She wrote in one of her last articles: »Of course I am a Czech, but above all I try to be a decent human being.«

FRANZ KAFKA (1883 – 1924)

The prose written by Franz Kafka, revered in some quarters as a cult phenomenon, met with little recognition during his lifetime. He was born as the son of a German-Jewish Prague businessman. The problematic relationship with his overbearing father is reflected in works such as »The Judgement« (1916) and »Letter to His Father« (1919). In 1906 Kafka completed his study of jurisprudence, and in 1908 he

Misunderstood genius writer

became an employee of the Prague Workers' Accident Insurance Company. The highly sensitive loner became close friends with the writers Max Brod and Franz Werfel. In 1917 Kafka developed tuberculosis, and five years later he retired on health grounds. In the summer of 1924 he died of tuberculosis of the larynx at the tender age of 41. Many of Kafka's writings – three fragmentary novels (»America«, 1912 – 1914; »The Trial«, 1914 – 1915«; »The Castle«, 1921 – 1922), and the diaries and letters which are essential for the understanding of his work were published posthumously by Max Brod – contrary to

Kafka's wishes expressed in his will. Only a few of his stories were published during his lifetime, including »A Country Doctor«, »The Judgement«, »In the Penal Colony«. The writer was buried in the New Jewish Cemetery on Israelská / Jana Želivského (Metro: Želivského in Žižkov. Not until World War II was over did Kafka's work find worldwide recognition. He was frowned upon by the communists for his allegorical description of power relations, evoking the »dictatorship of the proletariat«. Life under socialism meant living in a permanent state of anxiety, as nightmarish as a pulmonary disease. Kafka's works were placed on a blacklist in his home country in 1948. Today he is omnipresent in Prague.

CHARLES IV

Father of the nation, shining light, patron saint – victor in television's history show as the »greatest Czech of all time«: a somewhat ironic triumph, given that Charles IV actually hailed from the House of Luxembourg and was thus half a »foreigner«. His mother Elizabeth was the daughter of King Wencelas II, bequeathed, as it were, as a dowry with the Crown of the sanguinary King John of Luxembourg, the latter coming from Bohemian nobility. The reason for this unusual course of events: the Přemyslid dynasty was at an end, with no male heir. Following the short regency of John of Luxembourg – also known as John of Bohemia and »John the Blind« – whose eldest son Charles inherited the Bohemian Crown, the country lay plundered and neglected. Prague Castle fell into an inhabitable state of disrepair.

Bohemian King with an eye for the arts

This French book illustration depicts two crowned rulers at a feat in France: Charles IV and Charles V

Chosen by
God?

But Charles believed he had been chosen as King by God. He began by founding an educational institute – bearing his name – in Prague in 1348. The Karolinum is the oldest university in central Europe. With God's blessing, Charles commissioned the Charles Bridge, St Vitus Cathedral, the Franciscan monastery with the Church of Our Lady of the Snows, Prague's New Town (Nové Město) and, right in the centre, the Emmaus monastery as a kind of Slavic Vatican. The Old Town, rebuilt according to new plans laid down by Charles, is now protected by UNESCO, the layout having remained much the same. Yet in spite of such assiduity, the diminutive monarch did not forget the most important thing of all: demonstrating loyalty to the Pope. In return for being established as Roman Catholic »anti-king« of the German Empire, Pope Clement VI promised him that he would rule over the Holy Roman Empire, his coronation finally taking place in 1355. From the Baltic and the North Sea to the Mediterranean and the Adriatic: Prague would never again preside over such a vast array of territories as it did under Charles IV. This is probably why, historians surmise, the Czechs adore their father of the nation so much. Under his rule, the nation was a major power. With Charles on the throne, Prague stood alongside Constantinople and Rome as the third largest metropolis in Europe, celebrated in history as the »Golden City«. A dark shadow was cast over the brilliant Regent during the pogroms against the Jews during the plagues of 1348 to 1350. Having been falsely accused of poisoning wells, Jews collectively lost the protection which Charles had earlier offered them– he was seemingly more interested in collecting holy relics and conversing with God.

ALFONS MUCHA (1860 – 1939)

Graphic artist

The graphic artist and craftsman Alfons Mucha first worked as a decorative artist in Vienna, then studied in Munich and, from 1888, in Paris, where he became famous above all for his posters for actress Sarah Bernhardt. Mucha designed interiors, arts-and-crafts items, and book ornamentation. He had a decisive influence on Art Nouveau. After a period in the United States (1904 – 1910) he returned to Bohemia where he spent the rest of his life principally creating 20 paintings for the Slav Epic. Mucha was buried in Vyšehrad. A museum devoted to his work is located close to Wenceslas Square.

BOŽENA NĚMCOVÁ (1820 – 1862)

The »Czech
Virginia
Woolf«

Before you spend the rose pink five hundred note in Prague, be sure to take a closer look. This beautiful banknote is the only Czech currency dedicated to a woman of importance: Božena Němocová, author. Born in Vienna as daughter of a seigneurial coachman and christened Barbara Panklová, she was sent away at a young age to work as a maid in East Bohemia. Luckily for her, the lady of the house was a progressively minded duchess who, recognizing the girl's talent, educated her. Still, forced to wed a financial clerk, she found herself in an unhappy marriage. Her husband was a patriot who was subsequently transferred to Slovakia as punishment. Estranged from her husband, she remained in Prague without income, just about managing to support her four children. Her eldest son died in a tragic accident. Božena Němocová completes the circle of the Czech National Revival movement. She had affairs with several artists, including the composer Bedřich Smetana. She wrote short stories in an attempt to alleviate her growing existential hardship. Some of her writings were published. Already seriously ill, she looked back to the happy days of her youth. Her novel »Babička« – The Grandmother – is an idyllic eulogy of regional life and folk wisdom. Madeleine Albright mentions the book in her memoir. Success came, alas too late to save the author from a lonely and miserable death at the tender age of 42. The Grandmother has since been printed in 350 Czech editions and translated into almost 30 different languages.

JAN NERUDA (1834 – 1891)

The journalist and poet Jan Neruda was born in Prague's Malá Strana; the cobbled street Nerudova is named after him. He soon abandoned the study of jurisprudence and philosophy, begun in 1853, in favour of a literary career, and at the age of 22 he became feature section editor of the newspaper »Národní listy«. In 1866 he founded the periodical Květy (Flowers) with Hálek, and in 1873 Lumír, for a long time the leader in the field. Neruda is considered the founder of Czech feature writing. He also published several volumes of poetry, plays and travel sketches. His lively »Tales of the Little Quarter« below Hradčany (1878) tell of little people and great destinies.

Journalist and poet

PETER PARLER (CIRCA 1330 – 1399)

The sculptor and master builder Peter Parler was a key figure in the development of Gothic art in central Europe. He was born in Schwäbisch Gmünd, son of a respected cathedral architect, and in 1353 he was summoned to Prague by Charles IV in order to continue work on the choir of St Vitus Cathedral. Parler also built All Saints Chapel in the castle, and between 1380 and 1390 he designed Charles Bridge with the Old Town Bridge Tower. Its sculptures are also products of the Parler workshop, which can be shown to have influenced the development of the »Soft« style – characterized by elegant colouring and lines, a predilection for rich materials and the flowing rhythm of softly falling garments. The style is also known as International Gothic or, in Germany as »Beautiful« style. Examples of the Parler style are also found in the 21 portrait busts on the triforium of St Vitus Cathedral, which include a self-portrait of the artist. Parler's sons Wenzel and Johann continued work on St Vitus Cathedral. His nephew Heinrich Parler was a sculptor in Prague. Amongst other properties, Parler owned Hrzán Palace on Loretánská ulička and the Parler house on Hradčany Square.

LENKA REINEROVÁ (1916 – 2008)

Grande dame of German literature in Prague

Nobody knows the »Golden City« better than her. In her book »Dream Café of a Prague Woman« she reserves a table for all of her friends. Kafka, Brod, Werfel, Rilke, Kisch, Torberg. She is mentioned in the same breath as the last exponent of German language literature in Prague. A grand dame of the Golden Age, when almost everything in Prague revolved around leisure and intellect, art and imagination. Few of the world's metropolises have managed to belong to quite so many artists: we know Kafka's Prague, Mozart's, Smetana's, Havel's Prague. The Prague of Emperor Charles IV, of Rabbi Loew and Saint Wencelas. All of these together constitute the Prague of Lenka Reinerová. The autobiographical recollections of »The Scent of Almonds« reveal details of her own story. Born in the year 1916 into a German-Czech Jewish family, she worked from 1936 as a journalist on the Workers' Illustrated Newspaper – Arbeiter-Illustrierte-Zeitung (AIZ). Her entire family perished as the hands of the Nazis, she herself fled first to France and ultimately escaped via Morocco to Mexico. She returned to Europe with her husband, the writer and doctor Theodor Balk, after the Second World War, first living in Belgrade and then, in 1948, coming home to Prague. Four years later, the convinced communist fell victim to Stalin's purges and spent 15 months in a windowless prison cell before being banished to the provinces with her family. Rehabi-

MARCO POLO TIP

! *Remembering rather than forgetting*

In 2008, the year she died, Lenka Reinerová wrote a commemorative speech for the German Bundestag in which she looked back on the occupation of her homeland by the German Wehrmacht: »From this day on, Jewish citizens were no longer allowed out on the pavement, they were not allowed to sit on park benches. They were not allowed to use any means of transport nor public telephones, they were not permitted to enter the main post office, not even the cinema. At best, they did not exist at all.«

litated in 1964, she was hit by a publication ban in the aftermath of the Prague Spring. She was excluded from the Communist Party, lost her position at a publishing house and worked primarily as a simultaneous translator until the events of 1989. Thereafter, Prague romantics declared the author, who had won a number of prizes in the meantime, to be a cult figure. She died in Prague in 2008 at the age of 92, in the city where she continued her literary wanderings until the very end. She was fully aware of the less than romantic changes her hometown had undergone, but her love of Prague remained as strong as ever: there was always enough magic, enough charm to sustain this city's uniqueness. Her legacy goes beyond the books and memoirs she penned, works such as »Dream Café of a Prague Woman« and »Crazy Prague«. She also founded the Prague Literature Centre of German-speaking writers, of whom she was the last representative.

RAINER MARIA RILKE (1875 – 1926)

Rainer (actually René) Maria Rilke was born in house number 17 on Jindřišská. His career as an army officer was cut short by ill health, and he went on to study art, philosophy and literature in Prague, Munich and Berlin. In 1899 – 1900 two lengthy journeys took him to Italy and Russia. In 1900 Rilke settled in Worpswede and married the sculptress Clara Westhoff. The marriage lasted only one year, but they stayed in contact with one another nevertheless. In Paris he worked as Auguste Rodin's secretary, under whose influence he moved from the dreamy emotional lyric to the »object« poem. After breaking away from Rodin he travelled through Europe, North Africa, Egypt and Spain. From 1911 – 1912 he lived as guest of the Princess of Thurn and Taxis in Duino Castle close to Trieste, where he wrote his first Duino Elegies. It would take him until 1923 to complete them, in Muzot in Switzerland. He made Valais his home and this is where he died in 1926. His Two Prague Stories of 1899 recall the politically turbulent times around the turn of the previous century, Czech-German discord, and the latter-day Austrian Prague of the declining Danube monarchy.

Lyricist

BEDŘICH SMETANA (1824 – 1884)

The Czech composer Bedřich (Frederick) Smetana studied piano and music theory in Prague, then first tried his luck as a professional concert pianist, founding his own music school in the year 1848. After a five-year spell in Sweden he returned to his native city in 1861, where he was conductor at the National Theatre from 1866. Smetana is seen as the founder and most prominent protagonist of a Czech na-

Composer

tional style in opera and symphonic poems. His most famous work is the »My Country« cycle with The Vltava, Vyšehrad, Šárka, From Bohemia's Woods and Fields, Tábor and Blaník. (Premiere 1882). Although he was becoming increasingly deaf, Smetana did not give up composing. From the year 1882, he displayed symptoms of mental illness, by the time of his death he had lost his mind entirely.

ALBRECHT VON WALLENSTEIN (1583 – 1834)

Military leader and enigmatic genius

Albrecht Wenzel Eusebius von Waldstein, known as Wallenstein, the eponymous hero of Schiller's dramatic trilogy, was born on 24 September 1583 in the East Bohemian settlement of Heřmanice on the Elbe river. He was a complete orphan by the age of eleven and was taken in by a brother-in-law of his mother who sent him to be raised by the Bohemian Brethren, a pre-Reformation Christian community. From 1599 he studied theology for a short while at the Protestant University of Altdorf near Nuremberg, then embarked on a Grand Tour of Europe over a period of two years. In 1604 he joined a regiment of Imperial Bohemian foot soldiers as a cadet and converted to Catholicism not long after. Badly wounded in battle, his bravery did not go unnoticed and he was promoted to the rank of Feldhauptmann, or captain. So began the fairytale-like rise from a lowly member of the Bohemian landed gentry to one of the most famous commanders and (thanks to his keen business acumen and two »advantageous marriages«) one of the richest men of his time. In the end he fell victim to court intrigue, possibly as a consequence of the general's plan to depose Ferdinand II and make the throne of Bohemia his own, although this particular rumour was never substantiated. Either way, the Emperor had the general murdered in February 1634. Wallenstein's entire possessions and those of his intimates – all in all, roughly a quarter of Bohemian territory – were confiscated. The Emperor thus cancelled out his own substantial debts (owed mostly to Wallenstein), practically turning a political murder into one motivated by money.

Creation of a legend

To nip the outrage in the bud over his actions – and scorn was plentiful, even for the law of the land at that time – the Emperor spread vicious rumours about his generalissimo which throw the doors wide open to the stuff of legend to this very day. One of the more benign stories is that the commander was wont to consult horoscopes. In the Czech Republic after the events of 1989, in the search for democratic identity and unequivocally casting off the shackles of communism, the image of Wallenstein changed from controversial commander to »champion of peace in the Thirty Years' War« and »the first European of his era«. True enough, the »enigmatic genius« appears to have realized, halfway through the Thirty Years' War, that the killing had to come to an end as soon as possible. Hence his focus shifted from victory over the enemy to a mutually acceptable peace negotiation in which neither side would lose face.

FRANZ WERFEL (1890 – 1945)

The Austrian satirist Karl Kraus called them the »Arconauts«, the members of Prague's German language literary scene who gathered at Café Arco. It was here that Franz Werfel met with Max Brod, Franz Kafka and Egon Erwin Kisch, all destined to find fame in later years. Werfel himself was the son of a wealthy Jewish merchant family and launched his literary career with Expressionist lyric poetry and Symbolist drama, later moving on to historico-political realism. Among Werfel's best-known works are the novels Embezzled Heaven (1939) and Star of the Unborn (1945). He emigrated to France in 1938, then continued to the USA, where he died in 1945, in Californian exile. The house where Werfel was born stands in Nové Město (Havlíčova 11).

Expressionist writer

ENJOY PRAGUE

Where are the best places to go out? Which specialities of Czech cuisine should one sample? How is party life in the Golden City? What are the best addresses for shopping? We have put together some tips for you.

Accommodation

Partial to a Palace?

Patrician houses, Art Nouveau façades as far as the eye can see. Prague's hotel landscape could be a film set. Romantic rooms and splendid suites await beneath their intricate rooftops and ancient-looking turrets. How nice to would be to move from one to the next – feeling like a prince, a cardinal or perhaps even Mozart himself. Hotel nights in Prague can encourage such reveries.

Prague is, of course, also the city of Franz K., where a night in a hotel can swiftly take on nightmarish connotations. Romantic images of hotels seen on the internet do not always tell the whole story. The walls may shake as traffic rumbles past the building. Some establishments seem to be plagued by infernally rattling elevators and rumbling generators which switch on in the middle of the night, or fans which rattle and whir as they whip up a storm in the cramped courtyard. Kitchen vapours even reach some rooms or the water supply is reduced to a drip because someone, somewhere is taking a »rain shower«. Such mishaps cannot be ruled out when so many town houses are hastily converted into new hotels. Tourism is booming and time is money – hence, in recent times, some of the boldly coloured design hotels are not only minimalist in design, they are also minimalist when it comes to soundproofing, an expense often spared.

Nightmare or romance?

Be sure to read through the comments section when booking online – gushing praise (often written by the proprietors) on the one hand, scathing criticism on the other (some contributors do little else). The truth is probably somewhere inbetween. »Beautifully situated, friendly service, distinctive character« and photographs of palatial furniture. Sounds good, looks good and yet, it is only when arriving that the underwhelming view becomes apparent. Worst case scenario, the room looks out onto a raucous party alleyway behind the Church Of Our Lady Before Týn – beautifully situated in one sense, but not in another. Antique furniture may adorn your boutique hotel, but Mexican tequila bars and hard rock clubs are just across the street. The noise they make will rob you of your sleep – but at least you will have enough time to study the beautiful ceiling fresco.

Daylight robbery or bargain?

It makes sense to watch prices closely. Prices on the internet seem wildly unpredictable, going from 1000 Euro per night to 200 Euro

Prices

Kafka gave his first and only public reading (of *The Judgement*) in 1912 here, when Hotel Evropa was still known as »Archduke Stephan«.

from one day to the next – for the same room, it should be noted. Some hotels will charge quadruple rates for New Year's Eve, with many rooms only available for a minimum booking of three nights. With a little luck, however, it might just be possible to snap up a last minute deal, perhaps a 35 Euro dream room looking out over the rooftops of Prague.

Camping The campsites of Prague are usually between 5 to 10km/3 to 6 miles outside the city. Further information at www.camp.cz or the Prague information service at www.praguewelcome.cz.

Recommended accommodation

❶ etc. see map page 131/132

PRICE CATEGORIES
€	up to 80 €
€€	80 to 120 €
€€€	120 to 250 €
€€€€	250 € and over

Double room plus breakfast

? *Accommodation portals online*

MARCO ⊕ POLO INSIGHT

Hotels
www.booking.com
www.prag-cityguide.com
www.agoda.com
www.praguewelcome.cz
www.visitprague.cz

Bed and breakfast
www.wimdu.com
www.praguebedandbreakfast.
com
www.housetrip.com

LUXURY
❶ Mandarin Oriental €€€€
Lesser Quarter, Nebovidská 1
Tel. 233 088 888
www.mandarinoriental.com
This Benedictine monastery was secularized under Emperor Joseph II, then used as a hospital. In 1870

Prague newspaper editorial offices and printers moved in. After 1948, Communist propaganda material rolled off the presses. What remained of the public property was splendidly restored at a cost of some 100 million Euro. Today, beneath the cloister's high arches, spiritual powers are still close at hand – a former chapel now serves as a spa, to continue the reverent tradition. Where once the monks soujourned, aromatic ginger tea is now served to welcome guests for »Time Ritual« massages and treatments. The Lazar Suite was consecrated by His Holiness the Dalai Lama. Angelina Jolie has stayed here, a stone's throw from the picturesque alleys of the Lesser Quarter.

❷ Hilton Prague €€€€
Praha 8, Pobřežní 1
Tel. 224 84 11 11
www.hilton.com
Scale the heights to chill out, like in good old New York. The Cloud 9 sky bar fills up rapidly after work as the party begins on the Hilton roof. The Prague panorama of

100 towers glitters magically in the night at cocktail hour. Glass elevators glide up the interior façade, two restaurants and a lounge café are located on various levels. Construction on the Franco-Czech joint venture began during the Soviet Socialist era. Mitterand and Havel ceremoniously opened the hotel in 1991. Bill Clinton was the next head of state to visit. For Barack Obama, looking to accommodate his entire crew, the 780 room capacity was the deciding factor. By 6am he was already doing lengths of the indoor pool, the longest in any of Prague's hotels, measuring 12m/39ft. Light colours, high-grade natural wood and sleek leather in the rooms: a glass palace of comforts to the east of the Old Town.

Setting the table at the Kempinski

❼ Kempinski Hotel Hybernská €€€€
Hybernská 12, tel. 226 226 111
www.kempinski.com/en/prague/
When railway stations were built like temples for the gods, Prague's railway officials felt compelled to come up with something exemplary. The former Hibernian monastery matched their ambition. The modern reconstruction was quite revolutionary for the time, rising high above the original foundations and walls. Linear, graphically structured, in contrast to the Baroque profile of the lower levels, this was an out of the ordinary site for an exceptional hotel. Aesthetics, design and art are in harmony at the Kempinski in Prague. 61 of the 75 suites feature separate living and sleeping areas, as

well as walk-in wardrobes. A Nespresso machine is de rigeur. Should George Clooney himself turn up, he would not look at all out of place in this noble setting. The Powder Tower, Municipal House and Palladium shopping paradise are all within 200m/220 yards of this luxury residence. The tourist hub is not far away.

❶❶ The Augustine €€€€
Lesser Quarter, Letenská 12
Tel. 266 112 233
www.theaugustine.com
One of the world's ten most exclusive suites covers three floors in the tower of this Rocco Forte hotel – one floor is just for the bathroom. The bedroom boasts a 360° panoramic view of Prague – Hradčany can be admired without even getting out of bed. The price? Around 4000 € per night. Regular double rooms are fine too – and a lot less expensive (from 250 €).

❶❷ Four Seasons €€€€
Praha 1, Veleslavínova 2a
Tel. 221 427 000
www.fourseasons.com
Three buildings, Gothic, Renaissance and Baroque, linked by con-

High Life in Prague Insider Tip

Rooftop hotels pop up like colourful islands bedecked with parasols on the city panorama. At night, their illuminated roof terraces resemble dream ships cruising through the ocean of houses. The captivating views are matched by excellent gastronomy. The message is clear: first class is always at the top. Here are the top three rooftop hotels in Prague:

❽ Aria Hotel €€€€
Tržiště 9, tel. 225 334 761
www.codarestaurant.cz
Italian star design, imaginative dining opposite St Nicholas Church.

❾ U Zlaté Studně
(The Golden Well) €€€€
U Zlaté studně 4, tel. 257 011 213
www.goldenwell.cz
Magnificent panoramic views on the terrace from breakfast onwards.

❿ U Prince €€€
Old Town Square 29
Tel. 224 213 807
The star of Prague rooftop terraces (see below): Old Town Square and the Church of Our Lady Before Týn could not be any closer.

temporary design. Centrally located on the Vltava, the hotel is just a few steps from Charles Bridge and Prague's Old Town. The hotel contains over 162 rooms and suites, whilst the Allegro restaurant combines Italian cuisine with Czech specialities; an inviting riverside terrace is open in summer.

BELLE EPOQUE

❹ Grand Hotel Evropa €/€€
Praha 1, Václavské náměstí 25
Tel. 224 215 387
www. evropahotel.cz
No-one should expect old-fashioned comfort in this hotel in classic Art Nouveau style: time has left its mark on the 115 rooms. Steadfast nostalgia is required; otherwise, just try the Art Nouveau café.

⓭ Esplanade €€€€
Praha 1, Washingtonová 19
Tel. 224 501 111
www.esplanade.cz
The fine French restaurant alone may well inspire a visit to this exclusive 64-room hotel. Renovated in 1930s style, it is situated in a quiet spot opposite a park, near the main railway station.

⓯ Paříž €€€€
Praha 1, U Obecního domu 1
Tel. 222 195 195
www.hotel-pariz.cz
This venerable luxury hotel of 1907, situated behind the Municipal House, has 100 generously-sized rooms, two conference rooms and a stylish restaurant.

❸ Park Inn €€
New Town, Svobodova 1

Tel. 225 995 225
www.parkinn.com
A former printworks, this industrial building features an Art Déco façade from the year 1907. Those nostalgic for the East (so-called »Ostalgie«) will be happy to find a gigantic printing plate of Soviet cosmonaut Yuri Gagarin greeting them in the lobby. The Communist newspaper »Rudé Pravo« (The Red Truth), once printed here, put him on the cover on 13 April 1961 to celebrate his feats. Rooms are dominated by a dark shade of red, which complements the retro style of the functional design. The ruins of Vyšehrad fort are close by, inviting visitors to explore the legends of Prague's foundation.

⑯ Boscolo Hotel Carlo IV.
€€€
Praha 1, Senovážné náměstí 13
Tel. 224 593 033
www.boscolohotels.com
Originally a bank palace, it competes with the National Museum for splendour and scale. Upgraded by Roman luxury hotel group Boscolo, there is heavy leather furniture in the hall. Magnificent pilasters, crystal candelabras and exquisite Art Deco create an exalted atmosphere. The spacious rooms are furnished with antiques: this is what it must be like sleeping in the royal treasury. Gourmet cuisine with Italian flair.

⑰ The Icon Hotel & Lounge
€€€
New Town, V Jámě 6
Tel. 221 634 100
www.iconhotel.eu

A Madonna icon above the entrance watches over this 120 year old patrician house, not allowing the cardinal violet shade of the façade to distract her from her role as patron saint. All 31 rooms have been furnished with handmade beds from the Swedish company Hästens. Nice little touches such as Skype phone, an iPod docking station and biometric safe (fingerprint technology) add to the comfort. Well rested and well fed, thanks to the à la carte breakfast, one can begin to explore the city – Wencelas Square is easily reached via Lucerna Passage.

⑱ Kings Court
Old Town, U Obecního domu 3
Tel. 224 222 888
www.hotelkingscourt.cz
The Ministry of Industry and Trade moved into this impressive Art Nouveau palace in the year 1900. The rooms are extremely generous in size, most offering views of the bustling Republic Square. Spa enthusiasts will probably be less enthusiastic about the spa in the cellar.

BOUTIQUE
⑤ Le Palais €€€/€€€€
Praha 2, Vinohrady, U Zvonařky 1
Tel. 234 634 111
www.palaishotel.cz
Built around the year 1897, stucco, cartouches and ornaments adorn the grand cornices and pilasters of this patrician palace, complete with a corner tower adjoining the façade. The interior was designed by painter Luděk Marold, famous for the largest painting in the world, The Battle

of Lipany (1434). Cheerfully colourful, cozily appointed rooms,
bar, spa and restaurant have contributed to inclusion in the prestigious »Leading Small Hotels of
the World« list. The terrace boasts
an unusually open view into the
distance. Wencelas Square is nearby.

⑲ Maximilian €€€
Praha 1, Haštalská 14
Tel. 225 303 111
www.maximilianhotel.com
The hotel is close to the Convent
of St Agnes. Its 72 rooms are ex-
quisitely appointed – seminar
rooms are available for meetings
or conferences and the hotel has
an underground garage. Explore
the sights of the Old Town with
ease on foot from here.

⑳ The Three Ostriches
(U trí pštrosů)
Praha 1
Dražického náměstí 12
Tel. 257 288 888
www.upstrosu.cz
The pretty hotel »The Three Ostri-
ches« is just a few yards from
Charles Bridge. Early booking is
necessary in order to secure one
of the 18 romantic rooms, very
much in demand!

⑭ Roma €€ **Insider Tip**
Praha 1, Malá Strana
(Lesser Quarter)
Újezd 24
Tel. 222 500 222
www.hotelroma.cz
Close to Kampa Island, a sunny
hotel of the Mozart era, now a lis-
ted building, having been renova-
ted with meticulous attention to

detail. A modern atrium and designer wing have been added. Total
of 87 rooms, eight furnished with
antiques.

㉑ Eurostars David €€
New Town, Náplavní 6
Tel. 222 515 150
www.eurostarsdavid.com
Close to the Vltava: the exterior in
neo-Renaissance style, the interior
palatial, with stucco and ornamentation aplenty. Rooms in san-
dy and brown tones, deerskin at
the headboard end of the bed.
Orange Goliath lamps and black
David copies.

ECONOMY
❻ The Mosaic House €/€€
New Town, Odborů 4
Tel. 246 008 324
www.mosaichouse.com
Stay in a cool colour scheme:
three minimalist floors with a retro flair. This is how the future
might have been imagined in the
1920s/1930s, yet now feels bang
up to date.

㉒ Czech Inn €/€€
Vinohrady, Francouzská 76,
Tel. 267 267 600 or 267 267 612
www.czech-inn.com
Backpackers were yesterday, now
there are flashpackers: the deluxe
variety with money, laptops and
rucksacks, but nonconformist nevertheless. This white patrician
house is one of the best hostels in
Europe, with Scandinavian styled
dormitories for eight to twelve
people, as well as private rooms in
black and white design. Café Kavárna is where everyone comes
together: muesli greens, absinthe

drinkers, beer guzzlers, oenophiles, DJs, live bands, global travellers, Prague youth.

㉓ Purpur €

New Town, Řeznická 15
Tel. 731 118 113
www.purpurhotel.com
As the name suggests, purple is the dominant colour here: magenta bedding, curtains and walls. Pleasantly purist in design, the rooms are otherwise transparent: the shower is only separated from the bed by a glass wall. A balcony terrace on the fourth floor has a view of the New Town Hall.

㉔ STEP €

Vysočany, Malletova 1141
Tel. 272 178 350
www.hotelstep.cz
Eight storeys high, the concrete building looks a bit like a bread ben with orange and white stripes. Once a sports hotel for genuine Socialist athletes and renovated in 2007, it still has everything one might need for a warm-up: swimming pool, whirlpool, fitness studio, squash, indoor golf, bowling, billiards, all in the erstwhile industrial heart of Prague. Ostalgie (yearning for the East before the Wall came down) included.

㉕ Pivovar €

Vysočany, Freyova 1
Tel. 283 892 150
www.hotel-pivovar.cz
This former brewery has undergone simple renovations, the interior is spartan but not lacking in charm. The cellar features high, vaulted ceilings and thick walls. The surroundings amount to a post-Socialist document of history: this was once a workers' paradise.

Children in Prague

Fun, Games and Thrills

City tours can be exhausting at the best of times. For children, a packed sightseeing programme is not always their idea of fun. Prague, however, is relatively child-friendly in this regard, with much for kids to enjoy. The three islands in the Vltava offer some welcome respite from a trek around the city's high-lights.

One of these islands (close to Legion Bridge) is known, appositely enough, as Children's Island. It can be fun watching steamboats enter a lock here. A footbridge leads to playgrounds which, in the summer months, are pleasantly shaded by chestnut trees. Climbing apparatus, skateboard ramps and a small football pitch will keep kids of all ages interested.

Effortless pleasure

Prague also offers visitors young and old the chance to travel back in time. Imperial coaches ride through the well-maintained historic centre of the city, whilst boats over one hundred years old sail along the Vltava – both experiences feel like landing on the pages of an old picture book. One rare benefit: this is an effortless educational opportunity, a way to learn more about earlier times, how people lived in the past. History feels so close, so alive in Prague, but the future is also within reach: take the Prague Observatory, for example, mysteriously poised atop the old gallows hill. Back in the historical centre, families should allow themselves enough time to wander through the car-free alleyways and squares to enjoy the many buskers, junglers and artistes who turn the streets into al fresco stages during the summer.

MARCO ⊕ POLO TIP ❗

The cogs of time   **Insider Tip**

A red, iron needle reaches up to the sky on the Letná heights: the metronome, constructed in 1991 by Vratislav Novák on the site of the largest Stalin monument, demolished in 1962. The metronome was designed to symbolize the transience of time, which it most certainly does, but not in the way the artist intended it. The cogs of time have rusted, the timepiece has long since ceased to tick. Not to worry, the young folk of Prague have found their own use for it. They have suspended a wire between the base and the metronome and do their best to throw training shoes (the laces tied together) onto the wire: not easy to do, but great fun when the shoes land there. So remember: take an old pair with you to Prague!

Blowing bubbles outside the Church Of Our Lady Before Týn on Old Town Square – fun for everybody!

FUN IN THE MUSEUM
National Technical Museum

Národní technické muzeum
Prague 7 (Letná), Kostelní 42
Tel. 220 399 111, www.ntm.cz
Tue–Sun 9am–5pm, admission 50
Kč, children 20 Kč
The orbit of the metronome promises an exciting journey through
time into the wonderful world of
technology, with over 18,000 exhibits: vintage cars, locomotives,
plush carriages, colourful post office coaches and flying contrap-
tions suspended from the ceiling.

Toy Museum
Muzeum hraček, Hradčany

**Graffiti on the John Lennon wall
(Lesser Quarter)**

Burgrave's House, Jířská 6 (south
entrance)
Tel. 224 372 294
Daily 9.30am–5.30pm
Admission: 50 Kč, children 30 Kč
Old tin: chicken, dog, cat, beetle
and grandad on a motorcycle.
Snow White pouts. Aladdin's magic lamp shines. Barbie dolls, ted-
dy bears and robots (the word actually comes from the Russian
»rabota« for work). Founder of
this enchanting playroom is emig-
ré cartoonist Ivan Steiger: his collection is one of the most comprehensive of its kind in the world, a
pleasure for all ages.

Karel Zeman Museum

Lesser Quarter, Saská 3
(next to Charles Bridge)
Tel. 724 341 091, www.muzeum-
karlazemana.cz, daily 10am–5pm,
admission 200 Kč, children less
than one metre (3 ft 3) tall go
free.
The mercurial Karel Zeman was
the king of Czech animation. He
propelled Baron Munchausen
through the skies on a cannon-
ball, he animated Jules Verne's novel »20,000 Leagues Under the
Sea« for the silver screen. How he
managed it can be seen in the
museum studio. Visitors can even
experience a submarine voyage in
stormy weather.

STARGAZERS
Observatory, Petrín

Štefánika hvězdárna, Petrín
Tel. 257 320 540
www.observatory.cz
daily 11am–7pm, April–Sep also
9pm–11pm
Admission 65 Kč

Study the planets with the super-telescope, then watch computer animations to learn about the vital necessities of climate control.

ALWAYS ON THE MOVE
Little train rides
Departs from Old Town Square, April–Oct from 9am–6pm on the hour. The ride lasts for 50 minutes. Tickets cost 180 Kč, children up to the age of 12 ride for free. Discover Prague in Disneyland fashion, passing through the Jewish quarter, across the Vltava to the Lesser Quarter and back again.

The nostalgia tram 91
April–Nov, Sat, Sun and public holidays from noon to approx 5.30pm. Follow an abridged version of (tram) line 22 from the exhibition grounds to Charles Square, taking in all of the city's historic highlights: tickets 35 Kč.

By coach
The carriages line up all in a row outside the Old Town Hall. Their route takes them through the alleyways of Josefov and Prague's grand boulevard, Paris Avenue. A half hour ride will cost from 800 Kč for the whole family. Blankets on hand to keep passengers warm in winter.

By boat
Prague Venice company, Old Town, Křížovnické náměstí 3 Tel. 776 776 779, www.prazske-benatky.cz, Oct–March daily 10.30am–5pm (last boat), April–June and Sep only until 7pm, July and Aug until 9.30pm; jetties: Judita by the Old Town Charles Bridge Tower, landing stages at Hotel Four Seasons, Old Town, Platnéřská ulice, Čertovka, Lesser Quarter Charles Bridge Tower, Mánes, Lesser Quarter Vltava bank, Komárkovo nábřeží. Ticket prices: adults 290 Kč, children 145 Kč; 45 minute trip on historical ships, faithfully restored.

A SPECTACLE FOR ALL
Changing of the Guard at Prague Castle
Hradčanské námestí
www.hrad.cz
Straight out of a movie: with fanfares and a marching parade, the grand changing of the guard can be enjoyed at the Matthias Gate. The »smaller« changing of the guard takes place hourly at all of the gates.
May–Sep daily, 7am–8pm
Oct–April only until 6pm

»Magical Tour«
Old Town, St Michael's Mysterium Michalská 27, daily 10am–8pm. An insight into the history of Prague with a 45-minute multi-media show and special effects.

Wild riders on the Letná heights

Made out of Wood, but with Heart and Soul

Marionette theatre has a long tradition in the city on the Vltava: German, English, Dutch and Italian puppetmasters popularized the art as they travelled through Bohemia in the 18th century, entertaining the public with handmade marionettes and imaginatively presented stories.

As a rule, these journeymen carried a set of twelve wooden marionettes with them on their travels – six men, three female roles, Kaspárek (Punch), Death and the Devil. With their talent and dexterity, they breathed heart and soul into the wooden figures. In the 19th century, Prague developed into one of the most important centres of marionette theatre. The tradition has been passed down unbroken from one generation to another to this day. One of the best-known characters is the wily Honza, created by Matěj Kopecký. He may have appeared the fool at first, yet he was cleverer than the Habsburg authorities. This marionette is a precursor of Švejk, who would soon jump off the page and onto the stage into the marionette theatre. The first film adaptation of Švejk appeared in 1955, also using marionettes. Director Jiří Trnka is seen as the Czech Walt Disney. Prague's Barrandov Studios also produce animations.

Alongside Švejk, two further wooden figures attained cult status in the country: Spejbl and Hurvinek, father and son. The elder is stupid, the younger clever. Josef Skupa, their creator, carved them early in 1920 as a parody of bourgeois narrowmindedness, limitedness and stolidity. During the German occupation, Spejbl and Hurvinek took on the mantle of resistance fighters, until the Gestapo arrested puppetmaster Skupa in the year 1944. Even his marionettes were locked up.

Vengeance of Hell

Under Communism, Spejbl and Hurvinek were able to criticize Socialist everyday life, albeit gently, by implication. The tradition finally received the recognition it deserved after the Velvet Revolution, with the founding of the National Marionette Theatre in the city of Prague in 1991. The puppet version of »The Magic Flute« is not to be missed. When the Queen of the Night, suspended on her strings, belts out »The vengeance of Hell boils in my heart«, even Mozart will get goosebumps up in Heaven.

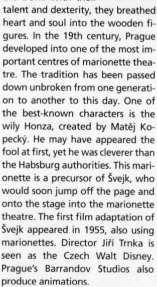

The puppetmaster's tradition is alive and well in Prague today. The marionettes are carved by hand in workshops like this one, belonging to Pavel Trulhar.

Entertainment

At Night, the Vltava Joins in the Dance

Watch the shadows. When they lengthen, the lights under the arcades begin to shine. The Prague scene in the Old Town can be found at legendary locations: jazz in 13th-century catacombs, classical music in Art Nouveau temples of the Belle Époque. Where the Philharmonic Orchestra should play has been the subject of debate in parliament. Dvořák, Mozart and Smetana have all held the conductor's baton in the opera house. Even Richard Wagner conducted in the Vltava city and Kafka was in the audience. Now it is your turn to enjoy Prague's nightlife.

Serenades sweep through beautiful gardens on balmy summer evenings. Grandiose Baroque churches resound not only to Vivaldi, but flourish with flamenco. Fresh young talent can often be heard in concert halls, Conservatories and the Academy of Music train their students to international standard. The syncopated rhythms of Prague are world-class.

The sound of Prague

Mozart's *Eine Kleine Nachtmusik* is the city's anthem, the serenade can be heard on every street corner: on CD, from loudspeakers or live, fiddled by brilliant buskers. And then, somewhere else, there's a crash and a bang as a hard rock band turns the volume up to the max at their open-air gig on Střelecký Island in the middle of the Vltava. Baroque music resonates in churches and cathedrals. The Church of St Nicholas in the Lesser Quarter plays host to concerts every evening in the high season. St Martin in the Wall, the Church of the Holy Saviour, St Salvator Church, St Francis Church, St George's Basilica at Prague Castle – all of them enrich secular music with their sacred spirit. Bach's strings sound like angels' wings rustling, Handel's Oratorios trumpet the last judgement: goosebumps guaranteed underneath the crucifix.

A colourful mix of styles

> **?** MARCO ⊕ POLO INSIGHT
>
> *What, when, where?*
>
> Prague's established culture tends to start early: the theatre at 7pm, concerts usually commence half an hour later. Jazz sessions kick in at 9pm, the bass in the clubs begins to rumble at 11pm and dances on until 5 in the morning, when an after-party promenade through the Old Town arcades provides a poetic conclusion to festivities as dawn approaches. Hollywood stars have told tales of such nights, hungover or otherwise.

A stroll across Charles Bridge before diving into Prague's diverse and colourful nightlife

Blue Notes and the Rest

Declaring a love of jazz in the city on the Vltava was, for many years, a symbol of opposition: against the Nazis, against the Communist establishment. The latter considered such blue notes to be »imperial destabilization of socialist morals«. Yet they were unable to suppress the sound of the times: »jazz is the music of the oppressed black people«, its supporters argued and claimed, in fine Svĕjk tradition: »we want nothing more than to show solidarity with the slaves of America«. One generation has now replaced another, with many of the superstars in Prague's vibrant contemporary jazz scene the sons of famous fathers.

These names are worth noting: Jiří Stivín Junior, the man with the flat cap. He brings as least 20 instruments to his gigs. A vast primeval forest of tones resides in his flutes, clarinets and pipes, one just needs to listen closely: birds, frogs, parrots, cicadas, screeching apes, rushing waterfalls – all the sounds of nature float around the stage. Jan Konopásek Junior has also played his way to cult status, a saxophone guru like his father before him. And Karel Růžička, king of the keyboard, has a talented son as well: Kája plays the tenor sax ever so sweetly.

Last Dance for the Monarchy

The tradition of blues, boogie and Dixieland in Prague goes all the way back to the reputedly »Golden Twenties«, with the birth of Czechoslovakia very much a part of the story. The Treaty of Pittsburgh saw the first independent Czechoslovakian state founded in 1918. The much-revered president Tomáš Garrigue Masaryk married a pianist from the United States. Prague station was renamed after Woodrow Wilson, the 28th President of the

United States of America. In the wake of the First World War, the American influence was enormous, contributing to the spiritual last dance for the monarchy. Blues and swing usurped the Viennese waltz. Ragtime à la Scott Joplin took over from Radetzky marches by the likes of »Old John« Strauss. Inspired by Broadway, the comic duo of Voskovec and Werich and the comedian Vlasta Burian performed »liberated theatre« (Osvobozene divadlo), whilst Jaroslav Ježek, a brilliant pioneer of swing, composed a Charleston soundtrack.

Clandestine Anthem

The Prague jazz scene grew from these roots over decades – in the 1940s, they tuned in to Bebop transmitted by the BBC from Broadcasting House, London. Political motives were certainly present, but not exclusively so. Live concerts by the Glenn Miller Orchestra were broadcast by the BBC at night – and a sworn community of Prague devotees listened in. The »Chattanooga Choo Choo« thus became the clandestine anthem of the resistance. In the 1950s, Benny Goodman discs smuggled in on the black market cost a whole month's salary. A price happily paid, if the money was there, in the interests of protest. The syncopated Sixties continued the freedom mission, with Karel Růžička (sax and keyboards), Miroslav Vitouš (bass), Karel Velebný (vibraphone) and the aforementioned Jan Konopásek on baritone sax all celebrated as national heroes.

These father figures of Czech modern jazz were crucial in proving that the Iron Curtain was not soundproofed.

Crossover on the Vltava

The scene changed rapidly once again after the Velvet Revolution. The AghaRTA jazz club was founded in the year 1991 and would play an integral role as Prague became a bridge between east and west and fruitful exchange was able to flourish. Chick Corea, Diana Krall, Maceo Parker and John Scofield, Spyro Gyra, McCoy Tyner and many more legends of the international jazz scene did a turn here. When a jazz fan comes to Prague, he saves himself a trip to New York. With a little bit of luck, someone like Wynton Marsalis might not only coax down the jazz stars from the firmament, but might also succeed in transporting fans to paradise when he plays Bach on the trumpet in the Church of St Nicholas.

AghaRTA: one of Prague's best jazz clubs, founder and promoter of the annual jazz festival which tempts international stars to the Golden City

Nightclubbing: Prague's dancefloors are undeniably hot – SaSaZu (on the left) and RadostFX (right).

New scene The experimental scene has established itself outside the centre, in former industrial districts. The SaSaZu disco complex in Prague 7 used to be a slaughterhouse. Bass rattles the metal air ducts in old production halls, new beat and techno reverbate under Dracula's chandeliers, guests lounge on Sleeping Beauty's plush fabrics. Emperor Rudolf II was himself a fan of the combination of art and kitsch. Prague's club architects feel similarly inspired.

Nightclubbing

❶ etc. plan page 131/132
unnumbered: off the map

BARS, CLUBS & CO.
❶ **Bar and Books Old Town**
Old Town, Týnská 19
Tel. 224 815 122
www.barandbooks.cz
Sun–Wed 5pm–3am
Thu–Sub 5pm–4am
Leather armchairs, mahogany, red wallpaper, a fine cocktail lounge with warm ambience by the lifestyle prophet Raju S. Mirchandandi.

❷ **Duplex**
Praha 1, Václavské náměstí 21
Tel. 732 221 111, www.duplex.cz
Mon–Thu 10pm–4am, Fri/Sat until 5am, Sun until 3am
A world-class club with industrial flair and loft atmosphere installed on the roof of one of the 1970s'

architectural sins. Exquisite dining, dancefloors on several levels, flirt zones for those intimate moments, a regular haunt of the in-crowd, fashionistas and the glitterati. »Big lips« himself Mick Jagger celebrated his 60th birthday here, President Václav Havel and his wife Dagmar were on the guest list. For even more kicks, take the free shuttle service to sister club Mecca, in a former production hall.

❸ **Hergetova cihelna**
Praha 1, Malá Strana Cihelná 2 b
Tel. 296 826 103, www.cihelna.com
daily 11.30pm–1am
Champagne and romance. The terrace of the old tileworks on the Vltava waterfront is the most beautiful place for lovers. With a view of Charles Bridge lit by flares, designer lounge with leather seating, 12m/39ft-long mahogany bar, vinotheque and chill-out music, sometimes played live or with DJs.

❹ **Klub lávka**
Praha 1, Staré Město, Novotného lávka 1, tel. 221 082288, www.lavka.cz
disco every night 9.30pm–5am, theatre performances begin at 7pm, Klub theatre, disco, tequila bar, dancefloor. The Vltava rushes underneath; the club is located on a barrage.

❺ **RadostFX**
Praha 2, New Town, Bělehradská 120
Tel. 603 193 711
www.radostfx.cz

Wed–Sun 10pm–6am
One of Prague's hottest clubs, the meeting place of »beautiful people« with lounge and restaurant.

❻ SaSaZu **Insider Tip**
Praha 7, Holešovice, Bubenské nábřeží 13,
tel. 284 097 455
www.sasazu.com
Lounge from noon, dancefloor from 10pm until open end. Trendy club in former slaughterhouse, advanced design, exotic chef Shahaf Shabtay, scene of the hottest parties.

❼ **Cloud 9 Sky Bar & Lounge**
Hilton Hotel, Praha 8, Karlín
Pobřežní 1
Tel. 224 842 999,
www.cloud9cz
Mon–Sat 6pm–2am
Glitzy bar deluxe on the rooftop terrace with a panoramic view reflected in mirror walls. Black marble sparkles, the entire interior is lavishly styled, all the way to the bathrooms. Charismatic cocktails. Exotic: melon juice with cranberries, spiced up with red chili pepper.

❽ **Solidní jistota (Solid security)**
Praha 2, New Town
Pštrossová 21
Tel. 725 984 964
www.soldnijistota.cz
Wed–Thu 8pm–2am
Fri–Sat 8pm–4am
At the heart of the new scene. Light, design, colours and the prettiest students in town. Explore stylish nightlife under the club's dome with an insider bonus.

Opera, theatre, cinema & co.

Eine Gefahr für die Moral?

The Estates Theatre opened its doors in the year 1781, right in front of Charles University, much to the chagrin of the latter's professors, who feared that fleet-footed soubrettes might corrupt the morals of their students. What a palaver! When Mozart's Marriage of Figaro came to town, the students emerged from the opera whistling the arias like the latest pop hits. And when Don Giovanni was premiered here in the year 1787, it proved a resounding success! Nevertheless, bedroom scenes were discussed between lectures. Today, the theatre is devoted primarily to the works of Mozart.

Music and pictures – Prague has plenty of both, always in especially atmospheric surroundings: opera sounds quite splendid in the erstwhile theatres of the aristocracy, Mozart's arias are more magical than ever when played in such delightful palaces. Serenades sound sweetest in ornate gardens on gentle summer evenings, Baroque churches are equally open to playing host to Vivaldi and flamenco and it does not always have to be expensive – many youthful talents perform in the city, seek them out! Performances begin at 7pm in Prague, which has one distinct advantage: if the first set is too early in the evening, there is every chance of catching the second set in a jazz club later on.

Highlights   With such an abundance of cultural offerings, here are a few highlights to begin with: enjoy »Mozartissimo« at the Estates Theatre, a selection of the finest operatic arias. The 100-piece Czech Philharmonic Orchestra plays at the Rudolfinum. Laterna Magika is an enchantingly imaginative experience, whilst the Agharta Jazz Centrum is one of the best clubs in town, an atmospheric medieval cellar graced with blue notes. Klezmer music in golden surroundings can be enjoyed in the Spanish Synagogue.

ADVANCE TICKET SALES
Bohemia Ticket International
Praha 1, Na Příkopě 16
Tel. 224 215 031
www.bohemiaticket.cz
Mon–Fri 9am–6pm, Sat until 5pm, Sun until 3pm

TicketPro
Passage Rokoko, Wencelas Square (Václavské námestí 38)
Tel. 234 704 234, www.ticketpro.cz
Mon–Fri 9am–2pm and 2.30pm–8pm

CLASSICAL MUSIC ·OPERA · BALLET · CONCERTS
National Theatre
(Národní divadlo)
Old Town, Národní třída 2
Tel. 224 901 668
www.narodni-divadlo.cz
Inaugurated in 1883 with Smetana's Libuše. Opera and ballet performances take turns.

State Opera (Státní opera)
New Town, Legerova 75
Tel. 224 901 780

Estates Theatre: František Antonín Nostic-Rieneck, a Bohemian patriot and generous patron of the arts, built this private theatre

www.sop.cz
Opera, ballet, festivals. The red carpet is rolled out for the Verdi Festival in August. Champagne sparkles on the al fresco balcony during the interval.

Estates Theatre
(Stavovské divadlo)
Old Town, Ovocný trh 1

Tel. 224 215 001
www.stavovskedivadlo.cz
Historical venue with Classicist façade. Mozart conducted here several times.

Rudolfinum
(Dvořák and Suk Hall)
Old Town, Alšovo nábřeži 12
Tel. 227 059 227

And the Eternal Desire ...

... for love endures (not only) in the theatre of magic. The giant glass cube is striking enough in itself, a stark contrast to the neo-Renaissance style of Prague's National Theatre, stopping most passers-by in their tracks. Built in the years 1977 to 1983, a ballet studio and the experimental stage for the Laterna Magika stand behind the honeycombed façade.

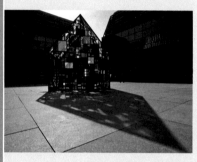

The Latin term for magic lantern was used for the first simple projection apparatus developed in the mid-17th century for glass slides. When the Lumière brothers in Paris cast the first moving images onto a screen with their cinematograph in the year 1895, many believed they were witnessing a »magic box« in action. These pioneering inventions with the pantomime effects of classic black light theatre, coupled with music and acting, and later with dance, were developed by director Alfred Radok (1914 – 1976) and scenographer Josed Svoboda (1921 to 2002) into their own astounding dream theatre, premiered in Brussels at the World's Fair in 1958.

The Laterna Magika transfixes the audience with a fantastical world of illusion

In Residence: New Stage

Since 1983 the illusionist proscenium has taken up residence in the New Stage (Nová Scéna) alongside the National Theatre, its bold glass façade designed by Karel Prager. Green marble slabs from Cuba adorn the interior, the understated auditorium opens up to the stage much like an amphitheatre. The audience holds its breath until this very day when a tram appears to rush towards them or when furniture is moved around by unseen magical hands and dan-

cers float through the air like birds. The multimedia spectacle has grown increasingly sophisticated, using the latest computer technology, scenery shifts apace – as if gravity has disappeared from the planet. The most successful production of all is called, appropriately enough, Wonderful Circus – still going strong with over 6000 performances since its inception in 1977.

Illusions, Bittersweet

The illusions of Prague's Laterna Magika can also baffle the senses with more contemporary material, as in the 2013 production Antikódy, a tribute to the poet president Václav Havel who died two years previously. The piece takes us back to the 1960s. Havel, played by Stanislav Abrahám, sits at his desk. His thoughts seem to fly out of the typewriter: Havel taps away on the keys, the word Člověk (human) multiplies in dozens of paraphrases. We, the audience, see only men, whether as actors, dancers or illusions. Why no women? Havel's typewriter rumbles louder and louder, like a Jumbo Jet, but the question goes unanswered. With a little luck, there is a chance to take a look inside the courtyard of the historic National Theatre after the performance, where a granite »Rusalka« stands: she portrays the unfortunate water nymph from Dvořak's opera of the same name, whose love of a mortal prince brought about her demise. Love is also at the heart of the Wonderful Circus – the unrequited love of a sad clown for a fragile and beautiful tightrope artist. A melancholy, bittersweet piece, sentimental yet not without hope. How does their story end? We have yet to find out.

The National Theatre is a noble stage for the high art of bel canto

www.ceskaphilharmonie.cz
This impressive structure rising up on the right-hand bank of the Vltava features an outside staircase, cast iron lanterns and museums in the eaves. Home of the Czech Philharmonic, one of Europe's finest orchestras. The concert hall boasts excellent acoustics and 1104 seats.

Municipal House
(Obecní dům)
Old Town, náměsti Republiky 5
Tel. 222 002 101
www.obecnidum.cz
Like a giant crown, the Art Nouveau palace dominates Republic Square. Home to the Prague Symphony Orchestra with its own programme of concerts (further information: www.fok.cz). Guest

ensembles also perform in Smetana Hall (1200 capacity).

Velký sál Lucerny
(Lucerna)
New Town, Vodičkova 36
Tel. 224 225 440
www.lucpra.com
Graced by stars and legends. No matter who is on stage, the beautiful Art Nouveau hall (4000 capacity) will remain long in the memory.

Barokní knihovní sál Collegium Marianum (monastery library)
Old Town, Melantrichova 19
Tel. 224 229 462
www.collegiummarianum.cz
Spiritual music of the 17th and 18 centuries, performed by the col-

lege ensemble under a splendid Baroque ceiling decorated with frescoes.

Spanish Synagogue
(Španělská synagoga)
Josefov, Vězeňska 1
Tel. 222 749 211
www.ticketstream.cz
From Bolero to Carmina Burana, Gerswhin to Klezmer groups, the Synagogue is a breathtaking backdrop to any soundtrack. Real gold glitters all around.

Czech Museum of Music
(České muzeum hudby)
Lesser Quarter, Karmelitská 2, Praha 1
Tel. 257 257 777, www.nm.cz
Formerly the stables for the police barracks, delightful classical music now resounds in the atrium, lit up in colour during performances.

MUSICAL ·PERFORMANCES
Hybernia
Old Town, náměstí Republiky 4
Tel. 221 419 420
www.hybernia.eu
A Classicist palace, originally built as a congress hall and now used for a varied range of events: the story of Golem as a musical, wild drummers or a suave Sinatra night, take your pick. Very much a »best of« programme.

All Colours Theatre ACT
Old Town, Rytířská 31
Tel. 224 212 810
www.blacktheatre.cz
Monks once dined under the Baroque dome. After 1948 the Communists used the refectory as a history museum. Since 1993, a

black cabinet theatre has been conjuring up illusionist performances from Faust to Frankenstein. Neon colours abound and amaze against the black background.

RockOpera Praha
Holešovice, Komunardů 1
www.rockopera.cz
A factory hall transformed into a stage (768 capacity). The ultimate progressive experience, where Greek tragedies metamorphose into modern rock operas. Oedipus and Antigone bathe in blood as vampires. In Czech, but not so difficult to follow.

Lod' Tajemství (Mystery Boat)
Moored at Výtoň (Palacký Bridge), tel. 603 340 770
www.formanstheatre.cz
The Forman twins' performance shows us just how absurd Jonah must have felt in the belly of the whale. Like father, like son: Miloš Forman, the brothers' father, won two Oscars for his Hollywood movies »One Flew Over The Cuckoo's Nest« and »Amadeus«.

Karlín Musical Theatre (Hudební divadlo v Karlín)
Praha 8, Křižíkova 10
Tel. 261 174 400, www.hdk.cz
Musicals like »Jesus Christ Superstar« in the district of Karlín.

MUSIC CLUBS
AghaRTA Jazz Centrum
Old Town, Železná 16
Tel. 222 211 275
www.agharta.cz
daily 7pm–1am
Bands on stage 9pm

The list of superstars who have performed here is endless – and it gets longer every year.

Blues sklep (blues lounge)
Old Town, Liliová 10
Tel. 608 848 074
www.bluessklep.cz
daily 7pm–2.30am
Sessions begin at 9pm
Boogie, blues, jazz, folk-rock, gypsy sounds – and great drinks.

Jazz Club Ungelt
Old Town, Týn 2
Tel. 224 895 787
Daily 8pm–1am
Jazz and bread and dripping, rock and crispy duck, funk and fusion with goulash in the cellar vaults of a former customs office. Local matador, the guitarist Luboš Andršt is a perennial institution in the Prague blues scene.

Jazzboat Kotva
Tel. 734 141 554
www.jazzboat.cz
Jazz, blues and funk on board, plus cocktails and catering from fingerfood to three course dinners. Departs at 8.30pm from pier 5 in Josefov, on the Pařížská boulevard by the Čech Bridge, tours until 11pm.

Jazz Dock Bar & Lounge
Smichov, Janáčkovo nábřeží 2
Tel. 774 058 838
www.jazzdock.cz
Daily 11am–4am, performances from 10pm.
A glass jazz pavilion on a floating pontoon. Such transparency fits the music: clanking, experimental, electronic. Many of those

asked to play here have reached cult status.

Lucerna Music Bar
New Town, Vodičkova 36
Tel. 224 217 108
www.musicbar.cz
daily 7pm–4am
Concerts from 8pm
Visiting bands on the famous names list are usually sold out weeks in advance. The good news is: when the concert finishes, a jam session begins.

MeetFactory
Smichov, Ke Sklárně 15
Tel. 251 551 796
www.meetfactory .cz
David Černý, chief provocateur of the Prague art scene, (▶MARCO-POLO Insight page 58) personally oversees this cultural factory, mixing exhibitions, theatre and music into one overall art happening – pretty crazy! Some visitors come to Prague just to check out these production halls.

Reduta
Old Town, Národní 20
Tel. 224 933 487
www.redutajazzclub.cz, daily from 9pm, shows start 9.30pm
Established in 1958, this cult location in Prague's jazz tradition is famous for Dixieland, Bebop, jazz and rock. Bill Clinton performed a legendary guest cameo when he visited Prague in 1994, spontaneously playing the sax while his presidential colleague Václav Havel played the drums. The live recording of this memorable event can still be purchased on CD at the club.

U Malého Glena (Little Glenn)
Lesser Quarter, Karmelitská 23
Tel. 257 531 717
www.malyglen.cz
Sessions daily from 9.30pm to half past midnight.
»Little Glenn« is an American, full name Glenn Spicker. He came to Prague as a bagel baker after the Velvet Revolution and is now a millionaire with two restaurants. This little club is his hobby, playing jazz, blues, ethno and fusion.

Klub U staré pani/The Old Lady (USP Jazz Lounge)
Old Town, Michalská 9
Tel. 603 551 680
www.jazzstarapani.cz, daily 7pm–2am, sessions from 9pm
Fresh talents and old masters in a mecca for glorious Czech swing and Bebop.

ROCK AND POP
Hard Rock Café
Praha 1, Malé náměstí 3
Tel. 224 229 529, www.hardrock.com, daily 11.30am–1am
Let it not be said that Prague does not rock. Talent competions as well as guest slots from stars like Alanis Morissette.

THEATRE
La Fabrika
Praha 7, Komunardů 30
Tel. 774 417 644
www.lafabrika.cz
Theatre, dance, concerts, films and exhibitions in a former factory.

Laterna Magika
New Town, Národní 4
Tel. 224 931 482
www.laterna.cz
Multivision with lasers, black cabinet theatre, video, mobiles, pantomime, ballet and dance (►MARCOPOLO Insight page 102/103)

CABARET
Rokoko Theatre (Divadlo Rokoko)
Praha 1, Wencelas Square, Václvské náměstí 38
Tel. 222 996 185
www.mestskadivadlaprazska.cz
Music and theatre

CHILDREN, YOUTH STAGES
National Marionette Theatre (Narodní divadlo marionet)
Praha 1, Žatecká 1
Tel. 224 819 322, http://mozart.cz (►MARCOPOLO Insight page 92/93)

Spejbl and Hurvínek
(Divaadlo Spejbla a Hurvínka)
Praha 6, Dejvická 38
Tel. 224 316 784
www.spejbl-hurvinek.cz
Puppet theatre with performances in different languages. (►MARCOPOLO Insight page 92/93)

CINEMA
Lucerna Cinema
Wencelas Square, Václavské náměstí 38
Tel. 602 329 906,
www.lucerna.cz/kino/php/
The cinema auditorium (454 seats) is the main attraction in the Art Deco palace built by President Havel's grandfather in the year 1908. The film plays second fiddle to the majestic balcony and ceiling. Nostalgia aplenty!

Festival Time

It began with a castle festival for Emperor Charles IV and is known today as »Prague Spring«, the oldest music festival in Europe. Prague's exceptional cultural agenda thus dates back many years, the historical backdrop lending events a unique quality. Even New Yorkers know where Europe's jazz capital lies – on the banks of the Vltava.

Prague as the event capital of Europe? Perhaps not in terms of size, but considering the sheer number of events, this ambitous goal may already have been attained. The city fathers are munificent when it comes to approving the use of Wencelas Square for festivals or allowing Old Town Square to be transformed into a giant dance floor – rarely has a town hall been so open-minded.

Event capital Prague

Fans of cultural niches will also find much to their liking in the city. Spiritually inclined voyagers on their way to the celestial spheres of the Orient should take time out for Prague's esoteric festival. This is very much the right place and the right time for the international gathering of spiritual minds to celebrate their motto: »Miluj svůj život« (»Love your life«). Prague was a magnet for spirits demons and ghosts as long ago as the imperial reign of Rudolf II.

Cultural niches

Music is the undisputed main attraction in the event capital of Prague. Classical or modern, Leoš Janáček or Iva Bittová. Prague Spring is no longer associated only with the political events of 1968, having also lent its name to the Czech Republic's most famous musical festival which takes place in May. No less famous among the jazz fraternity, the AghaRTA Prague Jazz Festival takes place in March. For many musicians, regardless of style or discipline, the words of Kaspar Zehnder in 2013, chief conductor of the Prague Philharmonic from 2005 to 2008 and now on the world's greatest stages, ring truer than ever: »To play in Prague is a matter of the heart«.

Music, music, music

The Golden City has much to offer cineastes: the Prague International Film Festival (Febiofest) in March introduces debut works, brave experimental, sociocritical or auteur films, the likes of which never make it into the multiplex cinemas. They may at some point appear on television, but deep into the night on the more obscure channels.

Film festival

Lesser Quarter Bridge Towers:
Prague's history as a contemporary event

Each year, the accomplished jury views up to 125 films which take part in the competition, often coming up with surprise winners from countries seldom seen on the podium elsewhere. Audiences revel in the individual charms of Turkey, Finland, Serbia, Kazakhstan instead of the more common Hollywood fare.

Official Holidays
1 January (New Year's Day), Easter Monday 1 May, (Labour Day) 8 May (Day of the Liberation of Prague, 1945), 5 July (Day of the Apostles to the Slavs, SS Cyril and Methodius), 6 July (Death of Jan Hus: burnt at the stake in Constance, 1415), 28 Sepember (Day of Bohemian patron saint Wenceslas), 28 October (Founding of Czechoslovakia, 1918), 17 November (Day of the Struggle for Freedom and Democracy), 24 December (Christmas Eve), 25 and 26 December (Christmas)

Calendar of events

A good overview
To find tickets for all kinds of events and to obtain a good overview of what's on, browse the following internet sites:
www.pragueeventscalendar.com, www.pragticketsinternational.com and www.praguecityline.com

JANUARY
New Year's Concert
The first musical highlight comes right at the beginning of the year: aficionados flock to the Municipal House for the New Year's concert given by the Prague Symphonic Orchestra.

Carnevale Praha
Jesters fools and masked revellers troop through the city's noble palaces, Art Nouveau halls and theatres. Carnival traditionally opens with a performance of Smetana's »Pražský karneval« which he composed just a few months before his death in the autumn of 1883, part of an unfinished symphonic suite.

FEBRUARY
Masopust (Czech for carnival)
The three last days before Ash Wednesday are known as Masopust (literally »without meat«). The Old Town of Prague is a sea

of masks, almost like a second Venice when carnival begins.

MARCH
Matějská pout' – St Matthew's Fair
Prague's oldest fairground comes to live with carousels, shooting galleries and ghost trains on the »Výstaviště« exhibition ground, an authentic Art Nouveau relic (www.matejskapout.cz).

AghaRTA Prague Jazz Festival
The syncopated season begins in March and lasts until October. International stars and newcomers play in Prague's medieval underworld on various stages, organized by the AghaRTA Jazz Club (www.agharta.cz).

Febiofest – International Film Festival
No Oscar nomination? Not on the Cannes reel? Too bizarre for Berlin? Then Prague is the logical place for a premiere. More charm than the Hollywood star circus (www.febiofest.cz).

APRIL
Hervis Half Marathon Prague
Handy preparation for the full marathon in May, the half marathon's 21 kilometres/ 13 miles begin and end at the Rudolfinum (www.praguemarathon.com).

MAY
Prague Spring
(Pražské Jaro)
There is music in the air: the traditional finale of the festival, renowned well beyond the country's borders, is Beethoven's Ninth with Schiller's Ode to Joy, »All men shall become brothers«, performed by the Czech Philharmonic in the Rudolfinum (www.festival.cz).

Prague Spring Music Festival: shortly before the concert begins in the Smetana Hall of the Municipal House

In the Leading Role: the Golden City

Prague is thought of as the Hollywood of the East. The reason why the film world descends on Prague is quite simple: Prague is a true master of metamorphosis, with a well-preserved Old Town which is more than capable of reviving epochs long since passed.

Tom Cruise loves Prague. He likes to choose his own locations, as he did when wandering through Prague's Old Town in preparation for the fourth instalment of »Mission Impossible –Ghost Protocol«. He found what he was looking for in the university district around Charles Square: the streets of Moscow – filmed in Prague, yet offering a convincing portrayal of the Russian capital. There are many other examples of Prague's talent for metamorphosis.

Hollywood of the East

The Czech film industry has been thriving for many years, not just since the Velvet Revolution. When the Barrandov Studios were founded in the 1930s at the foot of the castle, the real film business began. During the Nazi occupation, more and more Third Reich propaganda films were produced in Prague. Soviet productions took their place after the Second World War. In the mid-1960s, the censor-happy Communist officials of culture found themselves unable to subdue the »young and wild« protagonists of the Prague Film Academy, who were courageous enough to expose the daily horrors of life under Socialist rule. Forman, Chytilová, Juráček, Němec, Passer, Schorm – these were important names of the »new wave«, creating an internati-

onal sensation with content which was critical of the regime. The buzz reached Hollywood: in 1966 director Jiří Menzel won an Oscar for his film based on Bohumil Hrabal's novel »Closely Watched Trains«. 1983 saw the Iron Curtain open up surprisingly for Barbra Streisand: she was able to film the musical »Yentl«, the story of a Jewish girl, in Prague – the first American production in the Communist Eastern Bloc. A year later, Miloš Forman, a graduate of the Prague Film Academy, returned from his New York exile to film the essential Prague scenes for the definitive Prague film in the city's cinematic history: »Amadeus«. The film offered an authentic portrayal of Mozart's Prague and went on to win seven Oscars.

After the Velvet Revolution

The first American movie after the Velvet Revolution was Steven Soderbergh's 1991 »Kafka«. Since then, over 100 international productions have filmed in the city's labyrinthine alleys, romantic squares, on the castle slopes or under leafy avenues. Bollywood has also succumbed to the romantic charms of Prague: the panorama of this city of dreams is like a fairy tale to Indian audiences..

Top 10 Movie Locations

1 Rudolfinum, House of Artists: the monumental staircase, the balcony portal, the cast iron columns garlanded with lanterns and graced with muses can be seen in films such as »Mission Impossible«, »The League of Extraordinary Gentlemen«, »The Illusionist« and »The Omen«.

2 Hradčany Square: The castle gate and the entrance to the presidential chambers have featured in »Yentl«, »Amadeus«, »Les Misérables« and the Bollywood production »Rockstar«.

3 Strahov Monastery: The monks in »The Omen« ruminated beneath the splendid ceiling fresco in the library, Johnny Depp played Inspector Abberline in »From Hell« and James Bond was here in »Casino Royale«.

4 Charles Bridge: Stone saints heightened the dramatic tension in »Kafka«, »The Omen«, »Van Helsing«, »Blade II« and »Mission Impossible«.

5 Vltava: Making waves in the countdown for »Triple XXX«, Prague also played the role of the »forbidden city« in »Shanghai Knights«.

6 Old Town Square: Tom Cruise exploded a huge lobster aquarium here in »Mission Impossible«. Contract killer Nicholas Cage eliminated his first victim from the Astrological Clock in »Bangkok Dangerous«. Wesley Snipes passed through the medieval arcades as a kind of vampire terminator in »Blade II«.

7 National Museum: A diplomats' ball in »Mission Impossible«, a hotel lobby in James Bond's »Casino Royale«, opera house foyer in »The Omen«, faculty of medicine (in London) in »From Hell«.

8 Municipal House: Crystal chandeliers evoked authentic Parisian charm in »La Vie en Rose« and Bohumil Hrabal's »I Served the King of England«.

9 Kampa Island: Lichtenstein Palace doubled for the American embassy in »Mission Impossible« and for the Swiss embassy in Prague in »The Bourne Identity«.

10 Vítkov Hill: Prague's national monument is where James Bond kills double-crosser Dimitrios in »Casino Royale« (Miami Museum in the movie). Murder in the mausoleum – how apt!

Fit for the silver screen: the city, the river, the castle. And its lovers, of course.

Prague Volkswagen Marathon (previously PIM)

A city run for all the senses. The race begins with classical music and drummers keep the pace up. Dixie dictates the rhythm. Start and finishing line on Old Town Square (www.praguemarathon.cz).

Navalis

(Svatojánské Navalis)
In honour of St Nepomuk, patron saint of Charles Bridge, a celebratory regatta with decorated gondolas, allegorical dragon boats and Baroque ships – magically lit by lanterns and lampions in the evening (www.navalis.cz).

Khamoro

The world's largest Roma and Sinti festival, initiated by Václav Havel in 1999. Jazz, klezmer, flamenco, sitars – everything which makes gypsy culture so fascinating (www.khamoro.cz).

Prague Book Fair / Book World Prague

International publishers present their newest tomes (www.svetknihy.cz) whilst the Goethe Institute, Prague's Austrian Cultural Forum and the Swiss Embassy, supported by the Pro Helvetia cultural foundation, organize a literary programme »Das Buch« which runs concurrently.

JUNE

Prague Proms

Following the grandiose al fresco opener on Wencelas Square, a month of classical, pop and jazz music enriches the city – particularly impressive in the golden hall of the Žofín Palais.

United Islands

Střelecký ostrov, Kampa Island and Jazz Dock combine for a series of outdoor concerts, bringing a Woodstock vibe to the Vltava. A home game for Czech beat veterans (www.unitedislands.cz).

JUNE/JULY

New Prague Dance Festival

Classical and contemporary dance, hip-hop and experimental: this annual dance festival has plenty to offer friends and fans (www.praguedancefestival.cz).

JULY

Prague Folklore Days

Costumes, yodellers, musicians, dancers galore – they all come together for a great street party celebrating folk music under the open skies of Prague's Old Town (www.praguefestival.cz).

AUGUST

Lavka River Stage

Acrobats, jugglers, dancers, magicians of light, smoke and sound. Cirque Garuda's floating stage in front of Charles Bridge brings a touch of Las Vegas to Prague (www.lavkariverstage.cz).

Opera Barocca

When gods dance: a scenic music project with splendid costumes takes the audience back to the era of the Sun King. Staged in the pomp of the Clam-Gallas Palace (www.operabarocca.cz).

Verdi Festival

Prague State Opera celebrates bel canto, young opera stars and directors are given the chance to present themselves. A refreshingly unpretentious event, no dinner jacket required, no overbearing celebrity distractions (www.sop.cz).

SEPEMBER
Strings of Autumn festival

Autumn strings with jazz, classical, traditional and experimental tones. International performers play in various concert halls, one of the most enchanting being the atrium of the Czech Museum of Music (http://www.strunypodzimu.cz).

Dvořákova Praha

(Dvořák's Prague)
Czech music found fame throughout the world thanks to composer and conductor Dvořák. The festival in his name uses Prague's magnificent architecture as its sta-

ge: Rudolfinum, St Vitus Cathedral, the Spanish Hall in Prague Castle, the salon in Pálffy Palace (www.dvorakovapraha.cz).

OCTOBER
International Jazz Festival Praha

Breaking new ground in traditional garb: avant-garde and retro, freestyle and Sinatra or Stevie Wonder rearranged as swing. This melange rings sweet to the ears, a cult happening for over 30 years in Prague (Club Reduta and Lucerna Music Bar, www.jazzfestival-praha.cz).

NOVEMBER
Pearls of Music

Concerts in unusal and evocative settings: Palais Lobkowicz, St Nicholas Church and the Church of St James, the Baroque library of the Klementinum and Café Mozart (www.pragueexperience.com).

For the musically inclined members of the younger generation, Lichtenstein Palace in the Lesser Quarter houses the Prague Academy of Music

Free of charge and outdoors: buskers in the idyllic surroundings below the castle

DECEMBER
Christmas market on Old Town Square
The Christmas tree of the Republic: mulled wine, gingerbread, cinnamon and stars, rows and rows of charming stalls. To top it all, God sings down from heaven – Karel Gott, the »golden voice«.

»Hey, master, get up!«
Under the Baroque dome of St Nicholas and in St Salvator Church, the festive Pastoral Mass of Jan Jakub Ryba (the Czech J.S. Bach) rings out (www.ticketpro.cz).

New Year's Eve gala at the opera
Celebrate with the Strass operetta Die Fledermaus (»The Bat«) and dine on oysters, caviar and champagne as liveried valets glide around.

SPORTING EVENTS

Ice Hockey

Adopted from Canada and the USA, the Czechs are amongst Europe's pioneers in chasing the puck across the ice. When the sport made its debut at the 1920 Winter Olympics in Antwerp, the Czechoslovakian team won the bronze medal and stand third in the all-time rankings, behind Russia and Canada (2013 statistics). The Czechs, for their part, proudly claim to have taught the Russians »how to play ice hockey« given that a Czech coach trained the Soviet Union team who became world champions in 1956. In the grey years of the Communist dictatorship, matches against the Soviets were seen as a surreptitious form of »resistance«. The ČSSR team twice triumphed over the Russian »Zbornaja kommanda« during that period, winning the world championships in Prague in 1972 and again in Moscow (!) in 1985. Since 1993, there has been a Czech national team. Naturally, they won their first match against Team Russia 6:1, ushering in a hugely impressive run of success: in 1998 they won Olympic gold and in 1999, 2000 and 2001 they won the world championship – three times in succession. Two further world titles followed in 2005 and 2010, along with Olympic bronze in 2007. In 2011 and 2012 they

»only« finished third in the world championships. 14 teams compete in the EHL (Extraliga ledního hokeje) Czech championship.

Prague is very much on the map for travelling football fans. Sparta Prague is the Manchester United of the Czech Republic, a regular Champions League participant. Their eternal rivals, Slavia, generally hang around mid-table in the Gambrinus league, named, in the land of beer, after the Gambrinus brew. Soldiers no longer line up for Dukla Prague, the former army club in the socialist era, but the team has retained the name. Supporters further out of town are still devoted to legendary Prague clubs Viktoria (Viktorka) and Bohemia (Bohemka), in spite of their having dropped into the regional leagues. There are 125 registered football clubs in Prague altogether. Czech football fans still crave a world cup triumph, having twice been runners-up, albeit in 1934 and 1962. Still, many football fans would trade all the hockey titles for one football world trophy.

Football

ICE HOCKEY ADDRESSES

HC Sparta Praha
(Tesla aréna)
Praha 7, Za Elektrárnou 419
Tel. 266 727 454
www.hcsparta.cz

HC Slavia
Praha 10, Vladivostocká 10
www.hc-slavia.cz

O2 Arena
Praha 9, Vysočany »Zelený ostrov«
(Green Island) Ocelářská 460/2
Tickets tel. 266 121 122
www.sazkaticket.cz
Round as a saucer: the most modern multi-purpose venue in Europe, built for the ice hockey World Championship of 2004, in the record time of only two years. The ice rink can be transformed overnight into a stage.

FOOTBALL ADDRESSES

AC Sparta Prague
Praha 7, Milady Horákové 98
Tel. 296 111 336 or
296 111 400
www.sparta.cz

FK Viktoria Žižkov
Praha 3, Seifertova
Tel. 222 210 685
www.fkvz.cz Nicknamed »Viktorka«, the people's club from the working-class district of Žižkov. Usually fighting relegation.

SK Slavia Prague
Praha 10 Vladivostocká 2
Tel. 731 126 104
www.slavia.cz
Sparta's rival, and usually keeping them company in the top five of the table.

»Dobrou chut«

… means »bon appetit« in Czech and Prague is certainly a place with more than its share of culinary delights: classic Bohemian cuisine is booming in all manner of variations. Grandmother's recipes are back in fashion, with a new twist. Designers pull out all the stops to achieve the most original atmosphere. Art meets kitsch, hypermodern ambience confronts nostalgice interiors. Luxury and splendour dominate the top of the range. And panoramic Prague is the icing on the cake.

Bohemian cuisine is traditionally known for hearty, tasty dishes, many made with flour. Salads and vegetables were not, for many years, anywhere near the top of the menu, leading Josef Lada, the illustrator of the Švejk books, to voice his concern about the health of the nation some 100 years ago: mountains of dumplings, fatty meat and cream sauces far too rich. In one of his cartoons, a pig scampers out of the kitchen, ducks and geese flap their wings to escape the pots: run for your lives! The cook chases after them, brandishing a butcher's knife … whilst Lada poked fun at Bohemian cuisine, the author Karel Čapek offered this literary bon mot: »Delightful« though culinary Bohemia may be, it is also »suicide with a knife and fork«.

Suicide with a knife and fork?

Now for the good news: there are novel, excellent variations on this typical, traditional cuisine: Potrefená Husa (The Wounded Goose) is a modern restaurant chain run by the Prague brewery Staropramen, whose inns can be found on many a corner in the city centre – well worth dropping in. Beer bars, leather benches and rustically tiled walls add up to a trendy, yet cozy atmosphere with tasty national fare. Stern competition comes from the Kolkovna Group who have an ace up their sleeve: Pilsner Urquell. They serve a naturally cloudy beer, brewed in their own cauldron. Brass, chrome and old-fashioned posters from the founding years conjure up a nostalgic flair to match the indigenous cuisine.

Good and new: modern restaurant chains

It has to be said, at this juncture, that many of the Old Town alleys and leafy passages are littered with cheap menus and faded photographs of less than appetising offers from shoddy restaurants which do the heritage site of Prague no favours whatsover. Be prepared for a culture shock – and steer clear of the pungent fare along the »coronation road« and Old Town Square. The vaulted interiors may look inviting, but a disaster of gastronomical proportions may be the price to pay.

Mass production in the heritage site

Sweet temptations: the Art Nouveau café in the Municipal House

Typical Dishes

Hearty fare is the order of the day, nice and tasty for a »happy belly«. Delicious sauces, irresistible fruit dumplings and even the Italians love Prague Ham.

Česnečka (garlic soup): The powerful bulb can replenish spirits completely, hence this soup is often dished up as a hangover cure in Prague. Thickened with cheese, potato and onion, the aroma subsequently seeps through the pores. Garlic is hugely popular here: top chefs serve it as an appetiser cooked in olive oil, crispy and full of taste.

Goulash: The diced beef classic comes in many varieties in Czech cuisine. Karlsbad goulash is made with a heavy sauce – cream is a vital ingredient. The Znaimer version features the famous sweet and sour gherkins. Pilsner goulash is cooked with beer and leaves a spicy taste on the tongue. It would be politically incorrect to speak of »gypsy goulash«, but the recipe is still very much on the menu: spicy peppers, bacon and onion contribute to its distinctive taste. Only the name has changed.

Carp: Duck, pork and hare may be popular all year round, but »king of the kitchen« is »carp with grace«. Breaded or boiled, à la meunière or »black« with dark beer – the best way to enjoy carp is still the old fisherman's recipe – packed in mud and leaves, laid under the embers of the fire and then, when cooked, the crust is broken open and the white fish eaten with the fingers.

Pastries: Only Vienna comes close to Prague's riches when it comes to pastries: sweet dumpling, cream roll, kolach, vdolak, pancake, strudel, cream puff. Towers of tarts, cakes and slices filed with curd, nuts and poppy seeds. Powidltascherl, however, is the absolute champion – a plum jam turnover which is so delicious, any fan of pastries will be unable to resist!

Fruit dumpling: When God passed down national dishes to the people, the Czechs only received a pastry roll. »There's nothing in it«, they complained, so God relented and sent them a fruit orchard. Ever since, the Czechs have filled their potato flour or curd cheese dough with apricots, damsons, strawberries. Topped with melted butter, sugar, cinnamon or poppy seed, the veritable »icing on the cake« is a slightly salty goat's cheese crumble.

Prague Ham: Not cooked, but cured in brine and spiced with pepper, coriander and bayleaves, lending this speciality its mildly salty taste and smoky aroma. Traditionally served cold with horseradish and slices of sour gherkin. Warm, it can be baked in bread or eaten simply as a thick slice with mild mustard seed sauce and mashed potato.

Svíčková: A typical Czech dish, the slices of beef in »candle sirloin« are cut as straight as candles, hence the name. As soft as beef fillet, the traditional dish is served with light napkin dumplings, swimming in sweet and sour vegetable cream sauce, not too heavy, not too thin, not too fatty and not too bland. A spoonful of cranberries rounds things off nicely.

Utopenci: »Drunken men« are chunky little hot dogs pickled in oil and vinegar, found in every pub or tavern, usually in full display on the counter in a large preserving jar. Sometimes customers are allowed to help themselves. Liberally sprinkled with onion, accompanied by a slice of bread, »drunken men« amount to ideal preparation for sinking a drink or two. Cheers!

A Regal Head

»Pivo« is the magic word, Czech for beer – a winner on draught in Prague's many bars, pubs and taverns. But changes are afoot: a young generation of brewers is rebelling against their fathers' tradition. New labels are making their mark: Escape LImetka, Cool Grep, Zlatopramen Citrón. Pilsner Urquell still rules the export market, but the choice of unpasteurized, unfiltered, brews of distinctive flavour is on the rise. Microbreweries focussing on quality beers are emerging at quite a rate. Prague's next miracle is brewing…

The Czech Republic's international reputation for beer is largely due to the unrivalled hops which are cultivated today in North Bohemia around Žatec (Saaz), Roudnice, Úštěk and Dubá, collectively known as »North Bohemian hops«. Exported all over the world, most Czech beers are bottom-fermented. The basic types of beer are »světlé« (light) and »tmavé« (dark). Degrees Plato measurements refer to the density of beer, in other words, the concentration of sugars in the wort prior to fermentation, rather than measuring actual alcohol content.

The Rituals of Beer Culture

The appearance of a beer is important, first the colour and hue (Czechs observe a beer's »sparkle«). Thus begins the drinking ritual. Next, the head – how stable is it? If you can lay a coin on top, then the barman has done his job well. Lukás Svoboda, from the Old Town restaurant Lokál, was officially crowned world champion in this discipline in the year 2010. He now offers training courses to colleagues and keen amateurs (sign up at the bar).

Liquid gold is no longer drawn from the barrel, but from stainless steel tanks which are often on display, adding to a tavern's atmosphere. Newer, stylish beer bars also serve cans and bottles, as colourful as an alchemist's laboratory, along with exotic beer cocktails – just add a slice of pineapple. The mix is what matters, but there is also a clear difference in male and female preferences: studies reveal that men go for the world-famous Pilsner Urquell and Budweiser – and another favourite is Velkopopovický kozel. The ladies, meanwhile, prefer Primátor's Chipper Grapefruit beer from the little East Bohemian town of Náchod.

Liquid Gold

In the 19th century, there were approximately 120 breweries in the capital alone. Today some two dozen copper brewing kettles are still steaming in the cozy, nostalgic taverns around town. The inexorable trend towards global industrial breweries has even seen Pilsner Urquell snapped up by the South African/American conglomerate SAB Miller. České Budějovice in South Bohemia is still flying the flag for independence, however, they are their own Budvar bosses!

The Winning Combination

The Pilsner Urquell legend has Bavarian origins. In 1842, master brewer Josef Groll travelled from Vilshofen to Pilsen on a rescue mission to improve the poor beer quality. He experimented with different blends of the basic ingredients (water, barley malt, hops) until he struck the winning combination. His own invention, the bottom-fermented brew, proved a resounding success and soon made its way around the world, served in a similarly new style of tulip-shaped glass. It was named after the place it was created – Pils.

Matured in the Bottle

Visiting Prague without embarking on an extensive tour of the traditional watering holes would be like a love affair without any kissing. When it comes to beer, strength matters: the concentration of sugars in the wort.

Pilsner Urquell contains 12 degrees Plato, Prague Staropramen 10, 11. The Bernard family brewery, which can be traced back to the 16th century, introduced a beer which matures in the bottle like champagne. Its original swing-top and a clever marketing campaign also contributed to the success. Beer philosophies have been rewritten: Nowadays in the Czech Republic, »Bernard« is someone who dons a red wig and nose to listen to wild rock bands at Bernard music festivals. Lobkowicz, meanwhile, has retained a more aristocratic air. A real prince is responsible for this classy, yet bold, lager. His Hradčany palace is an inviting place to try it. Simply regal!

Every reason to laugh: Czechs are world champions in beer consumption per head

Marvellous atmosphere

There are, nevertheless, many culinary highlights to savour and good tips need not be overly expensive: the gourmet temples on the Vltava are certainly cheaper than those on the Seine. Prague's ambitious chefs reach for the Michelin stars and a number of restaurants have won nominations in the »romantic panorama« category. A golden hare under chandeliers or by candlelight, accompanied by classic Mozart melodies cannot fail to delight. And a Hradčany view will more than compensate for a less than spectacular dish.

TRADITIONAL DISHES

Meat and fish

The favourite meat of the Czechs is pork, prepared in many different ways. One national dish is roast pork, served with cabbage and dumplings. On festive occasions, crispy roast goose or duck may take the place of pork, the side dishes remaining the same. Game is often excellent, be it haunch of venison or larded saddle of hare. Further very important specialities are steamed beef, boiled pork belly, roast lung and various sorts of sausage (roast sausages, bacon sausages, Prague sausages, smoked sausages and knackwurst). Prague's boiled ham is rightly famous all over the world. Less frequently seen on the menu are fish dishes. However, scarcely any family can get by without the traditional carp at Christmas.

Heavy sauces

For all main dishes, sauces are considered very important. Sometimes this is seasoned gravy, possibly refined by the addition of cream. Both meat and vegetables are often accompanied by a white sauce, given a highly distinctive flavour by marjoram and caraway seeds.

Dumplings etc.

Bohemian cuisine is unthinkable without dumplings (▶MARCOPOLO Insight page 126/127). There are many varieties. Alongside semolina dumplings and noodles, dumplings made of potato or white bread are the most frequent side dishes. Bacon dumplings filled with cabbage or spinach, served with fried onions, are a favourite main dish, but the high point of Bohemian dumpling specialities is undoubtedly the fruit dumpling made with yeast dough, to which Franz Werfel devotes more than 1000 words in his novel The Pure in Heart. They can be filled with cherries, apricots, apples, blueberries or, most especially, plums. The dumplings are topped with hard, grated cream cheese or poppy seeds, and, last of all, melted butter.

Pastries and flour-based foods

There is a wide range of flour-based foods. Apfelstrudel and the variety of small cakes and doughnuts may be tempting, but the pancakes (palačinky) surpass them all. Made with egg-batter and filled with cream cheese, jam or chocolate, these pancakes are not as paper-thin as French crêpes, but just as delicious.

Prague delicacy: apple strudel with vanilla and chocolate sauce

TRADITIONAL DRINKS

»You don't need a bakery if there's a brewery« as they say in the bars of Prague. The Czechs may be a nation of beer drinkers, but they still maintain: »Wine is for the head, but in your belly the beer should be on its own« (►MARCOPOLO Insight page 122/123).   *Beer*

Did you know that the Czechs are the third-oldest winemakers in Europe? Father of the nation Emperor Charles IV imported vines from Burgundy in the mid-14th century to begin cultivation. Under the Habsburgs, the Bohemian vineyards of Lobkowicz produced the finest wines for the imperial table in Vienna. The winegrowing regions of Mělník, Litoměřice, Lovsice and Žernoseky became famous. In the French Rothschilds' stakes, the South Moravian viniculturists of Valtice, Lednice and Mikulov enjoy an excellent reputation, earned in recent years thanks to the winemaking project having been adopted as a national prestige project, rejuvenated after the barren years under socialist rule.   *Wine*

Bohemian Dumplings

They have to be tried once in Prague: Bohemian dumplings, the classic side dish for Prague's and Bohemia's favourite dish: roast pork. Don't be surprised, if you've never eaten them, that they come to the table in slices and that they are made with yeast – only one of the many variations of dumplings...

▶ **Making Bohemian dumplings** (český knedlík)
For the classical variety of the Bohemian dumpling wheat flour, eggs, water, salt and yeast are mixed to make a dough.

2 eggs

1 kg/2 lbs 3 oz wheat flour

300 ml/10 fl oz water

2 tsp salt

1 tsp sugar

1 cube fresh yeast

1 Combine all ingredients and knew thoroughly. The dough should be smooth and not sticky.

2 Place the dough in a bowl, cover it and let it rest in a warm place until air bubbles appear in the dough.

3 Cut the dough into four equally sized pieces and form each one into a loaf.

Dumpling varieties

Potato dumplings

Apricot dumplings
Thuringian dumplings
»Halbseidene« dumplings
Buckwheat dumplings
Poppy seed dumplings
Gnocchi di patate

Dumplings made with bread rolls

»Semmelknödel«
»Serviettenknödel«
Cheese dumplings
Spinach dumplings
Bacon dumplings

Quark dumplings
Plum dumplings
»Topfen« dumplings
Apricot dumplings

Flour dumplings

»Germknödel«
»Dampfnudeln«
Apple dumplings
»Klüten«

Dumplings made from farina
Farina dumplings
»Grießnockerl«

Dumplings made from matzo
Matzah balls

©BAEDEKER

4

Cook in lightly salted water for 20 – 25 min. in a sufficiently large pot.

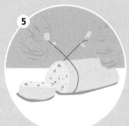

5

Use a piece of string to cut the hot dumplings into finger-thick pieces.

6

Dumplings are the ideal accompaniments for dishes with lots of gravy.

Not for losing weight
Dumplings with bread rolls 200g/7 oz = 340 kcal
»Serviettenknödel« 200g/7 oz = 390 kcal
»Germknödel« 330g/11.5 oz = 850 kcal

The president's digestive bitter

Gossips maintain that Miloš Zeman only won the presidential election in 2013 because of his prior admission: »I always drink beer with Becherovka«. Sometimes referred to as »Karlsbad's 13th spring«, this herbal liqueur is as popular as beer across the nation. Invented by a chemist named Josef Vitus Becher (1740 – 1840), the recipe has been kept a secret. Yellowish in colour, sticky and viscous, it tastes rather similar to cough medicine, but it will help to clear your stomach. In many of Prague's taverns, it is automatically brought to the table after a pork roast or braised beef ... »on the house!«, as the saying goes. Today Becherovka is mixed in cocktails – with tonic water it is known as »Beton«.

Both reds and whites prosper in the Bohemian and Moravian soil. The nation's champion is a hot topic of debate: is it »St Ludmila« from Mělník or the Muscatel from Bzenec in South Moravia? The Italians have their Chianti, the oenophiles of Prague their Frankovka: an earthy deep red, often poured from the barrel. Call into the Villa Richter below Hradčany to taste a Riesling or Pinot Noir, cultivated on the spot since 2008. This particular vineyard was founded by St Wencelas, so legend would have us believe, honoured to this day as Supremus Magistrum Vinum. With this seal of quality, Prague delivers the holy Wencelas wine to the Vatican.

Prague wine bars do serve wines with an international name, but principally home-grown wines are on offer. Among these are the famous »Ludmila« wine from the banks of the Elbe close to Mělník, and the Žernosecké and Primátorské varieties. Good-quality wines also come from the southern Moravian areas of Znaim, Mikulov (Nikolsburg), Velkopavlovické (Grosspawlowitz) and Valtické (Feldsberg), as well as from the region around Bratislava (Pressburg) in Slovakia.

Hard spirits produced in the country include: slivovice (plum schnaps) from Moravian Slovakia, meruňkovice (made from apricots), žitná or režná (corn schnaps) and jalovcová or borovička (juniper schnaps). After a heavy meal, many people swear by Karlovy Vary, an excellent herbal bitter (Becherovka, Baedeker Insight). The in-crowd drink it neat, on the rocks.

Coffee, tea The grand era of coffee house culture in Prague may be over – the city is no longer immune to the omnipresent Starbucks »to go« beakers – but coffeemania is still alive and frothing here. Latte, latte macchiato, cappuccino everywhere. Espresso is strong and black, usually bitter. The once popular Turkish style (complete with grounds) has disappeared, although at one time »Turek« was the nation's second favourite drink, after beer. Times change. Čaj (tea), mléko (milk) and juice are served all over.

Recommended pubs, restaurants and cafés

Michelin stars are not such a big deal for Prague folk. Gourmet attention, as everyone knows – including those who do not spend so much time in bars – has always been focussed on beer. Prague's new gastronomy, however, is recapturing former glories. Young chefs are returning to grandmother's Bohemian recipes, giving a modern, refined touch to meat, fish and poultry with »Bohemian light«. The coffee houses of Prague serve up similar fare to the confectioners of Paris and Vienna: sophisticated dishes and first-rate desserts. There is much for the eyes to feast on: stucco ceilings, simple vaults, an unfailingly harmonious ambience.

New Prague cuisine: Artichokes and Art Déco

❶ Etc. map page 131/132
Destinations outside the city are off the map
Price categories
for a main dish
€   15 – 20 €
€€   20 – 30 €
€€€   30 – 50 €
€€€€   50 – 100 €

WHERE TO DRINK BEER
❶ Kolkovna (Revenue Stamp Centre)
Josefov, V Kolkovně 8
Tel. 224 819 701
www.kolkovna-restaurant.cz
Mon–Sun 11am–midnight
A retro brewery bar and dumpling paradise. Pilsner Urquell lords it

Nostalgic microbrewery with brass and mahogany: Kolkovna

Hotels and Restaurants

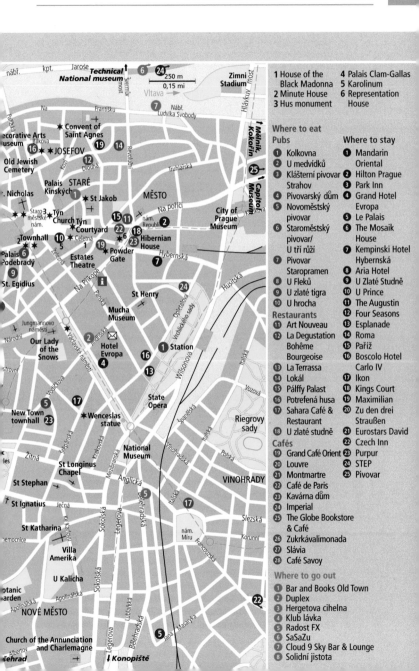

1 House of the Black Madonna
2 Minute House
3 Hus monument
4 Palais Clam-Gallas
5 Karolinum
6 Representation House

Where to eat

Pubs
1 Kolkovna
2 U medvídků
3 Klášterní pivovar Strahov
4 Pivovarský dům
5 Novoměstský pivovar
6 Staroměstský pivovar/ U tří růží
7 Pivovar Staropramen
8 U Fleků
9 U zlaté tigra
10 U hrocha

Restaurants
11 Art Nouveau
12 La Degustation Bohême Bourgeoise
13 La Terrassa
14 Lokál
15 Pálffy Palast
16 Potrefená husa
17 Sahara Café & Restaurant
18 U zlaté studně

Cafés
19 Grand Café Orient
20 Louvre
21 Montmartre
22 Café de Paris
23 Kavárna dům
24 Imperial
25 The Globe Bookstore & Café
26 Zukrkávalimonada
27 Slávia
28 Café Savoy

Where to go out
1 Bar and Books Old Town
2 Duplex
3 Hergetova cihelna
4 Klub lávka
5 Radost FX
6 SaSaZu
7 Cloud 9 Sky Bar & Lounge
8 Solidní jistota

Where to stay
1 Mandarin Oriental
2 Hilton Prague
3 Park Inn
4 Grand Hotel Evropa
5 Le Palais
6 The Mosaik House
7 Kempinski Hotel Hybernská
8 Aria Hotel
9 U Zlaté Studně
10 U Prince
11 The Augustin
12 Four Seasons
13 Esplanade
14 Roma
15 Paříž
16 Boscolo Hotel Carlo IV
17 Ikon
18 Kings Court
19 Maximilian
20 Zu den drei Straußen
21 Eurostars David
22 Czech Inn
23 Purpur
24 STEP
25 Pivovar

here, a strong, frothy bock beer served in foaming jugs – a darkish »13« with a recipe said to have come from the Vikings. A creamy brew with an explosively aromatic taste.

❷ U medvidků
(The Little Bear)
Old Town, Na Perštýně 7
Tel. 224 220 930
www.umedvidku.cz
Mon–Sun 11am–11pm
Ever heard of beer ice cream? This is the place to try it. Or, if you feel up to it, you can try the strongest brewed beer in the world, the golden brown X-Beer33, a rouge beer – reddish with a pink head. The cherry taste is not for everybody.

U Fleků: the Golden City's house brewery

❸ Klášterní pivovar Strahov (Strahov Monastery brewery)
Hradčany, Strahovské nádvoří 10, tel. 233 353 155
www.klasterni-pivovar.cz
Mon–Sun 10am–10pm
The naturally cloudy house beer in the cellar is just like the one brewed by the Benedictine monks back in 1505. The recipe was brought here from Bavaria. Traditional Budvar (Budweiser) is also served alongside St Norbert's lager and wheat beer.

❹ Pivovarský dům (brewery)
New Town, Ječná/Lipová 15
Tel. 296 216 666
www.gastroinfo.cz
Mon–Sun 11am–11pm
Searching for beers previously untried, this microbrewery comes up with a fresh surprise every month. Sour cherries, bananas, blueberries, stinging nettles, coffee, chocolate or chilli are among the ingredients added to the malt here. Only the naturally cloudy Stephan pils would pass the purity regulations (as used in Germany).

❺ Novoměstský pivovar (New Town Brewery)
New Toen, Vodičkova 20
Tel. 222 232 448
www.npivovar.cz
Mon–Sun 10am–11.30pm
The first tavern in Prague to begin leaving its beer unfiltered after the Velvet Revolution. There is a simple historical explanation to the name Levák (leftie), namely that the drainage pipe from the cauldron was on the left hand side.

When it became blocked, a new brewery technique was the result. The yeast has remained in the brew evers since the year 1434, when this providential accident happened.

❻ Staroměstský pivovar/ U tří růží (Old Town Brewery/The Three Roses)
Old Town, Husova 10
Tel. 225 226 650
www.u3r.cz
Mon–Thu and Sun 11am–11pm
Fri and Sat 11am–midnight
Opening this Old Prague style tavern was one of the last acts in office for the outgoing president Václav Klaus. His favourite pastry, a poppy strudel with plum puree, goes nicely with the dark beer served here.

❼ Pivovar Staropramen
Smíchov, Nádražni 84
Tel. 257 191 111
Mon–Sat 10am–6pm
Looking for a large beer factory? This is the place for time-honoured Prague brewing culture. The museum not only tells the story of the beer, but also serves samples, the nicest form of inspiration when it comes to ordering from the barman.

❽ U Fleků
Old Town, Křemencova 11
Tel. 224 934 019
http://en.ufleku.cz
A monument to Prague's history of beer: ever since the year 1499, without interruption, the dark »13« (Flekovské) has been brewed here according to the same recipe.

Hundred-year-old plane trees provide shade in the beer garden, where a 22m/72ft deep well stands. No genuine Prague citizen can pass by without sinking a quick half, standing at the bar. This is also a good spot to observe international drinking customs. Germans and Dutch bawl at each other, the Japanese bring their karaoke sets with them, Italians sing unisono as a choir, the Swedes as a quartet. The English are loudest of all – unless the Irish are in town.

❾ U zlaté tigra (The Golden Tiger)
Old Town, Husova 17
Tel. 602 238 502
www.uzlatehotygra.cz
This is what steel discipline looks like: no matter the weather, come rain or shine or snow – the Czech Hemingway of beer Bohumil Hrabal arrived at six on the dot every day at this favourite haunt of dissidents, literary legends, film and music makers. Václav Havel also brought his American counterpart Bill Clinton to this bar. At the long tables underneath impressive vaults, nine out of ten guests are sure to be regulars. If a stranger manages to down ten jugs, he is accepted as a new friend. The mystical-psychedelic rush to the head this achievement entails will not be so quickly forgotten. Nor will one forget the cutlets with potato cakes and spiced beer cheese – designed to fill your belly (and stay there). The cool Prazdroj 12° is stored in a deep, 13th-century cellar, giving it a unique taste.

❿ U hrocha (The Hippopotamus)
Lesser Quarter, Thunovská 10
Tel. 257 316 890
Mon–Sun 11am–11pm
Two rooms, divided by a vaulted corridor: the landlord established this tavern for Prague citizens to protect the »štamgast« (the »regular«, a similar word to that used in German), in his own nature reserve. Today, tourists wander in to see »real Prague people«. Brave enough to squeeze in between the archetypal characters? A little luck is also required, the place is usually packed. Diagonally opposite the tavern is the Czech parliament. Politicians possess a key for the rear entrance. Take note: Pilsner Urquell unites all parties.

RESTAURANTS

⓫ Art Nouveau €€€
Franco-Czech cuisine, Old Town in the Municipal House
Náměstí republiky 5
Tel. 222 002 770
Mon–Sun noon–11pm
www.franzouskarestaurace.cz
Luxus anno 1912: Art Déco does not come any more authentic than this, not even in Paris. Light floods in through tall windows into this XXL restaurant where the napkins stand to attention like penguins. Exquisite dishes are imaginatively served with honey and mustard sauce, walnut dressing, thyme, coriander and caramelized scallions. Movie scenes for »I Served the King of England« and »La Vie En Rose«, the Edith Piaf biopic, were filmed here. Remember to reserve a table in good time!

⓬ La Degustation Bohême Bourgeoise €€€€
Czech (haute) cuisine
Old Town
Haštalská 18
Tel. 222 311 234
Mon–Sun 6pm–11pm
www.ladegustation.cz
Oldřich Sahajdák ascended to star chef status in Prague by rediscovering »golden recipes« from the days of the monarchy. His new slant on the classics still maintains a down-to-earth Bohemian flavour. Diners can choose between a four or seven course menu in the pleasing surroundings under vaulted ceilings.

⓭ La Terrassa €€
Spanish fare with fish and meat aplenty, Smíchov Janáčkovo nábřeží, Dětský ostrov (Children's Island)
Tel. 604 300 300
Mon–Sun noon-midnight
www.laterrassa.cz
Sitting over the barrage as the waters of the Vltava rush by, the sensation of being on an island is intense. Steamboats pass through the locks right in front of the dinner table where tapas are served: Catalan Butifarra (sausage), grilled sardines in salsa verde,suckling pig from Salamanca and, of course, Crema Catalana. A nice touch, a few sun loungers are available for post-prandial relaxation.

⓮ Lokál €€
Traditional Bohemian cuisine
Old Town, Dlouhá 33
Tel. 222 316 265, Mon–Sat 11am–1am, Sun noon–10pm
www.ambi.cz

Final preparations for a successful evening in Pálffy Palace

White vaulted rooms offer a tableau of dark brown wood panelling, bulletproof glass shelves and stainless steel beer tanks. Svíčková (beer sirloin), black pudding with lentils, original Bohemian roast pork with kapusta (steamed cabbage) and napkin dumplings are so popular that there is often a wait for a table, even though 330 guests can dine here at one time.

⓵ Pálffy Palace €€€
Crossover, Lesser Quarter
Valdštejnská 14
Tel. 257 530 522
Daily 11am–11pm
www.palffy.cz
Has Don Giovanni called ahead to reserve a table? The décor would certainly suit him, with chandeliers and candlelight, silverware and priceless porcelain. The fine menus presented since 1994 include fish, hare, pheasant and guinea fowl in a sesame coat and red cabbage collar. The most tender of meats are ennobled with exotic herb titles. The summer terrace has the captivating flair of Lesser Quarter gardens, the sound of a harp accompanies birdsong. Don Giovanni should be here any minute.

⓶ Potrefená husa €
Regional fare
Josefov, Bílkova 5
Tel. 222 326 626
Daily 11am–midnight
www.potrefenahusa.com
If the »Wounded Goose« sign is hanging above the doorway, expect duck, pork and bacon

dumplings on the inside. Hearty fare with tasty sauces in remarkable surroundings characterized by Cubist beams, the original location of this restaurant chain which has gone on from strength to strength. A sort of Starbucks for typically Bohemian cooking with a trendy designer vibe.

⑰ Sahara Café & Restaurant €€€

Mediterranean-Arabic cuisine
Vinohrady, Náměstí míru 6
Tel. 222 514 987, Mon–Fri 11am–half past midnight, Saturday from noon to half past midnight, Sun noon to 11pm,
www.saharacafe.com
Thousand And One Nights in Art Nouveau Prague, harem curtains, a sultan's throne, pouffes, brass and mahogany. The culinary caravan travels through Spain and Morocco towards Lebanon, offering empanadas, houmous, kebabs, delicious lamb dishes and couscous to die for. The atmospheric Sahara soundtrack can be purchased on CD as a souvenir.

**⑱ U zlaté studně
(The Golden Well) €€€€**

Exquisite gourmet cuisine in the Lesser Quarter, U Zlaté studně 4
Tel. 257 533 322
Mon–Sun noon –11pm
www.terasauzlatestudne.cz
Keep it to yourself, this one is for insiders only: Barack and Michelle Obama are among those to have enjoyed the panoramic view of 100 towers included in a visit to this restaurant. Foodies will focus

on the duck with fig mousse, shrimps in mango sauce and poussin with chestnut puree – these creations are brought to the table on finest glassware. Master chef Pavel Sapík reaches for the highest gourmet stars, yet guests need not feel faint when the bill arrives.

CAFÉS

⑲ Grand Café Orient €

Old Town, Ovocný trh 19
Tel. 224 224 220
www.grandcafeorient.cz
Mon–Fri 9am–10pm
Sat/sun 10am–10pm
Complete cubism: cups, tables, lamps and mirrors – everything is authentic, all the way down to the ashtrays. The green and white striped décor of the café nicely matches the spinach pancakes served here. The entire U Černé Matky Boží with museum and café is protected as a listed building.

⑳ Louvre €

New Town, Národní 20
Tel. 224 930 949
www.cafelouvre.cz
Mon–Fri 8am–11.30pm
Sat/Sun 9am–11.30pm
A literary déjà-vu with red golden walls: Brod, Werfel, Kisch and Kafka are all here in spirit (and ambience), recalling the antepenultimate turn of the century. Notebooks and writing implements lie on the tables should visitors feel the urge to pen some lines of poetry. Connoisseurs keep quiet and savour the silent poetry

Louvre: focal point for Prague night owls and literati

of the Palatschinken filled with quark and rum raisins – a poem in itself!

㉑ Montmartre € Insider Tip
Old Town, Řetězová 7
Tel. 222 220 112
Mon–Fri 8am–11.30pm
Sat/Sun from noon
Kisch, Brod, Werfel, Hašek and other literary figues also frequented this locale along with demi-monde dames in feather boas. Some pieces of furniture from yesteryear have survived – those longing for the good old days will feel perfectly at home.

㉒ Café de Paris €€
Old Town, Hotel Paříž
U Obecního domu 1
Tel. 222 195 816
www.hotel-paris.cz

Egyptian décor at the Imperial

Mon–Sun 10am–10pm
Dark shades of Art Nouveau are mirrored in the tall windows, evoking nostalgic yearnings: dreams of the Belle Époque with apple strudel and café Viennois.

㉓ Kavárna Obecní dům €
New Town
Námestí republiky 5
Tel. 222 002 763
www.kavarnaod.cz
Mon–Sun 7.30-11pm
Prague's exuberant Art Nouveau reached its peak in the Municipal House: witness the breathtaking marble reliefs, stuccoed ceilings and cut glass chandeliers. The mountains of cake on the waiter's trolley are no less stupendous.

㉔ Imperial €€ Insider Tip
New Town, Na Poříčí 15
Tel. 246 011 600
www.hotel-imperial.cz
Mon–Sat 9am–midnight
Sun 9am–11pm
Back to the year 1914: a procession of the Nile's graces with the lions of Assyria, depicted on majolica tiles. The menu ranges from Prague/Viennese schnitzel and strudel to fragrant Asian cuisine. Viennese popular music played in the evenings.

㉕ The Globe Bookstore & Cafe €
New Town, Pštrossova 6
Tel. 224 934 203
www.globebookstore.cz
Sun–Wed 9.30–midnight
Thu–Sat until 11pm
In a former Prague cinema, two Americans practise their philosophy: »in books, truth, in coffee,

life«. A marvellous Art Nouveau ceiling arches above.

❷❻ Zukrkávalimonada €
Lesser Quarter, Lázeňská 7
Tel. 257 225 396
www.zukrkavalimonada.com
Mon–Sun 9am–7pm
This patisserie (with a small wholefood bistro) ushers in a new generation: cozy as a doll's house beneath a ceiling with wooden beams painted blue and white – a mere stone's throw from the well-trodden tourist trail, yet surprisingly tranquil and snug. The cakes are delightful – served by a lady who could have stepped straight out of the movie »Chocolat«. Sweet and dreamy.

❷❼ Slávia €
New Town, Smetanovo nábřeží 2
Tel. 224 218 493
www.cafeslavia.cz
Mon–Fri 8am–midnight,
Sat–Sun from 9am
A visit should be on everyone's list, but there's a hint of disappointment in spite of the glamour: the garish green image of the absinthe drinker, the 1930s lighting design, marble tables and leather furniture – all this literary panache is diminished by the hectic hustle and bustle. It feels like being on board a tramcar. Drop in, take a look, make your exit. The aroma of goulash and roast pork wafts through the air. Then there's the »little coffin« in the display cabinet – Rakvičky, a crispy and sugary pastry whose name derives from its form: hollow inside and topped

with cream, like a wreath. Taking a bite is a philosophical act: laughing in the face of death by eating it up. Speaking a little Czech helps at this point. A typical Slávia scene late in the evening can involve five psychiatrists discussing their work, surrounded by a captivated entourage. Illuminated Hradčany looks unreal in the distance and the National Theatre casts mystic shadows opposite while the tram ghosts by – the atmosphere in Café Slávia simply must be savoured on a night like this.

❷❽ Café Savoy €€€
Smíchov, Vítězná 5
Tel. 257 311 562
www.ambi.cz
Mon–Fri 8am–10.30pm
Sat–Sun 9am–10.30pm
The antipole to Café Slávia on the other side of the Vltava: greetings from Paris. Take a look at the luxuriantly gilded coffered ceiling, ornately painted by František Ženíšek, also responsible for the foyer of the National Theatre – the ceiling was hidden under plaster for over half a century. In the early 1950s, the Communist Party used this place as their registration office for new members. Oh' the irony, in what was once a haunt of the bourgoisie. A memory of those times is conjured up by the sight of delectable Prague ham, served warm with mashed potato. The fruit dumplings are so light, they almost hover above the plate. Covered with vanilla and chocolate sauce, thankfully they do not actually float away.

Museums

Kaleidoscope of the Arts

The entire Old Town resembles an open air museum, hence the enormous variety of art treasures to be admired here is hardly surprising. Many of them are presented in the most beautiful historical buildings of the city, adding to the marvellous experience of a visit to Prague's museums.

From old masters to the avant-garde ¬– there is a place for everything in the palaces of Prague. Beginning with the numerous branches of the National Museum and the National Gallery, to the Jewish Museum and the homages to significant artists and cultural talents in many other museums, Prague appeals to all tastes and interests.

Enormous variety

Prague's museums are usually open from Tuesday to Sunday, 10am to 5pm. The Jewish Museum is open on Mondays and closed on Saturdays. Children, students and senior citizens (aged 60 upwards) pay half price. Family tickets (two adults, two children, up to the age of 15) are also available. Photographs may be taken for a fee between 40 and 80 Kč.

Opening hours

Every year in June, some 29 of Prague's museums open their doors for a long night, an art marathon encompassing over 50 locations, with Charles IV and Rabbi Loew as spiritual companions. The programme can be previewed on the website www.prazskamuzejninoc.cz. Look for »my museum« and »my night« to prepare your own itinerary. Admission is free (so far), there is just a small donation required in the National Museum on Wencelas Square. With numbers now reaching a quarter of a million visitors, there is discussion of introducing a compulsory charge in future to offset the crowds. Altarpieces, dinosaur skeletons, vintage cars and much, much more can be viewed from sundown until the witching hour.

Long night

The magic of the night is especially strong in the Convent of St Agnes. Time travel by torchlight, beginning with the birth of Christ – the cycle of paintings is atmospherically illuminated. At half past eight, the Garden of Gethsemane is the next station, another medieval painting. A workshop is open to children, with pens, brushes and paints. The whole of Prague seems to be out and about on this night. Shuttle busses connect the museums and galleries along nine routes. The environs of the museums are otherwise closed to traffic. Coffee,

Family is the name Czech artist Karel Nepras (1932 – 2002) gave to his exhibit in the Kampa Museum

pizza, hot dogs and lemonade are served at kiosks. The party is finally over at one o'clock in the morning, but before the lights go out, most visitors have already decided to come back next year.

Prague's museums

ART
Prague City Gallery
page 192

Galerie Portheimka
page 299

Galerie Rudolfinum
Old Town, Alšovo nábřeží 12
Tue, Wed, Fri–Sun 10am–6pm
Thu until 8pm,
www.galerierudolfinum.cz

CONTEMPORARY ART AND
WORKS OF CLASSICAL
MODERNISM
House of the Stone Bell
page 267

Kampa Museum
page 220

Museum of Decorative Arts
page 245

Lapidarium
page 192

Mánes Gallery
page 239

Mucha Museum
page 241

Prague City Museum
page 295

National Gallery
page 247

National Museum
page 248

Wallenstein Riding School
page 325

Strahov Picture Gallery
page 306

CULTURAL HISTORY/
HISTORY
Jewish Museum
page 207

Museum of Communism
page 246

Náprstek Museum
Praha 1, Betlémské náměstí 1
Tues–Sun 9am–12.15pm, 1pm–
5.30pm free entry on first Friday
of the month
Ethnological collection of Asian,
African and American cultures

**National memorial for
victims of Heydrich reprisals**
in the crypt of the Church of SS
Cyril and Methodius
page 189

LITERATURE, THEATRE AND
MUSIC
Dvořák Museum
in the Villa Amerika, page 313

Franz Kafka Museum
in the former Herget brickworks
page 198

Mozart Museum
in the Villa Bertramka

Smetana Museum
on Smetana Quay

MILITARY
Military Museum
Praha 3, U památníku 2
Nov–April Mon–Fri 9.30am–5pm;
May–Oct Tue–Sun 10am–6pm,
www.militarymuseum.cz

OTHER MUSEUMS
**Museum of the Infant Jesus
of Prague**

Toy Museum

National Technical Museum

Wax Museum
daily 9am–8pm
Smetana, Dvořák, Mucha and
other illustrious personalities from
politics, sport, music and show
business.

! *Museums for free*   **Insider Tip**

MARCO⊕POLO TIP

On the first Wednesday of the
month from 3pm, the National
Gallery offers free entry until it
closes at 8pm. This is valid for all
permanent exhibitions: with a
sound plan, it is possible to cover
three of them in the five hours
available. No time to waste!

Shopping

Temples to Consumerism

Bohemian crystal, wooden toys, antique books – these used to be the most popular gifts taken home from Prague. Today, there are so many shopping possibilities, it is difficult to know where to start. In one of the new shopping centres? Luxury boutiques on the glittering boulevards? Or are we hunting for bargains? Perhaps a flea market will provide the answer to our quest.

Every world metropolis has a famous luxury mile. In Prague it is Pařížská – Paris Avenue. Based on Haussmann's Grands Boulevards, its construction went hand in hand with the restructuring of the Jewish ghetto in the late 19th century. Today, the magnificent buildings which line the street are replete with grand and wickedly expensive temptations. Objects of desire include must-have bags and accessories, boots and haute couture, glamorous names like Gucci, Dior, Chanel, Prada, Boss and Cartier.

Champs-Élysées on theVltava

To find a bag which will not break the bank, it is worth heading into the sidestreets of Josefov, the Jewish ghetto in the late 19th century, much as one would leave the boulevards of Paris to one side. Curiosities of all types can be unearthed in the maze of alleys behind the Church of Our Lady before Týn (particularly in Týnská ulička): old tin toys, time-honoured timepieces. Some shops are no bigger than telephone boxes, but filled to the brim with oddities. It can be great fun sifting through the wares.

A worthwhile detour

The city's shopping centre is Wencelas Square. The lower portion is known as »Golden Cross«, now lined with familiar chains as seen in so many other cities. What makes it attractive is the architecture and the atmosphere it conjures up: Art Nouveau columns, neo-Renaissance stucco. Ubiquitous cashmere polo necks look so different in the Prague retro setting, compared to the homogeneous shops of Berlin.

The mercantile heart of the city

The labyrinthine shopping arcades of the Old Town are a characteristic feature of Prague, with high ceilings and wide staircases. Much like a bazar, the Lucerna Passage in the palace of the same name – built in the years 1907 to 1921 according to plans drawn up by Václav Havel's grandfather, is a seven storey property on the west side of Wencelas Square, marked with a lantern (Latin: lucerna) as insignia. It branches out with three entrances in the New Town: Štěpánská 61,

Prague's passages

Window shopping in Paris Avenue, Prague's splendid luxury boulevard

Vodičkova 36 and Václavské náměstí 38 via Pasáž Rokoko. Less than ten minutes away, to the north, the Pasáž Černá-růže (Black Rose Passage) is an aesthetic concrete construction (New Town, Na Příkopě 12). The route passes Koruna Palace, (nominative determinism: koruna is Czech for crown) with an atrium boasting a mosaic of coloured glass (Václavské náměstí 1, www.koruna-palace.cz). New Town springs another surprise in the form of the mirrored passage in the Adria Palace, a rare example of Rondocubist style, a uniquely Czech variation on Art Déco (Národní 40).

Souvenirs, souvenirs Bohemian glass is famous the world over, beautifully cut in the past in glorious colours. It can still be found all through the Old Town alleys, degraded to the status of cheap tourist bait. Fortunately, there

is a vibrant new generation of glassblowing artists creating ambitious new forms with vivid imagination, a far cry from the archetypal boat and snowflake designs. Porcelain craftwork is also undergoing a transformation, lovely porcelain boots instead of bric-a-brac. Czech dolls and marionettes are extremely popular souvenirs, along with wooden toys and costume (Gablonzer) jewellery and, more recently, printed T-shirts, fool's caps, felt hats, joke articles. Swarovski crystals are similarly in demand – the family of this (patented) cut lead glass, famous the world over, can trace its ancestors back to Bohemia.

Popular souvenir: Bohemian cut glass at Moser in the Pasáž Černá-růže

Antiques and flea markets Alas, the wild days which followed the Velvet Revolution are over. Connoisseurs will no longer find Art Déco lamps for a few crowns. Expressionist art for a few hellers? No such luck in Prague today. The flea markets nevertheless afford an opportunity to indulge in social and historical studies. Here a Socialist »Hero of Labour« award, there a Red Army beret. Any valuable antiques which remain are worth their weight in gold to professional dealers.

Opening times »Your business is your home«, as the Jewish saying goes. Most of the shops on the tourist trip follow this adage, staying open until 10pm in the summer months. The same is true of the larger shopping centres. They even stay open on Sundays. The usual opening hours are as follows: Mon–Fri 10am–8pm, Sat 9am–5pm, Sun 10am–8pm.

Shopping addresses

SECOND-HAND BOOK DEALERS
Pražský Almanach (Prague Almanac)
Lesser Quarter, Újezd 26
Tel. 224 812 247, Mon–Fri 11am–6pm, Sat/Sun by appointment, www.artbook.cz
A treasure trove for picture books, illustrations and old photographs.

ANTIQUES
Antik Mucha
Old Town, Liliová 12
Tel. 222 221 523, Mon–Sat 10am–6pm
What remains of the Belle Époque: bronze dancers, colourful porcelain cats and much, much more.

ORGANIC CHEMIST
Botanicus
Old Town, Ungelt, Týnský dvůr 3
Tel. 234 767 446, daily 10am–6.30pm, www.botanicus.cz
The wonderfully »green« world of healthy cosmetics, natural beauty care and therapy products.

BOOKSHOP
Vitalis
Prague Castle, Zlatá ulička 22
Tel. 257 181 660
daily 10.30am–7pm
www.vitalis-verlag.com
The Kafka specialist presents his range at number 22, Golden Lane, a fitting address as this is where Franz Kafka spent much of his time writing.

DELICATESSEN
U Paukerta
New Town, Národní 17

Tel 224 222 615
www.janpaukert.cz, Mon–Fri 9am–7pm, Sat 10am–6pm
The »beetle« of Prague. Traditional Prague »decorated bread rolls« (obložené chlecbíčky) adorn the display case like jewels. Definitely worth a try!

DESIGN
Qubus
Old Town, Rámová 3
Tel. 222 313 151, Mon–Fri 10am–6pm, www.qubus.cz
The design maxim »form follows function« has been turned on its head here: a porcelain boot becomes a vase, a Baroque clock features a digital display, curiosities abound.

FLEA MARKET
Bleší trhy Praha
Vysočany (Prague 9), Kolbenova 9
Metro line B, station: Kolbenova
Tel. 777 121 387, Sat and Sun 7am–2pm, www.blesitrhy.cz
In the socialist era, the largest tram factory in the world stood here. The factory has long since disappeared and the 5000 sq m/53 800 sq ft site now hosts a market with a vast array of wares, where even busts of Marx or Le-

At Bleší trhy Praha flea market

nin medals may be purchased. Most fascinating of all is the lively panoply of characters found here.

GIFTS
Antěl
Lesser Quarter
U Lužickeho semináre 7
Tel. 251 554 008 or
Old Town, Celetná 29 (entrance at Rybná 1)
Tel. 224 815 085
www.antelglass.com
daily 10am–7pm
Karen Feldman from Chicago designs by far the most original and inventive artefacts, from retro-style glass to vintage bags from the 1920s or tin toys.

Palladium: everything under one roof

Moser
Old Town, Na Příkopě 12
Černá-růže Passage
Tel. 224 212 93
www.moser-glass.com
daily 10am–8pm (in winter Sat/Sun 10am–7pm)
Exquisite glass, vases and the like, with gold rims and ornate engravings – not cheap, but seconds are also on sale.

DEPARTMENT STORES
Anděl City
Praha 5, Smíchov, Radlická 1 b
daily 7am–midnight
Trendy corners offering cappuccino, bubbly and sushi – a hip place to shop, next door to the most spectacular new building in booming Smíchov: Jean Nouvel's »Golden Angel« – the name is a reference to the »House at the Golden Angel« which once stood here. The outline of a giant angel can be seen in the glass façade – or, to be precise, the outline of actor Bruno Ganz who played an angel in Wim Wenders' film »Wings of Desire«. Right next to metro line B.

Tesco
Praha 1, Národní třída 26
Mon–Fri 8am–9pm, Sat 9am–8pm, Sun 10am–7pm
Right beside metro station Národní třída, this is a good place to do some quick shopping, especially for food.

Palladium
Praha 1, Náměstí republiky 1
www.palladiumpraha.cz
Supermarket daily 9am–8pm
Sun until 9pm,

shopping gallery Sun–Wed 9am–9pm, Thu until Sat 9am–10pm
Shopping centre at the heart of the city with some 170 clothes stores, cafés and restaurants.

ART

Kunstkomora

Lesser Quarter, Lázeňská 9
Tel. 246 028 019
www.kunstkomora.cz
Tue–Sat 11am–7pm
Step back into the reign of mad Emperor Rudolf II. Exotic and fantastical oddities in a creepy chamber of horrors.

Gambra

Hradčany, Černínská 5
Tel. 220 514 785, Nov–Feb, Sat/Sung noon–5.30pm, March–Oct, Wed–Sun noon–5.30pm
www.gambra.jex.cz
The king of sharp-tongued satire. Not for the faint-hearted, Jan Švankmajer's creations in his surreal gallery are true works of horror.

HANDICRAFTS

Marionety pod lampou (Marionettes under the lantern)

Lesser Quarter, U Lužického semináře 5
Tel. 602 689 918
www.marionetty.com daily 10am–7pm
The marionettes cost a good 150 Euro apiece. Not cheap, but they are all different – each one has its own personality!

Studio Šípek

Old Town, Valentinská 11
Tel. 602 322 169
www.boreksipek.cz, Mon–Fri 10am–6pm, Sat/Sun 11am–5pm.

Prague designer Borek Šipek emigrated to Germany in 1968 and was brought back home in 1990 by Václav Havel to illuminate the interior of Prague Castle. Šipek is also responsible for Lagerfeld's lighting design in Paris. His Prague shop sells glass and designer décor.

Kubista

Old Town, House of the Black Madonna, Ovocný trh 19
Tel. 224 236 378, www.kubista.cz
Tue–Sun 10am–6.30pm
Cubism to go: postcards, pictures, books, wrapping paper, glass, ceramics, furniture, posters, metalwork, household textiles.

MARKETS

Havelský teh (Havel Market)

Old Town, Havelská, Mon–Fri 10am–7pm, Sat 8am–7pm, Sun 8am–6pm
Since the year 1260, this market – granted a licence by the king – has sold everything imaginable, nowadays ranging from cinnamon biscuits to fan merchandise.

FASHION

Klára Nademlýnska Boutique

Old Town, Dlouhá 3
www.klaranademlynska.cz
Tel. 224 818 769
Mon–Fri 10am–7pm, Sat 10am–6pm
A success story: she began as a simple saleswoman in Paris and went on to become a star designer in Prague.
Madame Nademlýnska designs silk dresses with Art Déco prints, delicate tops with beautiful Baroque patterns.

Tours and Guides

Discovering Prague

Prague for beginners. A sightseeing tour is a quick way to get one's bearings. Without having to search too far, one can spontaneously opt for one of the carriages or vintage cars waiting on Old Town Square, or start a guided tour from the Municipal House. Bicycle or Segway tours are trendy alternatives to the usual offers. Not forgetting the steamers which chug along the Vltava to musical accompaniment. Panoramic Prague swings in time to their beat.

Prague is a paradise for pedestrians, although it can be hard on the feet due to the rounded »cats' heads« cobbles, as they are known here. A decent pair of shoes is advisable. Orientation, meanwhile, is really easy: just make a note of a few key landmarks – the tower of the Old Town Hall, the Church of Our Lady Before Týn, the Powder Tower, St Nicholas Church. Dominating the city panorama is the Gothic spire of St Vitus Cathedral. Whichever route is followed, all roads should lead to Hradčany and the climb up the castle hill …

Prague on foot: a walk through the pedestrianized streets

Was it not suggested only recently that **riding a bicycle** in Prague was a crazy idea? If so, then half the city must be crazy by now. Riding a bike is »in« and Prague is fast becoming the Amsterdam of the Vltava. Not only for the potheads who enjoy the country's liberal attitude to drugs, but also for ecologically-minded pedal pushers. More and more bike lanes are appearing and some areas are now completely free of cars. One drawback is the proliferation of steps and stairs. Sometimes the only thing for it is to carry the bike up. »Citybike« has some 60 different models of bicycle (Czech: kolo) in stock and they also offer guided tours, with helmet, lock, map and drink included in the price. MP3 audio guides in various languages are available.

> **?** MARCO ⊕ POLO INSIGHT
>
> *Names and places: keep it brief!*
>
> What do the good people of Prague mean when they say »U koně« (»by the horse«)? That one could meet by the equestrian statue of St Wencelas on Wencelas Square. The Prague way is brief and to the point. Old Town Square (Staroměstské náměstí) is known as »Staromák«, Charles Square (Karlovo náměstí) »Karlák« and Wencelas Square (Václavské náměstí) simply as »Václavák«.

One relatively new addition to the range of speedy sightseeing solutions is the Segway. Trendy tourists now zip through the Old Town

Trendy wheels: Segway

The Golden City on the Vltava can also be discovered by boat

Changing of the guard on a Segway?

and Lesser Quarter on the motorized, self-balancing two-wheelers. The helmeted riders can be quite a comical sight on medieval alleys. It looks quite easy and elegant, but is it really? The answer has to be: yes! Staying upright is child's play, everything is calibrated electronically, no need to step on the gas. Tipping one's weight automatically moves the vehicle forwards. Tip slightly backwards and the vehicle slows down. A sharper movement backwards brings it to a halt, which it does in an instant – but remember to revert to an upright position, otherwise one will continue to reverse. It sounds more complicated than it is. Some basic instruction is given when hiring a chic electro-scooter. And off they go, the rock'n'rollers! They can cope with climbing steep alleys and descending park slopes. The city's sights fly by as if one were watching a historical drama.

Good to know: nobody is likely to steal your Segway if you stop for a coffee break. If you remove the Info Key Controlller, the vehicle is totally immobilized – ideal protection against theft. The motor is environmentally friendly and the batteries can run for up to 38km/24 miles, generating fresh electrical energy when braking or rolling downhill. They have a maximum speed of 20kmh/12.5mph – fast enough to get around, but not so fast as to miss Prague's most beautiful spots. A fun way to enjoy the city!

How about a vintage car?

Leather seats, carpet, as much legroom as in a tea parlour: taking to the streets of Prague in a vintage car from the »Golden Twenties« has a flair all of its own. Lovingly restored and polished to perfection, a nostalgic tour in such a vehicle will include all of the most important sightseeing spots. If passengers show more than a passing interest in what they see, the driver will be happy to elaborate.

Open-top vintage car ride through the city on the Vltava

The landing-stage for Vltava passenger ships is close to Palacký Bridge (Palackého most), on Rašínovo nábřeží quay. From May to Sepember boat tours organized by the Prague steamship company (Pražská paroplavební společnost) leave here every half hour; they offer a good overview of Prague (tel. 224 931 013, www.paroplavba. cz). In addition, boats depart from Palacký Bridge for recreational destinations around Prague with delightful scenery, such as Slapy Reservoir on the Vltava or Roztoky Castle. In addition to conventional boat trips on the Vltava, the EVD (»Evropská Vodní Doprava«), with its landing-stage by Čechův most (Čech Bridge) opposite Hotel Intercontinental, offers night cruises; it also hires out boats for special tours, corporate events or private parties by arrangement (tel. 224 810 030, www.evd.cz).

Making waves – by boat

WALKS WITH PRAGUE EXPERTS
Prague Walks
Old Town
Jungmanovo náměstí 20
Tel. 608 339 009
www.praguewalks.com

Tours on various themes, covering not only the typical sightseeing spots and stories, but also allowing enough time to convey deeper background knowledge and legends. Learn more about Golem and Co. in Josefov or follow the trail of Communism –

your guide will begin by singing the »Internationale«. Evening tours head for the haunted house or the coziest taverns. From 300 Kč per person, book a day in advance.

BICYCLE TOUR
Citybike hire
Old Town
Králodvorská 5
Tel. 776 180 284
www.citybike-prague.com
April–Oct, Mon–Sun 9am–7pm
The first two hours cost 300 Kč, each additional hour another 50 Kč. A full (24 hour) day costs 650 Kč, a themed ride like the »Castle Tour« 550 Kč. Helmet, bike lock, map and drink included in the price. MP3 audio guides available in various languages.

ROLL YOUR OWN TOUR
Prague Segway Tours
Lesser Quarter
Maltézské náměstí 7
Tel. 724 280 838
www.prague-segway-tours.com
Mon–Sun 9.30am–10pm
Individual rides from €49, group tours from €39 per person. Maltese Square is a good place to start. Beginners can get to grips with the balancing act before setting off. There is only one lively street to cross before heading out into greener surroundings. Laurenziberg, Strahov Monastery, Hradčany Square all offer ideal Segway terrain. In no time at all, one feels like a professional, weaving through the alleyways of the Lesser Quarter.

Prague by boat: twilight is the most atmospheric time for a Vltava cruise through the Golden City

VINTAGE CAR TOUR

3 Veterani
Tel. 603 521 700
Tel. 603 521 700
www.3veterani.cz

Prague by Oldtimer
Tel. 720 314 894
www.praguebyoldtimer.com
Locations: Old Town Square
(Staroměstské náměstí)/ corner of
Pařížska, Malé námestí (Little
Square), Malostranské námestí
(Lesser Town Square)
Vintage cars, as good as new,
built by cult manufacturers like
Škoda and Praga between the years of 1928 to 1932. Modern vehicles cannot compete with the
legroom these limousines offer in
the back. Prices range from 1200
Kč for 40 minutes to 1500 Kč for
an hour or 3000 Kč for two hours.
A »Prague by Night« tour (8pm–
10pm) costs 2000 Kč and an excursion to Karlštejn Castle (approx. 5 hours) 6000 Kč.

VLTAVA CRUISE

**Prague Steamboat Company
(Pražská paroplavební
společnost)**
Mooring: Rašinovo nábřeží (Jirásek
and Palackého Bridge)
Tel. 224 931 013, 224 930 017
www.paroplavba.cz

Prague Boats
Mooring: Na Frantísku, Czech
Bridge (Čechův most)
Tel. 224 810 030
or 224 810 032
www.evd.cz
Ship ahoy! Boats and steamers of
all shapes and sizes sail along the
Vltava, often hosting parties on
deck in the evenings, with jazz,
dance or folk music, good vibes
guaranteed. Some of these boats
are used for New Year's Eve parties, welcoming in the New Year
on the waves!

TOURS

Our tour recommendations will guide you through the Lesser Quarter, so rich in history, to the most important sights of the New Town, they will introduce you to the highlights on both banks of the Vltava and offer a few suggestions for excursions outside the city - such as the Emperor's residence, Karlštejn Castle (left).

Stern Castle
White Mountain
★★ HRADČANY
Royal
Belvedere Castle
★★ **Prague Castle**   garden
Hana
Pav
Chotec Park
Arch-bishop's Palace
St Vitus Cathedral
★ **King's Garden**
Palais Fürstenbersky
Capuchin Monastery
★ **Palais Sternbersky**
Palais Palffy
Palais Czezrnínský
★★ **Loreto Pilgrimage Shrine**
★ **Hradcany Square**
Klárov/Malostranská
Palais Schwarzenbersky
★ **Palais Valdštejnský**
Wallenstein Garden
★ **Strahov Monastery**
Nerudova
Palais Thun-Hohenštejnský
Palais Lichtenštejnský
Malà Strana Square
★★ **St Nicholas**
The Three Ostriches
★★ **Charles Bri**
Palais Vrtbovský
St Maria de Victoria
Lesser Quarter bridge tower
Old Tow bridge towe
★ Petřín
Palais Nostický
Kampa
Smetana Museum
★ **Petřín**
Petřín observatory
Tyršov House
Střelec ostrov
National Theatre
National Theatre
Lat Ma
Zofin
★ **Mánes gallery**
★ **Dancing House**
Emmaus monaster

Tours through Prague

Three walks and one tram tour will reveal the full spectrum of the city.

Tour 1 Lesser Quarter (Malá Strana)
From the Malostranské náměstí (Lesser Quarter Square) to Petřín
▶page 161

Tour 2 Prague New Town (Pražské Nové Město)
From the National Theatre to Vyšehrad
▶page 163

Tour 3 Prague by tram
The most comfortable way to tour the city
▶page 164

Tour 4 In Kafka's footsteps
Literary Prague – wherever one goes
▶page 168

1 House of the Black Madonna   2 Minute House   3 Hus monument   4 Palais Clam-Gallas   5 Karolinum   6 Representation House

✶ Letná Heights

National Technical Museum

Mělník, Kokořín ↑

500 m
0,3 mi
©BAEDEKER

Zimní Stadium

Vltava →

Poděbrady, Mladá Boleslav ↑

✶✶ Convent of Saint Agnes

Hotel Intercontinental

✶ Decorative Arts Museum

Bílkova · ✶✶ JOSEFOV

Kafkas 2nd flat

Rudolfinum

✶ Old Jewish Cemetery

Palais Kinských · STARÉ

Kafkas 1st flat

AUVA

City of Prague Museum

SS Cyrill and Methodius

afé Franze Kafke

Opelt Hs.

✶ St Jakob · MĚSTO

St. Nicholas **Birthplace**

✶✶ Tyn Church

✶ Tyn Courtyard

nám. Republiky

Klemen-tinum

U Minuty

✶ 6

Hibernian House

National Memorial on St Vitus Mountain

Palais Podebrady

Townhall 5

Karolinum

Powder Gate

Café Arco

✶ St Egidius

Estates Theatre

Mucha Museum

St Henry

Max Brod's flat

oly Cross-Rotunda (Old Town)

Milena Jesenská's flat

Assicurazione Generali

Station

t Ursula

Café Louvre

Our Lady of the Snows

Hotel Evropa

State Opera

New Town Townhall

Fleku

✶ **Charles Square**

✶ **Charles Square**

✶ Wenceslas statue

National Museum

Riegrovy sady

SS Cyrill and Methodius

St Longinus Chapel

VINOHRADY

St Stephan

✶ St Ignatius

nám. Miru

Slezská

New Jewish Cemetery

Faust House

St Katharina

Vinohrady

Villa Amerika

St John Nepomuk on the Rock

U Kalicha

French Street

Botanic Garden

NOVÉ MĚSTO

✶ **Vyšehrad**

Church of the Annunciation and Charlemagne

✶✶ **Vyšehrad**

Konopiště ↓

Kuban Square

✶✶ Kutná Hora

Getting Around in Prague

A trip to Prague is worthwhile even for a short weekend break. The average visitor to Prague stays three or four days, time enough to see the most important places. One thing that makes the modern metropolis attractive is that all the sights are very centrally located, and can easily be reached on foot. Finding one's way around is easy (the prominent towers are a help): not to be missed are Hradčany, Charles Bridge and the Old Town Square. The most comfortable way to get a really good look at the key attractions of the city is to hop on a number 22 tram (Tour 3). The Metro underground railway may be quicker, but there is far less to see. All the same, the Metro is a useful alternative on occasion.

The bus is the best means of transport for the outer suburbs. There is little point driving a car in Prague. Finding somewhere to park is problematic, but most places are well served by public transport. Better to call a taxi – ideally ask the hotel reception to book a radio cab. For the return journey, it is advisable to find out where cars from reputable taxi companies such as AAA, City Taxi and Taxi Praha are stationed.

The green lung of the city

The most intense way to experience the city remains on foot. And if the cobblestones should prove to be rather tough on the feet, then a break in one of Prague's green spaces. There are many to choose from, as Prague is not merely a paradise for pedestrians, it is also a »green city«. Over half of the city's urban space is dedicated to nature: wetlands, parks gardens, hills abundant with vegetation, guaranteed to attract »genuine Prague people« as opposed to mere tourists like oneself. Prague citizens love the green lung of their city. One of their favourite havens is the Franciscan Garden, a former monastery garden close to Wencelas Square and home to the city's oldest linden tree, some 500 years old. Others include the Old Botanical Garden (Stará botanická zahrada), immediately behind Charles University, Prague's »little Venice«, Kampa Park on the Vltava island of the same name and the Wallenstein Garden (Valdštejnská zahrada) below Hradčany. Meditative tranquility also flows through Saint Catherine's Garden (Kateřinská zahrada): mothers gently rock their prams and students take a break from lectures at the neighbouring Charles Uni-

Wonderfully atmospheric, also in winter: St Vitus Cathedral

versity. Whilst the mums dote on their babies, the scholars are hunched over their laptops. This is a place for veritable Prague connoisseurs.

Malá Strana (Lesser Quarter)   Tour 1

Duration: 1 day
Start: Malá Strana Square
Destination: Petřín

The best way to begin a visit to Prague is with a tour of Malá Strana (the Lesser or Little Quarter), taking in Prague Castle (Pražský hrad), the city's undisputed highlight, which alone requires half a day. Add to it Malá Strana Square (Malostranské náměstí), the Loreta and Strahov Monastery (Strahovský klášter), and the day is full.

Idyllic beginnings

Idyllic Malá Strana spreads out along the left bank of the Vltava. The imposing Church of **St Nicholas** in the middle of ❶***Malá Strana Square (Malostranské náměstí)** is considered a prime example of High Baroque architecture. The cobbled street ❷***Nerudova** is named after Jan Neruda, Czech author of Tales of the Little Quarter. It runs west from the square and is lined with magnificent late-Baroque burgher houses. Stroll along as far as the »Ke Hradu« turning – these steps lead up to Prague Castle. ❸***Hradčany** is the impressive high point of the tour, the official seat of the president of the Republic since 1918, home to the Royal Palace, St Vitus Cathedral, St George's Basilica and the valuable Bohemian Mannerism and Baroque collection in the adjacent Benedictine nunnery, as well as the famous Golden Lane. ❹***Hradčany Square (Hradčanské náměstí)** is flanked by the Archbishop's Palace and the former Schwarzenberský Palace with the Military History Museum. Not tired yet? Make a short detour through Loretánská Lane (Loretánská ulička) to the ❺***Loreta pilgrimage shrine** on Loreta Square (Loretánské náměstí). Those who still crave more can take a look at ❻***Strahov Monastery** (Strahovský klášter), highly recommended for its two library halls. If

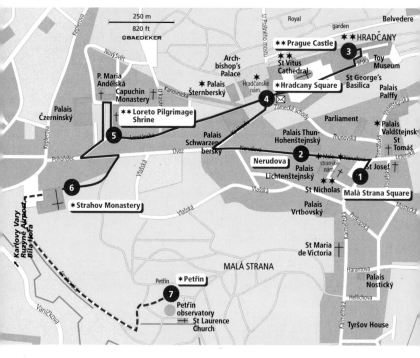

the stay in Prague is to last more than a couple of days, then this first day's tour can be shortened, saving the visit to **Hradčany** and the **Loreta** pilgrimage shrine for the morning of the second day. Then the afternoon can be spent on a visit to the famous library of **Strahov Monastery (Strahovský klášter)**, followed by a walk on the wooded ❼*Petřín hill. Look down from the Petřín viewing tower (Prague's Eiffel Tower) at all the sights seen so far.

Pražské Nové Město (Prague New Town)

Tour 2

Duration: half a day
Start: National Theatre
Destination: Vyšehrad

Touring Malá Strana and Staré Město will already have covered many of Prague's main sights, these being in close proximity to one another. The next walk goes further afield, but is no less interesting and is also manageable in half a day.

The tour starts at the ❶*National Theatre (Národní divadlo). Should the opportunity arise, it is worth taking a look at the interior, to which all the leading artists living in 19th-century Prague made a contribution. Continue south along the Vltava to pass first the island of Žofín/Slovanský ostrov, formed in the 18th century by natural silting, and the ❷*Manés gallery with the Šítka water tower. Today the Functionalist gallery puts on exhibitions of modern art. The ❸*Dancing House (Ginger & Fred) by architects Frank O. Gehry and Vlado Milunič is the next landmark on the walk, a Prague gem of contemporary architecture. Pause here, then turn east into Resslova, and pass the two churches of St Wenceslas on Na Zderaze (a 14th-century Gothic building) and SS Cyril and Methodius (a Baroque church by Kilian Ignaz Dientzenhofer; a national monument), to arrive at ❹Charles Square (Karlovo náměstí). This is the largest square in Prague, a traffic intersection point, yet more of a park than a square with all its greenery, and plenty of sights worth seeing: the Faustus House, the Baroque Church of St Ignatius by Carlo Lurago – especially the interior – and the New Town Hall, no longer used for its original purpose, but serving as a venue mostly for grand civic functions. Vyšehradská continues south from here, past ❺Emmaus Monastery (Klášter Emauzy), the Church of St John of Nepomuk on the Rock and the botanical garden. Have a look, in passing, at the Cubist apartment house by Josef Chochol below the fortress of

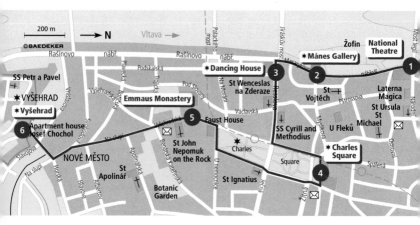

Vyšehrad. Many myths have been spun around ❻ **Vyšehrad (Prague upper castle)**. It offers a wonderful view of the city and the Vltava valley; it also has the Romanesque round chapel of St Martin, the collegiate church of SS Peter und Paul, and the memorial cemetery, all worth seeing.

Tour 3 **Prague by Tram**

Duration: 2 hours
Start: Mala Straná Square 9am
Destination: Mala Straná Square 11am

A classic: tram number 22 travels through all the ages of the city's history. To enjoy the ride to the full, climb aboard in the morning. The later in the day, the busier it gets.

On the right
track

It sounds English: tramvaj – Czech for tram. Number 22 rolls up every five minutes. Stand at the ❶ **Mala Straná Square stop (Malostranské náměstí)**, facing the mighty dome of the Church of St Nicholas, and board the tram heading to the right. The vehicle passes a blank wall protecting the ❷ **Wallenstein Garden (Valdštejnská zahrada)**. Beyond ❸ **Klárov station (Klárov/Malostranská)**, the route has a certain alpine flair. The tram crawls around a hairpin bend towards a dense backdrop of trees, recalling those times when kings would hunt on the wooded hill with a deer moat. Get off the tram at ❹ **Chotek Park (Chotkovy sady)** and admire the Singing Fountain in the ❺ **Royal Garden (Královská zahrada)**. A fairytale surprise awaits behind the Summer Palace or ❻ **Belvedere (Letohrádek královny Anny)**: an enchanted tableau of sprawling ferns and weeds, gigantic stone blocks which appear to »wander aimlessly« around. Swans glide across a small pond. Statues stand in a cave beside the water – figures from the novels of Julius Zeyer, to whom this fairytale park was dedicated in 1913.

Jump off tram number 22 before it reaches the end of the line: time to see the ❼ **Star Summer Palace (Obora Hvězda)**, appropriately shaped like a star. The castle stands on the ❽ **White Mountain (Bílá Hora)** and it was here that the Czechs' defining battle took place in the year 1620. Defeat here saw the country lose its independence and, as a consequence, its national identity.

Care for a castle?

The sprawling park is immensely popular with the citizens of Prague. For the return leg of the journey, find a seat on the right hand side of the carriage. Over the next 40 minutes, Prague's most significant architectural works will roll by as if on a movie screen: ❾ **St Vitus Cathedral (Svatovítská katedrala)**, the churches of the Lesser Quarter – then across the Legion Bridge to be greeted immediately by the ❿ **National Theatre (Národní divadlo)** on the corner. The streets of the New Town are predominantly lined with restored Art Nouveau houses. In the Vinohrady (literally, »vineyards«) district, the vista broadens out. Next stop: ⓫ **Peace Square (Náměstí Míru)**. Thanks to Prague's economic upsurge in the latter part of the 19th century, there are numerous showpieces of architecture to appreciate here. The tram rattles along ⓬ **French Street (Francouzská)** and there really is a resemblance to Paris. By way of contrast, Soviet-style socialist prefabricated buildings now come into view. ⓭ **Cuban Square (Kubánské náměstí)** may not yet have changed its name, but, unlike Havana, western company names are in evidence. Prague has come through the process of change. The satellite settlements have even been given a more colourful lick of paint. Prague residents love their »prefabs«, so they say.

Visitation: Mary on a tram

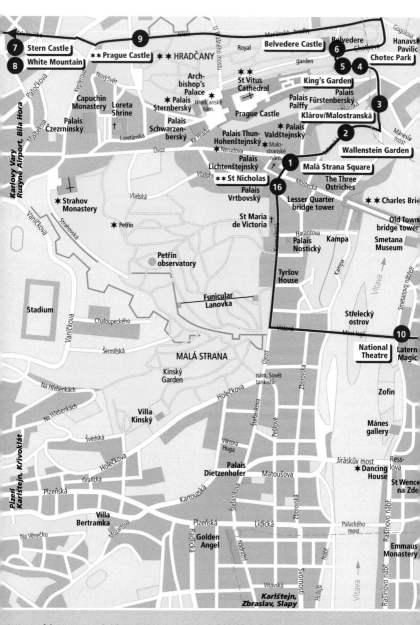

1 House of the
  Black Madonna

2 Minute House

3 Hus monument

4 Palais Clam-Gallas

5 Karolinum

6 Representation
  House

Letná Heights

National Technical Museum

Mělník, Kokořín

500 m
0,3 mi
©BAEDEKER

Podĕbrady, Mladá Boleslav

Vltava →

Zimni Stadium

Hlávkův most

Convent of Saint Agnes

Nábř. Ludvíka Svobody

Decorative Arts Museum

JOSEFOV

Old Jewish Cemetery

Pobřežní

Karlínské nám.

Rudol-finum

Palais Kinských

STARÉ

MĚSTO

City of Prague Museum

SS Cyril and Methodius

St Nicholas

Staro-městské nám.

St Jakob

nám. Republiky

Sokolovská

Klemen-tinum

Týn Church

Týn Courtyard

Celetná

Hibernian House

Bethlehem Chapel

Palais Podebrady

Townhall

Estates Theatre

Powder Gate

Hybernská

National Memorial on St Vitus Mountain

St Egidius

Příkope

Husitská

Holy Cross-Rotunda (Old Town)

Jungmannovo náměstí

St Henry

St Ursula

Our Lady of the Snows

Mucha Museum

Station

New Town townhall

New Town townhall

Hotel Evropa

State Opera

Riegrovy sady

U Fleků

15

Wenceslas statue

14 Charles

Charles Square

St Longinus Chapel

National Museum

VINOHRADY

SS Cyril and Methodius

St Stephan

Anglická

Square

St Ignatius

nám. Míru

Slezská

Vinohradská

Faust House

St Katharina

Villa Amerika

Vinohrady

11

French Street

St John Nepomuk on the Rock

U Kalicha

12

Francouzská

Botanic Garden

NOVÉ MĚSTO

Church of the Annunciation and Charlemagne

12

Kuban Square

Konopiště

Going back, looking ahead

Heading back with the number 22 tram, the lasting impression is of seeing everything from a different perspective. Fans of al fresco art will want to alight at ⓮**Charles Square (Karvolo náměstí)**, the largest square in the republic, covering an area of 80,000 sq m/860,000 sq ft – around 15 football pitches – and graced with more statues, sculptures, busts and monuments than any other site in Prague. The front side is dominated by the ⓯**New Town Hall (Novoměstská radnice)** – famous as the scene of the first Prague defenestration. Stormed by the Hussites in the year 1419, the incumbent mayor, two Catholic councillors and the judge were removed from office and flung out onto the street below. This precipitated a religious war which would shake half of Europe. Today, cafés, galleries and theatre scenes are seemingly untroubled by such distant events. Charles Square is vibrant with student life. Nevertheless, tram number 22 beckons us, ready to return to **Mala Straná Square (Malostranské náměstí)**, where the service terminates. Only now, coming back from the other side of Prague, does the irresistible magic of the Baroque strike home. Hurry up and buy tickets for a Bach recital in ⓰**St Nicholas Church (Chrám sv. Mikuláše)**. The music played here is unforgettable, no doubt about it.

Tour 4 # In Kafka's Footsteps

Duration: half a day
Start: Náměstí Franze Kafky (Franz Kafka Square)
Destination: New Jewish Cemetery or the Hunger Wall

The poet of melancholy liked to wander through the Old Town and the Jewish Quarter of Prague. What he saw and heard there would reappear in his writings. The city influenced the poet to such an extent that his works still resonate in the Prague of today. His life equally so. Time to retrace his steps.

Moving house

Yes, there really is a ❶**Kafka Square (Náměstí Franze Kafky)**. Kafka's place of birth is marked by a commemorative bust on the corner. He spent his first years as a child in a Renaissance house named after the owner, ❷**U Minuty**. Black and white sgraffito on the facade resembles book illustrations. The Kafka family moved house several times but remained close to the Old Town Square. They lived at two different addresses on Celetná street (Celetná ulice). ❸**Sixt's House (Sixtův dům)** is similarly ornate, built by the powerful Prague chancellor Sixt, an ancestor of the Munich-based car hire company bearing his name. The next family abode stood opposite, the Late Gothic

❹»At The Three Kings« (U tří kràlů), overlooking the shady courtyard of the **Church of Our Lady Before Týn (Týnský chrám).** Looking out of the window, Kafka found the view rather eerie, imagining shadows, perhaps even the devil, in the gloom. It is easy to imagine how he felt by taking a walk in the dark behind the Týn church.

For a while, Kafka's father Hermann ran his haberdashery from the **❺Goltz-Kinský Palace (Palác Kinských)** on the Old Town Square (today the shop sells CDs). Kafka himself was a student at the German grammar school at the rear of the building. The last place Kafka lived with his parents was **❻Oppeltův dům.** He delighted in the view, as he wrote to his sister

»Description of a Struggle«: Kafka monument by Jaroslav Róna (Spanish Synagogue)

Ottla, having moved into her room when she left to attend agricultural school. The roof of the house was set ablaze in May 1945 as the end of the war drew near. Nothing is left today of the gables and towers which once graced the structure. Still, here at this corner house is where Prague's luxury mile begins – Pařížská, lined with prestigious designer stores, just like in Paris. But we will shall ignore such distractions and turn left into the broad street named Široká. **❼Café Franz Kafka (Café Franze Kafky)** offers a literary fillip, in spite of lacking any authenticity to speak of. Kafka never set foot inside, although quotes on the walls evoke his presence. The Kafka trail continues along **❽Maiselova** as we recall Kafka's bemusement at brothels and synagogues standing side by side. The **❾Old-New Synagogue (Staronová synagoga)** did little to inspire religious reverence in him. Instead, to his ears, the cacophony of voices sounded more like the stock exchange. Nevertheless, he observed Shabbat here with his father every Saturday – he lived close by, where the **❿Hotel Intercontinental** now stands.

The next commemorative plaque can be found just a couple of streets further on: Kafka (also) lived at **⓫Bilková 10.** Hence it is possible to retrace his route to work, past the surrealist statue (the **⓬Kafka monument**) which now stands there to the richly ornate Art Nouveau house **⓭»At The Golden Pike« (U zlaté štiky),** where he also lived for some time. Just around the corner, in **⓮Masná**

The way to work

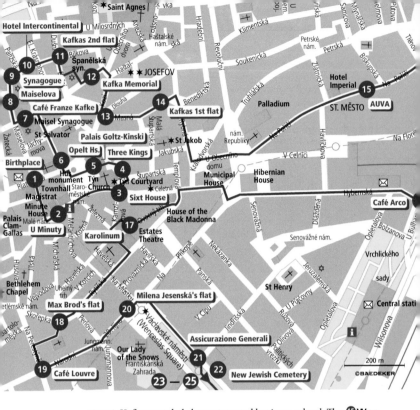

street, Kafka attended elementary and business school. The **⑮Workers Accident Insurance Institute**, where he worked until his premature retirement, impresses with splendid Art Deco features. The **⑯Arco Café** slumbers regrettably like Sleeping Beauty: once upon a time a meeting place for Prague's German literary scene, nobody seems to want to reopen the business today. Moving quickly on, then, to Charles University. Kafka graduated in law at **⑰Karolinum**. From here, he would often call in at **⑲Café Louvre**, invariably picking up his friend Max Brod, who lived in **⑱Skorépka street**, on the way there. On the way back, he could visit his girlfriend Milena Jesenská, who lived at number 13 on **⑳28th October street (ulice 28. října)**. Even without knowing it, most people stop in their tracks to look up at the imposing facade of the castle-like palace which rises before them. Wencelas Square is a mere 20 paces away. It was here that Kafka entered into employment for the first time, joining **㉑Assicurazioni Generali**, an Italian insurance company. A delightful scent emanates from Sephora, a luxury perfumery on the ground floor. There is a metro station out front. Dyed in the wool Kafka fans make the pilgrimage to his grave in the **㉒New**

Jewish Cemetery (from Želivského station on tram number 11, 19 or 26 to Vinohradské hřbitovy). Those more interested in Kafka's writing exile can use the same metro line but in the opposite direction, towards Malostranská. The address: Hradčany, ㉓**Golden Lane (Zlatá ulička)**, number 22, a tiny house where Kafka liked to write. The last Kafka station on the memory trail in the Lesser Quarter is the ㉔**Schoenborn Palace** (now the United States embassy, **Na tržišti**): the poet's health worsened considerably within these dank walls. Nonetheless, he summoned the strength to stroll along Charles IV's ㉕**Hunger Wall (Hladová zed´)**. As he walked, he kept thinking of the »Great Wall of China«. He never quite finished the story, but the message was clear: the abuse of power is – without exception – inhumane, whether it be in Peking or Prague.

Excursions

A few excursions in the vicinity of Prague can be rewarding, to **Chateau Troja** for instance, where 19th-century Czech painting is exhibited today, or to the **Baroque Břevnov Monastery**, or to the most famous medieval castle in Bohemia, **Karlštejn Castle**. On the **White Mountain**, where in 1620 a decisive battle took place in determining the fate of the Bohemian lands, stands **Star Summer Palace**, a hunting lodge set in a delightful park.

Outside the city

Within a radius of 70km/45mi around Prague there are castles and fortresses well worth making the effort to see, situated in wonderful countryside, as well as UNESCO world heritage locations and memorial sites. ***Konopiště Chateau** (Zámek Konopiště) is located approximately 44km/28mi south of Prague. Based on French chateaux, it was reconstructed in late-Gothic style, after which a Renaissance palace was added. Baroque elements were introduced in the 18th century. In 1887 Konopiště passed into the hands of Archduke Franz Ferdinand d'Este, later heir to the throne of Austria. He had the chateau remodelled as a magnificent palace. The exquisite interior decoration dates from that time, including the artefacts in the curious St George's Museum where there are numerous portrayals and images of the saint.

A iittle further afield

The picturesque mountain town of ****Kutná Hora**, which found fame and wealth through the discovery of silver deposits, lies approximately 70 km/44mi east of Prague; it has been granted UNESCO world heritage status. From the year 1300, the Kutná Hora silver mines were the basis for the minting of the **Prague groschen**, the most stable and best-known Bohemian coin of the Middle Ages.

Kutná Hora

This era of economic prosperity has left traces in the form of unique masterpieces of Gothic architecture, such as the **»Stone House« (Kamenný dům)**, which now houses the town museum. The Baroque **Ursuline nunnery** was built according to plans by Kilian Ignaz Dientzenhofer; František Maximilian Kaňka built the Baroque Church of **St John Nepomuk (Kostel svatého Jana Nepomuckého)**. The **Italian Court (Vlašský dvůr)**, the mint built in around 1300 and named after the first minters who came from Florence, was later a royal residence. The **fort (Hrádek)** was set up as a second mint shortly after it was built. The late Gothic Church of **St Barbara (Chrám svaté Barbory)** was begun by Peter Parler's workshop and completed in 1585. The ribbed vaulting in the impressive interior reveals the Renaissance influence and features numerous coats-of-arms. Mělník The skyline of **Mělník**, the centre of Bohemia's wine-growing industry 38km/25mi north of Prague, is dominated by the Gothic Church of **SS Peter und Paul**, and extensive castle grounds. Approximately 7km/4mi northwest, surrounded by vineyards on the right bank of the river Elbe, stands **Liběchov** with its 16th-century **castle**. 17km/10.5mi northeast, the Romantic/neo-Gothic **Kokolín Castle** rises up from dense woods above the charming Kokořín valley (Kokořínský důl). The river Pšovka flows through the valley, with cleft chalk cliffs on either side.

Terezín   The fortress town of Terezín was built by Maria Theresa and Joseph II – a prime Bohemian example of Classicist and Empire urban planning. During World War II the inhabitants were driven out by the Nazis and the town was turned into the Terezín ghetto. Starting in 1940, more than 140,000 Jews from all over Europe were deported to this concentration camp. Near the entrance to the fortress is a large national cemetery.

Zbraslav Castle   In the second half of the 13th century, Otokar II had a hunting lodge with chapel built at the confluence of the rivers Zbraslav Castle (Zámek Zbraslav) Vltava and Beraun, approximately 10km/6mi south of Prague; under King Wenceslas (Václav) II it was converted into a Cistercian monastery. Destroyed in the Hussite Wars, the monastery was rebuilt at the beginning of the 18th century and turned into a three-part castle complex at the beginning of the 20th century. The National Gallery's collection of Asian art is housed externally in Zbraslav Castle. (Tue–Sun 10am–6pm; Metro: Smíchovské, Bus: 129, 241, 243, 360, 255, www.ngprague.cz).

Karlštejn Castle   Created for Emperor Charles IV by French architect Matthias of Arras, also responsible for the cathedral in Prague, Karlštejn Castle (Hrad Karlštejn) stands on a 320m/1050ft high limestone cliff in a tributary valley of the Berounka river, some 30km/18mi southwest of

The church of St Barbara, influenced by French design, in the historical centre of Kutná Hora is a UNESCO World Heritage site

Prague. The fact that the ceremonial laying of the foundation stone was carried out by the Archbishop of Prague, Arnošt of Pardubice – unusual in itself in castle construction – indicates that Charles IV courted »loftier« ambitions for this complex based on three independent structures. Indeed, no military strategy dictated its construction, nor was it designed to serve a noble residence. Instead, its sole purpose was to store the treasures of the Holy Roman Empire of the German Nation, Bohemian royal insignia and stately relics of the Emperor. Severley damaged by Hussite attacks in 1422, it was subsequently restored and then conquered by the Swedes in 1648. Its appearance today dates back to the neo-Gothic restoration effected during the reign of Emperor Francis II in the 19th century and his son Ferdinand I.

SIGHTS FROM A TO Z

Prague is rich in stories and history, in art and culture, boasting a wealth of architectural treasures and contemporary testimonies to a vibrant metropolis at the heart of Europe. One of the many attractions is Charles Bridge, more than 500m/550yd long, not only the city's oldest surviving bridge to span the Vltava, but also the most beautiful.

Belvedere – Queen Anne's Summer Palace

✦ **D 3**

Location: Praha 1, Hradčany
Metro: Malostranská, Hradčanská
Tram: 22
Admission: 110 Kč, only open during exhibitions
www.ngprague.cz

Letohrádek Královský Anny

Ferdinand I had Belvedere, or the Summer Palace, built (1538 – 1563) for his wife Anna at the same time as the Royal Garden. Designed by **Paolo della Stella**, the Summer Palace is one of the finest examples of Italian Renaissance style north of the Alps. The arches of the arcade running right round the building rest on slender columns with voluted capitals. They are decorated with tendril moulding and reliefs with scenes from Greek mythology, hunting and rustic life. On the west side, between the second and third arches, there is an interesting scene: Ferdinand I presents his wife with a fig branch. The novel construction of the curved roof in the form of a ship's hull takes its lead from shipbuilding design. The palace was put at the disposal of the army at the end of the 18th century and was even used as an artillery laboratory until 1838, so the interior space has been altered to a considerable degree. Temporary exhibitions are currently on show in the palace.

Belvedere with the Singing Fountain in the foreground

West of Belvedere is the »Singing Fountain«. It was designed in the years 1564 – 1568 by Tomáš Jaroš and cast in bronze. When drops of water fall onto it, the resonating cavities of the bowl make a sound; lay an ear against the rim of the fountain to hear this special acoustic effect.

Singing Fountain

The Ball-Game Court was constructed between 1567 and 1569 by Bonifaz Wohlmut. The sgraffiti on the exterior show allegories of the elements, virtues and liberal arts. In front of the ball-game court is the statue group Night by Matthias Bernhard Braun (c1730); its companion piece (Day) was destroyed shortly after it was made, during the Prussian bombardment of Prague.

Ball-Game Court

❶ only open during exhibitions

South of Belvedere is Chotek Park (Chotkovy sady). This, Prague's second public park, was created in the years 1833 – 1841 on the initiative of city governor Count Chotek.

Chotek Park

Bethlehem Chapel (Betlémská kaple)

✦ E 4

Location: Praha 1, Staré Město, Betlémské n.
Tram: 6, 9, 18, 21, 22, 23
Metro: Národní tlída

Bethlehem Chapel is a simple building, originally Gothic. Between 1950 and 1953 it was rebuilt according to the first plans as found in old prints, descriptions and views, using designs by architect Jaroslav Fragner. This sacral building was declared a national monument of culture in 1962 and is one of the Czech Republic's most important historical religious monuments.

Faithful reconstruc-tion

❶ April–Oct Tue–Sun 10am–6.30pm Nov–March Tue–Sun 10am–5.30pm
Admission: 60 Kč

In the year 1391 Prague citizens wanted to found a church in which Mass would be celebrated in Czech. The Catholic authorities agreed only to the building of a Gothic chapel. This, however, could accommodate 3000; and its centre was not the altar, but the pulpit. Czech reformer **Jan Hus preached here** between 1402 and 1413. After his death in 1415 the chapel continued to be the spiritual centre of the Hussite movement.

Czech Mass

It was from this pulpit in the year 1521 that the German peasant leader Thomas Müntzer preached the establishment of a state of God

A book and a snack **Insider Tip**

Klub architektů is a favourite haunt of all Prague's keen readers. This multi-purpose oasis in Staré Město boasts a view of the Gothic Bethlehem Chapel where Jan Hus once preached. The specialist bookshop offers nourishment for the mind, while the medieval cellar caters for the body. Reservation recommended (daily 11.30am–midnight. Tel. 224 401 214, www.klubarchitektu. com).

based on equality and common property, and issued his Prague manifesto. During the years 1609 – 1620 the chapel belonged to the community of Bohemian Brothers. One of those active here was Senior Jan Cyrillus, later the father-in-law of the great educator of the people, Jan Amos Comenius. After Ferdinand II had defeated the »Winter King« Friedrich V of the Palatinate in 1620 at the Battle of the White Mountain – Roman Catholicism was the only religious faith allowed from 1627 – the Jesuits bought the chapel. In 1773 the order was dissolved, in 1786 the chapel was demolished down to its outer walls. On the inside of the church walls fragments of tracts by Masters Jan Hus and Jakoubek ze Stříbra can still be seen. In recent times students from the Academy of Visual Arts have decorated the walls with paintings, working from miniatures in the Jena Codex, Richenthal Chronicle and Velislav Bible. The reconstructed wooden pulpit, choir and oratory are also new. In Jan Hus's preacher's house above the chapel, exhibits document the reformer's life and work, and the architectural history of the chapel.

CHURCH OF ST GILES (KOSTEL SVATÉHO JILJÍ)

Splendid ceiling fresco

Husova třída leads north from Bethlehem Square. A short distance along on the right hand side is the Church of St Giles. The Romanesque building was remodelled in Gothic style between 1339 and 1371. Originally in the hands of Hussite Utraquists, the church was given to the Dominicans by Ferdinand II in 1625, after the Battle of the White Mountain. In 1733 the building was converted into Baroque style, probably according to designs by **Kilián Ignác Dientzenhofer**. Wenzel Lorenz Reiner was responsible for the Glorification of the Dominican Order of Preachers ceiling fresco. The subject enabled him to display the full array of his talents: he created a triumph of trompe-l'oeil architecture, with cupola and triangular portico in the process of collapsing, yet supported by St Dominic. Reiner also painted the altarpiece in the left side-aisle chapel. Here, too, is his tomb. The ornate confessionals are from the workshop of Richard Prachner. Concerts regularly take place in St Giles Church.

❶ Mon, Fri 4pm–6pm

Břevnov Monastery (Klášter Břevnov)

✳ Excursion

Location: Praha 6, Blevnov, Markétská 28
Bus: 108, 174, 180
Tram: 15, 23
Open to visitors only for guided tours at weekends: Oct–April at 10am and 2pm, May-Sept 10am, 2pm and 4pm
Admission: 50 Kč
www.brevnov.cz

5km/3mi from the city centre in the direction of Karlovy Vary (road no. 6) lies the district of Břevnov, with its Benedictine monastery of the same name. It was founded in 993 by Prince Boleslav II and St Adalbert (later bishop of Prague), and is the second Benedictine abbey, the earliest monastery in Bohemia. All that remained of the original Romanesque monastery church, built in the 11th century, was the chancel crypt. The Baroque complex seen today was developed under master builder **Kryštof Dientzenhofer**. First, St Margaret's Church was built (by 1716); four years later the monastery was completed. In order to visit the monastery today it is necessary to join a guided tour, which only run at weekends. Groups can also book during the week but unfortunately tours are conducted only in Czech, although a detailed brochure is available in English.

The oldest monastery in Bohemia

Entry to the monastery courtyard is through a beautiful portal (1740) by Kilián Ignác Dientzenhofer. A statue of St Benedict (by Karl Josef Hiernle) stands in the courtyard. The Baroque monastery buildings were begun in 1708 by Pavel Ignác Bayer and completed c1715 by Kryštof Dientzenhofer. The Prelate's Hall is outstanding; its ceiling fresco (St Günther's Peacock Miracle, 1727) is by Cosmas Damian Asam; Bernardo Spinetti designed the stucco work. There are fine paintings by A. Tuvora in the reception hall and Chinese salon.

Monastery grounds

The monastery's centrepiece is the Church of St Margaret (Kostel svaté Markéty). It, too, was built by Kryštof Dientzenhofer (completed c1720). The ceiling frescoes are by Johann Jakob Steinfels; the altar paintings by Peter Brandl. The depiction of St Margaret on the main altar is by Matthias Wenceslas Jäckel. A statue of St John Nepomuk outside the church (by Karl Josef Hiernle) commemorates Bohemia's patron saint. From Břevnov Monastery, tram no, 22 goes directly to Star Summer Palace on White Mountain.

Church of St Margaret

★ Celetná

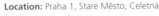

✦ E 4

Location: Praha 1, Staré Město, Celetná
(pedestrian zone)
Metro: Staroměstská, Màstek, Náměstí Republiky

Important link

Named after the medieval bakers of bread rolls, »calty«, Celetná has always been part of the link between Vltava ford, the Staré Město marketplaces, and the east of the Staré Město district. It was along this route that the »coronation procession« once ran, from the Powder Gate via Old Town Square and Charles Bridge, up to Prague Castle.

One of the finest palaces

Celetná has been very well restored (restorations were completed in 1987) and is lined with many important city palaces of Romanesque and Gothic origin, remodelled in Baroque style. No. 12 is one of the finest. The former **Hrzán Palace** was probably given its high Baroque appearance by Giovanni Battista Alliprandi in 1702. The sculptures on the front are thought to be from the workshop of Ferdinand Maximilian Brokoff. The Attica figures at no. 2, the **Sixt House**, close to Old Town Square, are attributed to Anton Braun. The family coat of arms above the doorway at no. 13 recalls the one-time owner of the Baroque **Caretto-Millesimo Palace**. Nos. 17 and 20: **Menhart House** features the »Spider« (**U pavouka**) wine tavern now, while **Buquoyský Palace** (no. 20) has belonged to Prague's Charles University since it was restyled in the 18th century. No. 22, the Classicist house next door known as »**The Vulture**« (**U zlatého supa**), is also used by the university. A statue of the Madonna (c1730) by Matthias Bernhard Braun adorns the Baroque façade of no. 23, »**U Schönfloku**«. No. 31, **Pachtovský Palace**, remodelled in the mid-18th century in Dientzenhofer Baroque style, is now an administrative building: the house sign of the »Madonna behind Bars« at no. 34 is a popular photo motif. It is the only remaining evidence of the former Baroque façade of the Cubist **House at the Black Madonna** (**U černé Matky Bož**) from the years 1911 and 1912. The house, designed by Josef Gočár with two recessed top floors, attests to Prague's own brand of Cubism, which – in contrast to Paris – extended to architecture. Almost contemporaneous with the Municipal House, whose decorative surfaces also owe a lot to Art Nouveau, the House at the Black Madonna is more progressive, with large front windows only possible within a ferroconcrete construction. Nevertheless, its sculptural emphasis preserves architectural harmony with the surrounding Baroque houses.

On the first floor – after almost 80 years – the erstwhile meeting place of artists, the Grand Café Orient has reopened. The **Cubist café** with a buffet bar, chandeliers and lamps designed by the very same Josef Gočár, is open every day until 10pm. Part of the Bohemian Royal court was located at no. 36 in the 14th century, before it became a mint in the 16th century.

The present building, **The Mint (U Mincovna)**, was built by mint-master František Josef Pachta of Rájov in the 18th century. A hundred years later the building was extended and given a neo-Baroque appearance. Celetná ends at the monumental **Powder Gate (▶Municipal House)**, part of the earlier Staré Město fortifications.

** Charles Bridge (Karlův most)

✦ **D 4**

Location: Praha 1, Staré Město, Karlàv most
Metro: Staroměstská, Malostranská
Tram: 17, 18

Charles Bridge is reserved for pedestrians; it links the two sides of the Vltava, Staré Město (Old Town) and Malá Strana (Lesser Quarter). From the bridge there is a wonderful view of the Vltava valley with its numerous bridges, of Shooters' Island and Slav Island (Žofín), and of Staré Město and Malá Strana themselves with Prague Castle. Beneath the west piers lies Kampa Island, which is separated from Malá Strana by the narrow Čertovka branch of the Vltava (»Prague's Venice«). In summer, the bridge is populated by painters, musicians and arts and crafts vendors. It rests on 16 piers and is 520m/570yd long and 10m/11yd wide. It was begun in 1357 under Charles IV by J. Ottl and completed in the early 15th century under Wenceslas IV by Peter Parler. The massive bridge towers on both banks, as well as the bridge itself, once served defensive purposes. Flood disasters have often damaged the fabric of the bridge – two arches had to be replaced in 1890 – yet have never caused it to collapse. In recent times, however, structural damage has been discovered. Restoration work is in progress, although the bridge remains accessible. The budget for repairs, around €11 million, has largely been covered by donations. With such **rich sculptural ornamentation**, Charles Bridge is hugely impressive.

Completed by Peter Parler

Created for the most part in the Baroque era, this »statue promenade« is one of Prague's loveliest architectural achievements, lending the city, in conjunction with the strict Gothic architecture of the bridge, a high degree of artistic appeal. In 1657 a bronze crucifix that had stood here since the 14th century was renovated; between 1706

Statue promenade

The Bridges over the Vltava River

15 bridges span the Vltava (Moldau) River on its 30km-long (18mi) course through the municipality of Prague. For four centuries there was only one bridge, the Charles Bridge, until a new means of transport, the railway, made building a bridge suited to trains necessary and the Negrelli Viaduct was built.

Troja tram bridge
built in 1977, 200 m/660 ft

Holešovice railway bridge
built in 1975, 187 m/617 ft

Hlávka Bridge
built in 1912, 400 m/1320 ft

Štefánik Bridge
built in 1951, 263 m/868/ft

Departure points for boat tours

Mánes Bridge
built in 1914,

Kampa Island
… was formed in the 12th cent. when a millstream was dug. Prague's shortest street at 27m/89ft, ul. Jiřího Červeného is located here.

① Boat tour »Little Venice«
The nostalgic mahogany boats with brass trim run between the Old City and Kampa Island, to the Čertovka (devil's stream) and back. It is a chance to see the Charles Bridge from underneath it (ticket 145 Kč).

www.prazskebenatky.cz

Vyšehrad railway bridge
built in 1901, 298 m/983 ft

② Ginger and Fred
This office building got its nickname because its shape looks like a dancing couple (Ginger Rogers and Fred Astaire).

©BAEDEKER

③ Vyšehrad
The first core of Prague, the seat of Duchess Libussa, towers over the right bank of the Vltava. The church of St Peter and Paul was only dedicated in 1902.

Barrandovský Bridge
built in 1988, 350 m/11

Bridge of the Barricade Fighters
built in1928, 220m/726ft

Bridge of the Barricade Fighters
It was originally called the Troja Bridge after the Troja city district that it leads to. It was renamed in memory of the Prague uprising in May of 1945 and the fighters who built a barricade on the bridge.

ň Bridge
t in 1928, 400m/1320ft

Negrelli Viaduct
built in 1850, 1110m/3660ft

Čech Bridge

Čech-Bridge
built in 1908,
170m/560ft

The only remaining Art nouveau bridge in the Czech Republic is a copy of the Pont Alexandre in Paris.

/614ft

Charles Bridge

Charles Bridge
begun in 1357,
516m/1702 ft

»Karlův most« is the oldest bridge across the Vltava River still in existence and connects the Old City with the Lesser Quarter.

Legion Bridge

egion Bridge
uilt in 1901, 360m/1188ft

The »main artery« across the Vltava connects the Lesser Quarter with the Old City and also offers a fabulous view of the Charles Bridge with the Hradčany in the background

irásek Bridge
uilt in 1933, 310m/1023ft

acký Bridge
lt in1878, 228m/752ft

▶ **Vltava River**

Sources	Warm Vltava (Bohemian Forest), Cold Vltava (Bavarian Forest)
Length	430km/260mi
Dams	72
Navigability	from Třebenice to where it runs into the Elbe

Sculptures on Charles Bridge

Lesser Quarter bridge towers

St Wenceslas
by J. K. Böhm, 1858

SS Cosmas and Damian
by J. O. Mayer, 1709

**SS John of Matha,
Felix of Valois and Ivan**
and figure of a Turk
by F. M. Brokoff, 1714

St Vitus
by F. M. Brokoff, 1714
marble sculpture

St Adalbert
by F. M. Brokoff, 1709
copy 1973

St Philip Benitius
by M. B. Mandl, 1714

St Luitgard
by M. B. Braun, 1710

St Kajetan
by F. M. Brokoff, 1709

St Nicholas of Tolentine
by J. F. Kohl, 1706
copy 1969

St Augustine
by J. F. Kohl, 1708
copy 1974

**SS Vincent Ferrer
and Procopius**
by F. M. Brokoff, 1712

St Judas Thaddaeus
by J. O. Mayer, 1708

St Francis Seraphicus
by E. Max, 1855

St Antony of Padua
by J. O. Mayer, 1707

SS Ludmila and Wenceslas
from workshop M. B. Braun
approx. 1730

St John Nepomuk
models by M. Rauchmüller and
J. Brokoff, 1683 bronze cast by W. H. Heroldt,
in Nuremberg

St Francis Borgia
by J. and F. M. Brokoff, 1710
restored 1937 by R. Vlach

**SS Wenceslas, Norbert
and Sigismund**
by J. Max, 1853

St Christopher
by E. Max, 1857

St John the Baptist
by J. Max, 1857

St Francis Xaver
by F. M. Brokoff, 1711
copy 1913

SS Cyril and Methodius
and three allegorical
figures (Bohemia, Moravia,
Slovakia), by K. Dvořák, 1938

St Joseph
by J. Max, 1854

St Anne with Mary and Child Jesus
by M. W. Jäckel, 1707

Pietà
by E. Max, 1859
originally, 1695

Bronze crucifix
cast 1629 by J. Hilger
erected 1657 as first bridge sculpture
Hebrew inscription 1696
figures by E. Max, 1861

**SS Barbara, Margaret
and Elizabeth**
by F. M. Brokoff, 1707

**Mary with SS Dominic
and Thomas Aquinas**
by M. W. Jäckel, 1708; copy 1961

St Ivo
by M. B. Braun, 1711
copy 1908

Mary and St Bernard
by M. W. Jäckel, 1709; copy

Old Town bridge tower

St John Nepomuk

St Luitgard

→ **N**

©BAEDEKER

and 1714, **26 statues were erected by famous artists** (Matthias Bernhard Braun, Johann Brokoff and his sons Michael Josef and Ferdinand Maximilian) and other sculptors. In the mid-19th century these were followed by **five further statues** by Josef Max and Emanuel Max; in 1938 the stone group of SS Cyril and Methodius (by Karel Dvolák) was added. The sandstone figures have suffered greatly through the ravages of time and environmental impact; in the meantime almost all have been replaced by copies. The only marble statue is that of St Philip Benizi. The most valuable in artistic terms is the chiselled sandstone figure of St Luitgard, a picture of mercy and grace: Christ leans down from the Cross to St Luitgard and allows her to kiss his wounds. The only statue cast in bronze is St John Nepomuk (in the middle of the bridge). It was cast in Nuremberg in 1683 from models by Matthias Rauchmüller and Johann Brokoff. Between the sixth and seventh piers of the bridge, a relief marks the spot from which St John Nepomuk was cast into the Vltava in 1393 on the orders of Wenceslas IV, because he had opposed the king in an ecclesiastical conflict. Canonized in 1729, he has been regarded since that time as Catholic Europe's »bridge saint«. The Crucifixion Group has a Hebrew inscription; in 1696 a Jew was sentenced by the regional tribunal to make this contribution as a punishment for blasphemy.

Old Town Bridge Tower (Staromestká mostecká) forms the eastern entrance to Charles Bridge, standing in fact on the first pier. Building started in 1357 and was completed at the beginning of the 15th century under King Wenceslas IV; the design was by the famous architect Peter Parler of the cathedral workshop. It is considered to be one of the finest Gothic towers in Central Europe. The figural decoration of Old Town Bridge Tower is one of the great accomplishments of Gothic sculpture in Bohemia (14th century). The tower was restored by Josef Mocker in the 19th century and given the roof it has today; its originally Gothic paintings were restored by Peter Maixner. Above the doorway arch on the east side are the emblems of all the lands ruled by the Luxembourg dynasty, and also the royal arms of Bohemia, the arms of the Roman emperor and the royal kingfisher, emblem of Wenceslas IV. The first storey is adorned by the kings Charles IV and Wenceslas IV, enthroned; between them, elevated a little, stands the figure of St Vitus. Above, a shield beneath a non-heraldic lion displays the St Wenceslas eagle. At the very top are the Bohemian patron saints Adalbert and Sigismund. **Old Town Bridge Tower**

❶ Jan–April, Oct–Dec daily 10am–7pm, May–Sept until 10pm
Admission 75 Kč

On the west side, Charles Bridge ends in the two Malá Strana Bridge Towers (Lesser Quarter Bridge Towers), which are linked by an archway. The lower tower (dating from the last quarter of the 12th cen- **Malá Strana Bridge Towers** tury) once formed part of the fortifications of the earlier Judith Bridge; in 1591 it was given Renaissance gables and ornamentation on the outer walls. The taller tower was built in the year 1464 at the behest of King George of Poděbrady, replacing an older Romanesque tower. Its late-Gothic architecture resembles that of Old Town Bridge Tower opposite, and some of its sculptural ornamentation replicates the style.

The fine Renaissance house **The Three Ostriches (U tří pštrosů)** at the Malá Strana end of Charles Bridge was built in 1597; remnants of the façade painting by Daniel Alexius of Květná (1606) still survive. The upper storey, in early-Baroque style, is by master builder Cril Geer (1657); the notable beamed ceilings in the dining-rooms date from the 17th century. A hotel and what is now a rather mediocre restaurant occupy the building today.

❶ April–Oct 10am– 6pm, admission 75 Kč

Prague, a winter fairy tale: here on Charles Bridge, adorned with sculptures and a fine view of the Old Town Bridge Tower

＊ Charles Square (Karlovo náměstí)

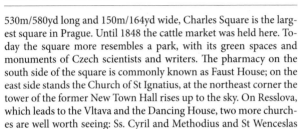

✳ E 5/6

Location: Praha 1, Nové Město
Metro: Karlovo náměstí
Tram: 3, 4, 6, 14, 18, 22, 24

530m/580yd long and 150m/164yd wide, Charles Square is the largest square in Prague. Until 1848 the cattle market was held here. Today the square more resembles a park, with its green spaces and monuments of Czech scientists and writers. The pharmacy on the south side of the square is commonly known as Faust House; on the east side stands the Church of St Ignatius, at the northeast corner the tower of the former New Town Hall rises up to the sky. On Resslova, which leads to the Vltava and the Dancing House, two more churches are well worth seeing: Ss. Cyril and Methodius and St Wenceslas on Na Zderaze.

Largest square in Prague

FAUST HOUSE (FAUSTŮV DŮM)

The Faust House, originally a late-Renaissance palace, was given a corner bastion when the fortifications were extended between 1606 and 1617, and was remodelled in Baroque style in the 18th century. Under Rudolf II (1576 to 1611), the **English alchemist Edward Kelley** carried out experiments to make gold here. When another chemist set up his laboratory in the house in the 18th century, one Mladota of Solopysky (hence also Mladota Palace), the legend arose that Dr Faustus had sold his soul to the devil, and was carried off to hell through the laboratory ceiling. Today – continuing an old tradition? – the pharmacy is located here.

Legendary laboratory

CHURCH OF ST IGNATIUS (KOSTEL SVATÉHO IGNÁCE)

The imperial master builder Carlo Lurago created this Baroque sacral building between 1665 and 1668 as a church of the former Jesuit college. Today it houses a clinic of the First Faculty of Medicine of Charles University. The grandiose doorway (1697 – 1699) with a statue of St Ignatius with an aureole (1671) on the tympanum is by Pavel Ignác Bayer. The other statues are by Tommaso Soldatti. The interior of the hall church is especially worth seeing, with rich stucco work and figures of saints by Soldatti. The Baroque high altar of faux

Sumptuous Jesuit church

Spring fever: Charles Square with the New Town Hall

marble (18th century) shows the Glorification of St Ignatius of Loyola (1688), a work by Johann Georg Heintsch, also responsible for the remarkable altarpieces. The painting Christ Imprisoned is by his teacher Karel Škréta; St Liborius is by Ignác Raab. The Calvary group beneath the organ loft is the work of Johann Anton Quittainer.

NEW TOWN HALL (NOVOMĚSTSKÁ RADNICE)

First Prague defenestration

The originally Gothic building on the northeast corner of Charles Square was erected as the town hall in 1348. After Hradčany, Malá Strana, Staré Město and Nové Město were joined together as one administrative unit and the offices centralized in Staré Město (1784), this former town hall served as prison, court of law and registry office. Today the building is used for ceremonial and cultural purposes. Work began on the corner tower, in 1452. It was altered several times and now contains a chapel. At the beginning of the 16th century the façade looking towards the square was given a Renaissance look. Empire elements were added in the 19th century; in 1906, it was reconstructed in the original Renaissance style. In earlier times Nové Město was inhabited predominantly by the poor. On 30 July 1419 the first Prague defenestration took place here: a crowd led by preacher Jan Želivský stormed the town hall, freed the Hussites imprisoned there and flung two Catholic councillors out of the window. This precipitated the Hussite Wars.

❶ Tue–Sun 10am–6pm, admission including tower viewing 50 Kč

The neo-Renaissance Czech Technical University building (no. 14) was erected in 1867 from designs by V.I. Ullmann. Allegories of Work and Science from A. Popp's workshop flank the entrance; the sculptures of ancient geniuses above the second-floor windows are by Josef Václav Myslbek (1879). Branching off from Charles Square, Resslova features the churches of Ss. Cyril and Methodius (Svatého Cyrila a Metoděje) and, diagonally opposite, St Wenceslas on Na Zderaze.

Czech Technical University

Originally dedicated to St Charles Borromeo, this Baroque structure (no. 9) was built around the year 1740 by Kilián Ignác Dientzenhofer. In 1935 it became a place of worship for the Greek Orthodox church. Stucco work by Michael Ignaz Palliardi adorns the interior. In June 1942 Czech resistance fighters who assassinated the »Deputy Reich Protector of Bohemia and Moravia«, Reinhard Heydrich, hid in the crypt after the attack. The gruesome reprisals which followed (»Heydrichiade«) saw entire communities slaughtered. On 10 June 1942 in **Lidice** and two weeks later in **Ležáky**, all male inhabitants were shot by the German SS. Women and children were sent separately to concentration camps, and the villages razed to the ground. Not a single resistance fighter survived the battle in and around the crypt (now the site of a **national memorial** commemorating the events).

Ss. Cyril and Methodius

❶ March–Oct Tue–Sun 10am–5pm, Nov–Feb until 4pm, admission 75 Kč

Since the year 1926, St Wenceslas on Na Zderaze (Kostel svatého Václava na Zderaze) has belonged to the Czech Hussite Church. It was originally the parish church of Zderaze, which later became part of Nové Město. The 14th-century Gothic building still has traces of a Romanesque nave and church tower. In the chancel are fragments of Gothic wall frescoes (Tree of Jesse), dating from around 1400. In 1586 and 1587 the church was provided with late-Gothic stellar vaulting by K. Mělnický. The wall frescoes depicting the legend of St Wenceslas (18th century) are attributed to Josef Hager.

St Wencelas on Na Zderaze

Charles University (Karolinum)

✳ E 4

Location: Praha 1, Staré Město,
Železná 9 (Pedestrian zone)
Metro: Màstek

Charles IV founded the Karolinum, which was named after him, on 7 April 1348. It was the first university in Central Europe. The most notable collegiate structure is Rotlev House (1370), added under the patron-

First university in Central Europe

age of Wenceslas IV in 1383, with its magnificent Gothic oriel windows that still survive today. The architecture of Charles University's other buildings ranges from Gothic to 20th-century. As early as 1409 the Karolinum's history as a universal university – teachers and students came from all over Europe – seemed to be at an end as, urged on by Master Jan Hus, King Wenceslas curtailed Germans' rights. Around 2000 students and many professors left the country. From this point, the reformer Hus held the post of rector (see the bronze statue by K. Lidický in the memorial courtyard) until, in the year 1412, the Catholic faculty spoke out against him and he had to flee to southern Bohemia. After the Bohemian nobility's revolt had been put down the Jesuits took over the running of the university. In addition to the oriel windows, two pieces of ribbed vaulting in the former arcade and a few recently uncovered Gothic elements have survived from the original building. Baroque alterations to the site were undertaken in 1718 by František Maximilian Kaňka. The heart of the Karolinum building is **the 17th-century aula**, which occupies two storeys and was extended (1946 – 1950) by Jaroslav Fragner. The Estates Theatre is located just a few yards from the Karolinum.

❶ Cloister open during exhibitions Mon–Sun 10am–6pm. Admission 120 Kč

St Gall's   St Gall's Church (Kostel svatého Havla) on Havelská, southwest of the Karolinum, was founded in 1232 at the same time as the southern German colony »Gallistadt«. It was one of four Staré Město parish churches completed by 1263. It was restructured in high Gothic style in 1353. Further alterations in the 18th century resulted in the apparently undulating façade and two towers. The Baroque interior has valuable altar paintings, and on the left a Pietà carved in wood, probably by Ferdinand Maximilian Brokoff. In the right side chapel is the tomb of painter Karel Škréta. From 1363, the Austrian reform preacher Konrad of Waldhausen was active in St Gall, at the wish of Charles IV; he was a predecessor of the great Czech reformer Jan Hus.

❶ Mon-Sun 11.30am–1pm

Church of the Assumption of the Virgin Mary and Charlemagne

✼ F 6

Location: Praha 1, Nové Město, Ke Karlovu 1
Metro: Vyšehrad, I. P. Pavlova
Tram: 6, 11

Octagonal plan, modelled on Aachen   ❶ Sun, public holidays 2pm–4.30pm

The Church of the Assumption of the Virgin Mary and Charlemagne (Kostel Nanebevzetí Panny Marie a Karla Velikého) is on Ke Karlovu, south of the Dvořák Museum located in Villa Amerika. Charles IV had this church with an octagonal groundplan built in 1358, on the model of the imperial chapel in Aachen. When it was dedicated to the Assumption of the Virgin Mary and Charlemagne in 1377, it had only a provisional roof. **Bonifaz Wohlmut** completed the stellar vaulting of the nave in 1575; it is considered one of Prague's most brilliant architectural achievements. Linked to it is the legend of the master builder who sold over his soul to the devil in order to be able to complete his work. From 1720, Kilián Ignác Dientzenhofer worked on the renovation of the church. Use of the former monastery church as a place of pilgrimage from the early 18th century, and the simultaneous installation of several chapels, very much diminished the originally Gothic character of the building. The Baroque cupolas were also a later addition.

Church of Our Lady Victorious

✴ **D 4**

Location: Praha 1, Malá Strana, Karmelitská
Tram: 12, 22
🕐 Mon–Sat 8.30am–7pm, Sun 8.30am–8pm
Museum of the Prague Infant Jesus: admission free

Not far from Maltézské náměstí (Maltese Square), at number 9 Karmelitská, stands the Church of Our Lady Victorious (Kostel Panny Marie Vítězné). It was built as a Carmelite monastery church in early Baroque style on the site of a Hussite church after the victory of imperial troops at the Battle of the White Mountain. The ground plan of the church is modelled on the Jesuit church »Il Gesù« in Rome. The altar by Franz Lauermann dates from 1776. It is adorned by statues by Peter Prachner and a small silver Christ Child casket (1741) by Jan Pakeni. Three of the altar pictures are by Peter Johann Brandl, namely those of St Simon, St Joseph and SS Joachim and Anne. The main altar (1723) is from the workshop of Johann Ferdinand Schor. In the catacombs beneath the church, closed to visitors, are the mummified remains of Carmelites and their benefactors, well preserved thanks to the circulation of air.

On the right side wall of the church hangs the »Prague Infant Jesus«, still the object of profound veneration today; it is a 50cm/20in-tall wax figure from Spain, given to the monastery in 1628 by Princess Polyxena Lobkowicz. It is supposed to have protected the city in a variety of ways: against plague and pillage, for instance, during the

* Prague Infant Jesus

Seven Years' War. Accordingly the Infant was not only deeply revered, but also showered with precious gifts: not least with a valuable gold and velvet dress by Maria Theresa. At that time there was an image of the Prague Infant Jesus in all Carmelite monasteries; today copies can be purchased in numerous shops – some nicely done, some nothing more than kitsch.

City Gallery Prague

❶ Mon–Sun 10am–8pm   **www.citygalleryprague.cz**
Admission: 120 Kč

Different locations in Prague   The City Gallery Prague (Galerie hlavního města Prahy), with its permanent collections and regularly changing exhibitions, focuses mainly on **Czech art of the 19th and 20th centuries**. The exhibitions can be found at different locations in Prague. In Troja Chateau there is a permanent exhibition of 19th-century Bohemian art with reference to European developments and the nation's past. The work of sculptor František Bílek (1872 – 1941) is shown in Bílkova vila (Praha 6, Mickiewiczova 1). A representative of both Symbolism and Art Nouveau, Bílek himself designed the villa (1911). The **House of the Golden Ring** (**U Zlatého prstenu**, Praha 1, Týnská 6) exhibits Czech art of the 20th century. Temporary exhibitions are presented in the **House of the Stone Bell** and in the town hall on Old Town Square.

✳ Convent of St Agnes (Anežký klášter)

 E 3

Location: Praha 1, Staré Město, U milosrdných 17
Metro: Staroměstská A)
Tram: 5, 8, 14
❶ Tue–Sun 10am–6pm
Admission: 150 Kč
www.ngprague.cz

A national monument   The Convent of St Agnes is one of Prague's most significant historic buildings, and has been declared a national monument. It is worth visiting not only because it is a magnificent example of early Gothic architecture: the National Gallery's collection of medieval art is housed here. The Convent of St Agnes was founded for the order of

Insider Tip

Don't miss!

- Master Theoderic: renowned for »beautiful Madonnas« (first wing)
- Master of Hohenfurth: panel paintings (whole room dedicated to him)
- Master of Třeboň (Wittingau): altar paintings with nine wing panels (whole room)
- Albrecht Altdorfer: *Martyrdom of St Florian* (last room)

the Poor Clares (Franciscan nuns) in 1234 by Princess Agnes, sister of King Wenceslas I, modelled on the foundation of St Clare of Assisi. Agnes subsequently entered the order herself and was the monastery's first abbess from 1235. She was canonized in 1989. By the year 1240 the monastery of Minorite friars had been established, with close links to the nunnery. In the years that followed, the churches of St Barbara (1250 – 1280) and St Francis (c1250) and the Franciscan convent were built, in the Cistercian Gothic style current in Burgundy.

Early Bohemian Gothic

The Church of the Holy Saviour (1275 – 1280) is considered the most important example of early Bohemian Gothic. Investigations have shown that the church was probably the burial place of the Přemyslid dynasty (capital sculptures of Přemyslid rulers). The presbytery and St Barbara's Church date from the 14th century; Baroque alterations to the church were undertaken in 1689. In the presbytery, archaeological researchers have uncovered the graves of King Wenceslas I, the convent's founder St Agnes (†1282) and further Přemyslids.

✴ NATIONAL GALLERY (NÁRODNÍ GALERIE) / COLLECTION

Exhibition of Medieval Art

The »Exhibition of Medieval Art in Bohemia and Central Europe (13th to 16th century)« is very well presented. Most of the sculptures and panel paintings come from Bohemian churches. Artists not known by name are designated according to their work and where they found. The Madonna is the most frequently recurring motif in medieval Bohemian art.

Panel painting and sculpture until the middle of the 14th century

The first part of the chronologically arranged exhibition is displayed in the monastery: it shows the development of panel painting and sculpture up to the middle of the 14th century. Following some early Gothic figures of the Madonna, a whole room is dedicated to the cycle produced by the **Master of Hohenfurth** (Mistr Vyšebrodského oltáře). Here the altar of the former Cistercian foundation is displayed; it dates from c1330 – 1350 and consists of nine panels. The cycle of scenes from the life of Christ, created by the Master of Hohenfurth with at least two further assistants, represents a new conception of spatiality through composition and three-dimensionality of figures and landscape, and a differentiated narrative style. This was influenced by Italian Trecento painting, especially that of Siena. Up to that time a style influenced by Anglo-French paintings had predominated in Bohemia. Next comes the room with works by **Master Theoderic**. The only artist here who is known by name is considered to represent the soft style of Bohemian Gothic painting. He created wall paintings and 128 panel paintings for Charles IV at Karlštejn Castle, of which six are on display (St Elizabeth, St Vitus, St Jerome, St Matthew, Pope Gregory, St Luke; mid-14th century). In this instance, too, Italian painting of the time influenced the style. The votive picture of Prague archbishop Johann Očko of Vlašim (c1370), with portrait-like pictures of Charles IV and Wenceslas IV, transcends the Soft style.

Master of Třeboň

The next room is devoted to what is now the fragmentary cycle of the Master of Třeboň (Mistr Třeboňského oltáře). The three panels of the winged altar, painted on both sides (only opened on feast days), show on the open side Christ on the Mount of Olives, the Entombment and Christ's Resurrection; on the reverse is a cycle of pictures of saints, also from the Master of Třeboň's workshop (he himself painted only the heads). There follow paintings and sculpture which demonstrate the development of late-Gothic art in Bohemia, with particular emphasis on the soft style. This style was most widely employed in the early 15th century and is represented, for instance, in the childlike *Madonna* by Český Krumlov (c1400) and in the Madonna from the Franciscan monastery in Plzeň.

New development in Bohemian painting

The Master of the Rajhrad Altarpiece (Mistr Rajhradského oltáře, early 15th century) initiated a new development in Bohemian painting with the almost caricature-like contortion of his crucifixion figures.

While Bohemia and especially Prague counted as important independent European centres of art in the 14th century, the influence of Central Europe increased in the 15th century. The works of the Master of the Litoměřice Altar (Litoměřice was responsible for decorating the upper part of the walls in the Wenceslas Chapel in St Vitus Cathedral with the saint's legend) show this clearly, as does the artist's *Madonna and Child* with the monogram IW; he was one of the most important pupils of Lucas Cranach the Elder. The exhibition ends with the works of the Master of the Lamentation of Christ from Žebrák and the altar shrine carved in wood by Master I.P. (c1520); the influence of Albrecht Dürer is discernible. These works, together with Albrecht Altdorfer's *Martyrdom of St Florian*, are in the last exhibition room.

✶ Dancing House (Tančicí dàm)

✦ E 5

Location: Praha 1, Nové Město, Rašínovo nábřeží 80/ corner of Resslova
Metro: Karlovo náměstí

One of the few examples of contemporary architecture in Prague is the »Dancing House«, a 1996 office block on the Vltava affectionately referred to by natives of the city as »Ginger & Fred« – after Ginger Rogers and Fred Astaire, the star couple of the American musical. Its two glass and concrete towers were for a long time considered controversial, but now, along with the castle or Old Town Square, they have become part of the Prague sightseeing programme.

Ginger & Fred

Dancing architecture

Croatian architect **Vlado Milunič** – who for years lived in a house alongside the empty plot, as did Václav Havel – found financial backing for his idea in a Dutch insurance company, and a collaborator in the Californian architect **Frank O. Gehry**, who brought greater incisiveness to the plans. The straight tower accentuates the street corner and behaves rather like a standing leg, while its glass counterpart snuggles up against it. This fluid movement recalls the Baroque style so prevalent in the city. The projecting windows and undulating surface of the façade guard against monotony, at the same time ensuring integration into the adjoining rows of houses. The airy stilts convey lightness, and set the ground floor back from the street. The building is literally crowned by a punched metal ball, the so-called *Head of Medusa*, that echoes the globe on Havel's house next door, and the neo-Gothic onion towers and oriel windows in the neighbourhood. Spectacular as the building looks from the outside, the interior conforms conventionally to its function as office block.

Emmaus Monastery (Emauzy)

E 6

Location: Praha 2, Nové Město, Vyšehradská
Metro: Karlovo náměstí
Tram: 3, 4, 7, 10, 14, 16, 17, 18, 21, 24
❶ April–Oct Mon–Fri 11am–5pm, May–Sept Mon–Sat 11am–5pm, Nov–March Mon–Fri 11am–2pm
Admission: 20 Kč

Emmaus Monastery (Monastery of the Slavs, Klášter na Slovanech) was closed in 1949 – the monastery and its Church of Our Lady were returned to the Benedictine order only in 1990. Charles IV founded the monastery in 1347 (with papal approval) for **Benedictines of the Slav rite** – Croatians, Serbs, Czechs and Russians. The language used to celebrate Mass was Old Church Slavonic, through which the church sought to extend its sphere in the relatively unexploited east. In the 14th century the monastery was an important cultural and educational centre; until 1546 it housed the Glagolithic part of the so-called Reims Gospel Book, on which the kings of France swore their coronation oath. In the year 1945 the building burnt down as a result of a US air attack. Only in 1967 was the restoration of the Gothic monastery church completed; the original towers were replaced by two modern intertwining concrete spires that stretch heavenwards like a pair of wings. Rough cement walls and undressed brick can be found inside.

Cloisters   The frescoes in the Gothic cloisters have been restored several times. They are among the most significant surviving works from the early Prague school of painting; as in late medieval Bibles of the Poor, important salvation events from the New Testament and scenes from the Old Testament are depicted in a total of 26 wall panels (dated c1360). Unfortunately, they are not especially well preserved.

Emmaus Monastery's Church of Our Lady was built in Gothic style between the years 1348 – 1372. It consists of three large aisles, equal in size. It underwent Baroque alterations in the 17th century, and then neo-Gothic remodelling. The concave spires of 1967 are the work of architect František M. Černý; they represent a compromise between Baroque towers and a pointed Gothic pediment.

Church of Our Lady

Diagonally opposite Emmaus Monastery is the Church of St John of Nepomuk on the Rock (Kostel svatého Jana Nepomuckého na Skalce, Vyšehradská 18). The central building with two towers and double flight of steps, built in around 1730 by Kilián Ignác Dientzenhofer, is one of the most beautiful late-Baroque churches. The fresco by Karel Kovář (1748) shows St John of Nepomuk's ascent into heaven. Johann Brokoff carved the wooden statue of the saint on the main altar; there is a bronze realization of the wooden model on Charles Bridge. The church is usually open during services only.

St John of Nepomuk on the Rock

Going south, Vyšehradská becomes Na Slupi, on which the entrance to the Botanical Garden (Botanická zahrada) is located. Laid out by the Florentine apothecary Angelo in the reign of Charles IV, the garden boasts a 600-year history and contains a multitude of native and exotic plants, along with a Japanese garden and rose garden. The university garden founded in Smíchov in 1775 was moved here in the year 1897.

Botanical Garden

❶ April daily 9am–6pm, May–Sept daily until 9pm and March daily until 5pm, Nov–Feb daily until 4pm, admission 50 Kč, www.botanicka.cz

Estates Theatre (Stavovské divadlo)

✦ E 4

Location: Praha 1, Staré Město, Železná 11
Metro: Můstek
www.stavovskedivadlo.cz

Count Anton of Nostitz-Rieneck had this, the first theatre in the Vltava valley, built in Classicist style in the years 1781 to 1783 from a design by Anton Haffenecker. East front and interior fittings are by architect Achill Wolf (1881). At the end of the 18th century the Nostitz Theatre was run by the Bohemian nobility as an »Estates Theatre«, from the mid-19th century as a »German regional theatre«. In 1945 it was re-named Tyl Theatre after the Czech dramatist and actor Josef Kajetán Tyl (1808 to 1856). In November 1991, after a seven-year renovation period, it was re-opened by the president of the republic at the time, Václav Havel, as the Estates Theatre. Today, the small theatre has

First theatre in the Vltava valley

become part of the Czech National Theatre. Three operas by Antonio Vivaldi, two operas by Gluck, and works by Jommelli, Rutini and Boroni were premiered at Prague's Estates Theatre. On 29 October 1787 the **first performance of Mozart's opera _Don Giovanni_** was staged here and was a resounding success. The event was recorded in literary form by Eduard Mörike, among others, in his work Mozart's Journey to Prague. In the years 1813 – 1816 composer Carl Maria von Weber (1786 – 1826) led the theatre orchestra; at a later date, Gustav Mahler and Carl Muck ran the theatre. The Charles University, the oldest university in Central Europe, is next door at number 9 Železná.

Franz Kafka Museum

✦ **D 4**

Location: Praha 1, Malá Strana, Cihelná 2b Hradčany
Tram: 1, 8, 12, 18, 20, 22
Metro: Malostranská
❶ Daily 10am–6pm

Admission: 180 Kč, concessions 120 Kč
Tel.: 257 53 53 73
www.kafkamuseum.cz

At the brickworks
Not far from Charles Bridge on the Lesser Quarter side, Hergets Brickworks (Hergetova Cihelna) was converted into a museum in 2005, dedicated to the life and works of Prague's most famous writer (▶MARCOPOLO Insight p.198). On display in Barcelona and New York for six years prior to the opening in Prague, the exhibition owes its existence to the private initiative of the Argentinian artist Juan Insua, who crafted a »symphonic unity« of word, image, light and music. The historical photographs and film recordings, manuscripts, newspaper cuttings, original letters and publications collected here are well worth a look.

Černý's Proudy
The same goes for the David Černý sculpture in front of the museum: _Proudy_ (2004) presents two naked bronze men urinating in a basin shaped like the Czech Republic.

Grand Priory Square (Velkopřevorské náměstí)

✦ **D 4**

Location: Praha 1, Malá Strana
Tram: 12, 22

Grand Priory Square is given its character by the two high Baroque palaces facing one another: that of the Grand Prior, and Buquoyský

Palace. North of Grand Priory Palace stands the Church of Our Lady Below the Chain. Further along Prokopská in a southerly direction is Nostitz Palace, on the south side of Maltese Square (Maltézské náměstí).

GRAND PRIORY PALACE

Today the Grand Priory Palace of the sovereign order of Maltese Knights (Palác maltézského velkopřevora) in Malá Strana is once again the seat of the order, jointly with its former convent at number 4 Lázeňská, and residence of the Maltese Grand Prior. The impressive Baroque rooms have wooden dado panelling, elaborate Baroque stoves and beautiful inlaid floors. Commissioned by Grand Prior Gundaker Poppo Count Dietrichstein, the Italian architect Bartolomeo Scotti constructed the double-winged corner palace between 1724 and 1728 by adapting the original Renaissance building and adding ornamental cornices, oriel windows, and a new doorway for the order. The vases and lamp-bearing statues in the stairwell are from the workshop of Matthias Bernhard Braun.

Impressive Baroque rooms

PALAIS BUQUOY

Standing opposite, Palais Buquoy (Buquoyský Palace, no. 486) today houses the French embassy. Commissioned by Marie Josefa von Thun (of the Valdštejn family), it was built in 1719 according to plans by Giovanni Santini-Aichl, probably in collaboration with František Maximilian Kaňka and extended in 1735. The ornamental moulding was done by Matthias Bernhard Braun. After the Buquoy family acquired the palace, the interior was decorated in neo-Baroque style. In the years 1889 – 1896, J. Schulz gave a neo-Renaissance look to the stairwell and rear wing; the two tapestries (16th and 18th century) in the large hall of the rear wing are worth seeing. Further alterations were made in 1904. The old, informal garden of the palace extends as far as Kampa Island.

Attractive tapestries

OUR LADY BELOW THE CHAIN

To the north of Grand Priory Palace is the Church of Our Lady Below the Chain (Kostel Panny Marie pod Řetězem, Lázeňská). It is one of the oldest Malá Strana churches, and was founded in 1169 with the former Maltese order monastery as the administrative headquarters of the order's Bohemian province. Remains of the Romanesque basilica, which burnt down in 1420, can be seen in the right-hand wall

One of the oldest Malá Strana churches

The City of K.

Aside from some travelling, sanatorium visits and a spell in Berlin late in life, Kafka rarely left the city of his birth. »Dear little mother with claws« was the name he gave to the city he both loved and loathed: for him, it symbolized, in much the same way as his occupation and family, the constraints of everyday life, preventing him from dedicating himself totally to literature. Nevertheless, Prague also offered him inspiration in so many forms. It is no coincidence that the city provides the backdrop to some of his most important works.

A look at the exhibition (on the left, a picture of Dora Diamant, Kafka's last great love)

During the Communist era, Kafka was persona non grata, but has since been rediscovered. In the summer of 2005, a museum dedicated to the man and his work opened alongside the Vltava river in the Lesser Quarter. The exhibition consists of two sections: Existential Space and Imaginary Topography. The first part examines how the city affected Kafka's writing and the traces of Prague which can be found in his work. »Prague contributes myth, obscure magic and provides a magnificent backdrop« as the exhibition submits, detecting the influence of the city on the poet in his diaries and extensive correspondence with relatives, friends, lovers and editors.

Part two of the exhibition looks at how Kafka himself portrayed the city in his work, a fascinating challenge given that Kafka rarely names the actual places or scenes he describes in his novels. It is possible to figure out some of the locations he uses, however – St Vitus cathedral is generally recognized as the anonymous cathedral in a key chapter of »The Trial«, the river in »The Judgement« as the Vltava. But Kafka was not particularly interested in accurately depicting his city. Instead, as the museum suggests, he sought to transform Prague into an »Imaginary Topography« in which nothing is quite what it seems. In other words, a metamorphosis of his city – in literature.

The museum is located inside a former brickworks on the bank of the Vltava in the Lesser Quarter

of the forecourt. The two massive towers were completed in the year 1389. In the 17th-century Carlo Lurago gave the presbytery its Baroque look, still evident today. Among the most notable features of the Baroque interior are the high altar painting (*The Assumption of Our Lady*) and a painting of St Barbara, both by Karel Škréta. The pulpit is by Johann Georg Bendl.

NOSTICKÝ PALACE

Noteworthy frescoes

The four-winged Nostický Palace on Maltese Square (no. 1, southwest of Grand Priory Square) – today the seat of various departments of the ministry of culture – fills the south side of the square. The palace was built between the years 1658 – 1660 in Baroque style, for Johann Hartwig of Nostitz (probably from plans by Francesco Caratti). It was enriched in 1720 by projecting dormer windows and statues of emperors from the Brokoff workshops (now copies), and after 1765 by the Rococo columned entrance by Anton Hafenecker. It is worth

Noble and dignified: the interior of Nostitz Palace, one of the earliest sacral buildings of Prague Baroque

taking a look at the courtyard and the ceiling frescoes in the halls with mythological motifs created by Wenceslas B. Ambrozzi around the year 1757.

❶ Open during exhibitions

★ Hradčany Square (Hradčanské náměstí)

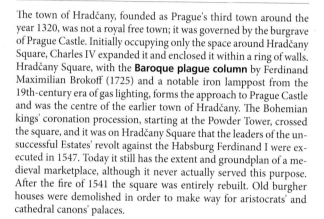

✦ C 4

Location: Praha 1, Hradčany
Metro: Hradčanská, Malostranská
Tram: 22

The town of Hradčany, founded as Prague's third town around the year 1320, was not a royal free town; it was governed by the burgrave of Prague Castle. Initially occupying only the space around Hradčany Square, Charles IV expanded it and enclosed it within a ring of walls. Hradčany Square, with the **Baroque plague column** by Ferdinand Maximilian Brokoff (1725) and a notable iron lamppost from the 19th-century era of gas lighting, forms the approach to Prague Castle and was the centre of the earlier town of Hradčany. The Bohemian kings' coronation procession, starting at the Powder Tower, crossed the square, and it was on Hradčany Square that the leaders of the unsuccessful Estates' revolt against the Habsburg Ferdinand I were executed in 1547. Today it still has the extent and groundplan of a medieval marketplace, although it never actually served this purpose. After the fire of 1541 the square was entirely rebuilt. Old burgher houses were demolished in order to make way for aristocrats' and cathedral canons' palaces.

No. 10, called the Saxon-Lauenburg residence, was the residence of the master builder of St Vitus Cathedral, Peter Parler, in 1372; he also owned Hrzán Palace on Loretánská. In the 18th century façade of this house and that of the adjoining number 9 were given a shared facing.

Parler House

In the centre of Hradčany Square stands the Marian plague column, erected in gratitude for the end of the epidemic in 1726. It was designed by Ferdinand Maximilian Brokoff (1688 – 1731). The figures on two levels at the foot of the column represent the saints: John Nepomuk, Elizabeth, Peter, Paul, Norbert, Florian, Charles Borromeo on the lower level; above them are Wenceslas, Vitus and Adalbert. The column is crowned by the figure of Maria Immaculata (Virgin of the Immaculate Conception; a popular Baroque motif), which was made after Brokoff's death, probably in his workshop.

Marian column

ARCHBISHOP'S PALACE (ARCIBISKUPSKÝ PALÁC)

From the Renaissance to Rococo The Archbishop's Palace (not open to the public) on the north side of the square originated as a Renaissance house, purchased by Ferdinand I from royal secretary Florian of Gryspek and conferred it on the first post-Hussite Catholic archbishop. In the years 1562 to 1564 it was altered, using plans by Hans Tirol, enlarged around 1600 and from 1675 to 1684 it was given a Baroque accent by the French architect Jean Baptiste Mathey, with a grandiose main portal (1676). Johann Joseph Wirch was responsible for its present Rococo appearance with the façade clad in marble facing (1763 – 1764). Two corner projections counterbalance the central projection, which is further accentuated by a shallow gable. The family coat of arms of Prince-Archbishop Anton Peter Count of Přichowitz crowns the sculptures by Ignaz Michael Platzner, of which Faith and Hope were replaced in the year 1888 by new works by T. Seidan. Wirch was also responsible for the late-Baroque interior. Nine tapestries by A. Desportes, made in the Parisian Atelier Neilson, address the theme of *Ancient and Modern India*. Particularly worthy of inspection, there is a wealth of wood carving and stucco ornamentation, two reliquary busts of apostles Peter and Paul in the chapel, as well as the collection of glass and porcelain. A passageway from the left doorway of the Archbishop's Palace leads to ▶Šternberský Palace with its collection of early European art.

PALAIS MARTINIC (MARTINICKÝ PALÁC)

On the northwest side of Hradčany Square stands Palais Martinic. The palace is privately owned and not open to the public. A café is open during the summer season on the ground floor. The renaissance building was erected at the end of the 16th century as a modest edifice with four wings for Andreas Teyfl. In 1624 it was taken over by Jaroslav Bořita z Martinic, one of those governors who went down in history because of the second Prague defenestration. Bořita Martinic added an upper storey with a renaissance gable and heraldic arms. The east front is decorated by figural renaissance sgraffiti with scenes from the life of Samson (from 15th-century German woodcuts) and from the life of Hercules (circa 1634). Similar sgraffiti from the 16th century and the first half of the 17th century have also been found on the front of the palace facing the square, with biblical scenes (including Joseph's flight from Potiphar's wife). Inside, take a look at the renaissance beam ceilings and the palace chapel with its richly ornamented renaissance vaulting.

www.martinickypalac.cz

TOSKÁNSKÝ PALACE

This two-storey, four-winged palace (no. 5) on the narrow west side of the square was built between 1689 and 1691 by the French architect Jean Baptiste Mathey for Michael Oswald Thun-Hohenstein. From 1718 to 1918 it was owned by the dukes of Tuscany; today it belongs to the Czech Republic's ministry for foreign affairs. The building's proportions appear well balanced against the cool aloofness of its surroundings. The early-Baroque front is ornamented with two pillared entrances and the dukes of Tuscany's heraldic arms on the wide space over the balconies; the tympanum carries six Baroque statues of the liberal arts by Johann Brokoff, father of Ferdinand Maximilian Brokoff, one of Prague's outstanding Baroque sculptors. The corner figure of St Michael fighting the dragon is by Ottavio Mosto from 1693.

Czech Republic Ministry for Foreign Affairs

SCHWARZENBERG PALACE (SCHWARZEN-BERSKÝ PALÁC)

The former Schwarzenberg Palace, which now houses the »Baroque in Bohemia« exhibition from the National Gallery, is one of the dominant features of the Hradčany skyline, along with the castle and Archbishop's Palace. Schwarzenberg Palace is a **prime example of northern Renaissance style**, with its richly adorned gables, projecting lunette sills based on the Lombardian model, refined diamond sgraffito décor modelled on north Italian (especially Venetian) graphic art in 1567, and representations of ancient gods and allegorical figures in the interior.

> **?** MARCO POLO INSIGHT
>
> *A popular candidate*
>
> Karel Schwarzenberg, born in the year 1937, may be known as »the old man« – but the nickname is a mark of respect. When he entered the presidential election race in 2013, opinion polls predicted he would take an 8% share of first round votes. In fact, he polled almost 46% and only lost to his rival Miloš Zeman in the second round runoff. Nevertheless, Schwarzenberg has no shortage of achievements to look back on. His unusual curriculum vitae includes the following: playboy, civil rights campaigner in Charta 77, Chancellor (chief of staff) under Václav Havel, Senator, Minister of Foreign Affairs (twice), party founder (TOP 09), majority shareholder in Becherovka, the national liqueur, castle owner and forest owner, amongst the foremost in Europe. Prince is one he can no longer use himself, as noble predicates are still prohibited in the Czech Republic, even after the Velvet Revolution.

Occupying the south corner of the square, the palace was created by the conversion of two Renaissance palaces. Alterations were undertaken in Empire style from 1800 to 1810 by F. Pavíček for Archbishop

Schwarzenberg Palace on Hradčany Square: »The square in front of
the royal castle … is surrounded by palaces« (Rainer Maria Rilke)

Salm – hence the initial »S« over the doorway. The right-hand part of
the building was constructed between 1545 and 1563 by Agostino
Galli.

Across three floors of the reconstructed palace, a **new permanent
exhibition from the National Gallery** presents over 160 sculptures
and 280 paintings of the late Renaissance and Baroque (late 16th century to the late 18th century) which were created in Bohemia. Sculptures by Matyáš Bernard Braun (1684 – 1738) and Ferdinand Maxi-
milián Brokoff (1688 – 1731), paintings by Karel Škréta (1610 – 1674),
Jan Petr Brandl (1669 –1735), Václav Vavřinec Reiner (1689 – 1743)
and Norbert Grund (1717 – 1767) are amongst the pieces on display,
as well as important works by Škréta, Brandl and Reiner from the
collection of A.I. Lobkowicz, examples of Mannerist (late 16th/early
17th century) and neo-Classicist (late 18th century) craftwork, liturgical artefacts, tableware, glass, porcelain, fans, textiles and jewellery.
Tempera frescoes (c1580) by an unknown artist adorn the ceiling of
the main hall on the second floor. They depict personifications and
allegories from Greek mythology (the Judgement of Paris, the Abduction of Helen, scenes from the Trojan war and the Flight of Ae-
neas from the burning city of Troy). In the neighbouring room the
Phaeton myth is shown. Two further rooms are decorated by paintings of Chronos and Persephone, Jupiter and Juno.

❶ Tue–Sun 10am–6pm, admission 150 Kč, concessions 80 Kč

Commissioned by Wilhelm Florentin von Salm-Salm (1793 –1810, Archbishop of Prague), the neighbouring Salm Palace was built in the years 1800 to 1810 on the south side of Hradčany Square. It too was taken over by the Schwarzenberg family in 1811 and now serves as exhibition space for the ▶National Gallery (p.247). Author Pavel Kohout lived in the Classicist noble palace until he emigrated in 1978.

Salm Palace (Salmovský palác)

❶ Tue–Sun 10am–6pm, admission 150 Kč, concessions 80 Kč, www.ngprague.cz

** Josefov

✦ E 4

Location: Praha 1, Staré Město, Maiselova etc.
Metro: Staroměstská
Tram: 17, 18

In existence since the 10th century, the Jewish community of Prague is one of the oldest and most signficant in the entire occident. Prague's Jews lived in their own district from the 13th century onwards around the Old-New Synagogue, which subsequently bemme a ghetto according to a papal decree which ruled that Jews had to live inside a walled settlement – separated from Christians. Little remains of this labyrinthine quarter of narrow alleyways and medieval houses: the former Jewish Town Hall, six synagogues and a section of the Old Jewish Cemetery have survived, whilst everything else was destroyed at the beginning of the 20th century to make way for modern Prague.   The Jewish community, today numbering some 1600 members, keeps the memory alive of the many tragedies, the fires, plague and terrible pogroms visited upon the Prague ghetto. Since 1906 they have also been the guardians of the Jewish Museum, founded by the Hebraist Salomon Hugo Lieben, in the northern part of the Old Town – it is one of the oldest Jewish museums in the world. It traces **a path through six historical sites** of the erstwhile Jewish town: The Maisel Synagogue, Klausen Synagogue, Pinkas Synagogue, Spanish Synagogue, the Old Jewish Cemetery and the Ceremonial Hall.

Jewish Museum

❶ April–Oct 9am–6pm Nov–March 9am–4.30pm (except Sat and Jewish holidays), www.jewishmuseum.cz

> **!** MARCO ⊕ POLO TIP
>
> *The eternal temptress*   **Insider Tip**
>
> By way of contrast to the Judaic programme: the small Galerie La Femme shows the diversity with which Prague's painters interpret the erotic, from Romanticism to Cubism. Whether blue-stockinged or emerging from the bath… (Bílkova 2, daily 10am–6pm; www.glf.cz).

Admission to all sites in Josefov with a combination ticket: 480 Kč, students 320 Kč, family ticket 480 Kč, admission to the Jewish Museum only: 300 Kč, students 200 Kč, family 300 Kč

Jewish Prague

The first Jews probably came to Prague in the 10th cent. They were persecuted and discriminated against across all centuries. Today the Jewish community of Prague has about 1,600 members.

▶ **The Jewish cemetery**
Jewish cemeteries are meant for eternity. Eternal rest is inviolable because the dead are waiting to be resurrected »at the end of days«. This led to some special characteristics:

The dead are always **buried in the ground**; the graves generally face Jerusalem.

Visitors lay **small stones** on the gravestones. This custom commemorates the time that the people of Israel spent in the wilderness, when graves were marked with heaps of stones.

The following inscriptions can be found on all gravestones:
P.N.: Poh nikbár (»here rests«) or Poh nitmán (»here lies buried«)

T.N.Z.W.H.: Te'hi Nischmató zrurá Bi'zrór Ha'Chajim (»May his soul be bound in the covenant of eternal life.«)

The graves are overgrown with **grass and ivy**. This is an expression of **mortality**.

The graves are **never levelled**. When space runs out another layer of earth is spread over the ground. Thus there are often several graves on top of each other.

▶ **Important Jewish cemeteries in Europe**

	since	burials
Old Jewish Cemetery in Vienna	1877	80,000
Cimeterio ebraico on the Lido in Venice	1389	unknown
Jewish Cemetery in Worms, Germany	1076	unknown
Jewish Cemetery in Hamburg-Altona, Germany	1611	8,000
Berlin-Weißensee	1880	115,000
New Jewish Cemetery in Lodz, Poland	1892	180,000

It kafkas and brods and werfels and kisches... is what Karl Kraus found. For him the German-Czech-Jewish Prague was the »ideal breeding ground for poetry«. Jewish authors from Prague:

GUSTAV MEYRINK
RAINER MARIA RILKE
MAX BROD
EGON ERWIN KISCH
FRANZ WERFEL
FRANZ KAFKA
VOSKOVEC & WERICH
FRIEDRICH TORBERG
JOHANNES URZIDIL
FELIX WELTSCH
LENKA REINEROVA

Rabbi Loew is supposed to have created the Golem from clay to protect Prague's Jews.

Rabbis and merchants
Rabbi Löw (1512/1525?–1609) Scholar, philosopher, father-figure to Prague's Jews. The Jewish legends of Prague go back to him.

Rabbi Pinkas (1535–1618) Rabbi of Prague and Cracow. The Pinkas Synagogue was named after him.

Mordechai Maisel (1528–1601) Court banker to Emperor Rudolf II, patron, philanthropist. He funded the Maisel Synagogue.

900

10th cent.
Jewish quarter in Prague first mentioned

Jewsih community of Prague
www.kehilaprag.cz

1096
Plundering by crusaders

around 1250
Pogrome by crusaders

around 1270
Old New Synagogue built

©BAEDEKER

1389
Pogrome, c. 3,000 dead

1535
Pinkas Synagogue built

1695
KlausenSynagogue built

1744
Maria Theresia orders expulsion

1851
The ghetto is called the »Josefstadt«

1939–1945
Occupation by Nazi Germany

1939
39,400 jews lived in Prague

31,860 were murdered by the Nazis

7,540 survived

MAISEL SYNAGOGUE (MAISELOVA SYNAGÓGA)

Primate of Prague's Jewish town

Mordecai Markus Maisel, Primate of Prague's »Jewish town« under Emperor Rudolf II, founded the synagogue that bears his name as a family house of prayer; the master builders were Joseph Wahl and Juda Goldschmied. After a fire in 1689 the building was renovated in Baroque style; from 1893 to 1905 Alfred Grotte modified it according to neo-Gothic notions. Only the general outline of a nave and two aisles and the women's gallery remained. The Jewish Museum shows the history of the Jews in Bohemia and Moravia from the 10th to the 18th century. The main points of emphasis are the beginnings of Jewish settlements in Bohemia and Moravia and the position of Jews in the Middle Ages, as well as the Renaissance era – which links in neatly with the founding of Maisel Synagogue.

✷ SPANISH SYNAGOGUE (ŠPANĚLSKÁ SYNAGÓGA)

Site of the oldest synagogue in Prague

The Spanish Synagogue occupies the site of the oldest synagogue in Prague (12th century), the so-called Old School (Stará škola), which was destroyed. The synagogue's name goes back to a group of Jews who fled to Prague from the Spanish Inquisition. In the following centuries the synagogue was burnt down several times, and built up again on each occasion. The Spanish Synagogue was given its present form between 1882 and 1893 by Vojtěch Ignác Ullmann; it is a central-plan building in Moorish style with impressive cupola and open galleries on three sides. The interior was designed with Granada's Alhambra in mind: oriental-type stucco work was introduced (1882/1883). Here, the second section of the history of the Jews in Bohemia and Moravia is displayed – from the Enlightenment to the present day.

PINKAS SYNAGOGUE (PINKASOVA SYNAGÓGA)

An architectural treasure

The Pinkas Synagogue arose on the south side of the Old Jewish Cemetery in a house bought by the leading family of the Jewish community, the Horovitz family, from Rabbi Pinkas in the 14th century. In 1535 Salman Munka Horovitz had a synagogue built in late-Gothic style; the reticulated vaulting dates from this time. Juda Goldschmied de Herz converted the synagogue in 1625 in late-Renaissance style, and extended it to include a women's gallery, vestibule and meeting room. The Pinkas Synagogue and the Old-New Synagogue are the oldest and, in terms of their architecture, the most important in Prague. Archaeological excavations have confirmed that

Don't miss! Insider Tip

- Mosaics inspired by the Alhambra in Granada (Spanish Synagogue, picture on the right)
- The names of 77,297 victims of the Holocaust etched into the wall with red ink (Pinkas Synagogue)
- The grave of Rabbi Löw, creator of Golem, with allegorical lion, bears and roses (Old Jewish Cemetery)
- Death of a Jew, cycle of 15 pictures of the observances of the burial fraternity (Old Jewish Cemetery, ceremonial hall)
- Anniversary lights, showing when to pray for the dead: 3 June, Franz Kafka (Old-New Synagogue)

the Pinkas Synagogue dates from the 11th or 12th century, and that there was once a ritual bath here. In the years 1950 to 1958 the **Memorial of the 77297** was erected in the synagogue, The number represents the victims of the Holocaust whose names are listed here. The building was closed at the end of the 1960s, the inscriptions on the walls having suffered from the effects of ground water. During the course of renovation work, an old well and a ritual bath were discovered. In the 1990s the names of the victims were once more inscribed on the synagogue walls. In the permanent display are children's drawings, exercise books, diaries, letters and lyric poetry from the Nazi concentration camp Theresienstadt (▶Terezín, p.172)

** OLD JEWISH CEMETERY (STARÝ ŽIDOVSKÝ HŘBITOV)

The Old Jewish Cemetery dates back to the beginning of the 15th century and is one of the most important surviving monuments of Josefov. The last burial took place in the year 1787. A new Jewish cemetery, the second-oldest, had already been established in the year 1680 in the ▶Žižkov district (p.330) on account of the plague (victims of the plague were not allowed to be interred in the existing graveyard). Kafka, who died on 3 June 1924, is among those buried in Žižkov, but in a more recent Jewish cemetery which was founded

Crowded gravestones

MARCO◉POLO INSIGHT

?

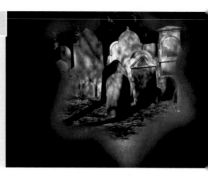

»House of eternity«

Reburial or relocation of graves, as is practised in Christian cemeteries, is unthinkable in a Jewish cemetery. Halakha, or Jewish Law, prohibits graves being touched, as the buried wait for the »ascension of the souls of the just«, as the Jewish historian Flavius Josephus (37 – c100) wrote, for an eternal life with God.

in 1890. Some 12,000 gravestones lie beneath the ash trees of the Old Jewish Cemetery, although far more are certainly buried here. According to Jewish law, graves may never be given up (▶MARCOPOLO Insight p.212) and, in spite of having been extended on several occasions, the limited space has proved too small for such large numbers. Fresh earth has been piled onto the existing graves in order to create new plots, so in some places there are up to nine layers, one on top of the other. Older gravestones have shifted closer to the surface, creating new arrangements of stones, giving the Old Jewish Cemetery in Prague its distinctive appearance.

Inscriptions and reliefs The Hebrew inscriptions on the gravestones name the deceased and the name of the father (for married women, also the husband's name), as well as date of death and of the funeral. Reliefs on the gravestones often depict either a visual image of the deceased person's name (stag, bear, carp, cockerel etc.) or his profession (physician's instruments, tailor's scissors etc.), and sometimes other symbols, such as blessing hands or pitchers (for members of priestly families), grapes (for the tribes of Israel), crowns, pine-cones or other motifs.

Famous gravestones The oldest gravestone, erected in 1439, marks the resting-place of scholar and poet Avigdor Kara, who lived through the pogrom of 1389 and wrote an elegy upon it. The most recent grave is that of Moses Beck from the year 1787. A sarcophagus in late-Renaissance style with chiselled lions and writing-tablets framed by arcades marks the grave of the learned **Chief Rabbi Jehuda Löw ben Bezalel**, known as Rabbi Löw who died in 1609, closely associated with the saga of the creation of Golem (▶MARCOPOLO Insight p.214). Further tombs which have been identified include those of the Primate of Prague's Jewish town, Mordecai Markus Maisel (died 1601), historian and astronomer David Gans (died 1613), scholar Joseph Schlomo Delmedigo (died 1655) and book-collector and scholar David Oppenheim (died 1736). One of the richest and loveliest is the grave-stone of Heudele Bassevi (died 1628), wife of Wallenstein's financier, the first Prague Jew to be elevated to the aristocracy.

The pebbles on the graves are laid there by relatives or friends. This custom dates back to the people of Israel's wandering through the desert under Moses, when the dead were covered with stones to protect them from wild animals. The faithful throw little messages onto the tomb of Chief Rabbi Jehuda Löw, hoping to invoke his help – it is said he can work miracles.

Ceremonial Hall

Beside the exit from the Old Jewish Cemetery is the neo-Roman-esque ceremonial hall of the Prague burial fraternity with a small tower, built in 1911/1912. The ceremonial hall was formerly used for obsequies and the mortuary was housed here. Now, the second part of the exhibition of Jewish Customs and Traditions is on display, including a 15-part cycle dedicated to the fraternity's observances by an unknown artist; it is dated 1780.

KLAUS SYNAGOGUE (KLAUSOVA SYNAGÓGA)

Rabbi Löw taught here

The Klaus Synagogue – its name derives from the Latin »clausum« (closure) – is located directly next to the exit from the Old Jewish Cemetery and ceremonial hall. Built in 1694 in Baroque style, re-modelled on the outside in 1884, the place of worship houses a permanent exhibition on the themes of Jewish traditions and customs. Rabbi Löw, one of the most important Jewish philosophers of the 16th century, taught in the Klaus Synagogue. The high prestige of the Klaus Synagogue was attributable to its size and to the fact that it was reserved for the burial fraternity.

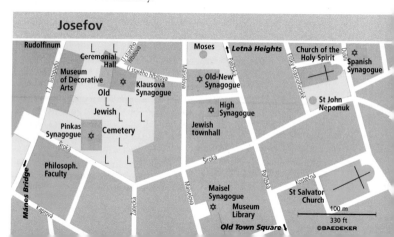

Golem, Graves and Scholars

Little has survived of the Prague district once inhabited by Jews – only a town hall, six synagogues and part of the old Jewish cemetery. Everything else was demolished at the beginning of the last century, to make way for a new city district.

The Maisel Synagogue of today, at Maiselova no. 10, replaced the magnificent structure which was destroyed in the great fire of 1689

At that point the crooked alleyways disappeared, where houses with such expressive names as »The Cold Hostelry«, »The Mousehole« and »No Time« had been crammed together. The rebuilding project was not to everyone's taste. Kafka, for example, found »the unhealthy old Jewish town … far more real than the new hygienic town around us«. But the story of the district has been kept alive – and not only by the small community of scarcely 1600 Jews who today once more celebrate religious services in Old-New Synagogue and run the Jewish museum. The old cemetery, with its crumbling funeral stelae is enormously fascinating. Those who find the plot where Rabbi Löw will invariably recall the legend of the gigantic Golem, said to have been created by the Rabbi out of clay at the end of the 16th century.

Soulless Matter

It was God's will that this soulless matter (»Golem« in Hebrew) should assist the rabbi and defend the persecuted Jews. In order to bring the creature to life, the rabbi placed in its mouth a parchment scroll bearing the unutterable name of God. Now the dumb creature worked week by week for the scholar, except on the Sabbath, when no Jewish believer may work. The inevitable happened: on one holy Sabbath the rabbi forgot to remove the scroll in order to let Golem rest. The giant was torn between his duty to work and his existence according to the will of God, which forbade him to work on this day, and he raged frantically.

With a mighty crash he smashed the furniture of the rabbi, who was just leading the community in the synagogue, singing the 92nd psalm. The people rushed out of the synagogue, but it was impossible to stop Golem. In order to avert the ultimate catastrophe, the rabbi threw himself upon Golem and pulled the sacred scroll away. Then he removed him – to this day, nobody knows quite where he took him – perhaps Golem turned to dust or clay in some attic or other. Or perhaps not: from time to time, on dark nights, Golem has reportedly been seen on the streets of Prague. Be that as it may, the rabbi had the community sing the 92nd psalm once more, and that has remained a tradition in Prague's synagogues to this day.

Scapegoats

Just as Golem could not protect the Jews in the long term, so also they received little help from other sources over the centuries. A good 100 years after the Jews first settled in Malá Strana in 995, the first pogrom was instigated by fanatical Crusaders.

In the twelfth century the Jews had to move from Malá Strana to the other side of the Vltava, where their settlement was enclosed by a wall, as laid down by the Third Lateran Council (1179). For centuries their history was marked by exclusion of this sort. It was never difficult for Christians to find a reason for a pogrom: for instance, Jews were blamed for the plague – after all, they succumbed to the disease far less frequently. People did not realize that their periodic relative exemption from this illness, which is spread by rat fleas, was attributable to Jewish ritual cleansing customs; they lived far more hygienically than did the Christians.

So-called Privileges

With very few exceptions, the so-called Christian benefactors who granted the Jewish ghetto short periods of security and self-determination did so only to enrich themselves: Rudolf II (1576 – 1611), for instance, annulled all the privileges he had granted the Jews in previous decades, at the very moment when the Jewish merchant Mordecai Markus Maisel died; Rudolf had been financially dependent on him. Moreover, the so-called privileges which the Jews enjoyed from time to time were usually only rights or permissions which other groups took for granted, such as the right to »protection against arbitrary persecution«, or permission to convey the dead without tax from one province to another. The Habsburg Joseph II (1765 – 1790), after whom the Jewish ghetto was renamed Josefov in 1861, is the only one of whom it can be said that he supported the Jews without considering his own advantage. Thanks to Joseph's enlightened attitude Josefov was recognized as a city district with equal rights, and the exclusion of Jews was temporarily suspended. However, at the beginning of the 19th century the former Jewish ghetto was almost entirely demolished to make way for new, larger houses and avenues as existed in Paris. The violent end of the Jewish community, repeatedly persecuted by pogroms, pillage and countless expulsions (under Ferdinand I in the 16th century and under Maria Theresa in the 18th century), came with the Nazis' racial fanaticism and programme of genocide. 90% of Bohemia and Moravia's Jews lost their lives between 1939 and 1945. Their names are inscribed in the Holocaust memorial to the 77,927 Czech Jews in Pinkas Synagogue.

Sightseeing in the Ghetto?

The Jewish community of Prague today numbers some 1600 members: there is a Jewish school, also attended by children from non-Jewish families, and a Jewish kindergarten. Two of the synagogues hold services during the week, whilst the Spanish Synagogue is used on High Holidays. Bearing in mind the history of the district, even the keenest of photographers amongst the tourists should adopt a degree or reverence and restraint. few Jews who still live in Prague see that their cultural memorials, made into a museum, now number among the city's main tourist attractions. On a quiet day out of season visitors to the synagogue and old cemetery area will find an enthralling magic in the ancient weathered gravestones, which have survived for centuries, though part or all may have sunk into the ground. Yet when masses of snapshot-seeking tourists crowd the paths of the old cemetery at the height of the season, one or other of the Jewish community may yearn for Golem, who would know how to restore peace.

A look inside the Old-New Synagogue (left) and the Klausen Synagogue (right)

★ OLD-NEW SYNAGOGUE (OLD-NEW SCHOOL, STARONOVÁ SYNAGÓGA)

Opposite the High Synagogue stands the Old-New Synagogue. The name actually derives from the Hebrew »altnai«, meaning »on condition that«. Behind this name lies a legend: for the building of Prague's synagogue, angels brought stones from the ruin of the temple in Jerusalem, but only »on condition that« these stones would be taken back to Jerusalem when the Messiah came to rebuild his temple. It is the only synagogue in Europe of this age that still serves as such. The oldest part of the building is the early-Gothic south hall, originally principal chamber of the house of prayer; in the 13th century it was extended by a double-aisled hall in Cistercian Gothic style. Its five-ribbed vaulting is unique in Bohemian architecture. The women's galleries were completed in the 17th and 18th centuries – only men may pray in the main hall.

The legend of the angels

The large flag was a present from Charles IV, who conferred the »lofty banner« on the Jewish community in 1358 as a sign of their privileges; today's flag is from the reign of Charles VI (1716). This red flag with the six-pointed Star of David and hat was the official banner of Prague's Jews, and it occurs on the capital's historic coat of arms, as third emblem from the right beside the Bohemian lion. This makes Prague the **only city in the world with a Jewish emblem in its heraldic arms**.

On the east side of the synagogue in a Torah shrine lies the Pentateuch parchment roll (the first five books of the Old Testament). In the centre is the raised pulpit, separated by lattice-work (15th century). The synagogue was renovated as early as 1618; further extensive reconstructions followed in 1883 and 1966. Legend has it that in the attic of the Old-New Synagogue lie the remains of Golem (▶MARCOPOLO Insight p.214). The tale of Golem is well served in literature by authors such as Gustav Meyrink (The Golem) and Egon Erwin Kisch (On Golem's Track). In the little park beside the Old-New Synagogue stands a statue of Moses by František Bílek (1872 – 1941).

❶ April–Oct Sun–Thu 9.30am–6pm, Fri 9.30am–5pm, Nov–March Sun–Thu 9.30am–4.30pm, Fri 9.30am–2pm, admission 200 Kč, students 140 Kč, families 200 Kč

Opposite the Old-New Synagogue, at no. 18 Maiselova on the corner of Pařížská, stands the former Jewish Town Hall (Židovská radnice). This is the seat of Prague's Jewish community and the council of Jewish communities in the Czech Republic, and is not open to the public. Mordecai Markus Maisel, court banker and mayor of the »Jewish town« under Emperor Rudolf II, donated this town hall to the Jewish community in around 1580. Building was undertaken in 1586 in Renaissance style; it was converted in Baroque style (1765) by Josef

Jewish Town Hall

Old-New Synagogue and the former Jewish town hall. The hands on the gable clock turn from right to left – as in Hebrew script

Schlesinger. The south extension dates from the first decade of the 20th century. The north gable beneath the wooden clock-tower has a clock with Hebrew numbers.

High Synagogue

Like the Jewish Town Hall, its once affiliated High Synagogue (Vysoká synagóga) at number 4 Červená is not open to the public. The synagogue was built in 1568 by Pankraz Roder, also on a square ground plan; in the 19th century it was separated from the town hall and provided with its own stairway and street access. The interior chamber was constructed on the first floor – hence »High« Synagogue. It was extended in the 17th century and re-designed in neo-Renaissance style in the 19th century. There is a contrast between this chamber with its magnificent stellar vaulting – a prime example of Jewish sacral building – and the synagogue's modest exterior.

Church of the Holy Saviour

The Church of the Holy Saviour (Kostel svatého Salvátora) in Salvátorská (accessible from Pařížská) was originally a Lutheran church; today it serves the Bohemian Brothers. It was built from 1611 to 1614 from designs by Swiss-born J. Christoph in Renaissance style; bought by the Pauline order (hermits of St Francis of Paola) around the mid-17th century, it was given a Baroque look, and in the year 1720 a tower was added. Protestants from all over Europe contributed to the construction costs.

Jungmann Square (Jungmannovo náměstí)

✳ E 4/5

Location: Praha 1, Staré Město
Metro: Màstek
Tram: 3, 9, 14, 24

On Jungmann Square stands the Jungmann monument (Jungmannův pomník), created by Ludvík Šimek in 1878. The writer, philosopher and linguistic researcher Josef Jungmann (1773 – 1847) was an important representative of the »rebirth« of Czech national sentiment during the Romantic era; he compiled an extensive Czech-German dictionary and wrote a history of Czech literature.

Our Lady of the Snows

The Church of Our Lady of the Snows (Kostel Panny Marie Sněžné) was commissioned in 1347 by Charles IV as a coronation and monastery church; it was intended to surpass St Vitus Cathedral (Prague Castle) in height. By 1397 only the 30m/98ft-high chancel was complete; on the north side was a fine Gothic doorway with numerous sculptures of saints. The building fell into decay from the 15th century; in 1611 the vaulting fell in, and the Franciscans replaced it with a Renaissance ceiling. The Baroque high altar (1625 – 1651) is the largest in any of Prague's churches. Above the left side altar hangs a painting by Václav Vavřinec Reiner, The Annunciation. The church played an important part in the Hussite movement. Jan Želivský preached here to the city's poor against the papal church, the aristocracy and the wealthy bourgeoisie. In 1419 Želivský stormed the town hall in Nové Město with the most radical of his supporters and flung the Catholic councillors out of the window. This so-called first Prague defenestration precipitated the Hussite Wars. Even after the murder of Želivský (in 1422), who lies buried here, the Church of Our Lady of the Snows continued to be a Hussite centre.

Franciscan garden

To the south of the Church of Our Lady of the Snows lies the green oasis of the Franciscan monastery garden (Františkánská zahrada). Passages link this public space to Wenceslas Square and to the streets Jungmannova, Palackého and Vodičkova.

Kampa

——————————————————— ✳ **D 4/5**

Location: Praha 1, Malá Strana, Kampa
Metro: Malostranská
Tram: 12, 22

Vltava river island

Separated from Malá Strana by the idyllic Čertovka arm of the Vltava (formerly also a dangerous stretch of river, hence the name »Devil's Stream«), the river island of Kampa forms the green strip on the Vltava's left bank, from Legií Bridge to Mánes Bridge. The west section of Charles Bridge passes over the island; some of the little houses on the island have their foundations supported on the arches of the original Judith Bridge. North of Charles Bridge, the Čertovka flows through two rows of houses, frequently referred to as »**Prague's Venice**« (Pražské Benátky). The cultivation of this initially boggy land to create several gardens did not begin until the 15th century. After this, the Čertovka was used to power several mills; some of the mill-wheels are on show near Charles Bridge and the bridge leading to Grand Priory Square.

The large wheel of **Grand Priory Mill** (late 16th century) has since been restored. There are potters' markets on Kampa Island, a pleasant place to stroll. It offers delightful views of the Vltava and Shooters' Island, of Charles Bridge and Staré Město, and of the waterfront gardens of some of the Malá Strana palaces, where a large park has been created through the amalgamation of previously separate palace gardens. Close to Charles Bridge is the late-Gothic statue of Roland, reconstructed by L. Simek in 1884. It once marked the border between Malá Strana, administered according to Magdeburg law, and Staré Město, where Nuremberg law prevailed.

KAMPA MUSEUM

This **museum for modern art** was founded on the initiative of Czech emigrant and patron of the arts Meda Mládek. Following the Velvet Revolution, she and her husband Jan bequeathed their private collection to the city of Prague. It was

Vltava river, as seen from Kampa island, an installation by the Italian »Cracking Art Group« in the foreground

made accessible to the public in September 2003 in the Sova's Mills, a 600-year-old building on the Vltava river island of Kampa. Along with paintings and drawings by František Kupka (1871 – 1957), a pioneer of abstract art, and Cubist statues by Otto Gutfreund (1189 – 1927), works by Jiří Kolář (1914 to 2002) and further Czech artists who were denigrated under Communism are on display. The roof is incorporated into the exhibition space, presenting two huge, inter-linked glass cubes by Czech sculptor Marian Karel. An armoured glass balcony appears to lead straight up into the Prague sky. Mill-stones, centuries old, can be found in the courtyard, whilst a giant chair stands on the Vltava river – a throne of fantasy.

❶ daily 10am –6pm, admission 160 Kč , www.museumkampa.com

Karlova

✦ E 4

Location: Praha 1, Staré Město
Metro: Staroměstská, Můstek
Tram: 17, 18

Karlova is part of the historic coronation route from Old Town Square to Charles Bridge. One of the thoroughfare's showpieces is the house at number 3, **The Golden Well**. Remains of masonry in the basement show that there was once a Romanesque building on this spot. The Renaissance façade seen today is embellished with a magnificent Baroque stucco relief from 1701 by Johann Ulrich Mayer

On the coronation route

which shows the saints Wenceslas, Rochus, Sebastian, Ignatius of Loyola, Franciscus Xaverius and Rosalia. There is an inviting wine tavern on the ground floor. The German astronomer Johannes Kepler lived at no. 4 from 1607-1612. he had been invited to come to Prague by Tycho Brahe in 1600 to be his assistant and took over his position when Brahe died in 1601. An ultramodern interior and the story of Prague's earliest coffee-house distinguish the pretty Renaissance house at number 18, **The Golden Serpent**. Here once dwelt the Armenian Deodatus Damajan, who sold coffee in Staré Město's narrow streets, and in the year 1714 opened Prague's first café in his house in Malá Strana.

Palais Pötting (no. 8), whose patron is recalled by his coat-of-arms impaled with those of his wife on the doorway of the Baroque façade, houses the Ta Fantastika theatre. At number 26, the State Conservatory's experimental theatre Disk resides.

Prague's first cinema was opened in 1907 by Viktor Ponrepo or, as the case may be, Dismas Šlambor in **The Blue Pike** (no. 20). Several shops on Karlova offer Bohemian glass, pillow lace and other arts and crafts, while beautiful antiquarian bookshops such as **Palais Colloredo-Mansfeld** (no. 2) and **The Stone Mermaid** (no. 14), extend an invitation to browse through rare publications.

** Karlštejn Castle (Hrad Karlštejn)
✦ Excursion

Location: 40km/25m southwest of Prague
Guided tours: March, Nov, Dec, Tue–Sun 9am–3pm, April and Oct until 4pm, May, June, Sept until 5pm, July, Aug until 6pm,
Admission: 270 Kč, photo pass 40 Kč
www.hradkarlstejn.cz

Bohemia's most famous medieval castle

North of the little wine-growing community of Karlštejn (population 1200) towers the mighty Hrad Karlštejn (formerly Karlův Týn), the most famous of Bohemia's medieval castles. From the car park outside the village it is an approximately 2 km/1.5 mi walk up to the terraced fortifications, which soar up from a wooded hill surrounded by limestone cliffs (319m/1050ft) above the slopes of a tributary valley of the river Berounka (Beraun). The castle is classified as a national monument of culture and is preserved with great care. It was built during the relatively short period between the years 1348 and 1357, in the reign of Emperor **Charles IV**, to house in safety the treasures of the Holy Roman Empire of the German Nation, the Bohemian royal insignia, numerous relics and important state documents. In all likelihood, the designs were provided by French architect **Matthias of Arras**. Severely damaged by Hussite attacks in 1422, it was repaired a

Charles IV's treasury: the laying of the foundation stone of Karlštejn Castle took place in the same year, 1348, as the founding of Prague New Town

few years later; it was restored with some alterations in the second half of the 16th century, and once again – with various alterations – by Friedrich Schmidt and Josef Mocker from 1887 to 1899.

The Burgrave Courtyard (Purkrabský dvůr) can be entered from the north through two tower buildings, approximately 100m/110yd apart. Here the guided tour (the only way to see inside) begins; visitors have to join a tour to view the castle. The four-floored Burgrave's House (Purkrabství) is on the south side of the courtyard; parts of it date back to the 15th century.

Burgrave Courtyard

At the extreme west end of the castle site stand some former farm buildings and the large Well Tower (Studniční věž) with a 90m/295ft-deep well and large scoop wheel.

Well Tower

To the east of the Burgrave Courtyard, through a large gate, lies the narrow Castle Courtyard (Hradní nádvoří). On the right is the Imperial Palace (Císařský palác), with steps going up on the extreme right-hand side. An antechamber leads into the Feudal Lords' Assembly Hall. The double-aisled hall has a coffered ceiling supported by four upright wooden beams. On the second floor, Charles IV's study, his

Imperial Palace

bedchamber with an altar picture by Tommaso da Modena, and the Imperial Chamber with precious wood-panelling are all that remains of the original Imperial apartments. The half-timbered top floor, initially the female domain, was replaced by wooden battlements when the castle was restored. Adjacent to the east side of the Imperial Palace stands St Nicholas Chapel.

Marian Tower Opposite the Imperial Palace stands the Marian Tower (Mariánská věž). On the second floor (access via stairs in the wall) is the Chapter Church of St Mary, with its painted beamed ceiling and wall frescoes that date back in part to the 14th century; they depict scenes from the Apocalypse and portray Charles IV. In the southwest corner of the Marian Tower is the vaulted Chapel of St Katherine; Charles IV had the original painted decoration replaced by plates of semi-precious stones set in the walls. Over the entrance is a painting of Emperor Charles IV and his wife Anna. In the altar niche an original picture of the Madonna has been preserved.

Great Tower On the uppermost level of the castle's rock foundation stands the enormous 37m/121ft-high Great Tower (Velká věž), which is linked to the Marian Tower by a wooden bridge – formerly a drawbridge. The Chapel of the Holy Cross (Kaple svatého Kříže) on the second floor was dedicated in 1360. A gilded iron screen divides it into two parts. Its markedly extensive vault is entirely gilded and covered with glass stars, creating the illusion of a canopy of the heavens. Above the candle rail on the walls (for 1330 candles) are more than 2200 semi-precious stones inlaid in gilded plasterwork and 128 painted wooden panels (1348 to 1367) by the Gothic Master Theoderic (largely now

Karlštejn Castle

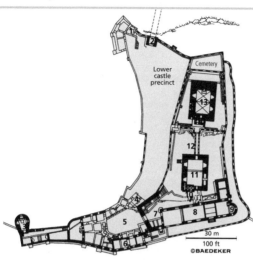

1 First gate (late 15th century) present-day entrance

2 Old castle gate

3 Well tower

4 Second gate (to Burgrave courtyard)

5 Burgrave courtyard

6 Burgrave house

7 Castle courtyard

8 Imperial Palace

9 St Nicholas Chapel

10 St Katherine's Chapel

11 Tower of Our Lady with Chapter Church of Our Lady

12 Wooden passage-way

13 Large tower with Chapel of the Cross

copies); today six of these panels are to be found in St Agnes Convent. The panels served to enclose reliquaries. Also by Master Theoderic are the paintings in the window embrasures. The imperial crown jewels (now in Vienna's Hofburg treasury), and later also the Bohemian royal insignia (now in the coronation chamber of St Vitus Cathedral at Prague Castle) were once kept in a niche behind the altar. Every year a solemn memorial Mass is celebrated in the castle in the early evening of 29 November, the anniversary of Charles IV's death.

Klementinum (Clementinum)

‡ E 4

Location: Praha 1, Staré Město, Kliôovnická, Platnéřská, Karlova
Metro: Staroměstská
Bus: 207
Tram: 17, 18

The former Jesuit college between Knights of the Cross Square and Mariánské Square is now the seat of the State Library of the Czech

State Library

Republic. It contains more than 5 million volumes, 6000 manuscripts – including the Codex Vyšehradiensis – and more than 4000 incunabula.

When Ferdinand I became ruler of Bohemia and Hungary in 1526 by right of his wife, he wished to reconvert the lands he had inherited to Catholicism, but without resorting to excessively rigorous methods; in 1556 he invited the Jesuits to Prague. They took over the monastery and church of St Clement from the Dominicans who had been there since 1232. An entire Staré Město district with more than 30 burgher houses, three churches and several gardens was demolished. Under the leadership of master builder Francesco Caratti and later František Maximilian Kaňka, the demolished buildings were replaced from 1578 with the buildings of the Klementinum. It was the largest building complex in the city after Prague Castle. In 1622 Charles University (►Karolinum) was joined to it.

The site of the clementinum includes five inner courtyards separated by various wings of the buildings, the churches of St Clement and the Holy Saviour (Knights of the Cross Square), the Vlašská Chapel – belonging to the Italian community – and an observatory (1751). The main façade of the collegiate building opposite the Church of St Francis goes back to the mid-17th century, and is decorated by richly structured stucco work in the form of shells, laurel, grimacing demons and busts of Roman emperors. Inside, it is well worth taking a look at the Jesuits' library (»Barokní sál«) on the first floor, built from designs by František Maximilian Kaňka and ornamented with ceiling frescoes by Johann Hiebl, which show the muses and biblical themes. In the centre, the painted cupola canopy grabs the attention, with the illusion of depth so dear to Baroque sensibility. Also worth seeing is the Mozart room with Rococo painting and bookshelves from the same era. The former Chapel of Mirrors was built in 1724 by František Maximilian Kaňka, and embellished with a ceiling fresco (pictures of the Virgin Mary) by Hiebel. Today it is used for chamber music concerts and exhibitions. The Mathematical Room with its collection of globes and table clocks is also interesting. In the southwest court the **Prague Student statue** commemorates the students' part in defending Charles Bridge against invading Swedes at the end of the Thirty Years' War (1648).

❶ Jan–March daily 10am–5pm, April, Oct–Dec daily until 6pm, May–Aug daily until 8pm. Admission to the library and observatory 150 Kč, plus Chapel of Mirrors 220 Kč. Tour plus concert 650 Kč

Church of St Clement

The Baroque Church of St Clement (Kostel svatého Klimenta) is part of the Klementinum site and is linked by an ironwork screen to the Italian Chapel. The church was built between 1711 and 1715. The sculptures inside number among the great treasures of Bohemian Baroque. Matthias Bernhard Braun created the eight sculptures of evangelists and fathers of the church, and also the wood carvings on the side altars, pulpit and confessional box. The altar picture is by Peter Brandl, and portrays St Linhart. Today, St Clement's serves the Greek Catholic community.

★ Knights of the Cross Square (Křižovnické náměstí)

⎯⎯⎯⎯⎯⎯⎯⎯⎯⎯⎯⎯⎯⎯⎯⎯⎯ ✕ **D/E 4**

Location: Praha 1, Staré Město, Kliôovnické náměstí
Tram: 17, 18

The traffic rushing across it nothwithstanding, the architectural lay-out of Knights of the Cross Square makes it one of the loveliest squares in Prague. It was laid out in the 16th century at the head of Charles Bridge, and the traditional Bohemian coronation procession crossed it. On the east side is the Church of the Holy Saviour, on the north is the Church of St Francis Seraphinus, which belongs to the Order of the Knights of the Cross. The Knights of the Cross with the Red Star was a military order which developed from a fraternity caring for the sick during the era of the Crusades, and expanded particularly in Silesia, Bohemia and Moravia.

One of the loveliest squares in Prague

On the east side of Knights of the Cross Square stands the Church of the Holy Saviour (Kostel svatého Salvátora), the Jesuit church originally included in the Klementinum complex. It was built between 1578 and 1601 in Renaissance style. Carlo Lurago and Francesco Caratti added the projecting Baroque doorway (1638 – 1659), for which Johann Georg Bendl provided the vases and statues of saints (1659). The statue of Christ on the tympanum is flanked by two evangelists on either side. The figures on the balustrade represent the four Fathers of the Church, framed in by two of the order's saints. In the central niche stands a figure of the Madonna. The towers, from a design by František Maximilian Kaňka, were not completed until 1714. The ceiling fresco by Karel Kovál shows the four continents known at the time (1748).

Church of the Holy Saviour

❶ Tue 6.30pm–8.30pm Thu 7.30pm–10pm Sun 1.30pm–3.30pm and 7.30pm–9.30pm

The Baroque Church of the Knights of the Cross (also: Church of St Francis Seraphinus, Kostel sv Františka Serafinského) was built between 1679 and 1689, from designs by Jean Baptiste Mathey, on the foundations of an early Gothic church, the remains of which still exist below ground level. The church commissioned by the Order of the Knights of the Cross was intended to equal, if not surpass, the architec-

Church of the Knights of the Cross

ture of the Church of the Holy Saviour that stood at the head of Charles Bridge and was a good 80 years older. This aim was indeed achieved, thanks not least to the high drum cupola which can be seen from afar. The niches in the façade are ornamented with figures of saints from the workshop of Matthias Wenceslas Jäckel in French pre-classical style. The angels at the top, now replaced by copies, are by Jäckel himself. The statues of the Mother of God and St John Nepomuk in front of the entrance are by Jan Antonín Quittainer; some features anticipate the Rococo style. To the side of the church is the Vintners' Column by Johann Georg Bendl with a statue of St Wenceslas (1676). In the richly ornamented interior the large cupola fresco of the Last Judgement by Wenzel Lorenz Reiner (1722) is especially noteworthy. The altar painting by Jan Kryštof Liška shows St Francis receiving the stigmata; the same artist was responsible for the cupola paintings of nativity scenes.

Charles V monument
Between Knights of the Cross Square and Old Town Bridge Tower (►Charles Bridge) stands a cast-iron monument to Charles IV , which was unveiled in 1848 to mark the 500th anniversary of Prague University.

✱ Lesser Quarter Square (Malostranské náměstí)
_____ ✧ **D 4**

Location: Praha 1, Malá Strana
Metro: Malostranská
Tram: 12, 22, 23

Erstwhile market below the castle
Lesser Quarter Square has been the centre of city life ever since Malá Strana was founded. It began as a market below Prague Castle. Nowadays it is divided into two smaller squares by the buildings around St Nicholas Church. It contains notable buildings such as Malá Strana Town Hall and the late-Baroque Kaiserstein Palace on the east side, as well as the Rococo »Stone Table« house next to the Church of St Nicholas. Each square used to have a well. The upper one was replaced in 1715 by a **plague column** with a Holy Trinity sculptural group and the Bohemian patron saint by Johann Ulrich Mayer and Ferdinand Geiger. The lower one was replaced in 1858 by a memorial to Austrian Field Marshal Radecký, exhibited today in the National Museum's Lapidarium (stone collection) in Stromovka Park.

Kaiserstein Palace
Kaiserstein Palace (U Petzoldů, no. 23) was reconstructed in the 1980s, but is not open to the public. Its predecessors were two 15th-century Gothic houses which were amalgamated in 1630 and rede-

Lesser Quarter Square

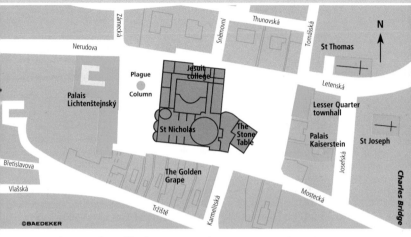

©BAEDEKER

signed in 1700 for Helfried Kaiserstein. The tympanum is adorned by allegories of the four seasons by Ottavio Mosto; the Kaiserstein coat-of-arms can be seen above the central first-floor window. At the beginning of the 20th century the famous opera diva Ema Destinnová (»Kittlová«, 1878 – 1930), partner of legendary tenor Enrico Caruso, lived in the palace; the »Destinnová« room serves as a reminder of the soprano singer.

The house at number 4 (U Zlatého hroznu) on the corner of Lesser Quarter Square and Karmelitská has been renovated to a high standard and is open to the public. It owes its Baroque appearance to radical alterations undertaken in the years 1707 to 1710.

The Golden Grape

The imposing Lichtenstein Palace is a focal point of the upper square, which was named Italian Square in the 17th century, and, since 1847, also St Stephen's Square. In 1591 Jan z Lobkowicz bought up five burgher houses and made them into one. In 1621 they became the property of Charles of Lichtenstein. The Classicist façade dates back to 1791. Today Lichtenštejnsky Palác houses the Prague Academy of Music.

Lichtenstein Palace

MALÁ STRANA TOWN HALL (MALOSTRANSKÁ RADNICE)

The former Malá Strana Town Hall acquired its municipal function at the end of the 15th century. The interior was altered in 1660, the

Site of important negotiations

exterior in the 19th century. It was here that the important negotiations concerning the **Bohemian edict of religious toleration** took place in 1575, amongst others. The building was given its current appearance during the late Renaissance (1617 to 1622); today it is used for cultural events. The doorway with the fine armorial bearings of the city was added in 1660. In the course of building work undertaken in the town hall's cellar vaults, valuable pre-1600 texts were discovered, including the »Lesser Quarter Hymnal« (1572), which is now preserved in the State Library.

✷✷ ST NICHOLAS (CHRÁM SVATÉHO MIKULÁŠE)

Former Jesuit church
The former Jesuit church was erected on the site of a Gothic church of the same name. Three generations of Prague's best Baroque architects were commissioned to build it. The great nave with side chapels, galleries and vaulting was the work of **Kryštof Dientzenhofer**, carried out between 1704 and 1711. Conveying the typically Baroque sense of life and vitality, the two-storey façade completed in 1710 is regarded as the greatest achievement of Bohemian Baroque. The coat-of-arms of the Count of Kolovrat above the main doorway and the statues of the fathers of the church on the balustrade are from the workshop of Johann Friedrich Kohl . The chancel with its 75m/246ft-high dome was built by Kilián Ignác Dientzenhofer from 1737 to 1751. Construction of the church was completed by Anselmo Lurago with the erection of the 79m/260ft bell-tower (1756).

❶ Nov–March 9am–4pm, April–Oct 9am–5pm, admission 70 Kč, concerts 490 Kč

Interior
The sumptuous interior of the church is regarded as a prime example of high Baroque. The overwhelming overall impression derives from the coloured stucco marble, rich sculptural ornamentation and outstanding frescoes. The large ceiling fresco above the nave was painted in 1760/1761 by Johann Lucas Kracker; it shows scenes from the life of St Nicholas. The dome fresco depicts the glorification of the saint and the Last Judgement (1752 – 1753), and is by Franz Xaver Palko, who also painted the wall frescoes in the chancel in collaboration with Joseph Hager. The sculptures in nave and choir, and the figure of St Nicholas on the main altar, are by Ignaz Franz Platzer the Elder; the mighty organ (1745) was made by Thomas Schwarz.
The artificial marble pulpit ornamented with gold is the work of Richard and Peter Prachner (1765); it is decorated in Rococo style with allegories of *Faith, Hope and Charity*, and with the *Beheading of John the Baptist*. The side altars in the transept have paintings by Johann Lucas Kracker, the *Visitation of the Virgin Mary* and *Death of St Joseph*, both dating from 1760. The altarpieces and ceiling paintings

MARCO ◉ POLO TIP

! *Big Brother is listening*   Insider Tip

During the Socialist era the Church of St Nicholas bell tower was used as a listening post by the State Security secret police. They tapped the embassies in the area with radio transmitters, and kept diplomats' windows under surveillance with binoculars. Now anyone can climb the so-called »earpiece« to enjoy the charming views of the Malá Strana rooftops. (April, May daily 10am –6pm, May Fri–Sat until 10pm, June–Oct until 7pm, Dec until 5pm).

in the side chapels, by Ignaz Raab, Franz Xaver Palko and others, are also worth seeing. The 150 sq m/1614 sq ft ceiling painting by Kracker is one of the largest of its kind in Europe. The Nicholas figure of the painted scenes is the 4th-century bishop of Myra in Asia Minor, who was seen in the Middle Ages as patron saint of municipal authorities and guardian of justice.

St Nicholas, surrounded by angels, dominates the action; he holds his episcopal staff in his left hand, while his right hand is raised in blessing. In another scene a priest is seen distributing little bottles with miracle-working oil presented as a gift by the saint. St Nicholas then gives money to a man whose poverty is forcing him to sell his daughter.

The painting on the right-hand side of the vault refers to a 14th-century martial conflict, in which St Nicholas's intervention saved three Romans from execution. On the left-hand side a coastal landscape is used to suggest that St Nicholas was also venerated as protector of seafarers and merchants. Pictures of coasts and seaports had a great appeal at the time. On the north side of the church are the cloisters of the former Jesuit order (13th/14th century), partially redesigned in Baroque style in the 17th century.

ST THOMAS (KOSTEL SVATÉHO TOMÁŠE)

On the northeast side of the square, at the point where Letenská branches off, stands the Church of St Thomas. The church, whose Gothic origins can still be clearly discerned in the buttresses on the outside walls of the presbytery, was founded in the year 1285 for the order of Augustinian Hermits, and completed by 1379, together with

Gothic origins

From the life of St Augustine: the ceiling frescoes inside the Church of St Thomas

the adjacent former Augustinian monastery (now an old people's home) and St Thomas Brewery. The restructuring in high Baroque style (1727 – 1731) was undertaken by Kilián Ignác Dientzenhofer. In a niche above the Renaissance doorway by Campione de Bossi (1617) stand statues of St Augustine and St Thomas, created by Hieronymus Kohl in 1684. The lavish interior, not open to visitors, contains paintings and statues by famous Bohemian artists. Wenzel Lorenz Reiner painted the ceiling fresco in the nave in 1730, with scenes from the life of St Augustine. The pictures from the St Thomas legend in the chancel and the dome are also by Reiner. Karel Škréta designed the main altar in 1731; the figures of saints are by Johann Anton Quittainer, Ferdinand Maximilian Brokoff and Ignaz Müller. Further works by Karel Škréta adorn the altars in the transept (St Thomas, 1671) and the chancel (Assumption of the Virgin Mary, 1644).

✳ Letná Gardens (Letenské sady)

✦ D/E 3

Location: Praha 6, Hradčany, Na baště sv. Tomáše, Praha 7, Holešovice, Kostelní
Tram: 1, 8, 12, 17, 18, 22, 26

Extensive parklands — Northeast of Prague Castle, above the left bank of the Vltava, are the Letná heights. It was here that the coronation of Ottokar II took place in 1261. In 1858 the plateau was given to the city authorities, who made it into a park. Steps lead up from Svatopluk Čech Bridge to the viewing platform of the fortress-like base of the Stalin monument that was dismantled in 1962 (30m/99ft high, and weighing 14,000 tons). The sculpture, once the largest in the world, had a short life-span: one year after its unveiling, Stalin was condemned by Khrushchev and the gigantic monument was blown up. In its place now stands an enormous metronome by Vratislav Novák and there is a fine view of Prague, Petřín hill and St Vitus Cathedral (Prague Castle).

Hanavský Pavilion got its name from the foundries of Count Hanavský, where the iron pavilion was made for the 1891 World's Fair from a design by Z. E. Fiala; in 1898 it was moved to Letná plateau and transformed into a restaurant with a panoramic view.

Hanavský Pavilion

The second pavilion is the one made for the Brussels Expo of 1958. Czechoslavakia's pavilion was re-erected here after the Expo was over. The prize-winning pavilion, with a restaurant inside, now offers little more than a good view of the historic city centre.

Czechoslovakia Pavilion

Lobkowicz Palace (Lobkovický palác)

✦ C 4

Location: Praha 1, Malá Strana, Vlašská 19
Tram: 12, 22

Today, Lobkowicz Palace is the home of the German embassy. The early Baroque building was erected at the beginning of the 18th century by Giovanni Battista Alliprandi; in 1769 it was redesigned by Michael Ignaz Palliardi and the side wings were raised. From 1753 the palace belonged to the Lobkowicz family, whose coat-of-arms appear on the gable. The finely structured façade with its impressive doorway is adorned by a tympanum complete with heraldry and symbols, and an attica with numerous statues. A ceiling fresco in the stairwell shows the triumph of peace over war; it is attributed to Johann Jakob Steinfels, as are more of the skilful paintings in the interior (c1720). The garden side is embellished by a projecting cylindrical building and the Sala terrena, a pilastered hall with three round-arch arcades opening onto the memorial courtyard. From the three-winged memorial courtyard at the back there is a way through a wrought-iron gate (with sculptures of the abduction of Proserpina and Oreithyia) to the garden terraces, established at the time of building and adapted at the end of the 18th century to a less formal English landscaping style.

Seat of the German Embassy

MARCO ⊕ POLO INSIGHT

? Go Trabi, go!

In October 1989 the building played host to momentous scenes when more than 4500 GDR citizens wanting to flee their country sought admission here. Their refusal to give up forced the authorities eventually to let them travel to the Federal Republic of Germany, but they had to leave their beloved Trabant cars behind. This historic event is commemorated by the bronze Trabant *Quo Vadis?* by David Černý which stands in the embassy's garden (1989).

Schoenborn Palace

Vlašská runs down along the foot of Petřín hill, and turns into the street called Tržiště. Here stands the spaciously laid out Schoenborn Palace (Schönbornský palác, no. 15) with its relatively unadorned and yet imposing façade. Today the palace is the home of the **American embassy** – it is not easy to gain access here, any more than to Lobkowicz Palace. Giovanni Santini-Aichl provided the four-winged building with gables and dormer windows, and the passage through to the courtyard with four giant statues, in about 1715. By the mid-17th century Schoenborn Palace garden was already famous. Its terraces rise from a checkerboard parterre to an arcaded gloriette (formerly a wine-press).

Loretánská Alley (Loretánská ulička)

✳ C 4

Location: Praha 1, Hradčany
Tram: 22, 23

Dwelling at number 1

Loretánská Alley is an alley running east-west between Hradčany Square in front of Prague Castle and Loreta Square in Malá Strana. Of historic interest is the dwelling at number 1, which until 1784 served as Hradčany Town Hall ; it was built at the beginning of the 17th century by K. Oemichen of Oberheim, following the promotion of Hradčany district to a royal town in 1598. Remains of the imperial coat-of-arms on the sgraffito façade and the Hradčany coat-of-arms over the doorway bear witness to this glittering era.

Hrzán Palace

Hrzán Palace (at number 9) also warrants a special mention; it was originally a Gothic house owned by master builder Peter Parler. In the mid-16th century the building was remodelled in Renaissance style, and in the late 18th century it was given its late-Baroque façade. At the beginning of the 20th century Ferdinand Engelmüller's (1867–1924) school of painting was located here, as commemorated by a bust in the courtyard. Refashioned for the last time in the mid-1950s, the palace is used today for official governmental and ceremonial purposes.

Loreta Square (Loretánské náměstí)

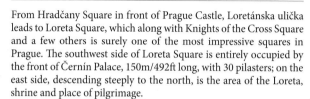

C 4

Location: Praha 1, Hradčany, Loretánské náměstí
Tram: 22, 23

From Hradčany Square in front of Prague Castle, Loretánska ulička leads to Loreta Square, which along with Knights of the Cross Square and a few others is surely one of the most impressive squares in Prague. The southwest side of Loreta Square is entirely occupied by the front of Černín Palace, 150m/492ft long, with 30 pilasters; on the east side, descending steeply to the north, is the area of the Loreta, shrine and place of pilgrimage.

Place of pilgrimage

** LORETA

The Loreta is the best-known pilgrimage destination in Bohemia. The Loreto cult – part of the Cult of the Virgin Mary – spread from Italy to Central Europe as early as the 15th century. It originated in the biblical story of the house of the Holy Family in Nazareth, where the archangel Gabriel announced the birth of Christ to the Virgin Mary. From the 13th century, a legend spread according to which the holy house (Casa Santa) was transported to Italy in order to protect it from infidels; this legend found great favour among Catholics in the Baroque era. During the Counter-Reformation, some 50 such places of pilgrimage were established in Bohemia on the model of the medieval Casa Santa Loreta shrine in an attempt to increase the popularity of Catholicism.

Part of the Cult of the Virgin Mary

❶ Tue–Sun 9am–12.15pm and 1pm–4.30pm, admission: 130 Kč
Photo pass 100 Kč, www.loreta.cz

Different architectural styles have left their mark on the Loreta. The Casa Santa was completed in 1631; the cloisters of 1634 were given a second storey after 1740. The façade is dated post-1721 and is

Architectural history

based on **designs by Kryštof and Kilián Ignác Dientzenhofer**. In erecting the main façade, the architects were charged with the task of creating a uniform front for the complex of buildings dating from different eras, and one which would offer an appropriate architectural response to the monumental Černín Palace on the opposite side of the square. Patrons of the façade were Count Philipp of Lobkowicz, Duke of Sagan, and his wife Eleonore Carolina; their impaled arms were inset over the main doorway by Johann Friedrich Kohl. In addition, the sculptor created the statue group of St Felix of Cantalice, St John Nepomuk, and probably also SS Francis and Anthony over the main portal (1721). For the somewhat older, early-Baroque bell tower, which dominates the façade, the Prague clockmaker P. Naumann in 1694 set up chimes with 27 bells (total weight approx. 1540kg/1.5 tons), purchased by wealthy merchant Eberhard of Glauchau in 1694 from the Amsterdam bell and gun-barrel foundry of Claude Fremy. In summer the bells ring out the Czech Marian hymn Tisíckrát pozdravujeme Tebe (»We greet thee a thousand times«) every hour.

Casa Santa In the middle of the cloisters, with their upward extension of arcades, stands Casa Santa, the architectural and spiritual centre of the pilgrimage complex; the patron was Countess Benigna Katharina of Lobkowicz (1626). The chapel's master builder was **Giovanni Battista Orsi** from Como; he completed it in 1631. The original painting on the façade was replaced from 1664 by sculptures and stucco reliefs modelled on those in Italy, with scenes from the life of the Virgin Mary, Old Testament prophets and pagan sibyls (G. Agosto, G. B. Colombo and Giovanni Battista Cometa; 1664). On the chapel's east wall, the Casa Santa legend is depicted. The interior is adorned with picture cycles from the Virgin Mary's life painted by Malá Strana artist František Kunz in 1695, as well as a silver altar and a Madonna carved out of lime-wood, encased in a silver wreath of winged angels attributed to Prague goldsmith Markus Hrbek. Casa Santa's silver adornments have a combined weight of more than 50kg/110lb.

Fountains In the courtyard, on either side of Casa Santa, are two fountains by Johann Michael Brüderle (1739 – 1740). Completed after Brüderle's death by Richard J. Prachner, they have now been replaced by copies. One shows the Assumption of the Virgin Mary; the other, the Resurrection of Christ.

Cloisters The ground level of the cloisters, begun in 1634, has vault frescoes by Felix Anton Scheffler (1750; restored 1882), with symbolic renderings of the Lauretanian litany. Against the arcade walls are several altars with pictures of saints by unknown artists of the late-Baroque era.

The Loreta Treasury is in the upper west passage of the cloisters. Mass   **Treasury**
vestments and liturgical items can be viewed here, also precious
monstrances from the 16th to the 18th century. These include: the
Small Pearl Monstrance, adorned with 266 diamonds and a ruby in
addition to pearls (1680); the Ring Monstrance of 1748 made of sil-
ver-gilt (492 diamonds, 186 rubies, a sapphire, 24 pearls, and emer-
alds, amethysts and garnets); and the famous sunburst Diamond
Monstrance (more than 6200 diamonds from the estate of Ludmilla
Eva Franziska Kolovrat), made in Vienna by court jewellers Matthias
Stegner and Johann Künischbauer in 1699.

There are seven cloister chapels. Of particular note are the chapels of   **Chapels**
St Francis Seraphinus (1717) and St Anthony of Padua (1710 – 1712),
both by Kryštof Dientzenhofer. The former has a main altar by Matthias Wenzel Jäckel with a picture of the saint from the workshop of
Prague's great Baroque painter, Peter Johann Brandl. Jäckel was a key
contributor to the sculpture in the Anthony of Padua chapel. He
made the altar, for which Sebastian Zeiler provided the paintings. On
the east side of Loreta in the middle of the cloisters is the Church of
the Nativity of Our Lord (Kostel Narození Páně). Begun by Kryštof
Dientzenhofer in 1717, work was continued by his son Kilian Ignaz
and completed in 1735 by Georg Aichbauer. The light interior is
dominated by a high altar with Nativity altarpiece by Johann Georg

The Casa Santa at the sacred Loreta site in Prague is based on the Santa
Casa di Loreto – the house of the Virgin Mary, according to legend

Heintsch. The ceiling fresco Christ in the Temple (1735 – 1736) by Wenzel Lorenz Reiner is painted in delicate colours, and shows the influence of Venetian illusionism on the artist. The ceiling frescoes Adoration of the Shepherds and Adoration of the Magi (1742) are the work of Johann Adam Schöpf, who headed the Prague painters' guild from 1740 to 1741.

ČERNÍN PALACE (ČZERNÍNSKÝ PALÁC)

Palace à l'italiana The monumental Černín Palace stands on the southwest corner of Loreta Square. Its 150m/492ft-long frontage with high diamond-patterned ashlar plinth and 29 colossal pilasters was commissioned in 1669, modelled on Palladian architecture by Count Humprecht Jan Černín of Chudenice, imperial ambassador to Venice. His son, Hermann Černín, completed the building in 1697. Italian builders and stonemasons were employed throughout, the most important being Francesco Caratti.

Alterations František Maximilian Kaňka carried out alterations on the palace after 1720. The adjacent formal gardens on the north side and the magnificent stairway with ceiling fresco (Fall of the Titans, 1718) by Wenzel Lorenz Reiner date from the same period. During the French occupation of Prague in 1741/1742 the building suffered grave damage; it was repaired by Anselmo Lurago between 1744 and 1749. Three new front doorways were added; the orangery in the garden was remodelled in Rococo style. In the mid-18th century Ignaz Franz Platzer created several sculptures for the palace. In 1851 the building was finally turned into a barracks. In the early 1930s it was restored, then becoming the seat of the Ministry of Foreign Affairs. Many citizens of Prague can recall the joke about the ministry which did the rounds under Socialism: »How many people actually work in this gigantic building? Around half of them!«

With the plain design typical of Capuchin architecture, this is the first **Capuchin** Capuchin monastery in Bohemia (Kapucínský klášter, 1600 – 1602) **monastery** and occupies the north side of Loreta Square, set down on a slightly lower level. A covered bridge-passage links the building with the Loreta Monastery opposite. Adjoining the monastery is a simple church of Our Lady which was once adorned with 14 Gothic panel paintings of unknown origin (now in the National Gallery).

Mánes Exhibition Hall

D 5/6

Location: Praha 1, Nové Město, Masarykovo nábřeží
Metro: Karlovo náměstí
Tram: 17, 21

❶ Tue–Sun
10am–6pm
Admission: 150 Kč
www.ncvu.cz

The Mánes Exhibition Hall (also known as the Mánes Gallery; no. 20) **No frills** was built between 1923 and 1930 in Constructivist style from designs by Otakar Novotný for the Mánes Artists' Society founded in 1898, on the site of the former Šítka mills. The exhibition hall's severe Functionalism contrasts sharply with the surrounding Art Nouveau and Classicist buildings, and with the water tower alongside it. The Mánes Artists' Society played an uncompromisingly modern role – just like the architecture of the time – which was of decisive importance in the opening up of Czech art to modernity. Today the building stages temporary exhibitions of contemporary art.

Beside the Mánes Gallery stands a 15th-century Renaissance tower **Renaissance** (Šítkovská věž), which has suffered from fires and bombardment and **tower** been restored several times; it contrasts nicely with the modern building. The Baroque roof dates from the end of the 18th century. The water tower is named after mill owner Jan Šítka (born 1451); since the late 15th century it has supplied the wells and fountains of upper Nové Město with water.

Žofín (also called Slav Island, Slovanský ostrov) came into existence **Žofín** in the 18th century through natural silting. From the 1830s the island developed into the centre of Prague's political and social life. Concerts, balls and congresses took place here – the latter especially in the revolution year of 1848. Famous composers such as Hector Berlioz and Franz Liszt performed their works here. The renovated neo-Renaissance building on the island dates from 1884. In the same year the Rudolfinum opened, and a good 25 years later the Municipal House; cultural life increasingly centred on these two buildings.

Mariánské Square (Mariánské náměstí)

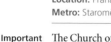

✦ **E 4**

Location: Praha 1, Staré Město
Metro: Staroměstská

Important site in the Reformation

The Church of the Virgin Mary on the Puddle once stood on Mariánské Square (Mariánské náměstí), which played an important role during the German Reformation. Following alterations made at the beginning of the twentieth century, only the south and west sides of the square were retained in their original form.

THE BLUE ROOM

Mr Ragtime

The smallest museum in the city is dedicated to Prague's »Mr Ragtime«. **Jaroslav Ježek** (1906 – 1942) famous for the legendary »Bugatti Step«, an irrepressible up-tempo number for piano and jazz orchestra, guaranteed to set the dance floor alight to this day. Ježek's piano room is designed in the Functionalist style of the 1930s and – as it is inside a private residence – can only be visited on Tuesdays from 1pm to 6pm.

❶ Kaprova 10, corner of Mariánské Square, admission 10 Kč, www.nm.cz

CLAM-GALLAS PALACE (CLAM-GALLASŮV PALÁC)

City archives

Today the former Clam-Gallas Palace houses the city archives (entrance from Husova třída, the road running south from Mariánské Square). The magnificent Baroque palace was built in 1707 according to plans by Viennese architect Johann Bernhard Fischer von Erlach; its patron was Johann Wenzel, Count von Gallas. Stone giants guard the doorway on Husova ulice, which intersects with Karlova, one of the sections of the Prague »coronation procession« route.

When the palace was renovated at the end of the 1980s it surprisingly transpired that the heads of the 3m/10ft-tall figures had been replaced by copies at the beginning of the 20th century. The doorway giants, parapet figures and fountain statue in the first courtyard are the work of Matthias Bernhard Braun.

Carlo Carlone created the stairwell frescoes in the years 1727 to 1730. He was also responsible for ceiling paintings in two rooms on the second floor (Olympus, Coronation of Art and Science), and in the library (Luna, Helios and Stars).

In the southeast corner of the square, close to the wall of the Clam-Gallas courtyard, stands the **fountain statue Vltava** by Václav Prachner (1812). The west side of Mariánské Square is bordered by the extensive complex of the former Jesuit college, the ▶Klementinum.

On the east side of Mariánské Square stands the **New Town Hall (Nová radnice)**, built in late Art Nouveau style between the years 1909 and 1912. Since 1945 this building has housed the chancellery of the mayor of Prague, the large meeting chamber, and municipal offices.

The two statues on the outer ends of the façade are by Ladislav Šaloun; they depict the Iron Knight and Chief Rabbi Löw (▶Josefov). The allegorical relief at the entrance to the town hall and the figures Auditing and Book-keeping are by Stanislav Sucharda; the groups Frugality, Strength and Perseverance on the balcony were designed by J. Mařatka.

❶ Tue–Sun 10am–6pm, admission for Opera Barocca 550 Kč

Impressive: a staircase in the Baroque splendour of Clam-Gallas Palace

Mucha Museum (Muchově muzeu)

✳ **E/F 4/5**

Location: Praha 1, Nové Město, Panská 7
Metro: Můstek
Tram: 3, 9, 14, 24
❶ daily 10am–6pm
Admission: 180 Kč
www.mucha.cz

This little museum is found in Kaunický palác at Panská 7, a street running parallel to Wencelas Square. The name of the Art Nouveau artist (1860 – 1939) is inextricably linked with the city, even though he was born in Ivančice, South Moravia.

Rejected by the Academy of Fine Arts in Prague, he worked painting theatrical scenery in Vienna before studying art in Munich and Paris. His big breakthrough virtually happened overnight when he designed a poster for the actress Sarah Bernhardt in the year 1894. »La divina« was so impressed, she offered him a contract for six years. Thereafter, Mucha's creations for the 1900 Universal Exhibition in Paris caused a sensation. He went on to teach in New York, Philadelphia and Chicago before returning home in 1910 to work on his Slav Epic, comprising 20 monumental paintings, which he bestowed to the state in 1928. By this time, the artist – once so scorned by the establishment – had made such an impression on the world of art that many spoke of »Mucha style« rather than Art Nouveau or Secession. The exhibition begins with the *Panneaux Décoratifs* which made Mucha famous: posters printed in Paris at the turn of the previous century, affordable because they were produced in large quantities, and they include Mucha's designs for Sarah Bernhardt which made him a high-profile representative of Parisian Art Nouveau. Alongside the few oil paintings, exhibits include photographs of models, sketches, notes and pastel drawings. Mucha's handbook for decorative artists, in which he recorded his designs, offers an insight into his creative ideas. Also of interest are the *Documents Décoratifs* and the *Figures Décoratives* (use of the human body as decorative element) which appeared three years later.

✱ Municipal House (Reprezentační dům)

✛ E/F 4

Location: Praha 1, Staré Město, Náměstí republiky 5
Metro: Náměstí Republiky
Tram: 5, 8, 14, 26

❶ Thu–Tue with guided tour at 11am, 1pm, 3pm
Admission: 290 Kč
www.obecni-dum.cz

Art Nouveau jewel   The Municipal House (Obecní dům) was built in the years 1906 to 1911 from designs by Antonín Balšánek and Osvald Polívka on the historic site where once the Royal Court had been established in 1380 and abandoned in 1547. It is considered the city's finest Art Nouveau building, with a restaurant steeped in tradition, a café, a wine tavern, exhibition rooms, offices and Prague's largest concert hall, the Smetana Hall (Smetanova síň, complete with organ), and is a typical example of Czech Secession architecture of the late 19th and early 20th centuries, with its

Over four hundred years of architectural history lie between the Powder Tower (on the left) and the Municipal House (on the right)

predilection for ornamentation, geometrical forms and elaborate detail, plant motifs and the ever-recurring theme of youth. A whole generation of artists contributed to the exterior and interior design. The façade ornamentation, the balcony pillar supports and the ceiling mouldings in the Smetana Hall are by Karel Novák; Ladislav Šaloun designed the allegories *Humiliation and Resurgence of the Nation* on the front, as well as Bohemian Dances and Vyšehrad on the Smetana Hall podium. The symbolic wall frescoes of the fine arts in Primator Hall were done by Alfons Mucha; in Rieger Hall there are paintings by Max Švabinský and in Palacký Hall stands a bust by Josef Václav Myslbek. Allegorical ornamentation also adorns Grégr Hall, while Sladkovský Hall was provided with landscape paintings by V.I. Ullmann.

MARCO ⊕ POLO TIP

! *Timeless fashion splendour* Insider Tip

The fairy tale of Cinderella revisited: Blanka, daughter of a poor glass cutter from the small Bohemian town of Světlá nad Sázavou, was alreadydrawing beautiful clothes as a child. In Prague she attended . In Prague she attended the Arts, Architecture and Design and met her prince, Makram Matragi from Lebanon, a student at the Czech Technical University. After they were married, he took her with him to the Orient. There, the Czech redhead enchanted the richest of the rich with her fashion creations, as imaginative as if they had been lifted from One Thousand and One Nights.
A permanent exhibition of Blanka Matragis dreamy robes, jewellery and porcelain can be admired in the Gaming Parlours of the Municipal House: Mon–Sun 10am–7pm Admission: 260 Kč, www.blanka.com

POWDER GATE (PRAŠNÁ BRÁNA)

This 65m/213ft late-Gothic tower, through which the southern trade route into Prague passed, was modelled on Old Town Bridge Tower (Charles Bridge) and formed part of the Staré Město fortifications. Building of this gate started in 1475; there was an earlier fortified gate here, built in the 13th century. Master builder M. Rejsek erected the tower for King Vladislav Jagiello. Vladislav lived initially in the adjacent royal court, no longer in existence; when he moved his residence back to Prague Castle the importance of the Powder Gate lessened. The present name arose in the 18th century when the gate served as a gunpowder store. When the city was besieged in 1757 by Frederick the Great of Prussia, the sculptural ornamentation was severely damaged. Josef Mocker undertook neo-Gothic renovations in 1875. The sculptures include portraits of Bohemian kings and patron saints. Inside, the **exhibition »Royal Court«**, spread over three floors, illustrates life in medieval Prague. The climb up 186 stone steps is rewarded by a very fine view of the city.

❶ Opening hours: April–Sept Mon–Sun 10am–10pm, Oct, March Mon–Sun 10am–8pm, Nov–Feb Mon–Sun 10am–6pm, admission: 75 Kč

The Hibernian House (U Hybernů) stands opposite the Municipal House and was originally a late-Baroque church, built in the years 1652 – 1659 by the monastery of Irish Franciscans (Hibernians) who had been there since 1629. The east and north wings of the monastery were added in the 18th century. After the dissolution of the monastery in 1786, and the closure of the church four years later, J. Zobel converted the church into a Customs House with Classicist façade (1808 – 1811), using plans by Georg Fischer; the sculptural ornamentation is by Franz Xaver Lederer (1811). In the early 1940s the interior of the Hibernian House was redesigned for exhibitions and cultural events.

Hibernian House

Museum of Decorative Arts

───────────────── ✦ E 4

Location: Praha 1, Staré Město, 17. listopadu 2
Metro: Staroměstská
Tram: 17, 18
❶ Wed–Sun 10am–6pm, Tue until 7pm
Admission: 120 Kč
www.upm.cz

The Museum of Decorative Arts (Uměleckoprůmyslové muzeum) on the west edge of the Old Jewish Cemetery (Josefov) was founded in 1884. The fin-de-siècle house was built under the supervision of architect Josef Schulz in neo-Renaissance style, 1897 to 1901 and is itself a work of art. It displays a world-famous collection of glass, porcelain and ceramics, as well as furniture (16th – 19th century) and gold artefacts (15th – 19th century). Further exhibition areas include textiles, measuring instruments, clocks, book-bindings, working drawings, small bronzes and coins in their historical development (going back in some cases to the 8th century AD). Temporary exhibitions are staged on occasion. The specialist art history and decorative arts library is also open to the public; it includes a collection of 15th-century manuscripts.

World-famous collection

Na příkopě
(On the Moat)

───────────────── ✦ E 4

Location: Praha 1, Staré Město (pedestrian zone)
Metro: Můstek, Náměstí Republiky

The street Na příkopě (On the Moat) is considered the liveliest in the city. It links the lower end of Wenceslas Square to the Square of the

Republic (Náměstí Republiky). Na příkopě, Wenceslas Square and Národní třída with their side-streets and lanes form the so-called »Golden Cross«, Prague's centre of business and commerce, with administrative and office buildings, banks, arcades, shops, hotels, restaurants and cafés. Once there really was a moat between the fortifications of Staré Město and Nové Město, flowing along what is now the Na příkopě pedestrian zone, but it was filled in as long ago as the year 1760. Looking from Wenceslas Square, Staré Město spreads out on the left, Nové Město on the right.

Distinctive buildings

The distinctive building on the corner of Na Příkopě and Na Můstku was built in the late 1970s for the administration of the **ČKD Praha machine factory**. A large clock from a previous building on the site crowns the gable of the modern steel construction. Completely renovated, it now houses shops and offices. Opposite, on the corner with Wenceslas Square, stands **House Koruna**, built in 1911 from a design by Antonín Pfeiffer. The three lower storeys are dominated by shop windows. A spacious passage links the two streets, and was the model for subsequent buildings in the vicinity. Nearby stands **Sylva-Taroucca Palace** (no. 10), a jewel of Bohemian late-Baroque housing a museum as well as a fast-food restaurant. Anselmo Lurago built the Baroque palace for the nobleman Ottavio Piccolomini in the years 1743 to 1751 from plans by Kilián Ignác Dientzenhofer. Under the influence of French Classicism, two courtyards, a garden with a riding-school and a gateway with pillars were created. Distinctive characteristics of Dientzenhofer's late style are discernible on the façade: alongside the triangular gable which crowns the three central axes of the nine-axis façade, two smaller gables arch over the middle axis of the two outer segments. Here Dientzenhofer allowed a measure of Rococo influence. The rich decorative structure of the façade with mythological sculpture and the ornamentation of the Rococo steps are by Ignaz Franz Platzer the Elder. The interior stucco is by Carlo Bossi. The frescoes on the stairwell vaulting (*Helios' chariot* and *Allegories of the Four Seasons*) are by Václav Bernard Ambrozzi. The neighbouring neo-Romanesque house **The Black Rose** (**U Černé růže**) once belonged to the University of Prague. German followers of the great reformer Jan Hus met here from 1411. Disciples of the Black Rose (such as Draendorf and Turnow) made a major contribution to the spread of Hussite beliefs in

Coming to terms with the past...

Insider Tip

...the Czech way. In the **Museum of Communism** in Savarin Palace (Na Příkopě no. 10), visitors can go on a guided tour of the country's recent history. The museum's theme runs through the entire exhibition: Communism - The Dream, The Reality, The Nightmare. The museum was founded by American businessman Glenn Spicker (daily 9am–9pm, www.muzeumkomunismu.cz, admission: 190 Kč).

Germany. In the mid 20th century a luxury arcade opened here; to-day the reconstructed palace is populated by elite stores, offices and apartments.

The only Empire-style church in Prague, the **Church of the Holy Cross** (**Kostel svatého Kříže**), was built in the years 1819 – 1821 by J. Fischer for the Piarist teaching order. The Piarist convent's former school buildings are on Panská street.

The house at number 20 on Na Příkopě is in Bohemian Renaissance style, decorated with allegorical mosaics from designs by Mikoláš Aleš and reliefs from the workshops of Celda Klouček and Stanislav Sucharda.

The Baroque palace, Příchovských, was built from 1695 to 1700 by Count Jean B. Vernier de Rougemont. It was known as the **German House** from 1875 to 1945 because Prague's German population met there; after World War II it was renamed **Slav House** (**Slovanský dům**). Late 19th-century alterations gave it a Classicist appearance; today the renovated building houses a shopping centre with restaurants, cafés, garden and a multiplex cinema (www.slovansky-dum. cz). House number 24 on Na přikopě is the **Palace of the Czech State Bank**, built between 1935 and 1942; In previous incarnations, this was a trade finance bank and the famous Blue Star and Black Horse hotels, where European celebrities (including Liszt and Chopin) lodged in the 19th century. It was in the Blue Star that the Treaty of Prague between Austria and Prussia was signed in 1866.

National Gallery (Národní galerie)

Location: various locations (see below)
www.ngprague.cz

The National Gallery in Prague was established thanks to the »Society of Patriotic Friends of the Arts«, a group of predominantly Bohemian nobles and affluent Grand Burghers who founded a picture gallery in 1796. The collection grew and the Prague gallery was opened in the year 1804, making it the second oldest in Europe (after the Louvre in Paris, which opened in 1793). Emperor Franz Josef I sponsored expansion works in 1902 and in 1918 the National Gallery was handed over to the state. Today its collections – around 14,000 paintings, 7600 sculptures, 243,000 prints, 61,000 drawings and 12,000 oriental exhibits – are spread around the following locations across the city:

Society of Patriotic Friends of the Arts

Veletržní Palace (▶p.311, 20th and 21st-century art)
St Agnes Convent (▶p.192, medieval Bohemian and Central European art)

St George's Convent at ▶Prague Castle (Bohemian art, reign of Rudolf II to Baroque era)
Salm Palace (▶p.207, monothematic, individual exhibitions)
Schwarzenberg Palace on Hradčany Square (▶p.205, »Baroque in Bohemia«)
Sternberg Palace (▶p.300, collection of European art from antiquity to late Baroque)
Wallenstein Riding School in Valdštejnská, belonging to Wallenstein Palace (▶p.325, temporary National Gallery exhibitions)

National Museum (Národní muzeum)

✦ F 5

Location: Praha 1, Nové Město, Václavské náměstí 68
Metro: Muzeum
Tram: 11
❶ The main building on Wencelas Square is closed for general renovation until 2016.
www.nm.cz

More than 13 million exhibits The National Museum was founded in the year 1818 when a Bohemian Enlightenment group – among them, Count Kašpar Maria Šternberk, Josef Dobrovský and František Palacký – called for a museum to be founded; it was initially made up of various private collections and was located in Sternberg Palace on Hradčany Square. Towards the end of the 19th century, the collections finally acquired a building of their own. The National Museum is the oldest museum in the Czech Republic and has more than 13 million exhibits. Its main building on Wencelas Square houses the museums' comprehensive collections on natural sciences, ethnography and archaeology, a library boasting 3.6 million volumes and a collection of coins. The building's poor condition is a result of a direct hit from a bomb in World War II, Soviet gunfire in the Prague Spring of 1968 and the construction of the metro in the 1970s. Comprehensive renovation work began in 2011, projected to be completed in 2016, at a cost of €190 million Euros.

The rectangular main building was built in the years 1885 – 1890 in neo-Renaissance style from designs by Josef Schulz. It is approached by a double ramp and a triple flight of steps. Corinthian columns and pilasters structure the façade vertically. The central projection and tower with four-sided segmental cupola emphasize the centre of the building; the corner projections are each superelevated by smaller octagonal cupolas. The interior has an impressive six-armed staircase

Some 70m/230ft high, the façade of the domed structure on
Wencelas Square is based on the Louvre in Paris

with an arcaded gallery. A lofty pantheon extending over two floors
displays statues and busts of famous Czech figures. In the arches beneath the cupola, allegories of science, art, inspiration and power can
be seen.

Further collections belonging to the National Museum are housed in
various buildings inside and outside the city: **Náprstek Museum** on
Beethoven Square in town presents Asian, African and American
cultures, the Czech Museum of Music, the ▶Smetana Museum, the
Dvořák Museum (▶Villa Amerika), the Musaion – an ethnographic
museum in the former summer palace of the Kinský in the district of
Smíchov – and the **Lapidarium**, featuring the original sculptures salvaged from Charles Bridge in the grounds.

**Further
collections**

NATIONAL MUSEUM – NEW BUILDING
(NÁRODNÍHO MUZEA – NOVA BUDOVA)

Temporary exhibitions

Built for the Stock Exchange in 138 and converted in 1948 to the seat of the Czechoslovakian parliament, the prestigious structure alongside the main building on Wencelas Square is also part of the National Museum. Karel Prager designed an extension in the 1960s which added an two-storey steel superstructure. An ironic twist of fate: in the complex where the Communist cabinet used to sit, Radio Free Europe took up residence after the Velvet Revolution – a radio station financed by the US government in the former headquarters of a totalitarian power. Natural sciences and historical themes are presented here in temporary exhibitions. There is also an opportunity to learn more about Czechoslovakia under the Communist dictatorship. The impressive view across the city afforded by the conference room – where only the highest-ranking officials previously gathered – justifies a visit on its own. Similarly enticing, the café is graced with the same leather furniture on which Communist ministers took a break in the 1970s.

❶ New Town, Vinohradská 1, daily 10am–6pm (closed first Tue in the month), admission 60 Kč, families 100 Kč, www.nm.cz

National Technical Museum
✦ E 3

Location: Praha 7, Holešovice, Kostelní 42
Tram: 1, 8, 25, 26
❶ Tue–Sun 10am–6pm, 1st Thursday in the month until 8pm
Admission: 170 Kč
www.ntm.cz

Národní technické muzeum

The National Technical Museum (Národní technické muzeum) has a lot to offer the visitor to Prague. Situated on the north slope of Letná plateau (Letná Gardens), the museum conveys a vivid picture of the development of cinematography, radio and television technology, transport and mining. The 600m/1970ft-long reproduction coal mine is particularly worth seeing. In the large hall are automobiles, aeroplanes and engines, as well as Emperor Franz Joseph's court train (two coaches). Ths was the vehicle in which the Austrian heir to the throne, Franz Ferdinand, and his wife travelled to Sarajevo on 28 June 1914, where the disastrous assassination took place that led after the July crisis to the outbreak of World War I. Some aeroplanes are also on display in the courtyard to the right of the museum.

National Theatre (Národní divadlo)

⟶ **D/E 5**

Location: Praha 1, Nové Město, Národní třída 2
Metro: Národní třída
Tram: 6, 9, 17, 18, 21, 22, 23
Visits by appointment: tel. 224 901 506
www.narodni-divadlo.cz

The Czech National Theatre was built in the years 1868 to 1881 by Josef Zítek in neo-Renaissance style, modelled on the Nostitz Theatre; it burnt down shortly after the first performance. Josef Schulz, a pupil of Zítek, had the theatre rebuilt within the space of only two years, using money donated by the general public in a wave of national sympathy. On 18 November 1883 the first season began with the festive premiere of Smetana's national opera Libuše, which was composed for the occasion. The theatre was founded during an epoch of national resurgence, and embodied »all the yearnings and leanings of a people returning to European culture and consciousness, full of energy, action and enthusiasm after long slumbers«. The foundation stone had been hewn from Říp mountain, from where founding father Čech took possession of Bohemia. **Neo-Renaissance style**

The exterior, restored between 1976 and 1983, is lavishly adorned; free-standing statues round off the silhouette of the monumental building. Bohuslav Schnirch created the two groups of figures on the north façade attica (goddesses of victory; Apollo and the muses); the allegories of opera and drama on the west side, and the statues of Záboj and Lumír in the north façade niches, are from the workshop of Anton Wagner (Vienna). The allegories of singspiel and drama above the side entrance are by artist Josef Václav Myslbek. The same sculptor subsequently provided the busts of famous people for the portrait gallery and the allegory of music for the large foyer (1913). **Exterior**

All the leading artists of the time were involved in the interior decoration. The frescoes in auditorium, loggia and presidential salon deal with mystical and historical themes, or the world of theatre. The ceiling fresco by František Ženíšek in the auditorium shows eight allegories of the arts. The lunettes on the loggia overlooking Národní třída are by Josef Tulka. The impressive painting *Golden Age, Decline and Revival of Art* by František Ženíšek adorns the large foyer on the first balcony. In collaboration with Mikoláš Aleš, Ženíšek also painted the 14-arch Homeland cycle and the four wall paintings Pagan Myth, *** Interior**

Golden Chapel above the Vltava

The National Theatre, a testament to Czech national identity, has been largely financed by donations from citizens. Ceremoniously opened in 1881 to great celebrations, it burned down just two months after completion. Restoration work began immediately and the second opening was celebrated as soon as 18 November 1883 – once again to the sound of Libuše, an opera by Prague's mythical founding father Smetana.

❶ Triga

The chariots of the Victory Goddess on the Prague National Theatre are drawn by a three-horse triga – without precedent in antiquity – a unique creation of the sculptor Bohuslav Schnirch.

❷ Façade

The portico in front of the building is defined by a columned loggia which adds weight to the entrance. On the side facing the bank of the Vltava there is a passage for carriages.

❸ Foyer

Mikoláš Aleš (1852 – 1913) designed the 14 lunettes in the foyer on the theme of Homeland. In the spirit of neo-Romanticism, they depict mythical figures and significant historical scenes of the Czech people. The ceiling fresco by František Ženíšek (1849 – 1916) glorifies the Golden Age, Decline and Revival of Art all at once. Bronze busts of Czech composers are also on display.

❹ Auditorium

The semi-circular auditorium is also adorned with František Ženíšek ceiling frescoes exalting the fine arts. 17,000 visitors can be accommodated on the auditorium's four levels.

Fire-fighting operations during the devastating National Theatre fire of 1881.

* Nerudova

✦ C/D 4

Location: Praha 1, Malá Strana
Metro: Malostranská
Tram: 12, 22

Nerudova, once the main approach leading steeply up to Prague Castle, begins at Lesser Quarter Square. Formerly known by the German name of »Spornergasse«, it is one of the loveliest of Prague's cobbled streets, lined with predominantly late-Baroque townhouses. In the years 1845 – 1857, the writer Jan Neruda lived in the **House of the Two Suns** (U dvou slunců, no. 47); a memorial plaque on the early-Baroque façade commemorates this fact.

Jan Neruda's house

Morzin Palace (Morzinský palác, no. 5) is one of the finest Baroque palaces in Malá Strana. For this building – now the seat of the Romanian embassy – three houses were amalgamated in 1714, merging the Baroque architecture of Giovanni (Johann Blasius) Santini-Aichl with the sculpture of Ferdinand Maximilian Brokoff. Heraldic figures of Moors, emblems of the aristocratic Morzin (Moor) family, support the balcony; over the doorway are allegories of day and night. The house front opposite is adorned by a Baroque sign of a red eagle carried by two cherubs. Three little criss-cross violins form the pretty house-sign (►MARCOPOLO Insight p.256/259) of no. 12, inhabited by Prague's violin-maker Edlinger family in the years 1667 – 1748; now it is an inviting wine tavern. The originally Gothic, subsequently Renaissance-style Valkoun House (Valkounský dům, no. 14) also owes its late-Baroque appearance to Giovanni Santini-Aichl. It is worth taking a look at further house signs, such as that on the Renaissance »Golden Bowl« (U zlaté číše, no. 16), and the Baroque »House of St John Nepomuk« (U svatého Jana Nepomuckého, no. 18).

Morzin Palace

Norbert Vinzenz Kolovrat was patron of the Baroque Thun-Hohenstein Palace, no. 20, which was built between 1710 and 1725, again from plans by Giovanni Santini-Aichl. Immigrant son of an Italian stonemason, he belonged from 1700 to the leading high Baroque artists in Bohemia; the radical blending of Gothic and Baroque elements is characteristic of his style. Today the palace is the seat of the Italian embassy. Linked to Slavata Palace on Thunovská, it has a fine doorway with two heraldic spread eagles (Kolovrat family coat-of-arms), and the Roman divinities Jupiter and Juno. In the direction of Prague Castle stands the Church of St Kajetan, built from plans by Jean Baptiste Mathey and probably also by Santini (1691 – 1717); it is also known by the German name of the Theatinerkirche.

Thun-Hohenstein Palace

Signs and Surprises

Wenn im hohen Mittelalter ein Fremder auf der Suche nach dem Haus seines Freundes durch die Straßen Prags lief, musste er sich mit ganz anderen Problemen befassen als mit dem verzwickten Auseinanderklappen eines patentgefalteten Stadtplans und dem nervenaufreibenden Suchen nach dem Straßennamen in einem überfüllten Planquadrat. Nein, der mittelalterliche Fremde musste nicht nur ohne einen Stadtplan, sondern auch ohne Hausnummern oder gar Straßennamen auskommen.

When a stranger walked through the streets of Prague in the High Middle Ages, looking for the house of a friend, he had to contend with problems very different from the complicated unfolding of a newly patented map of the city, or the exasperating search for a street name in an overfilled square on the map. The medieval stranger had to make do without city map, without house numbers, and even without street names.

At a time when even family names were still unknown it would have been odd to introduce modern means of orientation, quite apart from the fact that few streets were clearly demarcated, and the direction streets took could quickly change. Hereditary family names only became necessary when trade blossomed in the twelfth century and large cities evolved in which a precise distinction needed to be made between people, especially in matters of law. At the same time people started to want an unmistakable way of identifying their house, which would outlast a change in ownership. This prompted the individual and imaginative creation of so-called house signs, visual representations in stone, wood or metal, which were fixed like a coat-of-arms above the entrance to a house in order to identify it.

Initially the signs were mostly drawn from items in the vicinity of the house, »By the Chestnut Tree«, or »By the Bridge«, or from the owner's profession, trade or craft. The owner of the house »U tlí pštrosaů« (At the Three Ostriches) next to Charles Bridge, for example, enjoyed a flourishing trade with ostrich feathers.

There were also symbolic depictions of professions such as a key for a locksmith, scissors for a tailor, or the famous »Three Little Violins« in Nerudova for a violin-maker. In addition, biblical representations were very popular. A careful observer will still find house signs like »The Golden Angel« or »The House at the Black Madonna« in Celetná. Depictions of animals also served as house signs, such as »The Three Little Bears« or »The Green Frog«, as did plants, like »The Three Red Roses«, or celestial bodies, such as »The Two Suns«. Importance was attached also to the magical properties of numbers.

A Pleasant Reminder of the Past

Modern house numbers, anything but imaginative – let alone magical – were introduced in 1770 under Empress Maria Theresa, who imitated French models in this matter. Her reasons were purely pragmatic – to make life easier for military recruiting officers. Gradually the significance of certain signs and symbols faded into oblivion, so that people are now uncertain about the origin of house signs like »The Golden Serpent«. It is known, however, that some family and even street names derive from certain house signs. The reverse may also be true. Yet Prague still displays a further idiosyncrasy: the our present-day visitor would be dumbfounded if he was directed to look for the house of »The Golden Vulture« with no explanation. It's easier with numbers, but today the house signs remain a pleasant reminder of the past.

Inn signs (on the left, in Josefov), guild emblems or the patron saint of the house – the meaning of many house signs has been lost today. The »Three Little Violins« (top left) can be traced back to the family of a violin-maker by the name of Edlinger in Nerudova (number 12). The other signs depicted here were photographed in the same street.

walls of the houses regularly boast not one but two numbers. The less showy number on a blue background always indicates the normal numbering, whereas the one on a red background represents the property registration number. Beneath it the city district is indicated. Just as the medieval stranger would have been driven to despair by this complicated system, so also

| Literary and musical memories | The neighbouring house, the Ass at the Cradle (Osel u kolébky) is the setting for Neruda's story A Week in a Quiet House. The quaint, old Malá Strana pharmacy, restored in 1980, is found at the House of the Golden Lion (U zlatého lva, no. 32). The Baroque Bretfeld Palace (no. 33) is also called »Summer and Winter«; illustrious guests once lodged here, including Wolfgang Amadeus Mozart and Giacomo Casanova. The earliest Malá Strana pharmacy was located in the House of the Golden Horseshoe (U Zlaté podkovy, no. 34). The Baroque townhouse at number 49 (U Bílé labutě) has a house sign consisting of an elaborate white swan. From here, it is just a short distance up the Ke Hradu steps to Prague Castle. |

> **!** MARCO ● POLO TIP
>
> *Tales of the Lesser Quarter* **Insider Tip**
>
> In the 19th century, Nerudova provided the setting for Czech writer Jan Neruda's stories. His *Tales of the Lesser Quarter*, first published in the year 1878, give an affectionate picture of everyday life in the 19th century, along with petit-bourgeois superstitions, scandals and gossip. A good read! (published by Vitalis).

** Old Town Square (Staroměstské náměstí)

——————————————————————— ✦ E 4

Location: Praha 1, Staré Město, Staroměstské náměstí
Metro: Staroměstská (A)
Tram: 17, 18

| Central marketplace | Old Town Square is second only to Prague Castle in its significance in the history of Prague. The 9000sq m/2.2ac square, with the monumental memorial to reformer Jan Hus in the centre, began in the 11th and 12th centuries as a central marketplace for merchants. Over the centuries the square has witnessed historic moments, both tragic and glorious. It was on the route of the traditional Bohemian kings' coronation procession, from the Powder Gate (p.244) to Prague castle, but it was also a place of execution. In 1621 the leaders of the Estates' revolt were executed on Old Town Square; a bronze plaque on the Old Town Hall records the names of the 27 put to death. In more recent history, the citizens of Prague demonstrated here for an independent Czechoslovakia in 1918, and in 1945 an exultant crowd welcomed the victorious Red Army. Old Town Square was also the scene of the violent end of the Prague Spring in 1968, |

**Old Town Square with the Gothic Church of Our Lady Before Týn
in the background**

when Warsaw Pact troops marched in. In 1988, on the 20th anniversary of the Prague Spring, thousands took part in a protest march through Staré Město, the Old Town, in favour of liberty and civil rights.

Building and restoration

Late 1987 saw the completion of large-scale restoration of Old Town Square and its magnificent buildings, which include the Old Town Hall, Týn Church and school, Goltz-Kinský Palace and the Church of St Nicholas (Staré Město). Most of the façades around the square are now coloured in pastel tones. A brass plate charts in Latin and Czech the path of the meridian once used to calculate time in Prague.

Jan Hus Memorial

The colossal memorial dominates the centre of the square. It was commissioned in the year 1903 and unveiled in 1915, on the 500th anniversary of the death of Jan Hus. Ladislav Šaloun (1870 – 1946) designed the sculpture, which shows the reformer amidst the persecuted and exiled.

** OLD TOWN HALL (STAROMĚSTSKÁ RADNICE)

History

The former town hall is used today for cultural and social events (e.g. weddings), but has retained its »Old Town Hall« name. The history of the Old Town Hall – parts of which date from the 11th century – is one of individual burgher houses and perpetual building activity. In 1338 King John of Luxembourg granted the Staré Město inhabitants leave to build a town hall as their own administrative centre. The core was the **Stein corner house**, which was extended by a square tower in the year 1364. The oriel chapel on the northeast side of the tower was dedicated in the year 1381; seriously damaged in 1945, it was later partially restored. The mayor of Prague announced in 2007 that plans were being made to complete the restorations in the near future. A casket is embedded in the wall with earth from the Dukla Pass, where Czechs and Russians repelled the German troops in the year 1944. On the east side hangs a bronze memorial **plaque to the leaders of the Czech Protestant revolt** who were executed in 1621, and set into the paving are two crossed white swords with thorn wreath, the date of the execution and 27 small crosses. A bust by Karel Lidický commemorates the Hussite preacher **Jan Želivský** who was executed in 1422. The Gothic doorway on the south front had been completed as the main entrance by 1480. In addition, the **Křiž House** was bought around the year 1360. The lettering »Praga Caput Regni« (»Prague, capital of the kingdom«) above the Renaissance window dates from 1520. The third building, the Mikeš House, was added in 1458 (remodelled in neo-Renaissance style, 1878).

❶ Mon 11am–6pm, Tue–Sun from 9am, tower: Mon 11am–10pm, Tue–Sun from 9am, admission 75 Kč (full tour includes viewing of the 12 Apostles in the Astronomical Clock), tower (extra charge) 105 Kč

The Cock House

The Cock House (U kohouta) became part of the town hall complex in 1830; a Romanesque room has survived in the cellar. The Renaissance ceilings and wall paintings on the first floor are also notable. Building acquisition and activity did not cease until the end of the 19th century. The town hall was seriously damaged on the penultimate day of World War II, when last remaining units of German armed forces fired on the tower: the neo-Gothic extensions (east and north wings) and the city archives were destroyed. Today there is a small park on this spot. The south wing was entirely restored in the years 1978 – 1981. The council chamber on the second floor is still preserved in its original Gothic form (1470). In the large meeting hall are two paintings by Czech historical painter Václav Brožik: *Jan Hus before the Council of Constance* and *The Election of George of Poděbrady as King of Bohemia*. Paintings by Cyril Bouda (1901 – 1984) adorn the room where weddings are celebrated. The City of Prague Gallery is located in the cloisters. From the third floor there is access by lift or stairs to the 69m/226ft Town Hall Tower. Don't miss the panoramic view of Prague's Old Town from the viewing gallery.

> **MARCO POLO TIP**
>
> ❗ *Time to get married?* **Insider Tip**
>
> The registry office is also located in the Old Town Hall. The garlanded carriages, gleaming vintage cars and wedding ceremonies with confetti pouring out of the old lead windows are sure to put the happy couple in the right mood – no need to read the banns, passports and birth certificates will suffice. Couples wishing to get married in the Old Town Hall on a Saturday, however, should reserve at least two months in advance (tel. 221 097 469).

✳✳ Astronomical Clock (Orloj)

»On this clock it was possible to see the movements of the heavens throughout the whole year with the number of months, days and hours. Rising and setting of the stars, the longest and the shortest days, the equinoctia, the feast days for the whole year, the length of day and night, new and full moon and the quarters, the three different striking hours according to the whole and the half clock«. This is how the painter, copper engraver and art publisher Merian described the horologium clockface on the south side of the Town Hall Tower in 1650. Scarcely anything has changed in 500 years. The original construction of the clock is said to date from 1410, and in 1490 Master Hanuš of Charles University made additions to it. The story goes that the councillors had Hanuš blinded in order to prevent him from

City of 100 Towers ...

... is only one of Prague's many nicknames, of which »Golden City« is certainly the best known. This graphic shows the most distinctive buildings in Prague that markt he skyline, be they old or new, tower or monument.

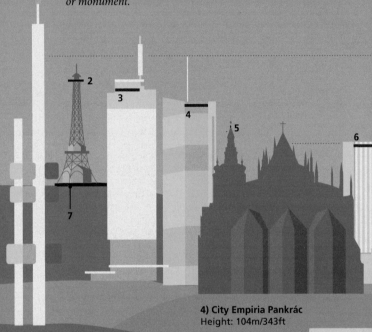

1) TVTower Žižkov
Height: 216m/713ft

2) Petřín (observation tower)
Height: 60m/198ft

3) City Tower Pankrác
Height: 109m/360ft

4) City Empiria Pankrác
Height: 104m/343ft

5) St Vitus Cathedral
Height: 96.5m/318.5ft

6) Panorama Hotel
Height: 79m/260ft

7) Petřín Hill
Height: 327m/1079ft

▶ TV Tower Žižkov	
Built in	1985–1992
Observation deck	100m/330ft
Function	transmission tower
Material	steel, concrete
Weight	11,800t

▶ Powder Tower	
Building started in	147
Roof added in	188
Function (former)	storage of gun powd
Material	sandstone, bri
Commissioned by	King Vladislaus

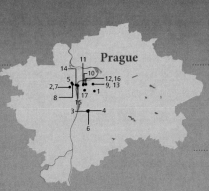

Prague

Height above sea level: 450m/1485ft

400m/1320ft

8) St Niklas Church
Height: 74m/244ft

9) Mausoleum at Vítkov Hill
Height: 31,5 m

10) Church of our Lady before Týn
Height: 80m/264ft

11) Old City Town Hall
Height: 69.5m/229ft

12) Powder Tower
Height: 65m/214ft

13) Jan Žižka
Height with base: 22m/72.6ft

14) Charles Bridge Tower (Lesser Quarter)
Height: 45m/148.5ft

350m/155ft

15) Charles Bridge Tower (Old City)
Height: 47m/155ft

16) Municipal House (dome)
Height: 45m/148.5ft

17) St Wenceslas
Height with base: 15.6m/51.5ft

300m/900ft

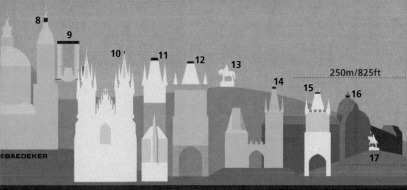

250m/825ft

©BAEDEKER

▶ Equestrian monument	Jan Žižka	▶ Equestrian monument	St Wenceslas
Built in	1930/1950	Built in	1912–1913
Heigth of figure	9m/28ft	Height of figure	7.2m/23.7ft
Design	Bohumil Kafka	Design	Josef Václav Myslbek
Material	bronze	Material	bronze (?)
Weight	16.5t	Weight	5.5t

making anything of the sort for any other city. Shortly before his death the blind man climbed the tower and stopped the clock mechanism before the Apostles' procession had begun. The clock stood still until 1551 – but here the legend ends: Jan Táborský restored the mechanism between 1552 – 1572.

The Astronomical Clock comprises three parts: Apostles' procession, clockface and calendar-wheel.

Apostles procession, clockface, calendar-wheel

The main attraction is the Apostles' procession with 19th-century figures that takes place each hour, on the hour from 9am to 9pm: with one hand Death pulls the passing-bell, with the other he lifts up the hourglass. The windows open, and Christ and the twelve Apostles move across. As the windows close, a cockerel flutters and crows in the niche and the hour chimes. A Turk shaking his head beside the clock, a miser gazing at his moneybags, and a vain man looking at his reflection in the mirror complement the allegory.

The clockface is divided into two circles. The upper one shows the movement of sun and moon, and the time. The lower one is subdivided into 24 segments and shows Bohemian time (from sunrise to sunset) in Arabic numerals.

The historical painter Josef Mánes (1820 – 1871) painted the scenes for the calendar-wheel. There are twelve round zodiac pictures, grouped around Prague's coat-of-arms, and scenes from rustic life for each of the months. The originals are on display in the Prague City Museum.

MINUTE HOUSE

Adjoining to the southwest is the Minute House (U minuty) with figural sgraffiti of biblical and mythological scenes. The house was built in around 1600; most of the sgraffiti were added in 1615, some later. The figure of a lion on the corner dates back to the 18th century. Through the arcades there is a passage to the smaller square of Malé náměstí.

Figural sgraffiti

Na Kamenci on the south side of Old Town Square is an originally Romanesque building with Gothic extensions; its late-Gothic doorway dates from the 16th century, the early Baroque façade from the 17th century. Next door to it is the early Baroque **House of the Blue Star** (U Modré hvězdy, no. 25), which has served wine since the 16th century. The **Golden Unicorn** (U Zlatého jednorožce, no. 20) outgrew its Romanesque form in the 14th century and was extended in late-Gothic style in 1496. The late-Baroque façade dates from the

Allegories of transience and desire adorn the Astronomical Clock at the Old Town Hall

18th century. A memorial plaque on the house commemorates the famous composer Bedřich Smetana, who founded his first music school here. The last of the magnificent Baroque houses on the south side of the square is the neo-Renaissance Štorchův dům, or Stork House (no. 16). Originally there a Gothic building here (14th/15th century); it was replaced in 1897 by today's building, according to plans by Friedrich Ohmann. The façade painting of *St Wenceslas on horseback* is by Mikoláš Aleš.

TÝN SCHOOL (TÝNSKÁ ŠKOLA)

Originally Gothic This originally Gothic building, with ribbed vaulting in the arcade on the east side, was extended in the mid-16th century in Venetian Renaissance style, and adorned with double gable. For four centuries, from the beginning of the 15th century, it housed the Týn parish school; in the mid-15th century the great master builder Matthias Rejsek of Prostějov taught here.

✳ CHURCH OF OUR LADY BEFORE TÝN (KOSTEL PANNY MARIE PŘED TÝNEM)

The Gothic Týn Church (Of Our Lady Before Týn) on Old Town Square is considered to be the emblem of Prague's Old Town. It is obscured a little by the school in front of it. Nevertheless, its two towers dominate the eastern side of the square. It was constructed with three aisles in 1365 to replace a Romanesque church. The chancel was completed in 1380; King George of Poděbrady had the façade with its high gabled roof built in 1460. At the time of the Hussite reform movement Týn Church was the Bohemian Utraquist centre in Prague.

Architecture A golden chalice was placed on the gable by King George of Poděbrady beside his statue to commemorate his coronation; it was replaced by a Madonna, for whose halo the chalice gold was used, after the Protestants' defeat at the Battle of the White Mountain (1620). The 80m/262ft towers, topped with delicate pinnacles, were built in 1463 – 1466 (north tower) and 1506 – 1511 (south tower). Noteworthy, too, is the north doorway with Gothic baldachin and tympanum from Peter Parler's workshop (Christ's Passion, copy).

Interior The interior seems a little gloomy in spite of the lofty Gothic chancel. The high altar at the end of the central aisle is very striking, with its splendid paintings *The Assumption* and *The Trinity* by Karel Škréta (1649). In the chapel to the north of the choir is a beautiful 15th-century Gothic Calvary group; the end of the south aisle is adorned by

Gothic corbels from the Parler workshop, busts of an unknown royal couple, and *Cyril and Methodius* in marble by Emanuel Max (1847). Moreover, there is a lovely Gothic pewter font here, dated 1414. The altar painting of St Adalbert on the first central column of the north aisle is also by Škréta, who created the paintings for the Annunciation altar and St Barbara altar after 1660, and the picture for the St Joseph altar (1664). A late-Gothic tabernacle (1493) by Master Matthias Rejsek of Prostějov overarches the neo-Gothic St Luke's altar (19th century); the altarpiece is by Josef Hellich. In the southern chancel pier is the red marble **tomb of Danish astronomer Tycho Brahe**

Tyn church

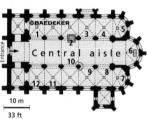

10 m

33 ft

1 St Adalbert altar
2 Late-Gothic baldachin
3 St Joseph altar
4 Annunciation altar
5 Calvary group
6 High altar
7 Gothic corbels, pewter font
8 St Barbara altar
9 Marble grave of Tycho Brahe
10 Renaissance altar
11 Gothic Madonna
12 St Wenceslas altar

(►Famous People), who was active at the court of Rudolf II. The two Latin sayings above the picture mean: »To be rather than to seem« and »Not power, not riches, only art is eternal«. The erstwhile court astronomer is shown in full armour; the artist responsible for the tomb is not known. The Gothic Madonna in the second chapel of the south aisle was created in about 1400. The relief of the baptism of Christ was made for the Renaissance altar at the beginning of the 17th century, the St Wenceslas altar picture at the end of the 17th century (A. Stevens).

❶ Tue–Sat 10am–1pm and 3pm–5pm, Sun 10.30am–noon
Obligatory 25Kč donation

Next to Týn School stands The Stone Bell (U Kamenného zvonu). The front of this house, with soaring Gothic windows, was covered by a neo-Gothic façade of 1899 until restoration work was undertaken in the 1960s. The history of the house began in the second half of the 13th century; the name »At the Stone Bell« is first recorded in a document of 1417. The probable patron was Queen Elisabeth, wife of John of Luxembourg. Alterations were made at the end of the 15th century, and further alterations ensured that from 1685 little remained to indicate the grand design of what was once a royal residence. After extensive reconstruction work, the building was restored in 1987 to its old Gothic shape.
The Galerie hlavního města Prahy (Prague City Gallery) puts on exhibitions (Tue–Sun 10am–6pm), concerts and lectures in The Stone Bell.
❶ Tue–Sun 10am–6pm, admission 120 Kč, www.ghmp.cz

At the Stone Bell

A Dientzenhofer was also responsible for St Nicholas

GOLTZ-KINSKÝ PALACE
(PALÁC GOLTZ-KINSKÝCH)

National Gallery

In the former Goltz-Kinský Palace (no. 12), directly next door to The Stone Bell, permanent exhibitions from the National Gallery are on display. Classical works and the art of Asia are currently on show. The late-Baroque building with impressive Rococo elements was erected on the foundations of an earlier Romanesque and subsequent early Gothic house (remains in the basement of the west wing). The designs for the palace commissioned in 1755 by Count Jan Arnost Goltz are by Kilián Ignác Dientzenhofer; his successor Anselmo Lurago completed the building in 1765. After only three years the palace passed to Prince Rudolf Kinských. Bertha von Suttner was born here almost 80 years later. The almost Classicist frontage on the square, with rich stucco work by G. Campione de Bossi and pilastered projections, has two triangular gables. A balcony supported by two pillared doorways runs across the wide façade. Four standing and four lying mythological sculptures by Ignaz Franz Platzer the Elder adorn the tympanum. The finely structured window surrounds are in Rococo style, with typical rock motif. The three side wings in Empire style were added later.

❶ Tue–Sun 10am–6pm, admission 150 Kč, www.ngprague.cz

CHURCH OF ST NICHOLAS IN THE OLD TOWN (KOSTEL SVATÉHO MIKULÁŠE)

The church of the erstwhile Benedictine monastery (Emmaus Monastery) belongs to the Czech Hussite church today. Designed by by Kilián Ignác Dientzenhofer, the splendidly light sacral building on the northwest corner of Old Town Square was built in Baroque style in the years 1732 – 1735, with a monumental south front, a long nave with side chapels and a cupola. The sculptured ornamentation is by Anton Braun, the rich stucco work by Bernardo Spinetti, the ceiling paintings (lives of St Nicholas and St Benedict) by Cosmas Damian Asam, who also painted the frescoes in the presbytery and side chapels. The crystal chandelier in the nave was provided in the late 19th century by the Harrachov glassworks. The statue of St Nicholas on the side façade is by B. Šimonovský, and was added in 1906. Since both monastery and church were secularized in 1787, the high altar, the pews and many of the paintings that were originally here are now in other churches.

> **! MARCO POLO TIP**
>
> *Kafka's Prague* **Insider Tip**
>
> A bronze plaque commemorates the Prague writer's birthplace, west of St Nicholas Church on »náměstí Franze Kafky« (no. 5). Opposite St Nicholas stood his school, and Kafka's parents had a haberdashery shop in Kinský Palace. No other writer has such close ties with the city (Tour 4, p.168).

❶ Mon–Sun 10am–6pm

Palace Gardens (Palácové zahrady)

✳ **D 4**

Location: Praha 1, Malá Strana, Valdštejnská
Metro: Malostranská
Tram: 12, 22
❶ April daily 10am–6pm May daily 10am–7pm June, July until 9pm Aug until 8pm Sept 10am–7pm Oct 10am–6pm
www.palacove zahrady.cz

The Palace Gardens beneath Prague Castle can be accessed from Valdštejnská 12 to 14, from Ledeburg Palace (Valdštejnské náměstí 3) and via the Garden on the Ramparts. By the beginning of the 16th century the southern slope beneath Prague Castle, for the most part vineyards and orchards, no longer had a part to play in defending the area. Various aristocratic families acquired the plots of land, some with buildings on them, in order to create Italianate Renaissance gar-   **Access via Valdštejnská**

Beautiful hillside location beneath Prague Castle

dens. After the 1648 siege of Malá Strana the ruined gardens were restored in Baroque style; this resulted in symmetrically placed monumental steps and balustraded terraces, with loggias, pavilions and galleries which afford a wonderful view of Malá Strana. The gardens are separated from one another by walls; steep steps lead up and down; at the top they are interconnected.

Giovanni Battista Alliprandi or František Maximilian Kaňka are the putative architects of **Ledeburg Garden** (Ledeburská zahrada) to the west, as they are of the palace of the same name on Valdštejnské náměstí. It is accessed by way of steps over the wall opposite the Sala terrena. Here stands a statue of Hercules fighting Cerberus. The garden's steep steps – geometrically constructed around a central axis – lead up to a pentagonal pavilion. To the east of Ledeburg Garden is the Small Pálffy Garden. The present layout of the Large Pálffy Garden dates back to 1751, created for Maria Anna of Fürstenberg. Steps lead to the lower terrace with a fountain. The central flight of steps lead up to the higher viewing terrace. To the east of the Large Pálffy Garden is the Kolovrat Garden. It has not been exploited in the same manner as the other gardens; after two houses were demolished in 1858 it was made into a terraced orchard.

Small Fürstenberg Garden

The Rococo garden is only partially accessible since the Small Fürstenberg Palace at the foot of the garden belongs to the Czech senate. It was laid out in the years 1784 – 1788, from plans designed by architect Michael Ignaz Palliardi. The centrally constructed steps lead from a gloriette at the bottom up past a loggia to a pavilion with viewing terrace.

☀ Petřín

※ **C/D 4/5**

Location: Praha 1, Malá Strana
Tram: 6, 9, 12, 22, 23
Funicular: Lanovka

The 327m/1079ft Petřín Hill forms a large park, a very pleasant place **Park**
for relaxing walks. Vineyards covered the hill from the 12th to the
19th century. The **Kinský Garden** was laid out in the southern part
of the park between 1825 and 1830, with a little pleasure palace. A
2km/1.2mi scenic walk begins in the garden of Strahov Monastery
and leads via the seminary garden to Kinský Garden. Alternatively
it is possible to reach the top of Petřín hill using the **funicular rail-**
way, the lower station being located just off Újezd. Close to the
midway stop an old vintner house was converted into an inn called
»Nebozízek« in 1984 – 1985, named after the vineyard first mentioned in documents of 1433. There is a marvellous view of Prague
from here. Petřín is an eastern foothill of the White Mountain; on it
are **Prague's Eiffel Tower** (Petřín lookout tower), the Church of St
Lawrence, the Štefánik Observatory, the Mirror Maze and »Hunger
Wall«.

The originally Romanesque Church of St Lawrence (Kostel svatého **Church of St**
Vavřince), first mentioned in 1135, was converted in Baroque style **Lawrence**
by Ignaz Palliardi between 1735 and 1770, who added a dome and
two towers. On the main altar a painting by J.C. Monnos (1693)
shows the martyrdom of the saint. The legend of the founding of St
Adalbert's Church on a heathen ritual site in 991 is depicted in the
sacristy ceiling fresco (1735). The German name of Petřín – Laurenziberg – derives from the patron saint of the church, which has belonged to the Old Catholic Church since 1994.

Close to the Church of St Lawrence stands a pavilion with a diorama **Mirror Maze**
of the *Battle of the Prague Students against the Swedes on Charles*
Bridge in the Year 1648 by Karl and Adolf Liebscher and Vojtěch
Bartoněk (1898). Beside it, a miniature wooden construction from
the former Charles Gate in Vyšehrad houses the Mirror Maze
(Bludiště), built at the same time as the lookout tower.
❶ Jan–March and Nov Sat, Sun 10am–6pm, April, Sept, Oct daily 10am–
7pm, May–Aug daily 10am–10pm, Dec daily 10am–6pm

In the summer of 1928 the first part of the Štefánik Observatory **Observatory**
(Štefániková hvězdárna) was opened to the public. Like the planetarium (Stromovka Park), the observatory puts on a range of astronomy events. There are regular guided tours and exhibitions and

! *Prague's Eiffel Tower*

The 60m/197ft iron tower with 299 steps was built for the Industrial Exhibition in Prague in 1891, a copy of the Eiffel Tower in Paris; until 1990 it was used for telecommunications. From the upper gallery there is a splendid panoramic view of the city. (April, Sept, Oct daily 10am–7pm, May–Aug until 10pm, Nov–March Sat, Sun 10am–6pm).

regular »Wednesday evening astronomy« programmes for the general public, in addition to introductory courses on astronomy and space travel, school courses and geographical lectures. Among the observatory's modern pieces of equipment are a 40cm/16in mirror telescope (by Carl Zeiss, Jena); worth noting are the earliest large (»King«) telescope and the original »comet seeker« light telescope. Stargazers can indulge in their hobby here every evening except Monday.

❶ Opening hours vary from month to month. For details, check the observatory's website: www.observatory.cz.

Hunger Wall From the peak of Petřín hill, the fortified city wall erected between the years 1360 and 1362 under Charles IV runs down to the foot of the hill. Legend has it that the ruler had it built by the poor to allow them to earn their daily crust. Hence the name »Hunger Wall«.

Kinský Square At the foot of Petřín hill lies Kinský Square (Náměstí Kinských), until 1991 Soviet Tank Square (Náměstí sovětských tankistů). It was named after tank no. 23, left here as a memorial to the liberation of Prague by General Dimitri Leljuschenko's tanks on 9 May 1945. On the initiative of the sculptor David Černý, the tank was symbolically painted pink in 1991, before the decision was taken to remove it.

Strahov Stadium Approximately 500m/550yd southwest of the lookout tower are several sports fields. The oldest and largest is the Strahov Stadium (Velký strahovský stadion), which was built for the Sokol gymnastics festival in the year 1926. During the era of Communist rule the stadium was enlarged several times, as the scene of Spartakiádas – the huge talent-spotting sports events organized in the former Communist/Socialist countries.

Poděbrady Palace (Palác Jiřího z Poděbrad)

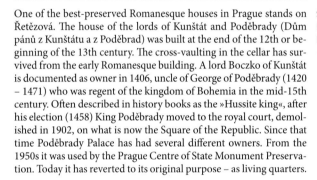

✦ E 4

Location: Praha 1, Staré Město, Retězová 3
Metro: Můstek
Tram: 17, 18
Gallery and café: daily 11am–11pm
Admission: 50 Kč
http://ukunstatu.cz

One of the best-preserved Romanesque houses in Prague stands on Řetězová. The house of the lords of Kunštát and Poděbrady (Dům pánů z Kunštátu a z Poděbrad) was built at the end of the 12th or beginning of the 13th century. The cross-vaulting in the cellar has survived from the early Romanesque building. A lord Boczko of Kunštát is documented as owner in 1406, uncle of George of Poděbrady (1420 – 1471) who was regent of the kingdom of Bohemia in the mid-15th century. Often described in history books as the »Hussite king«, after his election (1458) King Poděbrady moved to the royal court, demolished in 1902, on what is now the Square of the Republic. Since that time Poděbrady Palace has had several different owners. From the 1950s it was used by the Prague Centre of State Monument Preservation. Today it has reverted to its original purpose – as living quarters.

Secular Romanesque building

✶✶ Prague Castle (Pražský hrad)

✦ C/D 4

Location: Above the Vltava, to the northwest
Metro: Malostranská, Hradčanská
Tram: 22
Admission: 350 Kč (full tour: Old Royal Palace, Prague Castle historical exhibition, Basilica of St George, Golden Lane, Castle Gallery, Powder Tower, Rosenberg Palace, St Vitus Cathedral), 250 Kč (short tour: Old Royal Palace, Basilica of St George, Golden Lane, St Vitus Cathedral), Castle Gallery only 150 Kč
❶ April–Oct daily 9am–6pm Nov–March daily 9am–4pm
www.hrad.cz

Along with Charles Bridge and Josefov, Prague Castle (Pražský hrad, Hradčany) is one of the city's main attractions. Since 1918 it has been the official seat of the president of the republic. Prague Castle was founded in the late 9th century by the Přemyslids as a three-part wooden stronghold surrounded by an embankment. St Wenceslas

Seat of the president of the Republic

had a Romanesque rotunda built in honour of St Vitus on the spot where the Wenceslas Chapel stands today. In addition to the prince, the bishop of the newly founded diocese of Prague resided in the castle from 973. Under Břetislav I, in 1042, it was enclosed by a wall 2m/6.6ft thick; at the east and west ends, towers were built, and later on a gate was added on the south side. After 1135, Sobieslav I expanded the castle into an imperial palace in Romanesque style. The 30m/100ft »Black Tower« served as a prison. Work began on the central part of the former royal palace under Otokar II. After the end of the Hussite Wars, alterations were made under the Jagiellonian rulers and under King Vladislav (from 1471) and King Ludvík II (from 1516). In these phases the first Renaissance elements appeared, combined with late Gothic. Both Ferdinand I (emperor from 1556), who brought artists from Italy, the Netherlands and Germany to Prague, and Rudolf II enriched the castle and its immediate surroundings with magnificent Renaissance buildings. A great fire in 1541 necessitated further renovations. In 1614 Emperor Matthias commissioned the first secular Baroque building in Prague, the free-standing gate tower to the west. In the 18th century, at Maria Theresa's behest, this tower was incorporated into the building that framed the newly laid out first courtyard. The alterations made Prague Castle into an architectural whole, a distinctive feature anchored in the cityscape of Prague. After the coup d'etat of 1918 and the liberation of 1945, Prague Castle was adapted for ceremonial and cultural purposes.

! **MARCO◉POLO** TIP

Don't miss **Insider Tip**

- Changing of the Castle Guard on the hour and at noon with fanfares and flags (First Courtyard, Matthias Gate)
- St Vitus Cathedral: the most splendid building at Prague Castle
- Vladislav Hall: reticulated vaulting, the most beautiful hall in Prague Gothic style (Royal Palace)
- »Steep steps« 1920s Modernism by architect Josip Plečnik (Third Courtyard)
- »Kafka's house« tiny house at no. 22, Golden Lane (Third Courtyard)

FIRST COURTYARD (PRVNÍ NÁDVOŘÍ)

Access to the first and most recent of the three castle courtyards, also known as the Memorial Courtyard, is by way of Hradčany Square (Hradčanské náměstí), through a portcullis on which the »Battling Titans« (1786; copies since 1912) by Ignaz Franz Platzer the Elder are enthroned. The castle guards stand here, and the hourly changing of the guard attracts inquisitive crowds. The First Courtyard was constructed from 1756 to 1774 under Maria Theresa, from plans by Vienna's chief court architect Nikolaus Pacassi. Anselmo Lurago was in charge of the project. The plasterwork trophies above the cornices are further copies of works by Platzer. The most recent alterations were undertaken in the 1920s by Slovenian architect Josip Plečnik. He was commissioned by Tomáš G. Masaryk to renovate – in a simple yet distinguished manner – everything in the castle that could symbolize the independence of the state, and to lessen the threatening aspect of this seat of power.

Memorial Courtyard

Emperor Matthias had the Matthias Gate (Matyášova brána) built by Giovanni Maria Philippi in 1614 as a free-standing west entrance to Prague Castle. In 1760 the tower was combined with the newly erected castle frontage by Pacassi. Flights of steps, also by Pacassi (1765/1766), lead up from the gate to the castle's ceremonial rooms: the Throne Room, a room with paintings by Václav Brožík, the Mirror Room, the Music Room and the Reception Room. The residence of the president of the Czech Republic is also in this wing. The flagpoles in front of the Matthias Gate are pine trunks from Czech frontier forests – Josip Plečnik's idea.

Matthias Gate

SECOND COURTYARD (DRUHÉ NÁDVOŘÍ)

Entry to the Second Courtyard is through Matthias Gate. Over time the architecture was adapted in Renaissance and late-Baroque style, and the façades by Pacassi were made to match those in the First Courtyard. In the centre is a Baroque fountain, built by Francesco della Torre in the year 1686 and adorned with figures by Hieronymus Kohl. The wrought-iron grille covering the draw-well dates from 1702. An attempt was made in 1967 to lighten the severity of this courtyard by introducing a modern lion fountain (V. Makovský) and glittering granite paving (J. Fragner).

Fountain

On the north front of the Second Courtyard the Plečnik Hall was created in the years 1927 to 1931 by restructuring older parts of the building; together with the so-called Stair Hall it became the entrance hall for the Spanish Hall and Rudolf Gallery. From the Second Courtyard

Plečnik Hall

the Powder Bridge (spanning the Stag Moat) leads to a terrace walk (Mariánské hradby) which goes past the Royal Garden (accessible only in spring) and the former Ball-Game House to the Belvedere.

Castle Gallery

In 1965 the former Imperial Stables in the north wing and the ground floor of the west wing were converted to form the Castle Gallery (Obrazárna Pražského hradu), opened to the public following extensive renovations in 1997. In six rooms, paintings and sculptures are displayed from the former Rudolf Gallery and the Castle Gallery of Ferdinand II, which was formed later and subsequently broken up. Outstanding works in this collection of European and Czech art include the portrait of Emperor Matthias by Hans of Aachen (c1612); Titian's Young Woman at her Toilet; Tintoretto's Adulteress before Jesus; Veronese's St Katherine with the Angel; and Rubens' Assembly of the Gods at Olympus (c1602). In addition there are pictures by Bohemian Baroque artists (Jan Kupecký, Peter Johann Brandl) and a copy of a sculpture by Giovanni Battista Quadri (Adoration of the Magi). In the gallery rooms, remains have been discovered of a 9th-century Church of Our Lady, the earliest sacral building in Prague Castle.

Chapel of the Holy Cross

In the south corner of the Second Courtyard is the Chapel of the Holy Cross (Kaple svatého Kříže). Since 1961 it has served as treasury for St Vitus Cathedral. Here precious liturgical items are stored, such as Mass vestments, monstrances and relics; also St Wenceslas' coat of mail and St Stephen's sword. The Chapel of the Holy Cross was built

Hradčany (Prague Castle)

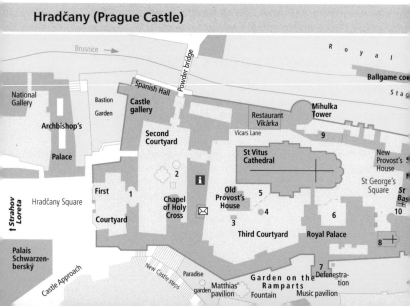

between 1756 and 1763 under the supervision of Anselmo Lurago. In the mid-19th century alterations were made (1852 – 1858) in an attempt to lighten the Classicist severity. Emanuel Max designed the statue of St John Nepomuk inside the chapel in 1854, and also the statues of SS Peter and Paul in the recesses. The sculptures on the high altar and side altars are from the workshop of Franz Ignaz Platzer, the central crucifixion painting on the high altar is by Franz Xaver Balko.

Admission: 300 Kč

THIRD COURTYARD (TŘETÍ NÁDVOŘÍ)

The Third Courtyard was once the centre of castle life. This is where the main route of the old Slav settlement began. The northern border of the Third Courtyard is St Vitus Cathedral. On the south side of the cathedral the walls of a Romanesque bishop's chapel can be seen, excavated from 1920 to 1928. Between 1750 and 1770 the older buildings of the royal estate (the former Renaissance palace of Rudolf II, the

Erstwhile centre of castle life

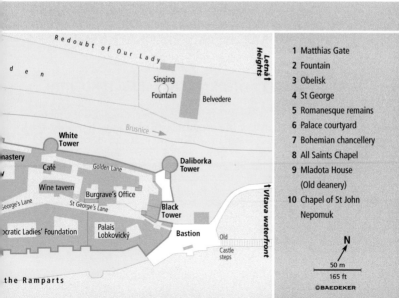

1 Matthias Gate
2 Fountain
3 Obelisk
4 St George
5 Romanesque remains
6 Palace courtyard
7 Bohemian chancellery
8 All Saints Chapel
9 Mladota House
   (Old deanery)
10 Chapel of St John
    Nepomuk

N

50 m
165 ft

©BAEDEKER

St George: masterpiece by the brothers Georg and Martin of Klausenburg

early Baroque queens' palace and Maximilian II's palace) were given a uniform façade by Nikolaus Pacassi. Beneath the balcony with lamp-bearing statues by Ignaz Platzer is the entrance to the president of the republic's chancellery. The Mrákotín granite obelisk on the south side of the former provost's lodging by Josip Plečnik (1928) commemorates the victims of the First World War. The equestrian statue of St George (a copy; the original stands in St George's Convent) is by the sculptors Georg and Martin of Klausenburg from the year 1373. Tomáš Jaroš restored the early Gothic sculpture after the castle fire of 1541. The pedestal in place today is by Josip Plečnik (1928). From the south wing of the Royal Palace the so-called »Bull Staircase« (Býčí schodiště) by Plečnik links the Third Courtyard to Paradise Garden. Stairs and pathway are inspired by Greek and Egyptian mythology.

Provost's lodging Adjoining the west side of St Vitus Cathedral is the former provost's lodging (Staré proboštství). It was originally a Romanesque bishop's palace, given its present Baroque form during 17th-century alterations. The statue of St Wenceslas is by Johann Georg Bendl from the year 1662.

** ST VITUS CATHEDRAL (CHRÁM SVATÉHO VÍTA)

Prague Castle's most magnificent building St Vitus Cathedral (▶MARCOPOLO Insight p.282) is the **metropolitan church of the archbishopric of Prague**. It occupies the site of a rotunda which Duke Wenceslas dedicated to St Vitus in 925. 135 years later Duke Spytihněv II donated a Romanesque basilica with double chancel. Charles IV began building the Gothic cathedral in 1344.

Architecture The east end was designed by French master builder Matthias of Arras, influenced by the older Gothic style of southern France (cathedrals of Narbonne and Toulouse). He was responsible for the chancel, 47m/154ft long and 39m/128ft high, of which only the lower parts were completed at the time of his death (1352). Peter Parler succeeded

Matthias of Arras and enriched the cathedral with the upward-soaring forms of German Gothic. Thereafter Parler's sons Wenzel and Johann took over (1399 – 1420); the entire chancel with ambulatory chapels and the foundations of the main tower are of this period. After the Hussite Wars Bonifaz Wohlmut and Hans of Tyrol (1560 – 1562) gave this 99m/325ft tower a Renaissance cupola with a parapet; in 1770 it was given its Baroque bulbiform roof (design by Nikolaus Pacassi). St Vitus Cathedral was was not completed until the early 20th century. From 1872 on, Josef Mocker oversaw work on the cathedral; drawing on Peter Parler's plans he began with the neo-Gothic west part of the main portal, which was completed under Kamil Hilbert in 1929. St Vitus Cathedral is not only the grandest church in Prague and Prague Castle's most magnificent building; with its external length of

Impressive: the West Portal of St Vitus Cathedral

124m/407ft, its transept width of 60m/197ft and height of 33m/108ft in the central aisle, it is also the largest church in Prague. The south tower with its Gothic, Baroque and Renaissance elements – accessible in the summer months – is architecturally unique and boasts the largest bell in Bohemia: the 1549 Sigismund bell, cast in bronze.

Exterior

The usual entrance to the cathedral is the west doorway. The upper part of the south doorway, also called the **Golden Gate** (Zlatá brána), has 14th-century glass mosaics (restored) showing the Last Judgement. At the top, Christ passing judgement on the world is depicted in a mandorla, flanked by Mary and John. Below him are the country's six patron saints, in two groups of three: Procopius, Sigismund and Vitus; Adalbert, Ludmila and Wenceslas. Below them are portraits of Charles IV and Elisabeth of Pomerania. At the side the apostles can be seen, and beneath them the righteous and the damned. Above is a 40,000-piece glass tracery window by Max Švabinský (1934), also depicting the Last Judgement.

Features

Between the pillared arcades and chancel windows runs the triforium gallery. In the outer triforium are busts of the cathedral's master builders, the family of Charles IV, and other contemporaries. The portrait gallery, emanating for the most part from the Parler workshop, is of great significance in art history: although the emperor still occupies the central position, the portrayal of master builders alongside spiritual and secular rulers attests to a novel self-assurance on the part of the late-Gothic artist; and the individualized facial characteristics of the subjects anticipate the Renaissance. There is no access to the triforium itself; indeed, most visitors to the church have never set eyes on it.

Organ loft Opposite the south doorway is the two-storey organ loft by Bonifaz Wohlmut from the years 1557 – 1561. After the cathedral was completed, the organ loft was moved from its original position inside the west façade to its current position in the north transept. The mighty organ (1757) has 6500 pipes.

Habsburg Mausoleum In front of the high altar, in the middle of the chancel, stands the white marble imperial monument by Alexander Collin; it is surrounded by a Renaissance grille and is difficult to get close to. It was begun in Innsbruck in 1556 as a memorial to Ferdinand I and his wife Anna Jagiello, and refashioned under Rudolf II not later than 1589. The figures on the covering plate are: Anna Jagiello, Ferdinand I (centre) and their son Maximilian II. Bohemian rulers and their wives who are buried in the crypt beneath the monument can be seen on the medallions on the sides. At the lower end is the figure of the risen Christ.

Wood reliefs On the north and south interior walls of the chancel ambulatory is a two-part wood relief by court carpenter Caspar Bechteler. It shows the plundering of the cathedral by the Hussites in 1619 and the flight of the »Winter King« Friedrich V of the Palatinate after the catastrophic defeat at the Battle of the White Mountain (1620). There is also an interesting view of Prague's townscape at the time.

Raised silver tomb of St John of Nepomuk In the south ambulatory is the splendid raised silver tomb of St John of Nepomuk, made in Vienna by Antonio Corradini and Johann Joseph Würth in the years 1733 to 1736 from a design by Joseph Emanuel Fischer von Erlach. Life-sized angels kneel on a marble pedestal, the sides of which are adorned with reliefs illustrating the saint's life. The angels support the saint's garlanded and richly decorated tomb. Nepomuk himself kneels on his sarcophagus and – gazing at the crucifix in his hands – he is transported above all worldly events. Later additions are the four silver figures on top (1746), which depict allegories of discretion, wisdom, might and justice, and the damask canopy borne aloft by angels, added in the year 1771.

Royal Oratory The Royal Oratory is attributed to Hans Spiess of Frankfurt. It is a rich late-Gothic installation, with frontage decorated by naturalisti-

Inside the Habsburg Mausoleum: the *Resurrected Christ* stands watch over the recumbent bodies of Ferdinand I's family

cally interwoven foliage. The interior design is based on two intersecting arches with pendent keystone. A passage links the oratory to the Royal Palace, so that the ruler could make his way directly to Mass. Depictions of miners on two pillars recall the source of the wealth that made the financing of the oratory possible.

The entrance to the Royal Crypt is in the chapel to the right of the oratory. In the passages, archaeological finds from the pre-Romanesque rotunda and Romanesque basilica are displayed. On the wall is a plan of the old Romanesque church. In the upper row of tombs lie George of Poděbrady (1420 – 1471, left), Charles IV (1316 – 1378, centre) and Ladislav Postumus (1440 – 1457, right). In the second row are the tombs of Wenceslas IV (1361 – 1419), his brother John of Görlitz (died 1396) and the shared sarcophagus of Charles IV's four wives; in the background is the tomb of Maria Amalia, daughter of Maria Theresa. Rudolf II (1552 – 1612) rests in the Renaissance pewter coffin; in the granite sarcophagus lie the children of Charles IV. The Royal Crypt was redesigned in the years 1928–1935. The exit from the crypt leads back to the nave, just in front of the chancel.

Royal Crypt

✦✦ *St Vitus Cathedral*

Although the foundations were laid in the year 1344, the cathedral was not completed until the beginning of the 20th century. Master builder Peter Parler from Schwäbisch Gmünd is responsible for many of its architectural highlights.

ⓘ Nov–Feb daily 9am–4pm
March–Oct daily 9am–6pm
Great South Tower closed
Free access to church interior
www.mekapha.cz/en

❶ Rose window
The west wall is dominated by a mighty rose window, 10m/32ft

❷ Wood relief
A two-part wood relief by Kaspar Bechteler in the ambulatory depicts the »Flight of the Winter King of the Palatinate« from Prague after the lost battle of the White Mountain. A panorama of the Vltava city is well worth seeing. It dates back to 1635 or earlier and reveals many interesting details.

❸ Tomb of Count Leopold Schlick
The marble tomb of Field Marshal Count Leopold Schlick was crafted by Franz Maximilian Kaňka (1674 –1766), based on a design by the architect Josef Emanuel Fischer von Erlach.

❹ Chapel of St Wencelas
The Chapel of St Wencelas is the most remarkable place in the cathedral. A stellar vault by Peter Parler crowns the rectangular base. The mortal remains of the saint are preserved here. The interior's significant ornamentation features over 1300 precious stones along the walls, beneath a cycle of paintings of Christs' Passion. Another cycle depicts 31 scenes from the life of St Wencelas, attributed to the Master of the Litoměřice Altarpiece.

❺ Golden Gate
The end wall of the cathedral entrance is decorated with a mosaic of the Last Judgement, with Jesus Christ enthroned at the centre in a mandorla.

❻ Cathedral, south vestibule
The three pointed arches of the Golden Gate open into the south vestibule of the cathedral, one of the most beautiful rooms in the whole building. Peter Parler strengthened the ribbed vaults, allowing them to hang freely in the air.

Alfon Mucha created the Art Nouveau *Cyril and Methodius* window in the third chapel of St Vitus Cathedral.

development of the building are clearly visible. A first ducal edifice of the 9th century was replaced in the 11th century by a Romanesque palace, which was remodelled in 1135 in the course of alterations to the whole castle site. From the mid-13th century, during the reign of Otokar II, it was enlarged all round, and under Emperor Charles IV further alterations were made. At the end of the 15th century Benedikt Ried undertook the last major alterations for Vladislav Jagiello. Until the end of the 16th century the Old Royal Palace was the ruler's seat. When the actual residence moved west under the Habsburgs, the palace rooms were turned into chancellery offices or storerooms. Parts of the Romanesque palace are preserved beneath Vladislav Hall on the ground floor and below; parts of the original castle fortifications are also visible. Above are the parts of the palace newly built by Přemysl Otokar II, Charles IV and Wenceslas IV. The centre of Vladislav Jagiello's new second floor, created by alteration and expansion, is Vladislav Hall – the pièce de résistance of secular castle buildings.

Passing through the central entrance beneath the balcony, and to the right of the eagle fountain by Francesco della Torre (1664), there is access via a vestibule to the Green Room. This was Charles IV's court of law, and from the 16th century seat of the high court and criminal court. The walls on the east side are decorated by Upper and Lower

Green Room

Royal Palace

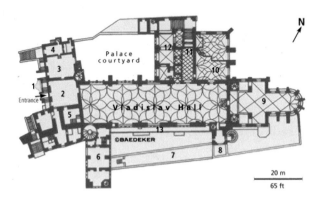

1 Eagle fountain
2 Antechamber (Small hall)
3 Green Room
4 Vladislav bedchamber
5 Romanesque tower
6 Bohemian chancellery
7 Theresian wing
8 Viewing terrace
9 All Saints Chapel
10 Diet
11 Riders' Staircase
12 New Appeal Court
13 Viewing gallery

Lausitz coats-of-arms; several coats-of-arms recall 18th-century owners. In 1963 the copy of the Baroque ceiling fresco Solomon's Judgement was transferred from the Burgrave's office to the Green Room. The Green Room connects to **Vladislav's Bedchamber** (also: Small Audience Room) and the **Land Roll repository**, the latter with fine late-Gothic polychrome-ribbed vaulting; the arms of Bohemia, Moravia, Silesia and Luxembourg are displayed, as is the royal monogram of Vladislav Jagiello, over the window. In the repository, the coats-of-arms of the high treasurers may be seen.

Vladislav Hall	Also called the Hall of Homage, Vladislav Hall is 62m/203ft long, 16m/52ft wide and 13m/43ft high. It was built in the years 1493 – 1503 by Benedikt Ried from Piesting, and with its late-Gothic reticulated vaulting is one of the most splendid parts of Prague Castle. The boldly composed ceiling, with ribs reaching far down into the room, has a delicacy and lightness from which the massive wall pilasters in no way detract. In spite of the Gothic vault, there is already a Renaissance flavour to its slightly superelevated proportions. The wooden floor probably dates from the late 18th century; three of the chandeliers date from the 16th century, the other two are copies. The hall was used mostly for ceremonial purposes. Here, Bohemia's kings were elected, the Diet met, and equestrian tournaments were held. Today, the president of the republic is sworn in here, whilst voting takes place in the Spanish Hall. Stairs lead up to a gallery from where one can look into the All Saints' Chapel.
Ludvík Wing	The Ludvík Wing adjoins Vladislav Hall. It was erected from 1502 – 1509 by Benedikt Ried for the Jagiellonians. A door in the southwest corner gives access to the rooms of the **Bohemian Chancellery**, on the same level as Vladislav Hall. The larger room with a Gothic vault was once the office of the governors of Bohemia. The smaller meeting-room is linked to the large one by a Renaissance doorway of 1509, on which Ludvík's monogram can be seen. It was from a window in this second room of the Bohemian Chancellery that in 1618 the imperial governors, Jaroslav Bořita z Martinic and Vilém Slavata of Chlum, together with their personal secretary, F. Fabricius, were thrown 15m/49ft down into the castle ditch below (where they escaped, however, with »mortal fear, their lives and a few scratches«). This **Second Prague Defenestration** was the signal for the start of the Bohemian revolt against the Habsburgs and precipitated the Thirty Years' War. A spiral staircase leads to the former chancellery of the imperial Hofrat. Here the 27 leaders of the Estates' revolt against the Habsburgs were sentenced to death on 19 June 1621, to be executed on Old Town Square. This was the end of the Estates' revolt which had begun with the defenestration of the governors one floor below. The door is ornamented with 17th-century inlay work; the

Remains of Romanesque wall paintings in the Basilica of St George illustrate New Jerusalem

interior is decorated in late-Renaissance style, with 17th/18th-century chancellery furnishings and tiled stove. The portrait of Spain's King Philip IV, to the left above the door, is a copy of a Velásquez painting.

From the south side of Vladislav Hall there is access to a viewing platform, looking onto the castle's south gardens. Beneath is the Theresian Wing, beyond which lies the Garden on the Ramparts. The view to the west is blocked by the Ludvík Wing.

Viewing platform

From the east side of Vladislav Hall a short staircase leads to All Saints' Chapel, built by Peter Parler from 1370 to 1387. After a fire in 1541, Queen Elisabeth, daughter of Maximilian II, had the chapel altered, enlarged and connected to Vladislav Hall between 1579 and 1580. Parler's reticulated vaulting, destroyed in the fire, was replaced by something simpler. The Renaissance doorway gives access to a gallery with view of the high altar (by Peter Prachner, c1750), adorned with an All Saints picture by Wenzel Lorenz Reiner of 1732. Unfortunately the angel triptych beneath the gallery, designed at the end of the 16th century by Hans of Aachen, cannot be seen. The carved tomb (1739) in the north section of the chapel, with relics of St Procopius, is by Franz Ignaz Weiss. The chapel originally served the erstwhile Theresian religious foundation for ladies of high rank (adjacent building to the east).

All Saints' Chapel

** *Royal Palace*

Until the 16th century, the Royal Palace was the seat of power. Its most important feature is Vladslav Hall, an impressive 62m/203ft long, 16m/52ft wide and 13m/42ft high.

❶ Nov–March daily 9am–4pm
April–Oct daily 9am–6pm
Access included in the ticket price for the full tour and short tour

❶ West façade

Following reconstruction under Maria Theresa, the west façade of the old royal palace was brought into line with the buildings of the third courtyard.

❷ Entrance

The entrance to the west wing, with late Gothic and Renaissance structures, leads past the Baroque eagle fountain, to which Jože Plečnik (1872–1957) added another fountain.

❸ Equestrian staircase

The equestrian staircase was for knights on horseback who were taking part in tournaments in the hall.

❹ Diet

Vladislav II commissioned Bohemian architect Benedikt Reid with the conversion of the palace (from 1454 to 1534). He also drew the plans for the Diet. After a fire, the late Gothic ribbed vaulting was restored by Bonifaz Wohlmut in the years 1559 to 1563. Apparently some members of the Diet preferred more pleasant activities to their duties. Baron von Roupow thought it necessary to admonish them during the reign of Friedrich of the Palatinate: »Wait a moment, gentlemen, and see to it that you do not waste your homeland while you are eating.«

❺ New Land Rolls Room

New land rolls were books in which the Diet's debates were recorded. These records amounted to laws.

❻ Vladislav Hall

Also designed by Benedikt Ried, this was the largest vaulted secular building in all of Central Europe at the time. The ambitious stellar vault diverts the load of some pillar supports two levels down.

❼ Panoramic terrace

From here there is a lovely view of the rooftops of the Lesser Quarter and the Vltava valley.

The Second Prague defenestration on 23 May 1618 precipitated the Thirty Years War

New Land Rolls Room

The first door in the north wall gives access to a spiral staircase which leads to the New Land Rolls Room on the first floor. The interior decoration dates from the 17th century, walls and ceilings are painted with arms of the Land Roll officials. The arms of Bohuslav of Michalowitz have been whitewashed, however; he was executed on account of his role in the Bohemian Estates' revolt. In the second room, the carved bookcase from the time of Rudolf II has reproductions of Land Rolls; the spines were coloured for classification purposes.

Diet

Before finally leaving Vladislav Hall by the Riders' Staircase doorway, it is worth passing through the rear door at the north end of the hall to enter the Diet, also built by Benedikt Ried (c1500). It was renovated between the years 1559 and 1563 by Bonifaz Wohlmut after a devastating fire, replicating late-Gothic ribbed vaulting. Busts commemorate the master builder and Emperor Ferdinand I, patron of the building. Built into the northwest corner is the parliamentary clerk's tribune, a Renaissance addition. Portraits of Habsburg rulers adorn the walls. The tiled stove by the entrance was made in the year 1836 in neo-Gothic style. Between the windows stands the similarly neo-Gothic royal throne (from the 19th century); the lion emblem above it dates from the 17th century. To the right of the throne sat the spiritual lords and highest officials of the realm, opposite aristocrats and knights. The balustraded space was reserved for representatives of the royal towns. The supreme court and the Estates met here until the year 1847.

Riders' Staircase

A special riders' staircase with Gothic ribbed vaulting was constructed for the tournaments that took place in Vladislav Hall. Via this staircase, alongside the entrance to the New Land Rolls room, the participants entered the hall on horseback. At the bottom of the riders' staircase to the right is the exit to St George's Square; to the left, a staircase leads down to the Gothic Palace.

Romanesque and Gothic Palace

In the Gothic Palace, though not always accessible, are the Old Land Rolls room, its massive vaulting supported by two low pillars, an arcade from the time of Přemysl Otokar II, the Gothic Hall with vault from the first half of the 14th century, Charles Hall; the old registry (also the palace kitchen) and the columned hall of Wenceslas IV with Gothic vaulting. Stairs lead from the palace courtyard to the lower floor, where 9th-century remains of castle fortifications can be seen.

BASILICA OF ST GEORGE (BAZILIKA SVATÉHO JIŘÍ)

Oldest sacral building in the castle

On the northeast side of George Square, opposite the chancel end of St Vitus Cathedral, is the twin-towered Romanesque Basilica of St George, the oldest surviving sacral building in the castle and the most important in Prague. The beginnings of the convent go right back to the 10th century. The basilica was begun in 912 by Duke Vratislav I, and dedicated around 925. Devastated by fire in the years 1142 and 1541, it was subsequently altered several times. The Baroque façade as seen today dates from 1670. Renovations in the years 1897 to 1907 and 1959 to 1962 restored the Romanesque character of the church: slender, white towers in the exterior silhouette, with alternating supporting columns and pillars inside, and three-arched galleries in the thick walls over the arcades create a harmonious whole.

Included in the full tour and the short tour, admission 350 Kč and 250 Kč respectively

West façade

The red-coloured façade is divided by pilasters on which the founders of the church and the monastery, Prince Vratislav I and abbess Mlada, are depicted. The Baroque chapel of St John of Nepomuk interrupts the harmony of the front. The statue of the saint on the tympanum is by Ferdinand Maximilian Brokoff. The south doorway (c1500) faces towards Jiřská; it is in early-Renaissance style, from the workshop of Benedikt Ried, and is adorned with a copy of a late-Gothic St George relief, the original of which is in the National Gallery.

Interior

The nave has 12th-century tribune windows, and the original arcading is from the 10th/11th century. In front of the entrance to the

Behind the Baroque obverse of the Basilica of St George, the most important Romanesque sacral building is concealed

crypt, a Baroque wrought-iron grille (c1730) encloses the sepulchre of Duke Boleslav II (died 999); to the right is the painted wooden tomb of Vratislav I (died 921). The crypt dates from the mid-12th century; the crossed vaulting is supported by pillars with cubiform capitals. In the raised chancel, reached by symmetrical double Baroque stairs, are remains of Romanesque ceiling frescoes of the New Jerusalem, dating from the beginning of the 13th century. Late-Renaissance frescoes (16th century) on the apse ceiling depict the *Coronation of the Virgin Mary*. Adjacent to the chancel on the south side is the Chapel of St Ludmila, separated by marble balustrade and grille. Built in the 13th century, the national patron saint's chapel was altered in the 14th century to receive her relics. In the Renaissance vault – the 14th-century extension had to be re-vaulted after a fire – is the sepulchre of Ludmila (murdered in 921) made in around 1380 by Peter Parler. Her life is depicted on the west wall of the chapel – difficult to see – in a fresco (1858) by J. V. Hellich. Further paintings from the late 16th century portray Christ, the Virgin Mary, the evangelists, and Bohemian sovereigns.

St John Nepomuk Chapel Adjoining the south side of the basilica František Maximilian Kaňka built St John Nepomuk Chapel from 1718 to 1722, now used as an exit from St George's Basilica. The saint is portrayed twice by Wenzel Lorenz Reiner: in the cupola frescoes of the Apotheosis of the Saint and in the altarpiece. The statues of St Adalbert and St Norbert in the chapel niches date from around the year 1730.

✴ CONVENT OF ST GEORGE (KLÁŠTER SVATÉHO JIŘÍ)

Bohemia's oldest monastic building Next to St George's Basilica stands the Benedictine Convent of St George, founded in 973 by Duke Boleslav II and his sister Mlada, the first abbess. The pre-Romanesque, Ottonian building is the oldest monastic building in Bohemia, consisting originally of one small building without cloisters. Following damage caused by raging fires during the siege of Prague Castle in 1142, and again in 1541, the monastery was altered and enlarged several times, given a Baroque look (1657 – 1680), and closed in 1782.

Included in the full tour and the short tour, admission 350 Kč and 250 Kč respectively

Permanent exhibition The permanent exhibition in the Convent of St George features **Czech painting, sculpture and applied art of the 19th century**. All the important fine art movements of the period are represented here against the background of developments in European art. One significant event in the history of the 19th century was the construction of Prague's National Theatre, created in an epoch of national renaissance. Numerous artists were involved in building and furnishing the theatre, including Julius Mařak, Mikoláš Aleš, František Ženíšek, Václav Brozík, Václav Hynais and Josef Václav Myslbek. In addition to works by these artists, the exhibition presents paintings by Josef Mánes, Adolf Kosárek and Jakub Schikaneder, restored sculptures from Zbraslav Castle which were damaged by flooding in the year 2002, and (in the chapel) Josef Václav Myslbek's outsized statues of Czech saints from the Saint Wencelas Monument on Wencelas Square.

🕐 Tue–Sun 10am–6pm

Further along the north passage is the original of the equestrian statue of St George, originally erected in the Third Courtyard of Prague Castle and now replaced there by a copy. The figure cast in bronze in 1373 by Martin and George of Klausenburg is regarded as the first free-standing sculpture – that is, detached from any architectural context – north of the Alps.

Equestrian statue of St George

✱ GOLDEN LANE (ZLATÁ ULIČKA)

Golden Lane – also known as Alchemists' Lane – runs from the castle fortifications built by Vladislav Jagiello to the old Burgrave's house; once it went all the way to the Convent of St George. Battlements linked the White Tower to Daliborka Tower. The surviving north frontage consists of picturesque cottages, which are built into the battlement arches. Rudolf II assigned them to his 24 castle guards, who practised a skilled craft in their spare time. The name »Alchemists' Lane« refers to Rudolf II's alchemists, who are traditionally said to have lived here and tried to produce gold – in actual fact, there is evidence that their laboratories were in Mihulka Tower (Alchemists' room). Later on, craftsmen and poor people lived in the cottages. It was in number 22 that Franz Kafka (▶Famous People) worked on stories and essays in the years 1916/1917 such as *A Country Doctor*, *Up in the Gallery*, *A Report for the Academy* and *A Message for the Emperor*. Today, souvenirs can be bought here in brightly coloured little houses, restored in 2010/2011.

Where Kafka came to write

Access only with a ticket for the full or short castle tour
Admission 350 Kč or 250 Kč

> **!** **MARCO POLO TIP**
>
> *Childhood memories*   **Insider Tip**
>
> Immensely appealing, by no means for children alone, the **Toy Museum** is situated in the former Burgrave's house behind Golden Lane (Museum Hraček), entrance from Jiřská). Crumpled old teddy bears await visitors large and small, along with more than 270 Barbie dolls, the earliest Märklin locomotives, aeroplanes, old airships and an abundance of metal toys (daily 9.30am–5.30pm). Admission 60 Kč

»...I carry up my dinner and usually stay there until midnight«
(Franz Kafka on his Golden Lane abode)

Garden on the Ramparts From the bastion, which offers a good view, there is access to the large Garden on the Ramparts. Two obelisks mark the spots where the imperial governors fell into what was then the moat on the occasion of the Second Prague Defenestration in 1618. Above the New Castle Steps – the quickest way up to the castle on foot – lies the Paradise Garden, with the Matthias Pavilion and a music pavilion.

Stag Moat The deep Stag Moat in the north of the castle precinct was once used to raise animals for the hunt. To the north of Stag Moat are the Royal Gardens; on the west side – in Lion's Court – Rudolf II kept lions, tigers and bears.

LOBKOWICZ PALACE (LOBKOVICKÝ PALÁC) IN PRAGUE CASTLE

Not to be confused with Palais Lobkowicz which houses the German Embassy, the Lobkowicz residence in Prague Castle was builf for Jaroslav of Pernštejn around the year 1550 and originally bore his name. In 1623 it passed via Polyxena Pernstštejn, Jaroslav's niece, to the House of Lobkowicz, who kept it in their possession until it was confiscated by the National Socialists. Shortly after the Second World War, the Palais was confiscated again, this time by the Communists, not to be returned to the Lobkowicz fanuly until after the Velvet Revolution. Today, it is the only privately owned palace on the grounds of Prague Castle.

Renovated over many years, the palace now houses a selection of **art from the Lobkowicz collection**. Valuable paintings are complemented by an array of historic musical instruments and original scores by famous composers such as Mozart and Beethoven. There is also an armoury to see, as well as a private St Wencelas chapel, maintained in its original 17th century condition.

❶ daily 10am–6pm, admission 275 Kč, www.lobkowiczypalac.cz

Prague City Museum

✦ F 4

Location: Praha 8, Karlín, Na poříčí 52
Tram: 3, 5, 8, 24
Metro: Florenc
Admission: 120 Kč
www.muzeumprahy.cz

Prague City Museum was completed in 1898 according to designs by Antonín Balšánek and Antonín Wiehl. The neo-Renaissance façade was decorated by various sculptors. In the stairway hangs the disk of the months that Josef Mánes created for the town hall's Astronomical Clock in Staré Město (Old Town Square). The City Museum, founded in 1884, offers a permanent exhibition concerning Prague's economic, architectural and cultural development. Alongside completely furnished rooms, historic costumes, ceramics and sculpture, the museum boasts a collection of Prague house-signs (▶MARCOPOLO Insight p.256/259). The 20sq m/215sq ft model of the city (1826 – 1834) by lithographer Antonín Langweil is most impressive.

Muzeum hlavního města Prahy

Rotunda of the Holy Cross (Rotunda svatého Kříže)

✦ E 5

Location: Praha 1, Staré Město, Karoliny Světlé/corner with Konviktská
Tram: 6, 9, 17, 18, 22
❶ Open only during church services

The Rotunda of the Holy Cross, just a few steps from the Vltava waterfront, is one of three surviving Romanesque rotundas (round

Romanesque rotundas

chapels) in Prague. It was built in about 1100. Scheduled for demolition, it was saved by an objection lodged by the Czech Society of Artists, and renovation work was undertaken in the years 1863 – 1865 by architect Vojtech Ignaz Ullmann and painter Bedlich Wachsmann, who also designed the new altar. Remains of Gothic wall frescoes inside the chapel depict the Coronation of Our Lady, supplemented by works from Soběslav Pinkas and František Sequens. The ironwork screen is by Josef Mánes, the paintings for the triumphal arch and apse by Peter Maixner.

Rudolfinum (Dům umělců)

E 4

Location: Praha 1, Staré Město, Náměstí Jana Palacha
Metro: Staroměstská
Tram: 17, 18
Gallery: Tue, Wed, Fri, Sun 10am–6pm Thu 10am–8pm
Café in the column hall: Tue–Sun 10am–7.30pm
Admission: 70 to 120 Kč
www.galerierudolfinum.cz

House of
Artists

The Rudolfinum (also: House of Artists; Dům umělců) is the **home of the Czech Philharmonic** (Česká Filharmonie); in addition, exhibitions and concerts are put on here, especially during the internationally renowned »Prague Spring« music event. The Rudolfinum

A broad, sweeping staircase leads up to the Rudolfinum.

was designed from 1876 to 1884 by the architects of the National Theatre, Josef Zítek and Josef Schulz, and named after the Austrian crown prince Rudolf. With the ▶National Theatre and the ▶National Museum it is one of Prague's most important neo-Renaissance buildings. Between 1919 and 1939 it was the seat of parliament, and there was also a picture gallery (now on show in Sternberg Palace). The interior of the Dvořák Hall was modelled on Gabriel's theatre at Versailles. An allegory of music by Anton Wagner adorns the main entrance (1885); the lion and sphinx statues are by Bohuslav Schnirch. The parapet features sculptures of famous artists and composers. In World War II the Rudolfinum served as headquarters for the occupying German forces. At this time, a famous case of »mistaken identity« occurred when Czech workers, ordered by the Germans to remove a statue of Jewish composer Felix Mendelssohn Bartholdy, actually carried out Hitler's favourite composer Richard Wagner ...

St Longinus Rotunda

✳ E 5

Location: Praha 1, Nové Město, Na Rybníčku
Metro: I. P. Pavlova Karlovo náměstí
Tram: 4, 6, 10, 16, 22
Guided tours: by request only (tel. 222 222 172)

The St Longinus Rotunda (Rotunda svatého Longina) was originally built in Romanesque style as Rybníček village church. The village, now attested to only by the street named after it, was absorbed into Nové Město after 1257. Up to the 14th century the rotunda was dedicated to St Stephen, but the Gothic parish church took his name when it was built (see below). In the 17th century the rotunda was given an open-structure lantern to replace the previous small tower. It is worth taking a look at the Baroque altar and the crucifixion scene with St Longinus. According to apocryphal documents associated with Pilate, Longinus was the Roman soldier, or captain, who pierced Christ's side with his lance. Longinus is said to have been active as bishop in Cappadocia following his conversion, and to have died a martyr's death.

CHURCH OF ST STEPHEN (KOSTEL SVATÉHO ŠTĚPÁNA)

From Na Rybníčku it is not far to Štěpánská, in which St Stephen's Church is located. Charles IV founded it in 1351 as the parish church for upper Nové Město; it was completed in 1394. The tower was not added until the beginning of the 15th century. In spite of restorations

Founded by Charles IV

(1876 and 1936), the Gothic exterior has been preserved. In addition to the Baroque interior decoration as a whole, it is worth noting the following in particular: the Gothic pewter font by B. Kovář (1462); the Gothic picture of the Madonna (1472); the late-Gothic stone pulpit (15th century); and three paintings, *St Rosalia* (c1660; second pillar on the right), *St Wenceslas* (c1650; left side of the chancel) and *Baptism of Christ* (1649; end of the left aisle) by Karel Škréta, as well as the tomb of Baroque sculptor Matthias Bernhard Braun (1684 – 1738).

Smetana Museum (Muzeum Bedřicha Smetany)
✦ D 4

Location: Praha 1
Metro: Staroměstská
Tram: 17, 18
❶ Wed–Mon 10am–noon, 12.30pm–5pm
Admission: 50 Kč
www.nm.cz

Named after the composer Bedřich Smetana (▶Famous people), the Smetanovo nábřeží embankment leads by way of a promenade from the National Theatre to a small peninsula before Charles Bridge, offering a splendid view of the bridge and Prague Castle. It passes the Emperor Francis I monument to the Old Town Water Tower (15th century). West of it is the Smetana Museum, which belongs to the ▶National Museum. It was established in 1936 in the former Prague waterworks, a neo-Renaissance building dating from 1883 and its sgrafitto décor is well worth seeing. The museum's exhibits include original manuscripts, letters, the famous composer's grand piano and numerous costumes from his operas. Concerts and lectures take place in the large hall. Outside the museum, on Novotného lávka, is the Smetana statue by J. Malejovský from the year 1984.

Smíchov (city district)
✦ B–D 6–7

Location: Praha 5
Metro: Anděl
Tram: 4, 6, 7, 9, 12, 16

Summer palaces for the aristocracy

The district of Smíchov lies west of the Vltava and was first discovered by the aristocracy in the 18th century, who built several summer palaces with lovely gardens here. Among them are Villa Bertramka, Villa Kinský with Kinský Gardens extending south of the Hunger Wall (Petřín), and the Dientzenhofer Summer Palace. In the 19th century the appearance of Smíchov was altered by the arrival of workers' dwellings and light industry. Yet the new industrial quarter had hardly arisen when it began its decline, becoming ever more dilapidated, because of emigration and factory closures.

Shopping in the »Golden Angel«

Only since the 1990s have efforts been made to upgrade the neglected district, which is now undergoing a transformation into a very attractive shopping and entertainment area: easy to reach from Metro station Anděl, **Prague's largest shopping centre** Obchodní centrum Nový Smíchov has more than 130 brand shops, an enormous supermarket, restaurants, cafés, bars and multiplex cinema, on the site of a former coach factory. No less gigantic is **Angel City** (Anděl City), a complex of offices, apartments, shops, restaurants, bowling and cinema with several screens. On the site of the former House of the Golden Angel (U Zlatého anděla), star architect Jean Nouvel created the Golden Angel (Zlatý Anděl) office and retail building with more than 13,000 sq m/140,000 sq ft of office space and 7000 sq m/75,000 sq ft of shop-floor space. Nouvel adorned the striking glass façade on the main street with a blown-up image of actor Bruno Ganz from the Wim Wenders film *Wings of Desire*, gazing down at the crowds of passers-by. The Angel also gave the shopping-centre its name. Alongside are quotations from poets whose names are closely connected with the city of Prague.

Angel over Prague

Kilián Ignác Dientzenhofer built this Baroque summer palace (Portheimka) at number 12 Štefánikova for his own family in the year 1725. The magnificent Bacchus Festival fresco (1729) on the ceiling of the central hall is by Wenzel Lorenz Reiner. In 1758 the summer palace became the property of Count Francis Buquoy, and in the 19th century it was purchased by Prague industrialist Porges von Portheim. Part of the palace was demolished in 1884 in order to make room for the new Church of St Wenceslas. Today, the **Galerie Portheimka** (www.galerie-portheimka.cz) is located here.

Dientzenhofer summer palace

State Opera (Státní opera Praha)

⚬ F 5

Location: Praha 1, Nové Město, Legerova 75
Metro: A, C Muzeum
Tram: 11 Muzeum
www.narodni-divadlo.cz/en/state-opera

Opening with Wagner

The Prague State Opera opened on 5 January 1888 with a performance of Wagner's opera The Master-Singers of Nuremberg and is a product of the rivalry between the Czech and German-speaking peoples of Prague. The former laid the foundations for »their« national theatre some twenty years earlier than the Germans, who then planned their own, much bigger stage. Today, the Prague State Opera – since 1992 an independent institution under this name, and a part of the ▶National Theatre since 2012 – concentrates primarily on bel canto and ballet.

Designed by the Viennese architects Ferdinand Fellner and Herrmann Helmer and constructed from around the year 1886, the house experienced its first golden era under the direction of Alexander von Zemlinsky, who enriched the city's operatic culture not only with works by Mozart, but of artists like Paul Hindemith, Erich Wolfgang Korngold, Ernst Krenek and Franz Schreker. Situated between the Art Nouveau railway station and Functionalist new building of the National Museum and separated from the centre by the Prague City Ring, this neo-Classicist structure boasts Corinthian pillars with galactic eagles on the gable in reference to antiquity. Portraits of German literary greats Goethe and Schiller adorn the façade alongside the chariot of Dionysus and the Muse of comedy, Thalia – recalling the German-Czech history of the building.

✷ Sternberg Palace (Šternberský palác)

⚬ C 4

Location: Praha 1, Hradčanské náměstí 15
Metro: Hradčanská, Malostranská
Tram: 12, 22

❶ Tue–Sun 10am–6pm
Admission: 150 Kč
www.ngprague.cz

Collection of European art

From Hradčany Square a passage in the left portal of the Archbishop's Palace leads to a steep lane down to Sternberg Palace, where the

Gustav Mahler and Richard Strauss – whose *Elektra* was premiered here in 1910 – stood on the conductor's stand here

National Gallery's collection of European art (Sbírka evropského umění od antiky do závěru baroka) from antiquity to late Baroque is housed. The palace was designed in high Baroque style by Domenico Martinelli and completed by Giovanni Battista Alliprandi (1698 – 1707). It is a four-winged building with a cylindrical projection, an inner courtyard enclosed by stuccoed walls, and ceiling paintings by Pompeus Aldovrandini. The collection shows works mainly by early Italian, Flemish and German painters. The palace was reopened, and the collection reorganized, after restoration work had been completed on a ceiling painting on the ground floor and other items.

Ground floor   The ground floor presents mostly 16th to 18th-century German and Austrian paintings. The acknowledged highlight is the picture painted by **Albrecht Dürer** for German merchants in Venice, the Feast of the Rosary: the *Blessed Virgin with Child*, crowned by angels, gives her blessing to Emperor Maximilian (kneeling on the right-hand side of the picture). Dürer immortalized himself in the painting, too (standing at the edge of the picture on the right with a sheet of paper in his hand). Further personalities of the age are likewise portrayed, such as Pope Julius II, but some are difficult to identify. It was Dürer's ability to combine Italian qualities such as generous composition and radiant colouring with close attention to detail that made the picture important; Emperor Rudolf purchased it and had it brought to Prague. There are also some works by Lucas Cranach the Elder (1472 – 1553) in Sternberg Palace, including the small *Portrait of an Old Man*, an example of the satirico-erotic genre in which unequal love is ridiculed. German and Austrian painting of the 17th and 18th centuries is represented, for instance, by the still-life painter Georg Flegel (1566 – 1638), in the utter realism of his *Cabinet Painting with Flowers, Fruit and Goblets*. Jakob Marell (1614 – 1681), a pupil of Flegel, even goes so far as to integrate his own self-portrait as a reflection in his *Vase with Flowers*. Johann Michael Rottmayr's virtuoso use of colour in his depiction of the *Death of Seneca* (pre-1695) creates a contrast between the serene resignation of Seneca in the face of death and the animation of the other figures.

> **MARCO POLO TIP**
>
> *Don't miss*   **Insider Tip**
>
> - Albrecht Dürer's Feast of the Rosary: highlight of the National Gallery (ground floor)
> - Jan »Mabuse« Grossaert's St Luke Drawing the Virgin: monumental altar picture (first floor)
> - Pieter Bruegel's Haymaking: one of five surviving pictures of the months (second floor)
> - Lion in inner courtyard: Bohemia's heraldic animal in impressive form

First floor   The first floor is mainly given over to painters of the 14th-century Florentine School. These include Giotto's pupil *Bernardo Daddi* (active 1327 – c1348), who has bequeathed to posterity, among other

things, a small portable altar for private meditation. Pietro Loren-
zetti (end of 13th century to 1348) was one of the leading Siena masters of the first half of the Trecento. Two panels portraying an unknown *Martyr Saint* and *St Anthony* are by him. There are also two
notable terracotta sculptures by Andrea della Robbia (1435 – 1525).
These are followed by Flemish masters of the 15th and16th centuries.
The triptych by Geertgen tot Sint Jans, *Adoration of the Magi* (c1490
– 1495), is one of the most important examples of Flemish painting.
Jan Gossaert, called Mabuse, displays clear traces of Italian influence
in *St Luke Drawing the Virgin* (around 1513). Gossaert had studied
ancient sculpture and Renaissance architecture in Italy.

Second floor

On the second floor are works by Italian, Spanish, French, Flemish
and Dutch artists of the 16th to 18th centuries. The French are represented, for instance, by Simon Vouet with his picture *Death of Lu-
cretia* (circa 1624/1625), whose light and dark effects show a marked
orientation towards Caravaggio's use of chiaroscuro. Italian painting
is represented, for instance, by Tintoretto's *St Jerome* (from around
1500). Tintoretto gives the Father of the Church an individualized
face, and shows him in cardinal's garb. The Flemish are represented
by such important artists as Jacob Jordaens and 17th-century landscape masters Joos de Momper (mountain scene with *Temptation of
Christ*) and David Tenniers the Younger. Of special note are the **numerous works by Peter Paul Rubens**, which include the *Portrait of
Commander-in-Chief Ambrosius Spinola* (c1627), who had himself
immortalized in full armour. Further portraits, notably those by
Rembrandt and Franz Hals, attest to the mastery of the Dutch and
Flemish.

** Strahov Monastery (Strahovský klášter)

✦ C 4

Location: Praha 1, Hradčany, Strahovské nádvoří 132
Tram: 22, 23

The **second-oldest monastery in Prague** was built by Duke Vladislav II at the request of Jindřich Zdík, bishop of Olmütz, for the Premonstratensian order. Its name, Strahov, derives from the location of
the monastery on a hill above Malá Strana, at the entrance to Prague
Castle (strahovat = guard). After a great fire in 1258, which destroyed
the first library, the monastery was renovated in Gothic style. In 1360
Charles IV brought the monastery – till then outside the city gates –
within the city walls. In the 15th century the Gothic renovations were

interrupted by the bloody Hussite Wars. The monastery flourished most under abbots Jan Lohel, Kašpar of Questenberk and Kryšpín Fuk, who worked hard on the generous remodelling in Renaissance style. At the end of the Thirty Years' War the monastery was ransacked by Swedish soldiers. After the Peace of Westphalia a new library – the Theological Hall – was set up in 1671 with a core of newly acquired books. Between 1682 and 1689 the whole area was given a Baroque appearance, overseen by architect Jean Baptiste Mathey. Broad landscaping, gardens and fruit trees framed the whole complex in a fitting manner. Through the Austrian Wars of Succession the monastery once more suffered severe damage, in 1741; the repairs took more than four decades. They were completed with the Classical Philosophical Hall, the most important Prague building of Emperor Joseph II's era. Remains of the original Romanesque foundations were exposed during careful restoration work undertaken between 1950 and 1954.

Monastery grounds Entry to the monastery courtyard is either direct, through passage and steps at number 8, or, more rewardingly, by passing this entrance and going up a short ramp at the west end of the square and through a Baroque gate (1742), crowned in the middle by a statue of St Norbert, founder of the Premonstratensian order. The statue, dating from 1719, is by Johann Anton Quittainer. In the courtyard, immediately to the left, is the former Chapel of St Roch (Kaple svatého Rocha). Rudolf II had the chapel built (1603 – 1617) in gratitude for the city's being spared the plague in 1599. Today there is a gallery here, also used for concerts.

Church of the Assumption of Our Lady Straight ahead, beyond the St Norbert Column, is the 17th-century Church of the Assumption of Our Lady (Kostel Nanebevzetí Panny Marie), with a richly fitted Baroque interior of the mid-18th century (restored in the 1970s). The stucco cartouches by Michael Ignaz Palliardi contain Marian pictures by Josef Kramolín and Ignaz Raab; the main altar, from the year 1768, is by Jan Lauermann with a relief of saints by Ignaz Franz Platzer the Elder. In the Pappenheim Chapel in the right side aisle is the tomb of imperial cavalry general Gottfried Heinrich Pappenheim (1594 – 1632, killed at the Battle of Lützen). Adjacent to the church stand the monastery buildings, in part Romanesque, with a library and a cloister.

MONASTERY LIBRARY

Precious inventory The historic monastery library belongs once again to the Premonstratensian order. Among the precious holdings of this unique library, with approximately 280,000 volumes dating from the 9th to the 18th centuries, are some 2500 incunabula, 5000 manuscripts and numerous historical maps. The extent of the collection, readily made

Amongst the most valuable manuscripts in the Theological Hall of the library is the Strahov Evangeliary from the 9th/10th century

available to secular scholars, was one of the contributory factors in emperor JosephII's decision ath the end of the 18th century to preserve the monastic community.

❶ daily 9am–noon and 1pm–5pm, www.strahovskyklaster.cz

Particularly worthy of note are the richly stuccoed Theological Hall, painted in the years 1723 – 1727 by Strahov monk Siard Nosecký, with early-Baroque barrel vault by Giovanni Domenico Orsi de Orsini, and the Philosophical Hall, located in a Classical extension (west wing) in the years 1782 – 1784 by Michael Ignaz Palliardi. In decorating the Theological Hall, monk Siard Nosecký was inspired by abbot Hieronymus Hirnheim's De typo generis humani (1670 – 1679), and by biblical quotations. The 25 frescoes symbolize the struggle for wisdom in relation to the love of scholarship and literature. The southern part of the vault shows The Assumption of Mary; there then follows a celebration of the building of the library. Next appears Christ teaching in the temple, then the creation of the earth, and finally a depiction of the limits of human reason confronted with the complexity of the world, shown by five questioners gathered round a globe. There is a self-portrait of the artist in a window embrasure on the right. Along the length of the hall, terrestrial and celestial globes alternate; three come from the workshop of the famous Flemish cartographer Willem Blaeus.

** Theological Hall

**Philosophical Hall

The dimensions of the Philosophical Hall – 32m/105ft long, 10m/33ft wide and 14m/46ft high – were calculated to accommodate the richly carved bookcases (Jan Lachhofer) from Louka Monastery in Southern Moravia. Arching over the hall is a mighty ceiling fresco, in which Franz Anton Maulbertsch (1724 – 1796), from Langenargen on Lake Constance, depicts scenes from the intellectual history of mankind in the allegorical style of the Vienna Academy. In the middle of the hall an old case houses the six-volume botanical work Les Liliacées and the four-volume treatise Le Musée Francais, both gifts of the French Empress Marie Louise in the year 1812. The marble bust of Emperor Francis I was created by Franz Xaver Lederer around the year 1800. This hall is currently undergoing renovation for the first time in 300 years. Neither hall is open to visitors, but both can be observed from the doorway.

Library treasures

The **Strahov Evangeliary** (9th/10th century) is an Ottonian Renaissance work of art from the circle of the Trier School. The Latin text was written in golden uncials on 218 parchment folios; later the manuscript was embellished with four elaborate gospel illustrations. This manuscript, the St Mark Torsi and the famous **Codex Vyšehradiensis** belong to the earliest surviving manuscripts in Central Europe. Further highly notable items are the Historia Anglorum, the account of Friedrich Barbarossa's Italian campaign, the partially preserved Dalimil Chronicle, the Doxan Bible, the late-Gothic Schelmenberg Bible (Pontifical of Albrecht of Sternberg from the time of Charles IV), and writings by Tomaš of Štítné and Jan Hus. Dating from the 15th century are the Strahov Herbarium, a Latin lexicon and the medical books of Magister Ambrož. The 16th and 17th centuries are represented by works of the Utraquists, the Unitas fratrum, and Catholic literature. Travel narratives, atlases, alchemical works, astronomical treatises by Tycho Brahe, Johannes Kepler and Nicolaus Copernicus, oriental manuscripts and other bibliographical curiosities continue the long list of valuable holdings.

Strahov Picture Gallery

The Strahov Picture Gallery (Strahovská obrazárna) on the first floor of the cloisters contains one of the most important monastic collections, from the Gothic era to the 19th century. The exhibits include Gothic art from Bohemia and Moravia, with such pieces as the **Strahov Madonna** from the workshop of the Master of Hohenfurth and the **Strahov Retable** by the Master of the Litoměřice Altar, of which, however, only the panels with the Annunciation, Nativity and Flight into Egypt have survived. Among the painters at the court of Rudolf II were Joseph Heintz the Elder and Bartholomäus Spranger, whose works are just as well worth seeing as the Baroque and Rococo works, or those of the first half of the 19th century.

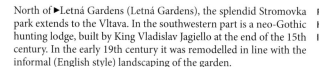

Stromovka

✦ D – F 2

Location: Praha 7, Holešovice
Tram: 5, 12, 17

North of ▶Letná Gardens (Letná Gardens), the splendid Stromovka park extends to the Vltava. In the southwestern part is a neo-Gothic hunting lodge, built by King Vladislav Jagiello at the end of the 15th century. In the early 19th century it was remodelled in line with the informal (English style) landscaping of the garden.

Park and hunting lodge

EXHIBITION GROUNDS (VÝSTAVIŠTĚ)

In the southeastern part of the park, exhibition grounds were laid out for the Jubilee exhibition of 1891 and ethnographic exhibition of 1895, based on plans by **Antonín Wiehl**; since 1918 the Prague trade fairs have been held here. At the beginning of the 1950s the grounds were extended to become a recreational park. The Industry Palace (Průmyslový palác), built in about 1900 from designs by **Bedlich Münzberger** and **Josef Fanta** is an immensely imposing iron construction.

Iron construction

Until the opening of the ▶Vyšehrad Palace of Culture, congresses and conferences took place here. The left wing burned down in 2008 and is currently undergoing reconstruction. The façade of Prague pavilion shows figures from Bohemian history; it was also constructed in the late 19th/early 20th century, by G. Zoula, with allegorical sculptures by F. Hergesell. Today the pavilion houses the National Museum's **Lapidarium** (collection of stone works), with notable 11th–19th-century architectural and sculptural exhibits. The originals of many sculptures in and around Prague that have been replaced by copies over the years – in order to protect them from inclement weather – can be viewed here, including the Charles Bridge statues by Braun and Brokoff (closed for redevelopment work since the end of 2010). The round **pavilion** (Maroldovo panorama) with the *Battle of Lipany* diorama was designed by J. Koula in 1908. Inside is a painting by L. Marolds (1898) of the Hussite battle of 30 May 1434. The **planetarium** was

The old industrial palace with its fountain

built (1960–1962) from a design by J. Fragner on circular foundations. At around the same time, the former engineering exhibition
pavilion (1907) was converted into a **sports hall** with seating for
18,500 spectators. Around 1990 the **Kliôíkova fountain** was built,
which is illuminated very impressively in the evening, as were an am-
pitheatre and several pavilions.

Lapidarium: May–Oct Wed 10am–4pm, Thu–Sun noon–6pm, admission 50
Kč

Maroldovo panorama: April–Oct Sat, Sun 10am–5pm, admission 25 Kč
Mon–Fri Sun 9am–6pm, Sat 9am–8pm, admission 120 Kč

Troja Chateau (Letohrádek Troja · Trojský zámek)

— ✳ Excusrsion

Location: Praha 7, Trója
Bus: 112
❶ April–Oct Tue–Sun 10am–6pm, Fri 1pm–6pm
Park open until 7pm, closed Nov–March
Admission: 120 Kč

Battle of the giants

North of ▶Stromovka Park – in the outlying district of Troja – is the
Baroque Troja Chateau, built in the years 1679 to 1685 by Jean Baptiste Mathey. The magnificent steps up to the entrance were added
later; their decorative figures (a gi-
gantomachia, or battle of the giants) are by two pairs of brothers,
Johann Georg and Paul Herrmann
from Dresden, and Johann Josef
and Ferdinand Maximilian Brokoff. Figures and steps form one
entity, yet no figure is required to
sacrifice its individuality. On the
inner side the figures gradually rise
up, mirroring the movement from
bottom to top, until they finally
stand upright. On the outer balustrade are busts, allegories of the
times of day, continents and elements. Notable features of the interior are the Imperial Hall with wall
and ceiling frescoes created between the years 1691 and 1697 by
Flemish artist Abraham Godin,

Baroque delights at the gates of Prague

and the mythological frescoes by the Italians Giovanni and Giovanni Francesco Marchetti in the side rooms. Early Baroque vases and 17th-century busts adorn the terrace.

Today, the restored chateau houses an exhibition from the City Gallery Prague, including 19th-century Czech painting (www.city galleryprague.cz).

City Gallery Prague

Directly to the west of Troja Chateau is Prague's Zoological Garden. It was set up in 1931 in an area of 45ha/111ac of meadows, groves, gorges and cliffs; differences in altitude are overcome by a chair-lift (Lanovka). Today more than 3800 animals are kept in an area of almost 60ha/148ac – more than 540 different species, including mammals, fish and other creatures – from all over the world. After the flood of 2002 destroyed almost half of the area, new enclosures and buildings appropriate to the different species were built. The zoo has had notable success in breeding original Przewalski wild horses – predecessors of the domestic horse – now a rarity in the wild. In the terrarium visitors can observe tortoises, cobras, rattlesnakes and a rare sauria species.

Zoologická zahrada

❶ Praha 7, U Trojskeho zamku 3/120, March daily 9am–5pm April, May, Sept, Oct until 6pm June–Aug until 7pm Nov–Feb until 4pm, admission: 200 Kč, www.zoopraha.cz

* Týn Courtyard (Týnský dvůr)

──────────────────── ✳ **E 4**

Location: Praha 1, Staré Město, Týnský dvůr (Ungelt)
Metro: Staroměstská, Màstek
Tram: 5, 14, 26

The medieval marketplace of Týn courtyard – extensively renovated on several occasions since the 1920s – was opened to the public in 1996. It's name derives from the toll that once had to be paid here. The creation of a princely farmstead dates back to the 11th century. Under the ruler's protection, for which dues were payable, foreign merchants stored, sold and levied tolls on their goods until 1773.

Medieval marketplace

The most important building in the courtyard is the Renaissance Granovský Palace with an open first-floor loggia (1560), which served as lodgings for visiting merchants. The loggia wall paintings depict biblical and mythological scenes. The doorway bears the date, 1560, and the coat-of-arms of the Granovský family. The adjoining 14th–19th-century burgher houses are also worth seeing.

Granovský Palace

Fountain sculptures in Týn Courtyard, the medieval layout of which has remained unchanged until today

CHURCH OF ST JAMES
(KOSTEL SVATÉHO JAKUBA)

Church of the former Minorite monastery

East of Týn courtyard, on the corner of Malá Štupartská and Jakub-ská, stands the Church of St James – founded in 1232 as church of the former Minorite monastery (on the north side). In 1366 the church burnt down, and was then rebuilt in Gothic style; the current Baroque architecture was created between 1689 and 1739, the work of master builder Jan Šimon Pánek, who succeeded in creating a consummate model of Baroque remodelling of Gothic architecture. The stucco front with SS James, Francis and Anthony of Padua is by Ottavio Mosto. The interior is of particular note, divided by delicately moulded pilasters, with 21 altars. With the exception of St Vitus Cathedral (Prague Castle), St James's is the longest church in Prague and, on account of its rich ornamentation, one of the most beautiful. Wenzel Lorenz Reiner painted the Martyrdom of St James for the high altar, while Franz Guido Voget created the ceiling frescoes (Life of Mary, Glorification of the Trinity). The Baroque tomb of Count Vratislav of Mitrovic was designed by Johann Bernhard Fischer von Erlach and executed by Ferdinand Maximilian Brokoff between the years of 1714 and 1716. The arrangement of the figures recalls the

Pietà: the count reclines on the sarcophagus, supported by the shoulders of a female figure. Since the church acoustics are very good, concerts are often given here. Adjacent to the north side of the church are the cloisters of the Minorite monastery, itself remodelled in Gothic and later in Baroque style. Today it houses an art school.

❶ Mon–Sun 9.30am–noon and 2pm–4pm, Fri until 3.30pm

Veletržní Palace (Veletržní palác)

Location: Praha 7, Holešovice, Dukelských Hrdinů 47
Tram: 5, 12, 17
❶ Tue–Sun 10am–6pm
Admission: 190 Kč
www.ngprague.cz

This enormous palace, with eight storeys and around 40,000 cubic metres / 1.4 million cubic feet of usable space, was built as long ago as 1924 to 1928 by architects Oldřich Tyl and Josef Fuchs. The building was conceived as part of a trade fair complex, and was initially to be followed by further buildings. Although it was the only one to be realized, the Functionalist building is a supreme achievement of the era.

Functionalist achievement of the era

Le Corbusier spoke admiringly of Veletržní Palace in 1928, with its multi-level exhibition spaces grouped around an enormous glass-roofed industrial hall. Especially impressive is the »Small Hall« – not so very small, with seven floors, an open gallery, and a further glass roof. From the beginning of the 1950s Veletržní Palace was used for administrative purposes. After it had been gutted by fire in the 1970s, the authorities decided that it should be reconstructed to house a large part of the art collections of the ▶National Gallery.

Veletržní Palace now presents **art of the 20th and 21st centuries**. The wide-ranging exhibition draws not only on painting, but also on various themes in architecture, film and design to present a picture of the intellectual and cultural creativity of the period. Much of the display is devoted to Czech painting and sculpture, represented in works by Alfons Maria Mucha, Josef Šíma, František Kupka, Emil Filla, Jindřich Štýrský, Stanislav Kolíbal, Otto Gutfreund, Vincenc Makovský, Hana Wichterlová and others. Yet French art, too, is uniquely hon-

Cubic furniture

MARCO POLO TIP

! *Don't miss* **Insider Tip**

- František Kupka: *Fugue in Two Colours*, representative of the abstract art movement (3rd floor)
- Jan Zrzavý: *Cleopatra II*, Prague's Picasso (3rd floor)
- Pablo Picasso: *Violin, Glass, Pipe and Inkpot* (1912), first painting in the style of Cubism (3rd floor)
- Josef Svoboda, scenographer and stage designer, Oscar for Amadeus (2nd floor)
- František Drtikol, avant-garde photography of the 1920s (2nd floor)
- Gustav Klimt: *Virgin in Gold* (1st floor)
- *Trpaslík*: Prague's tallest dwarf, almost 3m/10ft, in the internet café (ground floor)

oured: the Veletržní Palace collection is one of the most extensive in the world. In part it was acquired by the Czechoslovakian state as early as 1923, purchased after a Mánes Union of Fine Arts exhibition.

Key works are **19 pictures by Picasso** as well as numerous Impressionist works, including pictures by Renoir, Gauguin, van Gogh, Pissarro, Monet, Cézanne, Rousseau, Matisse and Sisley. The National Gallery also owns several Rodin sculptures. The museum is further enriched by outstanding sculptures and paintings by Kokoschka, Klimt, Schiele, Klee, de Chirico, Miró, Munch and others.

On the second floor of Veletržní Palace is the **Lidice collection**, with works by 52 German artists. In 1967 the Berlin gallery owner René Block organized an exhibition »Hommage à Lidice« for a projected museum in the town. In July 1968 Block brought works donated by renowned artists Joseph Beuys, Dieter Roth, Wolf Vostell and others to Prague, where they were shown in a gallery. After the upheavals caused by the arrival of Warsaw Pact troops they were thought to have disappeared. Three decades later, in the spring of 1997 they were rediscovered, and supplemented by the work of 31 artists of the younger generation, thanks once again to Block's initiative. Both components of the collection are now on show here, since the projected museum in Lidice is yet to be completed due to insufficient funds.

Villa Amerika (Letohrádek Amerika)

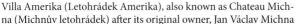

✴ E 5/6

Location: Praha 2, Nové Město, Ke Karlovu 20
Metro: I. P. Pavlova
Bus: 148
Tram: 4, 6, 16, 22
❶ April–Sept Tue–Sun 10am–1.30pm and 2pm–5.30pm
Oct–March 9.30am–5pm
Admission: 50 Kč

Villa Amerika (Letohrádek Amerika), also known as Chateau Michna (Michnův letohrádek) after its original owner, Jan Václav Michna **Chateau Michna**
of Vacínov, today houses the
Dvořák Museum. Kilián Ignác Dientzenhofer built the Baroque chateau from 1717 to 1720 as a summer residence for Count Michna.
The elaborate architecture and
structuring of the front make the
villa one of Prague's finest secular
buildings of the Baroque era. The
original Baroque wrought-iron gate
at the entrance has been replaced
by a copy. Inside, the frescoes were
created by Johann Ferdinand Schor
in 1720. The workshop of Anton
Braun provided the sculptural ornamentation in the garden around
1730. The **Dvořák Museum** has
musical scores and documents relating to the important composer
Antonín Dvořák (▶Famous People), notably his correspondence
with Hans von Bülow and Johannes
Brahms.

A house in verdant surroundings: Villa Amerika

The former church of St Catherine's Monastery (Bývalý kostel svaté **Prague**
Kateřiny) is not far from Villa Amerika. It is located on Kateřinská; **Minaret**
the entrance is on Viničná, but the church is not open to the public
at present. When the church was remodelled in 1737 – 1741,
František Maximilian Kaňka incorporated the Gothic tower into the
new Baroque part of the building. Because of its slender form the
octagonal tower is sometimes referred to as the »Prague minaret«.

The interior is adorned with frescoes by Wenzel Lorenz Reiner (Life of St Catherine) and stucco work by Bernardo Spinetti. The regional psychiatric hospital is located in the former monastery complex.

Villa Bertramka (Letohrádek Bertramka)

✳ C 6

Location: Praha 5, Smíchov, Mozartova 2/169
Metro: Anděl
Tram: 4, 7, 9
❶ April–Oct daily 9am–6pm Nov–March daily 9.30am–4pm
Museum admission: 50 Kč
www.bertramka.com

Mozart's Prague refuge

The story of this residence began in the 17th century, when Malá Strana master-brewer Jan František Pimskorn had the villa built. At the beginning of the 18th century it passed into the ownership of František Bertram of Bertram, after whom it has been named ever since. During the years 1784 to 1795 it belonged to opera singer Josefa Dušková, wife of the composer and music pedagogue František Xaver Dušek. Wolfgang Amadeus Mozart lodged in the musicians' household during his frequent visits to Prague in these years. In the mid-19th century the Popelkas – father and son – made it into a Mozart memorial house; sculptor Tomáš Seidan created a bust of the composer for the garden.

Mozart Museum

Inside the Villa Bertramka, it is possible to see the rooms where Mozart slept and worked. Original Mozart scores and historic posters are on display, as well some of his letters, including correspondence with G. Jacquin – and 13 of the maestro's hairs! The Smetana, Dvořák (Villa Amerika) and Mozart Museums form an independent music department of the ▶National Museum.
❶ Daily 10am–6pm, www.mozartovaobec.cz, admission: 50 Kč

Dispute over the estate

Contrary to the rumours in circulation: Villa Bertramka is still open. There is, however, a lively dispute over the estate involving the Mozart Society now in situ and the previous owners. Kafka himself could not have dreamed up a more absurd scenario than the hurling of insults between the parties as they jostle for position to be the rightful guardians of Mozart's heritage in Prague – more detail can be found on the website www.mozartovaobec.cz. The beloved summer serenades, in which musicians performed and sang in the garden of the Villa Bertramka in period costume no longer take place.

»My Praguers Understand Me …«

… enthused Wolfgang Amadeus Mozart (1756 –1791) following the rapturous reception for his Le nozze die Figaro at the National Theatre in December 1786. The Italian librettist Lorenzo Da Ponte who, besides »Figaro«, wrote the libretti for two further Mozart operas (Don Giovanni in 1787 and Così fan tutte in 1790) was astounded by the level of enthusiasm with which Mozart's music was received in the city on the Vltava.

Da Ponte was particularly surprised to see that the works were »completely understood at the first performance« … unlike elsewhere. Mozart in Prague was, thus, a case of love at first sight, so to speak, and this was by no means restricted to just his music. »Everywhere he went«, a contemporary report noted, »and wherever he was seen, the fervent Praguers met him with respect and love.«

Prague or Vienna?

Such affection for Mozart was surely reciprocated – but man cannot live on praise alone. Hence Mozart returned time and again to the less-favoured, yet considerably more lucrative city of Vienna. He dedicated his Prague Symphony (KV504) to the city on the Vltava and the concert scene Bella mia fiamma, addio! (KV 528) to the lady of the house at Villa Bertramka, Josefa Dušková. His opera Don Giovanni was premiered in the Estates Theatre on 29 October 1787. Four years later, commissioned by impresario Guardasoni, Mozart composed the opera La clemenza di Tito for the Czech Estates on the occasion of the coronation of Leopold II as King of Bohemia. Mozart attended the premiere in the year 1791, shortly before his death. This was his final visit to Prague.

Mozart's music is always playing somewhere in the city on the Vltava – often by musicians in period costume.

Villa Kinský
(Letohrádek Kinských)

✳ B – D 6 – 7

Location: Praha 5 (Smíchov), Kinského zahrada 98
Tram: 6, 9, 12, 20 Švandovo divaldo
Bus: 176 Kobrova

❶ Tue–Sun 10am–6pm
Admission: 70 Kč
www.nm.cz

Musaion – section of the National Museum

As the musical Dušek couple accommodated such illustrious guests as Wolfgang Amadeus Mozart in their ▶Villa Bertramka, the Kinský family also has a summer residence in ▶Smíchov. Count Rudolf Kinský acquired the plot of land in 1825 where vines had earlier grown. Two years later, he commissioned the Viennese architect Heinrich Koch to design a villa in Empire style, which was completed in 1831. Ownership of the estate was transferred to the municipality in 1901 and the park was opened to the public. The following year, it hosted the famous Prague Exhibition which featured works by the French sculptor Auguste Rodin. The Villa Kinský is still an art trove today – and, as the name suggests, a temple for muses. Since 1922, the Musaion has been home to the National Museum's ethnographical collection of some 200,000 artefacts, one of the most valuable of its kind in Europe.

Villa Richter
(Letohrádek Richterova)

✳ D 3

Location: Praha 1 Malá Strana, Na Opyši 5
Tram: 12, 22
❶ Daily 10am–11pm
www.villarichter.cz

One of Prague's most noteworthy Classicist villas

Close to Prague Castle, at the heart of the **Saint Wencelas Vineyard**, which offers a wonderful view of the city, stands Villa Richter. Constructed by the architect J. Peschka in the year 1832, it is one of Prague's most noteworthy Classicist villas. After the Second World War, it was occupied by the Cuban embassy. Since 2008, both the vineyard and the villa, now boasting three restaurants, have been open to the public (accessible from the Old Castle Stairs or via the Black Tower gate). The Saint Wencelas Vineyard is one of the oldest vinicultural sites in Bohemia, dating back to the 10th century. The winemaking history of Bohemia is related on panels on the site. Wine festivals are celebrated here, not only in September.

Vinohrady

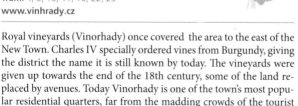

✦ J 5

Location: Praha 2, Vinohrady
Metro: A, C
Bus: 135
Tram: 4, 6, 10, 11, 16, 22, 23
www.vinhrady.cz

Royal vineyards (Vinorhady) once covered the area to the east of the New Town. Charles IV specially ordered vines from Burgundy, giving the district the name it is still known by today. The vineyards were given up towards the end of the 18th century, some of the land replaced by avenues. Today Vinorhady is one of the town's most popular residential quarters, far from the madding crowds of the tourist spots. This is a lovely place for a stroll by day and for a drink in one or two of the pubs by night. The smaller streets between the main thoroughfares of Vinohradská, Korunní and Francouzská are dotted

Vines from Burgundy

Church of the Most Sacred Heart of Our Lord – with its unusually wide tower in Vinohrady

with many individual shops, bric-a-brac, cafés and restaurants, wine cellars and bars. There is a popular beer garden in Rieger Park (Riegerovy sady), the largest and most attractive park in Vinohrady.

St Ludmila Church

Geographical and commercial centrepiece of the district is **Peace Square** (Náměstí míru), dominated by the neo-Gothic St Ludmila Church. This brick, three-aisled basilica with a transept and two striking, 60m/196ft high towers, was constructed from 1888 to 1892 from a blueprint by the architect Josef Mocker. The interior features work by the leading Czech artists of the period, the sculptor Josef Václav Myslbek and painter František Ženíšek. The mortal remains of patron saints Ludmila and Wencelas rest here.

Church of the Most Sacred Heart of Our Lord

The first drawings for the brick construction of the Church of the Most Sacred Heart of Our Lord (Kostel Největějšího srdce Páně) were sketched by the Slovenian architect Jože Plečnik (1872–1957) as early as 1921, although the foundations were only laid in 1928 and the church consecrated another four years later. Plečnik's eclectic style saw his draw inspiration from early Christian architecture, fused with a modern design idiom. The main body of the single-nave church is 13m/42ft high, with brickwork reaching two thirds of the way up its cube-like exterior, the windowed upper third in white plaster. The most striking element is a 42m/138ft high tower, monolithic in appearance, dominated by a 7.6m/25ft diameter glazed clock. Inside, a concrete ramp invites visitors to the top of the clock tower.

Vrtba Palace (Vrtbovský palác)

D 4

Location: Praha 1, Malá Strana, Karmelitská/Tržiště
Metro: Malostranská
Tram: 12, 22
www.vrtbovska.cz

Prague's most beautiful Baroque garden

Head east from Lobkowicz into Karmelitská (today the main traffic thoroughfare in the Lesser Quarter) to find Vrtba Palace, created in the years 1627 to 1631 when two Burgher houses were joined together. The more northerly of the two belonged to Kryštof Harant z Polžic a Bezdružic, one of Bohemia's most important composers, who was executed on 21 June 1621, Prague's Day of Blood, as a member of the Protestant Revolt. The new owner, Sezima von Vrtba, bridged the narrow passageway between the two Burgher houses by adding a portal. It was still possible to use the path, however, which led into one of the most beautiful Baroque gardens in central Europe. The ***Vrtba Garden** is one of the most outstanding achievements of Ba-

The Vrtba Garden with Baroque sculptures and the Church of Our Lady Victorious, Malá Strana.

roque garden architecture in Central Europe It was designed by František Maximilian Kaňka (1674 –1766). Wenzel Lorenz Reiner (1689 – 1743) did the paintings for the Sala terrena; at the entrance to the former vineyard are statues of Bacchus and Ceres by Matthias Bernhard Braun, created around 1730. On the double steps, Baroque vases alternate with mythological sculptures. From the topmost terrace there is a spectacular view of St Nicholas Church (▶Lesser Quarter Square) and the Old Town.

❶ Garden April–Oct daily 10am–6pm, admission: 60 Kč

** Vyšehrad

✦ E 6/7

Location: Praha 1, Vyšehrad
Metro: Vyšehrad
Bus: 148
Tram: 3, 7, 18, 24
www.praha-vysehrad.cz

Legend has it that Princess Libuše lived at Vyšehrad rock (Vyšehrad = stronghold). The earliest Přemyslid rulers are also said to have resided here (▶city history). In Adalbert Stifter's late work Witiko, a historical novel set in the early period of Bohemian history, Vyšehrad is one scene of the action. Duke Soběslav lies on his deathbed and young Witiko is in Prague to gather information at his behest, the great having gathered in Vyšehrad to determine the succes-

Legendary royal residence

MARCO ⊕ POLO TIP

Step back in time ... **Insider Tip**

to the era of the Přemyslid rulers – by strolling along the Vyšehrad fortifications and open your eyes to the Vltava valley. Beneath the ramparts masonry can be seen, sometimes designated »Libuše's bath« – the remains of a medieval palace which once stood here. According to legend, Libuše dallied here with her lovers and pushed them through a crack in the rock down into the Vltava if they failed to please.

sion: »There on a rock beside the Vltava, before her waters reach Prague, stood the fortress Vyšehrad. It was built while the original forest still covered all these hills beside the Vltava, long before the hero Zaboy lived, or the singer Lumir. And then came Krok, and had his golden seat on the sacred hill. Thereafter it was Libuše, his favourite child amongst all the sisters, and she married the ploughman Přemysl, and she had the first wooden stake cut for the castle of Prague. And from her came numerous progeny, and they ruled over the peoples. One of them received Christian baptism, because Christ was born and brought holy faith into the world. He was called Duke Bořivoj and his grandson was St Wenceslas, and his wife St Ludmila.«

History Vyšehrad was probably founded in the 10th century as the second Prague stronghold. There is no historical evidence of a fortified site until the time of King Vratislav (1061–1092), who moved his residence here from Prague Castle. At that time Prague Castle was a bishop's see. Vratislav had a stone fortress and several churches built on the rock above the Vltava (SS Peter and Paul, St Lawrence), and founded the collegiate chapter, which for a long time was an important centre of learning. It was here that the Codex Vyšehradiensis was written, which is now preserved in the manuscript department of the Klementinum. The only surviving building from this era is the round chapel of St Martin. Soběslav I continued building, but after his death in the year 1140 Vyšehrad rapidly grew less important. The Bohemian rulers moved their permanent residence back to Prague Castle. It blossomed once again under Charles IV, who commissioned extensive renovation works. Between 1348 and 1350 a Gothic ring of fortifications, joined to the city walls, was built around the complex. During the Hussite Wars, in the year 1420, almost all of Vyšehrad's buildings were destroyed. During the second half of the 15th century, craftsmen founded the »Free Town on Mount Vyšehrad«. In the late 17th century Vyšehrad was extended in its present form as Baroque fortress, and the citizens' houses were demolished. The fortress was closed as such in 1866, Vyšehrad became one of Prague's districts and the cemetery was extended; in 1911 Vyšehrad was razed to the ground. Only the fortress walls remained. Vyšehrad with all its legends was a favourite theme for fine artists, composers and writers. Well-known works include Bedřich Smetana's opera Libuše, Mendelssohn's Libussa's Prophecy and Franz Grillparzer's play Libussa.

The best way to get to Vyšehrad is via Vratislavova, entering the complex from the north through the Cihelná brána gateway (1848); from there, the path to the right leads to a copy of the equestrian statue of St Wenceslas by Johann Georg Bendel (1678). From the gateway, »V pevnosti« leads to the left, past the Chapel of Our Lady, to the Romanesque round chapel of St Martin (Rotunda svatého Martina), the **oldest architectural monument in Prague**, which dates back to the time of King Vratislav. After Vyšehrad was made into a fortress, the church was used as a gunpowder store; it was renovated in 1878. Leaving the chapel, »K rotundě« leads to the chapter deanery, behind which are the foundations of the Romanesque basilica of St Lawrence.

St Martin

The towers of the chapter church of **Ss. Peter and Paul** (Kostel svatého Petra a Pavla), added only in 1902 from designs by Josef Mocker and F. Mikš, are today the emblem of Vyšehrad. The church itself dates from the second half of the 11th century. In the reign of Charles IV it was altered to become a basilica with nave and two aisles, and in the 16th century it was modified again in Renaissance style. At the beginning of the 18th century František Maximilian Kaňka oversaw the conversion to Baroque, and the church was given its neo-Gothic style in the years 1885 – 1887. Significant items in the interior are, above all, an 11th-century Romanesque stone coffin (St Longinus' tomb), and a panel painting from the year 1355 with the so-called *Rain Madonna,*

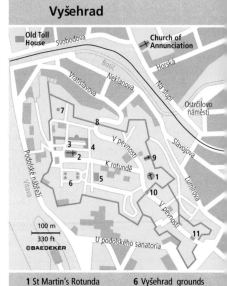

Vyšehrad

Old Toll House
Svobodova
Church of Annunciation
Botič
Vratislavova
Neklanova
Horská
Na slupi
Ostrčilovo náměstí
Podolské nábřeží
Vltava
7
8
3
4
2
V pevnosti
9
K rotundě
1
Slavojova
Lumírova
6
5
10
V pevnosti
100 m
330 ft
©BAEDEKER
U podolského sanatoria
11

1 St Martin's Rotunda
2 Chapter church of SS Peter and Paul
3 Memorial cemetery
4 Slavín
5 St Lawrence Chapel
6 Vyšehrad grounds
7 St Wenceslas
8 Chotek gate
9 Chapel of Our Lady
10 Leopold gate
11 Tabor gate

Final resting place of important figures: the Vyšehrad memorial cemetery, established in the 19th century

believed to protect against drought; this Marian picture is thought to have come from Emperor Rudolf II's collection. The main altar by Josef Mocker is adorned by figures of four saints (SS Peter and Paul, SS Cyril and Methodius), created by F. Hrubeš at the end of the 19th century. The wall frescoes with stylized plant décor were designed by husband and wife František and Marie Urban in the years 1902 and 1903.

❶ Tue–Sun 9am–noon and 1pm–5pm

Vyšehrad The church of SS Peter and Paul is bordered on the north by the memorial cemetery (Vyšehradský hřbitov). When the fortress as such was given up in 1866, the medieval churchyard was extended to become a national memorial for representatives of art and culture. Composers Bedřich Smetana and Antonín Dvořák, writers Božena Němcová, Karel Čapek and Jan Neruda, and painter Mikoláš Aleš are among those buried in the cemetery and cemetery arcades. The »Slavín« monument, a work by Antonín Wiehl and Josef Maudr, is the resting-place of sculptors Josef Václav Myslbek, Bohumil Kafka and Ladislav Šaloun, painter Alfons Mucha and violinist Jan Kubelík, among others.

❶ Mon–Fri 8am–3pm

Vyšehrad grounds South of the chapter church a Baroque gate opens onto the grounds of Vyšehrad. Four groups of statues crafted in the years 1881 to 1897 by Josef Václav Myslbek present figures from various Czech legends:

Přemysl and Libuše, Lumír and Song, Slavoj and Záboj, Ctirad and Šárka. Made to be viewed from below, the sculptures originally stood on the pylons of Palacky Bridge. Some damage was done to them in 1945, and after reconstruction and restoration they were placed in this new location, where, however, much of their original impact is lost. At the southeast end of Vyšehrad is the Leopold gate (Leopoldova brána), and beyond it the early-Baroque projecting Tábor gate (Táborská brána), part of the earlier fortifications. Between them lies the remains of the Peak Gate (Špička), which now houses an information office, shop and tourist facilities.

Beneath Vyšehrad, at number 30 Neklanova, is one of the most famous examples of Cubist architecture. The apartment house by Josef Chochol, one of Prague's best-known Cubist architects (▶MARCO-POLO Insight p.326/329), was built in the years 1911 to 1913. The house stands in an angle where two streets converge and sticks out like a wedge. The façade flows in vertical and horizontal lines, especially through the jagged accentuations which project from the flat surface. The movement reaches its peak at the top, emphasized all the more by the cornice that juts out.

Josef Chochol apartment house

** Wallenstein Palace (Valdštejnský palác)

✦ **D 4**

Location: Praha 1, Malá Strana, Valdštejnské náměstí
Metro: Malostranská
Tram: 12, 22
❶ Open to the public on the first Sat and Sun each month 10am–6pm
Admission: free

Laid out on an exceedingly grand scale, the most magnificent of Prague's aristocratic residences was built in the years 1624 to 1630 for Albrecht of Wallenstein (Famous people), one and the same as depicted in Schiller's trilogy, one of the wealthiest noblemen of the time, imperial generalissimo and later Duke of Friedland (murdered in the year 1634 as a consequence of court intrigue). Wallenstein had 25 houses, three gardens and a city gate demolished in order to build the city's first Baroque palace opposite Prague Castle. The designs were by Andrea Spezza and Giovanni Pieroni, while supervision of the building project was entrusted to Giovanni Battista Marini.

Prague's most magnificent residence

A ceiling fresco in the central Knights' Hall of this imposing residence shows Albrecht of Wallenstein as the god Mars on his trium-

Interior

! *Heavenly violins*

The belligerent general Wallenstein loved music. The 17th-century Sala terrena, modelled on buildings in Florence, protects the chamber orchestra and has fine acoustics. When Prague Castle is floodlit in the evenings, the magical setting is complete. The garden has seating. Concerts usually commence at 7pm. Tickets: tel. 257 010 401.

phal chariot (B. Bianco, 1630). In the other rooms are an equestrian portrait of Wallenstein (F. Leux, 1631) and 19th-century paintings with motifs from antiquity by Peter Maixner. The palace chapel contains Prague's earliest Baroque altar, created by E. Heidelberger. Today, Wallenstein Palace is the **seat of the Czech senate** and open to visitors for only one weekend a month.

No ordinary lordly seat In his famous Wallenstein biography, Büchner prize winner Golo Mann describes the scale and splendour of the Wallenstein residence: »The front is Bohemian Italian, modelled on Palazzo Farnese ... In order to grasp the true dimensions of Wallenstein Palace it is necessary to inspect the inner courtyards and park. From the square, only the façade is visible ... The rest, the entirety, was no ordinary lordly seat. It was an autarchy, a mini-empire amidst the bustle of the city, enclosed by outbuildings and a fortress-like park wall. Once Wallenstein's coach had entered the yard to the left of the front, he had everything he required; a chapel for his prayers; a riding-course at the lower end of the park; a bathing grotto with crystals, shells and stalactites, of paramount importance; and paths between statues and fountains.«

WALLENSTEIN GARDEN (VALDŠTEJNSKÁ ZAHRADA)

The Wallenstein Garden was designed in Italian Baroque style with grottoes, a pool and an aviary. Access is from Letenská. The paths and fountain are embellished by copies of bronze statues by the Flemish sculptor Adriaen de Vries , who was working in Prague at the time. The originals were carried off by the Swedes during the Thirty Years' War; they are at Drottningholm Castle near Stockholm. On the west side of the garden is the Sala terrena, designed by Giovanni Pieroni. It is adorned with frescoes by Baccio del Bianco.

❶ April, May, Sept, Oct, Mon–Fri 7.30am–6pm, Sat, Sun from 10am
June-Aug Mon–Fri 7.30am–7pm, Sat, Sun from 10am

VALDŠTEJNSKÁ

On Valdštejnská running north from Wallenstein Palace Baroque Prague is still fully in evidence. On the left-hand side rises Pálffy Palace (no. 14), now the conservatoire; two doors before that (no. 12) is the entrance to the Palace Gardens beneath Prague Castle. A few steps away (no. 10) is Kolovrat Palace (18th century, now part of the Ministry of Culture); next to it is Fürstenberg Palace, built between 1743 and 1747 (no. 8; now the Polish embassy).

Pálffy Palace, Kolovrat

Diagonally opposite, on the right-hand side of Valdštejnská, is the former Wallenstein riding school (Valdštejnská jízdárna), where the National Gallery puts on temporary exhibitions.

Wallenstein riding school

❶ Tue–Sun 10am–6pm, admission 150 Kč

★ Wenceslas Square (Václavské náměstí)

✳ E/F 4/5

Location: Praha 1, Nové Město, Václavské náměstí
Metro: Můstek, Muzeum
Tram: 3, 9, 14, 24

When Nové Město was founded, Charles IV had the square developed as a horse market; it was given its present name in 1848. However the 750m/820yd-long and 60m/66yd-wide Wenceslas Square is more like a boulevard. It is one of the vibrant centres of modern Prague, surrounded by hotels rich in tradition such as the Art Nouveau »Evropa«, by stores and shopping passages, restaurants and cafés, cinemas and cabaret venues. With the streets ▶Na příkopé, Na Můstku, 28. října and Národní it forms the »Golden Cross«, within which the city's business and social life have developed most intensively.

Modern centre and site of historical significance

Many key events in recent political history have taken place on Wenceslas Square (in 1969 the self-immolation of Jan Palach and Jan Zajíc; in the years 1988 and especially 1989, numerous demonstrations against the regime; (▶city history).

Angles and Diagonals ...

... or Cubism, Bohemian style. Celetná, with its carefully restored Baroque and Rococo palaces, is among the most beautiful streets in Prague's historic centre. One of the few buildings that does not fit the pattern is the house on the corner of the fruit market, named »The House at the Black Madonna« after the Marian plaque on its façade – the house sign from the Baroque building that used to stand here.

The building makes a sober, functionalist first impression; it was designed by Josef Gočár in 1911/1912 as a retail store for wholesaler František Josef Herbst. Constructed with steel skeleton – discernible in the large, scarcely interrupted surfaces of the windows and the variable disposition of interior spaces – it represents the most modern architecture in Prague at the beginning of the 20th century.

Yet that is not all. Closer inspection reveals various details that cannot easily be slotted into any architectural style, such as the rounded windows, slanting eaves, and deeply recessed entrance which is framed by a pair of pillars with pointed tops and hexagonal capitals. The round stairwell with its glass dome is also unusual for its wrought-iron stair railing, and creates an illusion of plasticity with its spiralling, twisting cubes.

Improvements of the postmodern age? By no means. Rather, these curious details express a style known otherwise only from painting – Cubism. For a few years in Prague – and only here – there arose Cubist architecture and Cubist design. The new style had arisen in 1906/1907 in Paris, where Picasso and Braque brought about the break with traditional conventions of painting.

Departure from ...

One of Cubism's most important formal innovations was the departure from central perspective in favour of a presentation that brought different views of an object into the picture. Since the Cubists held that every object could be reduced to a few basic cubic forms, they dissolved the object into individual geometrical and plastic forms, which were anchored in the painting without spatial coherence. The Cubists no longer

Right and on the right hand side: staircase and Café Orient on the first floor of the Cubist »House at the Black Madonna«.

wanted to reproduce the look of things; rather, they wanted to make possible a new view of them, and of their essence.

... Central Perspective

In Prague, as elsewhere, there were heated discussions about the new art from France. People were familiar with paintings by the famous Picasso and Braque either from journeys to Paris or through the collection of art historian Vincenc Kramar, who systematically bought French avant- garde works from 1910 onwards. In Prague it was above all the younger generation who were enthusiastic about Cubism, men such as sculptor Otto Gutfreund, architects Josef Gočár, Josef Chochol and Pavel Janák, and painters Emil Filla, Bohumil Kubišta and Václav Špála.

Between 1920 and 1925 more than 30 Cubist houses were built in the city, of which 27 still survive. Only a small distance from the centre, in Vyšehrad district, several apartment blocks and villas were built with Cubist façades designed by Josef Chochol (Neklanova 30 and Libušina 49, among others). The peak of his achievement is the apartment block at Neklanova 30, completed in 1914. Like the objects in a Cubist painting, this building flouts a one-dimensional view. The formal centre is the corner of the building, simultaneously the corner of two streets, where the sides converge at an acute angle, as in a ship's prow.

Prague's Cubists designed complete interiors – from the doorknob, through balustrades and lamps, to sofas, cupboards, desks and carpets. Nor did avant-garde design stop there: vases, sugar bowls and coat hooks were also given the treatment. The Prague Workshops founded in 1912 produced avantgarde furniture of undeniable originality – whether one would choose (or be able) to sit on them, however, is quite another matter.

Wencelas Square: witness to dramatic events in history

✳ WENCELAS MONUMENT (POMNÍK SVATÉHO VÁCLAVA)

Patron saint of Bohemia

At the southeast end of Wenceslas Square, in front of the National Museum, stands the Wenceslas Monument created in the years 1912 and 1913 by Josef Václav Myslbek. Wenceslas, who ruled from the year 921 as Duke of Bohemia, was murdered in 935 by his brother Boleslav I. Reports of miracles caused him to become patron saint of Bohemia – in his honour, 28 September is celebrated as a national holiday in the Czech Republic. Although Wenceslas' murder probably resulted from the power struggle between Saxons and Bavarians in Bohemia, he is nonetheless revered as a martyr. His name was so popular among the Czechs that the writer Johann Fischart (1546 – 1590) commented after one of his journeys: »Bohemians are called Wenceslas, Poles are called Stanislav.«

Bohemia's first female martyr

The equestrian statue of the duke is surrounded by the figures of four further patron saints of the country. On the right in the front is St Ludmila (»loved by the people«), grandmother of St Wenceslas and wife of the first duke of Bohemia to receive a Christian baptism. When she was murdered by pagan opponents she became Bohemia's first female martyr. On the left in the front is St Procopius, at the back are St Agnes (Anežka) and St Adalbert (Vojtěch) of Prague. There is another Wenceslas statue on Knights of the Cross Square (Vintner Column with sculpture of St Wenceslas), one more can be found in Vyšehrad (equestrian statue).

White Mountain

✳ **Excursion**

Location: Praha 6, Blevnov, Bílá Hora
Bus: 108, 174, 179, 180, 191
Tram: 1, 2, 18, 22

It was on the bare limestone heights (318m/1043ft above sea level) that rise up on the western edge of the city and are now partially built over that the Battle of the White Mountain took place on 8 November 1620 . The battle had decisive consequences for the destiny of the Bohemian lands under the Habsburgs. Within a single hour the army of the Bohemian Protestant Estates, an army of mercenaries led by Count Matthias von Thun, was defeated by the Catholic League led by Maximilian of Bavaria. The Palatine Elector Friedrich V – the »Winter King« 1619 to 1620 – had recently been elected king of Bohemia by the Estates according to a new constitution (which made Bohemia into an elective monarchy), and now had to flee; this meant that the country lost its independence, until 1918! A chapel was later erected on the battle site, which K. Luna converted in the 18th century into a Church of our Lady Victorious. A little way to the north, a monument recalls the Battle of the White Mountain.

Site of pivotal battle

STAR SUMMER PALACE (LETOHRÁDEK HVĚZDA)

In the former star zoo (Obora Hvězda) on the slopes of the hill stands Star Summer Palace. King Ferdinand I had established a hunting park in Malejov forest in 1530 and later royal festivities and shooting matches took place there as well. In 1797 the game enclosure was turned into an informal park with wide promenades; it took its name from the hunting lodge that had been erected here, known as star lodge.

Six-pointed star plan

The castle lies north of the main avenue. The unusual, externally modest renaissance building with hexagonal ground plan was commissioned by Archduke Ferdinand of Tyrol as a hunting lodge and constructed by Italian master builders in the years 1555 to 1558; it served as a residence for his wife-to-be, Philippine Welser from Augsburg, who came from a patrician family in that city. Later the castle was used to store gun powder.

Inside are delightful Italian stucco decorations by Giovanni Campione and Andrea Avostali from the years 1556 to 1563, which show 334 scenes from Greek mythology (Aenas and Anchises, Bacchantes, sea divinities) and Roman history (Mucius Scaevola, Horatius Cocles, Marcus Curtius). The glazed renaissance tiles in the former dining room on the second floor are also worth seeing.

❶ April–Oct Tue–Sun 10am–5pm May–Sept Tue–Sun daily 10am–6pm, admission: 60 Kč

Museum of Czech literature
Since the restoration of the castle, it has housed an exhibition of czech history recalling the battle of the White Mountain (lower floor, ground floor). There are also displays curated by the Museum of Czech literature, which change every year. Sometimes concerts and lectures on literature are arranged.

Žižkov (city district)

──────────── ✦ G – J 4 – 5

Location: Praha 3, 8 Žižkov
Metro: Line A, Jiřího z Poděbrad, Flora, Želivského
Tram: 1, 2, 18, 22

The original Prague
The district of Žižkov, east of the city centre, has developed from workers' quarters to a location popular with Prague's middle classes. In the Czech Republic, as elsewhere, life is shifting more and more from the metropolitan centre to the outskirts – for instance, to Žižkov. Prices for food and accommodation in the centre are no longer affordable for most Czechs. Žižkov is **well known for its bars**, where the atmosphere is better than in the centre. In the meantime tourists have also discovered this district at the foot of Vítkov (St Vitus) Hill, especially the area between Husitská and Seifertova. It was on Vítkov Hill that the Hussites under Jan Žižka vanquished the numerically superior troops under King Sigismund in 1420.

Vítkov Monument
The Vítkov National Monument (Národní památník na hoře Vítkově) is best approached via the streets Wilsonova, Husitská třída and U Památníku (At the monument), and finally by climbing the steps. The memorial was erected in the years 1929 to 1932, but not completed until after 1948. The tall granite-faced stone marks the Tomb of the Unknown Soldier. In addition, until 1990 this served as memorial burial-place for top Communist Party officials. After the Velvet Revolution the mausoleum was closed. Wrangling over proprietary rights endured for almost two decades. When the National Museum was granted ownership, renovation works were completed in record time.Since November 2009, this collosal monument has been open

to the public and serves as a warning against all forms of totalitarianism. The Tomb of the Unknown Soldier is located in the catacombs, in a newly refurbished ceremonial space. There is a rather haunting air to the rooms where the embalmed and decaying body of Communist president Klement Gottwald was once treated by doctors. A mighty organ stands in the vast festival hall which is not yet, however, a part of the Prague concert programme. A series of exhibitions should breathe more life into a site weighed down by history. »Beatlemania«, the first exhibition, was a resounding success. The rooftop café has been given a facelift and justifies climbing the hill for an unusual view of Prague. On the terrace is the equestrian statue of the victorious Hussite general Jan Žižka of Trocnov. The monumental sculpture is the largest equestrian bronze in the world, 9m/30ft high, with a weight of 16.5 tons. It was created in 1930 by Bohumil Kafka, but not cast until 1950.

❶ April–Oct Wed–Sun 10am–6pm, Nov–March Thu–Sun 10am–6pm
Admission: 110 Kč

Prague TV Tower

Today the 216m/709ft-high TV tower is a distinctive feature of Prague's skyline. Situated about 800m/875yd south of Vítkov Hill, it was built in the years 1987 to 1990, and soars up in bizarre architectural forms. A panorama restaurant is situated at a height of 66m/216ft (www.tower.cz). Stylized sculptures of crawling children ascend the concrete base of the tower – one of the most famous works by David Černý (▶MARCOPOLO Insight p.58/59).

❶ Daily 11am–11pm

New Jewish Cemetery

Directly at the foot of the TV tower, the New Jewish Cemetery (Nový židovský hřbitov) is the second oldest Jewish graveyard in the city. It was established in 1680 following an outbreak of the plague, as victims of the plague were not allowed to be interred in the existing graveyard. An epidemic in the second half of the 18th century led to the same thing happening again. It was not until 1787 that is came into full use, when the Josefov cemetery had clearly become too small; but only until 1890, at which point another new Jewish cemetery was established a few streets further east, where Franz Kafka and his parents are buried.

❶ Metro A, Želivského, access via Izraelskà street, April–Sept Sun–Thu 9am–5pm, Friday until 2pm, Oct–March Sun–Thu 9am–4pm, Friday until 2pm

PRACTICAL INFORMATION

What is the best way to get to Prague? Which documents do you need to take with you, what is the local currency and where can one find out more about the city on the Vltava?

Arrival · Before the Journey

HOW TO GET THERE

By car
The motorway network is still under construction. 744km/462mi are already completed 2100km/1300mi are planned in total. There is a seamless route from Germany via the D5 Rozvadov (Waidhaus) border crossing for those driving from Nuremberg or Munich. A section of the D8 at Ústi nad Laben (Aussig an der Elbe) to Dresden and Berlin is not yet finished. Slow progress is made on country roads to Austria. The D1 to Brno is hopelessly overloaded and the road itself is in quite poor condition.

Tolls
Tolls are payable on all Czech motorways. A vignette for cars costs 1500 Kč for a whole year, 440 Kč for a month, 310 Kč for a week.

Internet updates
Updates on roadworks and traffic jams: www.dalnice.cz, interactive information on Prague traffic can be found at www.dopravniinfo.cz

Driving in the city
Driving to Prague is relatively quick and easy, but the problems begin in the city. The centre is largely closed to cars and traffic jams reach apocalyptic proportions. Parking spaces are licensed exclusively to local residents. Garages cost between 15 and 25 Euro per day, which can make a stay a considerably more expensive undertaking. Beware of simply parking in the outskirts, your car can just as easily end up in the scrapyard. Vehicles are routinely broken into and dismantled piece by piece, or stolen in one piece. Taking care of the paperwork at the police station neither improves matters nor one's mood.

Coach travel
Coaches provides a less expensive alternative to the car, with regular connections from many cities further west – for as little as 19 Euro. Prague's bus station is adjacent to the Florenc Metro station. Wencelas Square is only minutes away on Metro Lines B and C.

By train
There are attractive offers to be found for those travelling by rail. Tickets from Berlin to Prague are often available for just 29 Euro, from Hamburg for 39 Euro or just 19 Euro from Dresden. Austria tells a similar story: 29 Euro from Vienna, 39 Euro from Salzburg. Using an Interrail pass (valid for 3 days) from Zurich will cost a mere 59 Euro – the journey lasts for almost 14 hours, however. Trains from Prague's main railway station (Wilsonovo nádraží) head southeast, Praha-Holešovice trains head northeast. The two railway stations are connected by Metro Line C. Remember to check your ticket before you get ready to leave – your station of departure may not be the same one you arrived at!

Eurolines Ltd.
Florenc bus staion
Křižikova 2b, Prague, Karlin
Metro line B: Florenc
Tel. 245 005 245
www.elines.cz.cz
Reservations from Prague

52 Grosvenor Gardens
London SW1W 0UA
Tel. 0870 514 3219
www.eurolines.com

Bohemia Euroexpress
Florenc bus station
Křižikova 6
CZ-186 00 Praha 8

Tel. 224 218 680
Reservations for departures from
Prague

TIMETABLE INFORMATION
České Dráhy
Czech Railways
Tel. 840 112 113
www.cd.cz

International Rail
08700 84 14 10
www.internationalrail.com
Seat 61
(online journey planning)
www.seat61.com

By air Those who are flexible when it comes to choosing dates of travel should be able to find competitive prices on budget airline flights.
A plan to change the name of Prague's Ruzyně airport to Letiště Václava Havla (proper names are also declined in Czech) almost led to a governmental crisis – a typical mishap in Czech politics. Having landed, the safest bet is to book a taxi at the information desk in the arrivals hall. This is more likely to secure a bona fide driver with a fixed price of around 18 Euro: www.taxiterminal.cz – another company might charge as much as 30 Euro for a ride to the city centright More adventurous types might want to try their luck on bus number 119 or 179, connecting to Metro Line A which leads to the city – total journey time approximately 40 minutes, not really slower than a taxi ride.

ENTRY AND DEPARTURE REGULATIONS

Travel documents Since 21 September 2007, the Czech Republic has been part of the Schengen Area of the European Union, removing border controls between Germany, Austria, Poland and Slovakia. Passports should nevertheless be on hand when entering the country for stays of up to 90 days, as well as children's passports if not included on their parents' documents.
Drivers require their driving licence, vehicle registration document, and green international insurance card. Vehicles must display an oval plaque indicating nationality, or EU plaque.

Pets

According to EU regulations, dogs and cats are required to have an official veterinary pet passport for journeys within the EU. This must contain an official veterinary health certificate (issued not more than 30 days before travelling), a rabies vaccination certificate issued at least 20 days and not more than eleven months before entering the country, and a passport photograph. In addition, the animal must be identified by microchip or tattoo. A muzzle and a lead are compulsory. Hotel accommodation can be a problem – many hotels will not accept pets, or will charge a supplement if they do. Dogs must be kept on a lead on all beaches and in nature reserves.

Customs regulations

Did you enjoy your Budweiser or your Pilsner Urquell? You can take 110 litres of beer home with you. Ten litres of Moravian Slivovitz or Karlovy Vary Becherovka (herbal bitter) are permitted. There is no limit for wine or for Prague ham and Marienbad wafers, but the maximum for sparkling wine is 60 litres. Other goods may be taken out of the country up to a value of 300 Euro (by road) or 430 Euro (by air or by sea). Children under the age of 15 are allowed to take declarable goods with them up to a value of 175 Euro. Works of art and antiques require a certificate to confirm that they are not stolen goods. Tobacco allowances are as follows: 800 cigarettes or 200 cigars.

TRAVEL INSURANCE

Health insurance

Citizens of EU countries are entitled to treatment in the Czech Republic under the local regulations. International health insurance certificates are no longer in use, but a health insurance card has been available to EU since 2005. Even with this card, some of the costs must be paid by the patient, hence it is advisable to take out extra insurance. Upon presentation of receipts, the health insurance at home covers the costs – but not for all treatments. Citizens of non-EU countries must pay for medical treatment and medicine themselves and should take out private health insurance.

Emergency

Emergency calls
Tel. 112

Fire brigade
Tel. 150

Police
Tel. 158

Breakdowns
page 349

Etiquette

Keep calm. There is refined English humour, black humour and gallows humour. But Prague humour tops them all. It starts off in fine British spirit, turns black, and finally hangs like a rogue on the gallows. Don't be quick to take offense in Prague; after all, as the saying goes: »Czechs aren't friendly, but they are human«. So, although you may often encounter rudeness, you will never experience inhumanity. In spite of EU expansion towards the east, the exact geographical position of this nation needs to be observed. The Czechs do not regard themselves as belonging to the east. Indeed, they insist that »in Eastern Europe, we are closest to the west«. Links with the west are constantly emphasized, as is Prague's position at »the heart of central Europe«. Attending to these nuances of geography will improve relations no end. Anyone who knows that »Rosamunde«, the world's most famous polka, really comes from Bohemia will quickly make friends of the Czechs. Any proud Czech will refuse to hear a word said against their country's folk music. Brass is as essential a part of Czech culture as the bagpipes are to Scotland's. Moreover, the polka is immortal!

> **! MARCO POLO TIP**
>
> *Fun with Švejk – better not!* **Insider Tip**
>
> So you are in a Prague pub and make a witty remark about Švejk, then end up waiting an age for your beer? That can indeed happen, as the good folk of Prague react rather abrasively to quips about the erstwhile figurehead of the Czech nation. His loss of status in the wake of the Velvet Revolution marks a crucial paradigm shift in Czech national consciousness. A recent poll of the top 100 Czechs featured neither Švejk nor his literary progenitor Jaroslav Hašek. Passive resistance by »playing dumb« is a thing of the past. In the modern Czech state, the good soldier Švejk has been well and truly demobbed.

It is not the done thing to criticize Czech cooking! Even when the culinary offering in front of you is not quite your thing, it would be incredibly impolite to compare it unfavourably with the cuisine at home. Czech beer is, of course, the best in the world! No arguments theright »Na zdraví« – cheers!

Communism as a topic is closed, it should be noted. Today's themes are corruption, the failure of politics, ice hockey, football – and Greece, the Czechs' favourite holiday destination!

For some time now, Prague has been a popular destination for stag nights. Groups of young British men descending on the city to take advantage of the cheap beer and other nocturnal attractions have earned an unfavourable reputation among the locals. Stag parties are increasingly being banned from the bars of the Old Town. Walking shirtless and inebriated through the city centre chanting football slogans is frowned upon, to say the least. Still, there is some tolerance of the mostly harmless if raucous Brits: »They drink, they spend money, they go home,« is the philosophical reaction of many Prague residents. Even as august a figure as Prague's chief of police is on record as saying that he »prefers drunken Britons to sober Germans«.

Health

In the event of illness, first consult your hotel reception or tour leader. Seriously ill foreign visitors are treated in outpatient clinics or in hospital (Czech = nemocnice). The standard of medical care is generally fine.

EMERGENCY SERVICES
Medical emergency service
Tel. 155

Accident emergency service
Tel. 12 30,
12 40

Emergency calls
page 336

Doctors on call
Praha 1
Palackého 5
Tel. 224 949 181

Dentists on call
Praha 1
Palackého 5
Tel. 224 946 981, 1 41 22
Mon–Fri 7pm–7am
Sat, Sun 24-hour service

EMERGENCY HOSPITALS
Na Homolce
(foreign languages spoken)

Praha 5
Roentgenova 2
(From Metro station Anděl (line B) with 167 bus to the final stop)
Tel. 257 271 111
www.homolka.cz

First-aid assistance is available in emergencies and usually free of charge. In the event of illness, anyone can receive treatment in any hospital; in Na Homolce hospital there is a special department for foreign private patients, with swimming pool and cafeteria.

PHARMACIES WITH
24-HOUR SERVICE
Lékarna U Svaté Ludmily
Praha 2
Belgická 37
Tel. 224 237 207

Lékarna Palackého
Praha 1
Palackého 5
Tel. 224 946 982

Information

IMPORTANT ADDRESSES
UK (AND REPUBLIC OF IRELAND)
Czech Tourism
13 Harley St, London W1G 9QG
Tel. 020 7631 0427
Tel. 09063 640641 for brochures
www.czechtourism.com

USA
Czech Tourism
1109 Madison Ave
New York, NY 10028
Tel. 212 288 0830
www.czechtourism.com

CANADA
Czech Tourist Authority
2 Bloor Street West, Suite 1500
Toronto, Ontario M4W 3E2
Tel. 416 363 9928
www.czechtourism.com

PRAGUE
Čedok
Na příkopě 18,
11135 Praha 1
Tel. 224 197 641
Fax 224 216 324 387
Enquiries of all sorts, reservations for rail, bus and airline tickets; bureau de change, city tours, excursions and tickets for cultural events; meeting place for »Historic Prague« morning tours, day trips and guided walks.

Prague Information Service
Rytiřská 31, Praha 1
Staroměstská radnice (Old Town Hall),
Staroměstské náměstí 1
Tel. 221 714 444
www.praguewelcome.cz

There are further information offices at the main railway station (Hlavní nádraží), the airport (Letiště Praha) and, from April to October, in Malá Strana Bridge Tower (Malostranká mostecká věž).

Listings are given monthly in Downtown magazine, with information on cinema and theatre programmes, concerts, exhibitions and other events. Prague's cinema listings and details of other events can be found at www.prague.tv. Prague in your pocket appears every three months; a good guide with useful addresses, information and tips: www.inyourpocket.com.

CZECH EMBASSIES
In the UK
26-30 Kensington Palace Gardens
London W8 4QY
Tel. 020 7243 1115 Fax 020 7727 9654
Email: london@embassy.mzv.cz
www.mzv.cz/london/

In Australia
8 Culgoa Circuit, O'Malley
Canberra, ACT 2606
Tel. (61-2) 62901386 Fax (61-2) 62900006
Email: canberra@embassy.mzv.cz

In Canada
251 Cooper St.
Ottawa, Ontario K2P0G2
Tel. (613) 562-3875 Fax (613) 562-3878
Email: ottawa@embassy.mzv.cz

In the Republic of Ireland
57 Northumberland Road
Ballsbridge, Dublin 4

Tel. +353 1 668 1135
Fax +353 1 668 1660
Email: dublin@embassy.mzv.cz

In New Zealand
Honorary Consulate of the
Czech Republic
Level 1
110 Customs Street West
P.O.Box 106-740
1010 Auckland
Tel. +64 9 306 5883
Email: auckland@honorary.mzv.cz

In the USA
3900 Spring of Freedom St. NW
Washington, DC 20008
Tel. (202) 274-9100
Fax (202) 966-8540
Email: washington@embassy.mzv.cz

FOREIGN EMBASSIES
IN PRAGUE
British embassy
Thunovská 14, Malá Strana
Tel. 257 402 111
www.britain.cz

Australian embassy
6th floor, Klimentská 10, Nové Město,
Tel. 296 578 350
www.embassy.gov.au/cz.html

Canadian embassy
Muchova 6, Bubeneč
Tel. 272 101 800
www.canada.cz

Irish embassy
Tržiště 13, Malá Strana
Tel. 257 530 061
Email: pragueembassy@dfa.ie

New Zealand embassy
Dykova 19, Vinohrady

Tel. 222 514 672
Email: egermayer@nzconsul.cz

United States embassy
Tržiště 15, Malá Strana
Tel. 257 022 000
www.usembassy.cz

INTERNET
www.mzv.cz
The Ministry for Foreign Affairs home-
page offers basic information about the
country.

www.myczechrepublic.com
The easy to follow pages of this online
city guide provide a fine overview of
Prague's places of interest.

www.zamky-hrady.cz
Information about castles and palaces in
the vicinity of Prague; supplements the
list at www.pis.cz.

INTERNET CAFÉS
PG Cyber Café
Praha 5,
Village Cinemas, Anděl
Tel. 420 774 225 500
www.pgcybercafe.cz
Mon–Fri 9am–5pm,
Sat, Sun from 10am

Spika
Praha 1, Dlážděná 4
Tel. 224 21 15 21
http://netcafé.spika.cz
An inexpensive place to spend 15 minutes surfing the internet during the
week.

Blue@Mail
Praha 1,
Konviktská 8
www.cz99.cz

Language

In Czech the main stress is always on the first syllable, whereby l and r as semi-vowels also carry a stress, even when vowels follow (e.g. Vltava; Brno). In words without a vowel, r carries the stress (e.g. prst/ finger). Czech distinguishes clearly between long and short vowels. Long vowels have an accent (á, é, í) or a small ring (ů). Y is always pronounced i. A hook above the letter ě indicates the pronunciation ye (as in yet). Both parts of diphthongs (aj, áj, ej, au, ou) are pronounced distinctly, the intonation stressed on the first part, with j as semi-vowel y (e.g. kraj/land, auto/car). The diacritics are characteristic; these are: č (pronounced ch), š (like sh), ž (like s in treasure), ř (like r + ž).

Rules of pronunciation

Czech Language Guide

At a glance

Say ...?	mluvíte ...?
... English?	... anglicky?
... French?	... francouzsky?
... German?	... německy?
I don't understand	nerozumín
yes, indeed	ano
no	ne
please!	prosím!
thank you!	děkuji!
excuse me!/sorry	promiňte!
can you please help me?	Prosím vás, můžete mi pomoci?
good morning!	dobré jitro!
good evening!	dobrý večer!
good night!	dobrou noc!
goodbye!	na shledanou!
man/woman	pán/paní

Out and about

where is ...?	kde je ...?
street, lane	třída/ulice
road to ...	cesta do ...
square	náměstí
travel agent	cestovní kancelář
bank	banka
bureau de change	směnárna

railway station	nádraží
church	kostel
cathedral	chrám
museum	muzeum
when?	kdy?
castle	zámek
open	otevřeno
closed	zavřeno

Accommodation

hotel	hotel
I would like ...	chtěl bych/chtěla bych
room	pokoj
single room	jednolůžkový pokoj
twin-bed room	dvoulůžkový pokoj
key	klíč
toilet	toaleta, záchod
bath	koupelna
guesthouse	hostinec

Illness

doctor	lékař
chemist	lékárna
I have a temperaturight	Mám horečku.
It hurts heright	Mám bolesti tady.

Traffic

no entry!	průjezd zakázán!
one-way traffic	jednosměrná ulice
diversion	objížd'ka
beware!	pozor!
There has been an accident!	stala se nehoda!
right	napravo, vpravo
left	nalevo, vlevo
straight on	přímo
above	nahoře
below	dole

Weekdays

Monday	pondělí
Tuesday	úterý
Wednesday	středa
Thursday	čtvrtek
Friday	pátek
Saturday	sobota

| Sunday | neděle |
| public holiday | svátek |

Numerals

1	jeden, jedna, jedno	3	trí
2	dva, dvě, dvě	4	čtyři
5	pět	18	osmnáct
6	šest	19	devatenáct
7	sedm	20	dvacet
8	osm	30	třicet
9	devět	40	čyřicet
10	deset	50	padesát
11	jedenáct	60	šedesát
12	dvanáct	70	sedmdesát
13	třínáct	80	osmdesát
14	čtrnáct	90	devadesát
15	patnáct	100	sto
16	šestnáct	1000	tisíc
17	sedmnást	million	milión

Breakfast (snidan)

black coffee	černá káva
coffee with milk	bílá káva
tea with milk	čaj s mlékem
hot chocolate	čokoláda
fruit-juice	džus
eggs and bacon	vejce na slanině
bread	chleba
butter	máslo
sliced sausage	salám
jam	džem

Soups (polévky)

potato soup	bramborová polévka
white cabbage soup with sausage	zelná s klobásou
onion soup	cibulová

Main dishes

roast pork	vepřová
roast duck	kachna pečená
Wiener schnitzel	smažený řízek
breaded carp	kapr smaženy
roast goose	pečená husa
goulash	guláš
fish	ryby

zigane/gipsy-style (with vegetables)	po cikánsku
trout	pstruh

Side dishes

sauerkraut	zelí
red cabbage	červené zelí
potato dumplings	bramborové knedlíky
bacon dumplings	špekové knedlíky
boiled potatoes	vařené brambory
chips/fries	smažené hranolky
potato salad	bramborový salát
white cabbage salad	zelný
mixed salad	míchaný

Desserts

fruit dumplings	ovocné knedlíky
pancakes	palačinky
... with fruit and cream	... s ovocem a se šlehačkou
cream puff	Větrník se šlehačkou

Literary recommendations

Novels and stories, biographies and memoirs

Albright, Madeleine: *Prague Winter: A Personal Story of Remembrance and War*; Harper Collins (2012). The first woman to become Secretary of State, about which she wrote in her earlier book »Madam Secretary: a memoir« (2003), reflects intimately on her Jewish-Czech origins and the fate of her family.

Brod, Max: *Tycho Brahe's Path to God*; Northwestern University Press; New Ed edition (2007). This historical novel appeared in 1916; Max Brod presents Johannes Kepler and Tycho Brahe not as historic individuals, but as representatives of opposing cosmologies.

Eco, Umberto: *The Prague Cemetery*; Harvill Secker (2011). The story mainly takes place in Paris, but the ghosts conjured up and brought to literary life by Umberto Eco dwell in the shadows of the Prague Ghetto – fertile ground for anti-Semitism and conspiracy theories. »The Prague Cemetery« was voted book of the year 2011 in the Czech Republic.

Hašek, Jaroslav: *The Good Soldier Švejk*; Penguin Classics (2005). Under the guise of imbecility, the courageous soldier Švejk confuses everything and reduces war to absurdity – a wondrous symbol of resistance against authority.

Hrabal, Bohumil: *I Served the King of England*; New Directions (2007). First-person narrative of a gradual ascent to hotel ownership, from Czechoslovakia in the 1930s until shortly after the end of the Communist regime. Realizing that it is worth lifting himself above his lowly origins, the protagonist's claim to have served the king of England eventually leads to his serving the emperor of Abyssinia.

Kisch, Egon Erwin: *The Raging Reporter*; Purdue University Press (1987). The journalistic style Kisch developed between 1906 and 1913 as local reporter in Prague is characterized by a certain distance and objectivity. In the early 1920s he travelled widely in Europe, aiming to document the lives of ordinary people, the »hoi polloi« in an interesting and entertaining style which would be easy and quick to read.

Kundera, Milan: *The Unbearable Lightness of Being*; Harper Perennial Modern Classics (1999); ISIS Audio Books; Unabridged edition (1999), read by Jonathan Oliver. Against the backdrop of political events and the invasion of Warsaw Pact troops, the love story of Prague surgeon Tomaš and waitress Teresa leads to Zürich and back.

Meyrink, Gustav: *The Golem*; Dedalus (2000). Like many other writers before him who in one way or another used the Golem legend as subject matter, Prague writer Meyrink (1868 to 1932) also tackled the myth of the artificially created, dumb human being. Created from clay by Rabbi Löw, in Meyrink's novel it becomes a symbol of the Jewish people.

Neruda, Jan: *Tales of the Lesser Quarter*, Baedeker Recommendation page 258

Sherwood, Frances: *The Book of Splendour*; W. W. Norton & Company (2003). Whilst Emperor Rudolf II, residing in Prague Castle, has scholars search for the elixir of immortality, the sage Rabbi Löw creates Golem. But Jossel, as he calls him, is no soulless lump of clay. When he falls in love with Jewish dressmaker Rachel, there are consequences for the whole of Prague. Set in 1601.

Topol, Jáchym: *City, Sister, Silver*; Catbird Press (2000). Topol's challenging debut (in translation) captures the post-communist world and its social dislocation. Dark, horrific and hallucinatory, this three parter is influenced by Meyrink's The Golem and Dante's Inferno. His 1997 debut »Angel Exit« about a drug addict dropout in the 1990s, in the working class district of Smíchov has been made into a film, but the book has yet to be translated into English.

Werfel, Franz: *The House of Mourning*. The story of the Prague brothel »Gogo«, a house with more on offer behind the curtain than ladies of the night and champagne – a vignette of bourgeois life in Prague before the First World War (currently not in print in English).

Keane, John: *Václav Havel*; Basic Books (2001). More than 70 people, including Havel's brother Ivan, contributed over a six-year period to the meticulous assembling of dates, details and documents. This is Havel's life as mirror image of political events, and at the same time a close-up view of the Czech nation's inner life. Well researched and well written.

Media

Czech daily newspapers

The most popular Czech daily is Blesk (Lightning), a typical tabloid. Other papers with a big circulation are Mladá fronta Dnes (Today) and Lidové Noviny (People's Paper). Almost all the dailies belong to Swiss, German or French publishing houses.

International press

The critical commentary of the English-language Prague Post appears weekly on a Wednesday. The Prague Daily Monitor provides daily news in English on Czech politics, business and markets, sports, and Prague events. The Prague Tribune is a monthly magazine focusing on lifestyle and business in the Czech Republic.

Money

Currency

Although their membership of the EU stipulates signing up to the single currency, the Czechs seem in no great hurry to comply. »We should be ready in 2016« the Czech parliament has announced – rather equivocally. Until then, the national currency remains the Koruna Česka (Czech crown), abbreviated to Kč. The crown is freely convertible. The following banknotes are in circulation: 50, 100,

200, 500, 1000, 2000 and 5000 Kč. There are coins for 1, 2, 5, 10, 20 and 50 Kč. There are 100 haléř to the crown.

It is worth comparing charges before changing money: bureaux de change, travel agents and hotels often charge very high fees.

It is possible to get money round the clock at the numerous cashpoints (Czech: bankomat) in Prague with credit cards and bank cards. Most international credit cards are accepted by banks, hotels, restaurants, car-hire firms and many retailers.

?	*Exchange rates*
	1 EUR = 27.00 CZK
	100 CZK = 3.70 EUR
	1 GBP = 35.40 CZK
	100 CZK = 2.82 GBP
	1 USD = 24.75 CZK
	100 CZK = 4.03 USD
	Current exchange rates on the internet: www.oanda.com

MARCO ⊕ POLO INSIGHT

Post and Communications

Postage stamps (známky) are obtainable from post offices, tobacconists and newsagents. Postage to all European countries for letters up to 20g/0.7oz and postcards is 17 Kč.

Stamps and postage

Phone cards are available from Telefónica O2, Ditel and Smartcall. Cards with different numbers of units (150 Kč, 200 Kč , 300 Kč, 500 Kč, 600 Kč and 1000 Kč) are obtainable from newsagents, post offices, hotels and travel agents. Local calls from public telephone kiosks cost 5 Kč.

Telephone

Czech mobile networks are provided throughout the country via T-Mobile CZ, Telefónica O2 and Vodafone. Sometimes it is worth comparing prices and connecting manually, in order to minimize roaming charges.

Mobile phone

DIALLING CODES
Dialling codes to Prague
from the Czech Republic 0
from the UK and Republic of Ireland:
Tel. 00 42 0
from the USA, Canada and Australia:
Tel. 00 11 42 0

Dialling codes from Prague
to the UK: tel. 00 44
to the Republic of Ireland: Tel. 00 353

to the USA and Canada: tel. 00 1
to Australia: tel. 00 61
The 0 that precedes the subsequent local area code is omitted.

DIRECTORY ENQUIRIES
National
Tel. 11 80

International
Tel. 11 81

Prices and Discounts

Discounts A Prague Card is available for two (880 Kč), three (990 Kč) or four days (1200 Kč). This gives access to more than 40 of the most important sites and museums in Prague. The card, complete with an information pack, is available from the Tourist Information Centre or Čedok (information). A Prague Card & Prague Transport Pass includes free bus, tram, Metro and train for a designated period (2 days/1100 Kč, 3 days/1320 Kč, 4 days/1640 Kč). Also available with an information brochure from the Tourist Information Centre or Čedok (information).

MARCO❂POLO INSIGHT

? *How much does it cost?*

- Simple meal: from 8€
- 3 course meal: from 25€
- 0.5 litre beer: 1.40€
- Tram ticket: from 1€
- Double room: from 60€
- Restaurant prices p.7
- Hotel prices p.7

Time

In the winter, Prague follows Central European time (CET). For the period from April to September, the Czech Republic has introduced summer time (Central European time + 1 h).

Transport

BY CAR

Traffic regulations Traffic regulations in the Czech Republic are the same as in most other European countries. There are heavy penalties for non-compliance. There is a zero tolerance alcohol limit. The maximum speed on motorways and expressways for cars, motorcycles and camper vans up to 3.5t is 80mph/130kmh (camper vans over 3.5t and cars with trailer 50mph/80kmh); on country roads for cars, motorcycles and camper vans up to 3.5t, 55mph/90kmh (camper vans over 3.5t and cars with trailer 50mph/80kmh); in built-up areas the limit is 30mph/50kmh unless otherwise indicated.

Taxis Look out for the »yellow angels« when you need a taxi. It is advisable to take one of the vehicles painted yellow – marked with a red hand with thumb pointing upwards – which wait for passengers at taxi ranks. The »Fair Place« message they bear indicates that this particu-

BUS & RAIL
www.dpp.cz
www.dp-praha.cz
Homepages of Prague public transport,
also in English

www.jizdnirady.cz
Timetables and ticket offices of Czech
bus companies

www.vlak-bus.cz
Official website of Czech rail and bus
companies, with timetable, rail connections and bus prices for the entire Czech
Republic.

HELP ON THE ROAD
Ústlední automotoklub (UAMK)
Na strži 9, CZ-14002 Praha 4
Tel. 261 104 401
Tel. 12 30 (breakdown service)
www.uamk.cz

Road maintenance (Silniční Služba)
Opletalova 21, CZ-11000 Praha 1
Tel. 2 22 24, 12 57

lar cab company has signed up for fair charges and their taximeters
have not been tampered with. The initial fee is 40 Kč plus 28 Kč for
each additional kilometright Waiting time is charged at 6 Kč per minute. Receipts are printed automatically.

Reduced prices are available for bookings made in advance. AAA   Discounts
Taxi (the yellow cabs): tel. 140 14, advance booking tel. 222 333 222;
Halotaxi (can be ordered by mobile phone all over Prague):
244 114 411, text message bookings 776 114 411.

BY BOAT

The landing-stage for Vltava passenger ships is close to Palacký Bridge   Excursions on
(Palackého most), on Rašínovo nábřeží quay. From May to September   the Vltava
boat tours organized by the Prague steamship company (Pražská paroplavební společnost) leave here every half-hour; they offer a good
overview of Prague (tel. 224 931 013, www.paroplavba.cz). In addition, boats depart from Palacký Bridge for recreational destinations
around Prague with delightful scenery, such as Roz toky Castle. In
addition to conventional boat trips on the Vltava, »Evropská Vodní
Doprava«, with its landing stage by Čechův most opposite Hotel Intercontinental, offers night cruises; it also hires out boats for special
tours or private parties by arrangement (tel. 224 810 030, www.evd.cz).

PUBLIC TRANSPORT IN THE CITY

The Prague Metro has been in service since 1974. The three lines – A,   Metro
B and C – cover 59km of track. Trains run from 5am to midnight,

?

Ticket prices: how much for how far?

There are two basic tariffs. A 32 Kč ticket is valid for an unlimited number of journeys in 90 minutes. Short journeys (maximum 5 stops) within 30 minutes cost 24 Kč. Day passes are available for 110 Kč, 3 days (72 hours) for 310 Kč. Children generally travel for half price.

running at three minute intervals at peak times. Ticket machines can be found in all stations, but exact change is required – otherwise excess coins pop back out. Tickets are also obtainable in kiosks and newspaper stands. Hotel concierges often have some at reception as well.

The green **line A** stops at all of the must-see tourist sites, from the Old Town Square and under the Vltava to the Lesser Quarter and up to Prague Castle. The Metro station for the castle is still some distance from the castle itself – alternatively, the number 22 tram takes passengers right up to the Second Courtyard.

Line B, the yellow route, runs through the city from east to west, crossing the A line at Můstek station and C at Florenc. Riding from Republic Square to Národní, the national boulevard, takes just seven minutes.

Line C connects Prague's three railway stations, Nádraźí Holešovice, Masarykovo nádraźí and the main railway station Hlavní nádraźí at Wencelas Squaright It then continues to the old Vyšehrad fort. It is possible to change to the A line at Muzeum station beneath the National Museum.

Tram Prague's tram network is so dense, there is a stop on almost every corner in the city centright Regular service runs between 4.30am and a quarter past midnight on all mapped out lines. Tram numbers 51 to 59 continue through the night on joint tracks (marked at the tram stops).

Bus Visitors to Prague will not find the bus so useful, as they usually run from the Metro and tram termini to the outskirts.

Funicular Erected in honour of the General Land Centennial Exhibition of 1891, the funicular climbs daily from 9am to 11.30pm from the Újezd valley station in the Lesser Quarter to the Petřín hill station; 32 Kč.

Travellers with Disabilities

Bezbariérový přístup is Czech for barrier-free, indicating where disabled access is guaranteed. Many of Prague's museums, concert halls and theatres are equipped with wheelchair-friendly lifts, shown on

ADDRESSES
RADAR (UK)
12 City Forum, 250 City Road
London EC1V 8AF
Tel. 020 7250 3222 Fax: 020 7250 0212
www.radar.org.uk

Mobility International USA
132 E. Broadway, Suite 343
Eugene, Oregon USA 97401
Tel. (541) 343-1284
Fax: (541) 343-6812
www.miusa.org

Sdruôení zdravotn: postiôených
Praha 8, Karlínské námĕstí 12
Tel. 224 81 69 07

Czech Rail
Tel. 224 61 56 33
www.cd.cz

Prague Heritage Reservation
City map for persons with reduced mobility. Available at the Prague Information Service (PIS)
Old Town, Staromĕstské námĕstí 1
(Old Town Hall at Old Town Square)
Tel. 221 714 444
www.praguewelcome.cz
tourinfo@pis.cz

Taxi service for disabled passengers
Tel. 776 440 044
www.taxiprovozickarightcz

websites with pictograms. Accessible toilets can be found on most public squares and at the main tourist sites. Suitable Metro station entrances are marked accordingly. Traffic lights often feature a button which can adjust the green signal to wheelchair pace. A number of tram lines are equipped with low level entry. It is worth remembering that Prague is rather hilly, with steep alleys in the Lesser Quarter and steps leading up the castle. Special maps are available illustrating easier terrain for travellers with disabilities.

Index

List of Maps and Illustrations

Photo Credits

Publisher's Information

1st Edition 2016
Worldwide Distribution: Marco Polo
Travel Publishing Ltd
Pinewood, Chineham Business Park
Crockford Lane, Chineham
Basingstoke, Hampshire RG24 8AL,
United Kingdom.

Photos, illlustrations, maps::
167 photos, 24 maps and and illustra-
tions, one large map
Text:
Dr. Madeleine Reincke and
Thomas Veszelits, with contributions by
Barbara Branscheid, Jutta Buness, Rainer
Eisenschmid, Robert Fischer, Sabine
Herre, Dr. František Kafka, Dr. Otakar
Mohyla and Andrea Wurth
Editing:
John Sykes, Robert Taylor
Translation: David Andersen, Barbara
Schmidt-Runkel, John Sykes, Robert
Taylor
Cartography:
Franz Huber, Munich;
MAIRDUMONT Ostfildern (large map)
3D illustrations:
jangled nerves, Stuttgart
Infographics:
Golden Section Graphics GmbH, Berlin
Design:
independent Medien-Design, Munich
Editor-in-chief:
Rainer Eisenschmid, Mairdumont
Ostfildern

Printed in China

Despite all of our authors' thorough
research, errors can creep in. The publishers do not accept any liability for thi
Whether you want to praise, alert us to
errors or give us a personal tip Please
contact us by email or post:

MARCO POLO Travel Publishing Ltd
Pinewood, Chineham Business Park
Crockford Lane, Chineham
Basingstoke, Hampshire RG24 8AL
United Kingdom
Email: sales@marcopolouk.com

FSC
www.fsc.org
MIX
Paper from
responsible sources
FSC® C011918

Curious Prague

So many things in Prague are so different. Some of them are rather curious. Here is a small selection.

►Pilfering President

Václav Klaus, Czech president from 2003 to 2013, set a unique record in March 2011: he became a Youtube star for a whole week. The clip showed him on a state visit to Chile, signing a treaty alongside the Chilean president – then surreptitiously pocketing the bejewelled fountain pen. A cameraman caught this memorable trick on film and the clip registered over 1 million hits online.

►Ritual pointers

The Jewish Museum in Prague has an unparalleled collection – not only in terms of its sheer size, boasting 4054 Thora mantles and 1042 Menorahs, but also on account of a particular curiosity: the 1165 pointers which are on display. They are shaped like a hand with an outstretched index finger, used to read the Torah scrolls. Why? Because it is not permitted to touch the sacred pages.

►Under the microscope

The smallest book ever printed in Prague is a prayer book with the Lord's Prayer in seven languages: only 6x6mm/quarter of an inch squaright It can be marvelled at in the library of Strahov Monastery.

►Crawling rarity

The idiosyncratic Emperor Rudolf II was a shopping addict! In addition to the predictable works of art, jewellery, precious stones and paintings, he hoarded pewter tankards, stuffed owls and preserved bear claws just as ardently. His mania for collecting ruined the treasury, although it is hard to place a value on all of his exhibits. One item in his collection, a stag beetle measuring 7.5cm/3 inches, found fame much, much later. It was named »Insect of the Year in 2012«. So Rudolf did have a knack for tracking down rarities after all…

►Dance of the Vampires

Its dome is the most striking feature of the Lesser Quarter: crowning Dientzenhofer's Baroque Church of St Nicholas, the 3000 sq m/3600 sq yd interior of which contains magnificent frescoes depicting scenes from the Bible. Together with suspended holy statues, the church provided the perfect setting for the vampire thriller »Van Helsing«. An orgiastic Dracula ball, of all things, was staged within these holy walls. If some religious believers were outraged at the spectacle, the church authorities adopted a more pragmatic approach in granting access to the filmmakers: »The means justify the end. We urgently need the money to renovate the church«.